# Tamil

# *Tamil*

## A BIOGRAPHY

DAVID SHULMAN

*The Belknap Press of Harvard University Press*
CAMBRIDGE, MASSACHUSETTS
LONDON, ENGLAND
2016

Printed in the United States of America

First Printing

*Library of Congress Cataloging-in-Publication Data*
Names: Shulman, David Dean, 1949– author.
Title: Tamil : a biography / David Shulman.
Description: Cambridge, Massachusetts : The Belknap Press of Harvard University Press, 2016. | Includes bibliographical references and index.
Identifiers: LCCN 2016008042 | ISBN 9780674059924 (alk. paper)
Subjects: LCSH: Tamil (Indic people)—Intellectual life. | Tamil (Indic people)—History. | Tamil language—History. | Tamil literature—History and criticism. | Tamil poetry—History and criticism. | India—Civilization.
Classification: LCC DS432.T3 S46 2016 | DDC 305.894/811—dc23
LC record available at http://lccn.loc.gov/2016008042

Book design by Dean Bornstein

For Yigal, Sashi, and Ramacandra Reddy

*sasneham*

# Contents

# Preface

A language is never a thing, even if its speakers sometimes do whatever they can to turn it into one—to make it an "it." The ideas people have about their language may be things, and as such may have a history; even so, the language will always exceed those ideas and, given certain basic conditions, will continue to grow and thus to fulfill the organic, uncertain, and lively destiny encoded in its grammar. Old languages like Tamil, given to intense reflection over many centuries, write their own autobiographies, in many media, though we may not know how to read them. Sometimes they ask the assistance of a ghostwriter, a biographer, like me.

Everywhere one looks at language, at every point that we touch it, we see movement, aliveness, and singular forms of self-expression—usually not amenable to translation. In the Jerusalem school of linguistics we were taught that there is nothing trivial in language, nothing too minute to be studied and explored. There is, implicit in each point and part, the logic of a system held together from inside and of the world that lives inside that world. I doubt that these worlds are representational in any meaningful sense, but I think they do speak to us. You don't need to know Tamil to hear them.

This is not the book a historical linguist would have written. It is more of a cultural history of Tamil, with particular focus on the understandings and perceptions about the language that came to the surface over the two thousand years of its documented existence. There are thus two stories running concurrently: one about the ways Tamil evolved in itself, generating grammars of speaking and singing and thinking, and one about major expressive—especially poetic and literary—drives and themes, seen in a broad historical perspective that makes space for continuities. I thought it would be a very short book, essayistic and nonlinear, but Tamil thought otherwise.

The best part of writing it was discovering texts I had never read, or had read long ago and mostly forgotten, or to which I had paid too little attention (in other words, most Tamil texts). I was regularly astonished.

Most of these works, many of them masterpieces of human civilization by any standard, belong to the past thousand years or so of Tamil. This means that a certain dissonance has probably found its way into the heart of the book. It is one thing to look at Tamil from the vantage point of the year 1000, or the year 1500; another thing to look backward from 2016 toward both the distant and the recent past. These rival perspectives, largely incompatible, are, in a sense, what this book is about. They are its *pŏruḷ*—the hidden stuff of meaning, not always spelled out explicitly.

I hesitated before agreeing to write. Almost everything about Tamil is contentious. Some of the most important questions cannot be answered. We have rather tentative notions about chronology and, in this generation, fierce disputes about identity (not my favorite word). I have had to leave vast swaths of Tamil out of these pages for want of knowledge and want of space. Almost every Tamil reader will see, perhaps before all else, what is missing.

The book is built like a concert, or a composition, *kriti,* in the Carnatic style. It has an opening *ālāpana,* largely focused on grammar; a *pallava* refrain that speaks of in-ness; an *anupallavi* secondary refrain about *uyir,* the core of the Tamil person; and several *caraṇam* verses, each with its own primary subject and time period, eventually culminating in a modern *rāga-mālikā* rapidly running through diverse rāga-scales with a meditative *tillāṉā* at the end. The refrain, also the *anupallavi,* naturally recurs frequently throughout the composition with its *caraṇam* variations, as in the performance of any *kriti.* Any reader who manages to read the whole book, if such a person miraculously appears, will notice a certain set of patterns and melodies. Sadly, unlike the compositions of Muttusvwamy Dikshitar and others, this *kriti* is unlikely to be conducive to the manifestation of any god or goddess.

Now there are those to be thanked, too many to be mentioned. Still: First among them is my first Tamil teacher and guru, John Ralston Marr, whose love for all things Tamil infused every line of poetry we read. A. Kandiah also taught me, gently and firmly, in those early years. I was fortunate to read many challenging texts with V. S. Rajam in the course of a sabbatical year in Baltimore and Philadelphia. Many good friends on several continents, including two new generations of brilliant scholars of Tamil, sent me their essays and books, read and commented on chapters as they took shape, corrected my errors, and kept up my spirits when the task seemed impossible: Jean-Luc Chevillard, Archana Venkatesan, Vasudha Narayanan, Blake Wentworth, S. Ramakrishnan, Emmanuel Francis, Talavajjhala Sashi Shekhar, Yigal Bronner, Jennifer Clare, Sascha Ebeling, and the ever-generous and insightful Whitney Cox. François Gros very helpfully discussed issues of dating. George Hart sent me his wonderful new translation of *Akanāṉūṟu.* I thank Sivan Goren for our sessions reading *Līlā-tilakam* and Venugopala Panicker for sharing his tremendous knowledge of south Indian linguistics. Ilanit Loewy Shacham plied me with scans of rare Tamil books from the infinitely capacious Regenstein Library—when she had far better things to do with her time. Charles Hallisey, who has taught so many of us how to read, read this book in draft and gave me faith that it has some value.

This book, like several of its predecessors, was finished in the utopian space of the Israel Institute for Advanced Studies. I want to thank the devoted staff of the institute and its director, Professor Michal Linial, for nurturing that space. I wish to thank the Israel Science Foundation and the University Grant Commission in India for a joint grant that contributed to the writing of this book. I thank Brian Ostrander of Westchester Publishing Services, and Heather Hughes, Louise Robbins, and Stephanie Vyce at Harvard University Press for help and encouragement at every stage. My editor, Sharmila Sen, gently and firmly nudged me into writing this book, and now that it's written, I'm more than grateful to her. As always, my wife, Eileen, who has shared the Tamil adventure from the start and who knows how to sing the *kritis* so they melt my mind, gave of her munificent nature; my sons and grandchildren willy-nilly put up with my frequent absentmindedness and physical absences.

And there are the infinite absences to be borne in heart and mind as long as there are mountains and rivers: Abbie Ziffren, Norman Cutler, K. Paramasivam, K. Kailasapathy, Kamil Zvelebil, Thirupur S. Ramu, Gopal Aiyar, Bernard Bate, and many others whom I was not lucky enough to know in person.

I dedicate this work to three soul-friends, connoisseurs, and teachers: Yigal Bronner, Tallavajhalla Sashi Sekhar, and Karri Ramacandra Reddy. I hope they can hear its music.

# Note on Transliteration

I have tried to minimize the dots and dashes that embellish scholarly writing on Sanskrit and Tamil, though I found that I could not dispense with them altogether. Place names are without diacritic marks. The names of modern Tamil authors generally appear using the English spellings they themselves adopted. Very common and familiar names, or some modern ones that have many English equivalents—Kamban, Caminat'aiyar, and Minatcicuntaram Pillai, also deity names—appear in phonetic approximation without diacritics. The Sanskrit retroflex sibilant ṣ is marked as *sh*. Vocalic ṛ appears as *ri*.

For readers who would like to try to pronounce words and names in the Tamil way, the following rules may be helpful:

Consonant-stops, such as *k, t, ṭ,* and *p,* are unvoiced in initial position and also when doubled. Within a word, between two vowels, they tend to become fricatives: thus *k* turns into a *ch* sound like in German. Initial and intervocalic *c* is pronounced like *s* in the Tamil of Chennai (but like English *ch* or *sh* farther south, and in several dialects). After nasals, consonant-stops are always voiced: *nk=ng, nc=nj, nt=nd,* and so on. There are no voiced initial consonants in Tamil except in borrowed words. Also, unlike Sanskrit and nearly all other South Asian languages with the exception of the Munda and Tibeto-Burmese family, Tamil has no aspirates. Gemination is phonemic: a doubled consonant is twice as long as a single one. Long vowels are double the length of short vowels. The short vowels *ĕ* and *ŏ* are distinctive to Dravidian.

All translations in this book are my own unless otherwise noted.

# Tamil

ONE

# Beginnings

*Ālāpana*

## What Is Tamil?

The word or name "Tamil" ends in a sound proudly seen by its speakers as characteristic of this language. Linguists transcribe it as *ḻ*. It would be best if you, the reader, were simply to hear it uttered by a native speaker, but I can try to describe it. The tongue slides backwards in the mouth without stopping the flow of air, and the result is an *r*-like sound (a retroflex liquid in the terminology of the grammarians) somewhat similar to the way many Americans pronounce the *r* in "girl." The sound survives in colloquial speech in most Tamil dialects and in Tamil's sister language Malayalam, spoken in Kerala. A few Tamil dialects have transformed it to a retroflex *ḷ* in certain phonetic environments, but in formal contexts—speeches, news broadcasts, recitation or singing of verses, and the like—you can always hear the original sound, which adds a pleasant purring quality to what may sound like the rapid rushing of a rivulet, for Tamil, like other south Indian languages, is among the most rapidly spoken of human languages. When I first heard it, many years ago, I wasn't sure that it was really akin to what one calls "language," and even today I find it hard to believe that the human tongue is capable of such swift twists and turns. That said, I hasten to add that to my ears Tamil, both in everyday speech and in contexts of formal recitation, is always a delicious, bewitching, incantational music, unlike any other that I have heard.

Indeed, "music," or "the Tamil that is music," *icaittamiḻ*, is one of the meanings of the name itself in the ancient grammatical and poetic sources. More specifically, this music-Tamil is one of three categorical divisions, along with *iyaltamiḻ*, that is, the "natural" (literary) language, and *nāṭakattamiḻ*, the Tamil of (dramatic) performance. The normative texts thus like to speak of *muttamiḻ*, the threefold Tamil. But this slightly mechanical division is very far from summing up the meaning of the term "Tamil." We would, I think, be better to think of more comprehensive definitions, such as the following:

1. Tamil is, first, the name of an ancient language, spoken today by some eighty million people in south India, Sri Lanka, and a large diaspora that includes Malaysia, Singapore, Fiji, South Africa, Paris, Toronto, and many other sites throughout the world. This language is attested from at least the first century B.C., though its roots go back much farther into the past, as we will see. Among the South Asian languages, Tamil is perhaps the only case of a very ancient language that still survives as a vibrant mother-tongue for tens of millions of speakers.
2. Tamil is a certain body of knowledge, some of it technical, much of it intrinsic to an ancient culture and sensibility well documented in a continuous literary tradition going back many centuries. Specifically, *tamiḻ* means something like "knowing how to love"—in the manner of the classical love poetry with its conventions, its heroes and heroines, its powerful expressive and suggestive techniques. Thus the great poet Cuntaramūrtti Nāyaṉār (you will have to get used to these long names) says to his god, the beautiful but unpredictable Lord Śiva, at a temple called Tiruppainnili: "Do you know proper Tamil?"[1] He means by this: "Do you know how to behave properly as a male lover should? Can you understand the hints and implicit meanings that a proficient lover ought to be able to decipher?" The poet has some doubts about this, for in the next line he says to the god:

   > Why are you just standing there
   > with a red-eyed serpent
   > dancing in your hand?

In fact, "Tamil" as a body of knowledge has a still wider application, so that "to know Tamil" can also mean "to be a civilized being." We could say that "Tamil" in this sense is a kind of grammar, not merely of the language in its spoken and written forms but of the ways of life that have been created and lived out by its speakers.

3. Here we already touch on the next, much wider sense of the term. Tamil was one of the languages of a great south Indian civilization and, as such, of one of the most creative geographical domains in historical South Asia. Some people would say that this civilization reached its apogee in the Chola period, roughly from 850 to 1200, when Tamil speakers ruled a state that brought large parts of the southern subcontinent under its control; this period is often seen as "classical," in several senses of this word. Others, like me, might think that no less vibrant and significant achievements of south Indian civilization began long before the Chola period and continued on right up to the early modern age. Here is a topic we will want to explore in this book. In general, I think of Tamil as a living being—impetuous, sensitive, passionate, whimsical, in constant movement—hence worthy of a biography. There is also reason to put aside the dynastic-political periodizations that are still prevalent for south Indian history in favor of more organic, thematic continuities that cut through the periods of dynastic rule.

The cultural role of Tamil is not, in any case, truly analogous to that of, say, Latin for the Roman Empire or of Sanskrit for what Sheldon Pollock has called the "Sanskrit Cosmopolis," that is, the vast swath of Asia within which Sanskrit grammar and the political ideology couched in Sanskrit had a pervasive and stable presence for well over a thousand years. Nor was Tamil ever the sole or, for that matter, even the clearly predominant language of the south Indian civilization that I'm referring to. It shared pride of place with other languages such as Sanskrit, the various Prakrits, Telugu, Kannada, and Malayalam. I will thus refrain, in this book, from speaking about a "Tamil civilization," which seems to me a modern, nationalist construction bearing little relation to any historical reality. We can, nevertheless, agree that the Tamil language and its particular themes, images, and traditions informed and in many ways shaped an extraordinarily long-lived, heterogeneous, and richly elaborated culture or series of cultures along with the political and social orders that emerged out of those cultural matrices.

4. Tamil is, at its most basic, an intoxicating, godly fragrance *(tĕyvat tamiḻ maṇam).* It is thus something light, delicate, and pervasive, an existential undercurrent flowing through everything that lives, and as such intimately linked to the human faculty of memory and to musical poetry as the voice of memory and awareness.[2] Not everyone can take in or recognize this fragrance, but the First Sage, Agastya, did and, overcome by its power, proceeded to write a grammar of this sweet vital force after learning to speak and understand with the help of Lord Śiva.[3] Moreover, as a fragrant breath of air Tamil is also, by definition, both "bright" or golden *(cĕn tamiḻ)* and cool *(taṇ ṭamiḻ),* like all good things in south India.[4] Blake Wentworth has shown that in the very earliest strata of Tamil literature, the so-called Sangam corpus, the word "Tamil" is regularly paired with the idea of something deliciously cool.[5] Incidentally, like Tamil itself, the Tamil land has a gentle nature *(mĕlliyal).*[6]
5. Finally—or perhaps this should have been our point of departure—Tamil is a living goddess, her body constituted by the phonemes (in their oral and also written forms) that make up the language and its grammar, in the wide sense of the latter term intimated above. Tamil, that is, is entirely permeated by divine forces that are accessible to those who know the language and that may be amenable to pragmatic uses that can make, or change, a world.

Does the word *tamiḻ* have an accepted etymology? Do we know what it originally meant? Unfortunately, the answer is no. The medieval lexicons, such as the *Piṅkala nikaṇṭu* (10: 580), say *tamiḻ* means "sweetness" *(iṉimai)* and also "coolness" or, literally, "waterness" *(nīrmai),*[7] two associations we have already noted. Modern dictionaries such as the *Madras Tamil Lexicon* follow this gloss, adding others. Kamil Zvelebil, after an exhaustive discussion of the problem, suggests an etymology from the root *taku,* "to be fit or proper" (medial *k* being capable of elision or of shifting to *m,* and *–iḻ* being seen as a nominalizing ending). Thus *tamiḻ* would mean "the excellent [resounding] process," "the proper [process of] speaking."[8] I find this far-fetched, but no less so than other suggestions, for example S. V. Subrahmanian's, deriving the word from the reflexive pronoun *tam:* thus "*our own* (sweet sound)." The

*Tamil Lexicon* suggests that the name goes back to *tami*, "solitude," "loneliness"—so this would be a rare case of a language calling itself lonely or, perhaps, singular.

Whatever the correct etymology, *tamiḻ* clearly underlies the Sanskrit word *draviḍa*. The Sanskrit word reveals the attempt by speakers of Sanskrit or other north Indian languages to capture two distinctive Tamil sounds: the initial *t*, which is pronounced with the tongue slightly backed up and touching the back of the teeth and the alveolar ridge—thus a sharper sound than Sanskrit *t*—and the final retroflex *ḻ*, which I have already discussed. Classical Sanskrit uses *draviḍa* both to refer to Tamil speakers specifically and, at times, to indicate south Indians generally: in the royal palace at Ujjayini in central India, in the mid-first millennium A.D., lightly armed servants were mostly men identified by their home region as "Āndhra, Draviḍa, and Sinhala" (the Draviḍas presumably speaking Tamil);[9] the great prose writer and poetician Daṇḍin (seventh century), himself a Tamilian, tells a story located *draviḍeṣu*—in the Tamil country;[10] and the topos of the "Draviḍa ascetic" *(drāviḍa-dhārmika)* became something of a cliché in Sanskrit narratives.[11]

Sanskrit *drāviḍa* (with long initial *ā*; also *dramiḷa*, middle-Indic *damiḷa*) has given us the name of the language family to which Tamil belongs: Dravidian. The existence of such a family, like the existence of the Indo-European family of languages stretching from Calcutta to Iceland, is a modern discovery.[12] Credit for identifying the major south Indian languages as a distinct family, unrelated to Sanskrit, goes to Francis Whyte Ellis (1777–1819), a British savant-cum-administrator linked to the vibrant early days of College Fort St. George in Madras. Ellis established that Tamil (both colloquial and literary), Telugu, Malayalam, and Kannada were close relatives; he published his findings as a "Note to Introduction" to Alexander Duncan Campbell's *Teloogoo Grammar* (1816).[13] However, the first attempt to produce a comparative overview of the Dravidian languages was carried out a generation later by Bishop Robert Caldwell in his *Comparative Grammar of the Dravidian or South Indian Family of Languages* (1856). By Caldwell's time, the number of recognized Dravidian languages had grown; today we count some three dozen, most of them tribal languages with relatively few speakers, apart from the four major literary languages of Tamil,

Telugu (the language of the states of Andhra Pradesh and Telangana), Kannada (the language of Karnataka), and Malayalam (the language of Kerala). To do justice to medieval south Indian scholarship, we should mention that *Līlā-tilakam,* probably a fifteenth- or sixteenth-century grammar in Sanskrit of the mixed language of Kerala known as Maṇi-pravāḷam,[14] already recognized that the spoken languages of Kerala and the southern Tamil regions were close to one another and deserved to be called "Dramiḍa" (that is, "Tamil"); but the learned author of the *Līlā-tilakam* excludes the "Karṇṇāṭa and Āndhra" languages from this category (though he admits that some people would include them) since they are too far removed from the language of the "Tamil Veda," that is, the Vaishṇava poet Nammāḻvār's canonical *Tiruvāymŏḻi* poems.[15]

More precisely, Tamil belongs to what is called South Dravidian and is thus relatively close to its sister languages, Kannada and Malayalam. There has been a tendency among historical linguists to think of Malayalam as having diverged directly from Tamil (the Tamil spoken from ancient times in what is today Kerala), perhaps as late as the thirteenth century. But this view is almost certainly wrong. Tamil and Malayalam must have separated from one another at a much earlier stage, perhaps around the middle of the first millennium A.D., as we can see from several surviving archaic features of Malayalam.[16] The South Dravidian branch is clearly marked off from what is now usually called South-Central Dravidian (following Bh. Krishnamurti), which includes the major language Telugu and several important tribal languages such as Gondi, Koya, Pengo, and Chenchu. Although Tamil and Telugu are syntactically very close—as, for that matter, are Tamil and classical Sanskrit (and also Hindustani)—their phonology and morphology are highly distinct. Tamil and Telugu are not mutually intelligible; Malayalam and Tamil may be, with practice (Malayali speakers exposed to Tamil films acquire a passive knowledge of Tamil very quickly, though the reverse seems to be less common). In border areas, of course, such as Kanyakumari District in Tamil Nadu or Palghat in Kerala—the historic geographic link between the Tamil country and the Malabar coast—and in Chittor District in southern Andhra, where Tamil and Telugu freely mix, very large numbers of bilinguals and multilinguals are in evidence. Multilingualism was, I think, in any case extremely prevalent in premodern south India; the creation of language-based states in 1956 largely destroyed this once-normative fluency in many languages and their respective cultures.

Tamil is more distantly related to Central and North Dravidian, the latter including the far-flung language Brahui, still spoken by a few hundred speakers in today's Pakistan. Modern Tamil nationalists like to think that the existence of Brahui constitutes proof that Dravidian languages were once prevalent throughout the subcontinent and thus greeted the Vedic Sanskrit speakers on their arrival. More on this later.

## Tamil Syntax: What It Feels Like to Live in Tamil

Like other Dravidian languages, Tamil is agglutinative. This term means that suffixes are added sequentially, usually without substantial modification of the initial stem, to specify meaning and syntactic function. For example, look at the word *maram,* "tree." To pluralize, we add the plural suffix *-kaḷ:* thus, *maraṅkaḷ,* "trees." (The final *m* of the singular adapts itself to the initial *k* of the suffix, becoming the nasal that English uses in "bank," for example—though this velar nasal is nonphonemic in English.) Now suppose we want to refer to "trees" as a direct object of a verb, as in: "(I see) the trees." We add the object marker *ai: maraṅkaḷai (ppārkkiṟeṉ).* This suffix is habitually classed as the accusative case, akin to the cases *(vibhakti)* of Sanskrit, though this nomenclature is not really well suited to Dravidian. Similarly, we can add other suffixes to the plural form to fulfill other syntactic functions: *maraṅkaḷoṭu,* "with the trees"; *maraṅkaḷil,* "among the trees"; *maraṅkaḷiliruntu,* "from among the trees" (this form is actually composed of two suffixes, *il + iruntu*); and so on.

Now suppose we want to qualify further the trees-as-object, for example by adding the conjunctive particle *-um,* "and": *maraṅkaḷaiyum āṟṟaiyum pārkkiṟeṉ,* "I see the trees *and* the river." By now we have a sequence of three suffixes added to the initial noun stem. This is a simple example of agglutination at work. The process differs markedly from the way nominal suffixes work in Sanskrit and Indo-European generally, where substantial modifications of the stem are followed by varying case-specific suffixes: thus *vṛkṣa,* "tree" becomes *vṛkṣāḥ* ("trees," nominative), *vṛkṣān* ("trees," accusative), and so on; and the regular cumulation of suffixes is not the norm. It would be easy to show similar differences in the verbal systems of the two families.

Even more striking are the predominant syntactic patterns of Dravidian languages, which are what linguists call "left-branching"—that is, modifiers, including entire clauses, generally *precede* the modified (the term arbitrarily assumes that one is speaking or reading in a left-to-right mode). Since English, like most Indo-European languages (but not classical Sanskrit), is mostly "right-branching," Tamil sentences often follow an order that appears as a precise inversion of the English sentence. Look, for example, at an English sentence like the following:

> *This book, which I, a professor of Indology in Jerusalem, have written about Tamil, [which is] a south Indian language spoken by millions, seems to be getting off to a slow start.*

Every time more information is added it comes *after* the modified noun (and is situated graphically to the right of the latter). Now consider the following Tamil sentence:

> *civapĕrumāṉ puṟṟ'iṭaṅ kŏṇṭu pūṅkoyilil ĕḻunt'aruḷiyirukkiṉṟa mikka pĕrumaiyai uṭaiyatum atuve [tiruvārūr].*[17]
>
> It [the temple town of Tiruvarur] has the distinction of having Lord Śiva ensconced in its beautiful temple, in the anthill he [originally] took for his home.

In English this basically equational sentence [X=Y] is naturally top-heavy toward the right: the "distinction" is modified by a gerund clause, which issues into another subordinate relative clause ("in the anthill he took for his home," the relative pronoun "that" has fallen away). But in Tamil, everything is weighted to the left, before the "distinction," which is modified by what is called in Tamil a *pĕyar ĕccam* or "residue of a noun," often the equivalent of a relative clause in English; and this entire syntactic chunk includes, as its initial segment, a nonfinite verb *(kŏṇṭu)* that feeds into the verb of the *pĕyar ĕccam* ("being ensconced"). Here is how the sentence looks in its Tamil order, with the emphatic subject, "it," coming at the end:

> *[The] Lord Śiva—having taken the anthill for his home—in the beautiful temple-ensconced distinction*—having / has—it.

The italicized portion is a single complex clause modifying "distinction." What kind of distinction? The Lord-Śiva-in-the-beautiful-temple-ensconced distinction. In general, Tamil sentences work in this order: modifiers of one kind or another usually precede what they modify, so that the elaboration or characterization of any given noun is present, aurally and cognitively, before one knows for sure what is being described.

Despite what linguists sometimes claim, classical Sanskrit, for all its Indo-European origins, has largely assimilated this left-branching syntax (which we also see in the modern vernaculars of north India), along with various specific syntactical patterns prevalent in Dravidian.[18] There is much more to say about the radical changes in Sanskrit syntax, in both poetry and prose, in the post-Vedic era and their resonances with Dravidian patterns of sentence building. But for now, let me simply note that left-branching sentences appear to demand a somewhat different set of mental processes than do right-branching ones, where expansion of the basic content or its modification can unfold in the linear sequence in which the words are spoken. In Tamil and other south Indian languages, the sentence as a whole often crystallizes, to some extent, in the speaker's mind *before* utterance begins—as we can see by the way speakers of these languages sometimes use proleptic devices to announce what the sentence is about to say, thereby easing the listener's task of comprehension and alleviating the otherwise typical syntactic tension built into the statement ("Would you like to know what that man said to me yesterday? He said that . . ."). Without slipping into some version of Whorfian determinism, I think it is still possible to argue that these left-branching structures, and the strong sense of the prefashioned sentence as a whole that they imply, may underlie the fifth-century Sanskrit philosopher Bhartrihari's great discovery of the sentence as the primary and holistic unit of speech, rather than the word or the morpheme; for Bhartrihari, words, as we normally think of them, are pure fictions. A left-branching linguistic metaphysics also has implications for our understanding of classical Tamil poetry and poetics, as we will see.

This book is not meant to teach the reader how to speak Tamil; but I would like you, nonetheless, to have at least some sense of what it feels like to live inside this language and to use its particular expressive features to subtle effect. Among these, in particular, are the very rich forms of modality and aspect, both lexical and morphological, that all Dravidian—in fact, all South Asian—languages offer their speakers. To taste something of the flavor of what this means, consider the following paragraph from a very fine short story by Na. Muthuswamy, *Naṭappu*, "Happening," describing how the narrator as a three-year-old child fell into a well in the village:

> The bucket (for drawing water) was sitting on the cement ring circling the well. . . . I wanted to steep the cloth I held in my hand in water from the bucket and then scrub it against the stone that was placed there for that purpose. But I couldn't reach the bucket. Also, I couldn't climb up onto the ring. Apparently, I must have climbed up on the stone for scrubbing and from there onto the ring. It seems there was no water in the bucket. Without water, how could I scrub the cloth? I probably thought that at least I might be able to play inside the bucket. I climbed into the bucket and sat there for a while. It was a pretty big bucket, enough to hide a three-year-old child inside it. Grandmother, I thought to myself, must not see me on her way back from the heap of grain in the courtyard. I guess I may have peeked out to see if she was coming. Probably the cement pillar to which the pulley and its support were attached blocked my view. So it's quite possible that I stretched my neck out to see past the pillar—to see if she was coming. But I must have held fast to the rim of the bucket. The bucket must have tilted and fallen into the well. The bucket descended with me still inside. It seems that I held on hard to the bucket as it fell. . . . Just as when you stand near a well as evening falls and, staring downward, can't see the bottom, my memory grows dark today. They say that they lowered a lantern tied to a rope into the well and saw me there.[19]

Muthuswamy's narrator is struggling to remember what cannot be recalled; at almost every step he has to reconstruct the lost sequence of events. As a result, this lyrical yet simple prose passage is peppered with finely shaded modal forms of several types. Sometimes an explicit verb colors the hypothetical statement: "It seems that" *(toṉṟukiṉṟatu)*. Sometimes we have a direct word of supposition: "It's as if" or "it must have been the case that" *(polum)* or "it's possible that" *(kūṭum)*. Most of the modal forms, however, are built into the agglutinative verbal strings. For example:

*viḷaiyāṭavāvatu ceyyalām* ("at least I might be able to play," with verbal suffix *-alām,* of possibility / potential / desire, added to the verbal root)

*ĕṉakkut toṉṟiyirukka veṇṭum* ("I probably thought" < auxiliary verb *veṇṭum,* "to want, need, must do" + modal verb *toṉṟu + irukka* "would have": so, literally, "It must be that I would have thought")

*nāṉ ĕtti pārtt'irukkalām* ("I guess I may have peeked out," again with the modal suffix *[kk]]alām;* literally, "It could be that I would have pcckcd out")

*pārttārkaḷām* ("They say that they saw me there," < reported speech with *–ām* tacked on to a past-tense verb)

And so on. Tamil easily allows such hypothetical statements, as well as counterfactuals, expressive wishes, anxieties, blessings, and curses, by means of a subtle menu of semantic, lexical, and morphological modality. Quite often one finds two or more modal forms compounded sequentially: "the thought that most probably would have occurred to me. . . ." Of course, English and other languages are quite capable of articulating such ontic and cognitive nuances with their own various means; but Tamil modality is strongly integrated into the verbal strings with their potentially very precise and often cumulative sets of nuance. Thus denotative factuality, though no less present in Tamil than in other languages, can very rapidly slip into semifactual or entirely nonfactual expression carried by both morphological and lexical means. If one adds to this particularly thick set of modal devices the omnipresent aspectual morphology of the Tamil verb—that is, the use of verbal chains, or so-called auxiliary verbs, to define the action as either fully completed or as continuing in one of several possible patterns, in all three tenses—the result is a supple, systemic expressivity beautifully suited to specifying what happens in the sentence (in particular, the nature and meaning of an action either as enacted in external space or as transpiring, or undergoing interpretation, somewhere in the mind). Native speakers bend this expressive potential to their intentions with often astonishing richness and precision. In the specific case of Muthuswamy's prose, the repeated modal devices create an atmosphere of dreamlike semimemory, as befits his narrator's attempt to recapture the long-lost awareness of a three-year-old child.

Within this wealth of modal and aspectual means, verbs of being and becoming occupy a central space. Several of the modal forms just mentioned require the use of the important verb of coming into being, *ā / āku*.[20] This omnipresent verb contrasts with, but can also combine with, *uṇḍu,* from *uḷ,*[21] the root for being or having; this root gives us the noun *uṇmai,* "existence," "reality," "truth." A second, homonymous root *uḷ*[22] refers to whatever is inside, interior—hence, *uḷḷam,* "heart," "mind," and *uḷḷu / uḷku,* "to think." But these two *uḷ*'s often fuse in popular understanding: in some sense, in Tamil "to be" is "to be inside," and truth, too, is a kind of innerness, as we shall see. Another root for "being" is *iru* (also "to sit"), extremely common as a "light verb" or auxiliary to produce, for example, a sense of temporal depth (perfect and future perfect tenses). If we combine *uṇḍu* with *āku* we get the composite verb *uṇḍāku,* "to come into being"—or, adding the auxiliary *iru, uṇḍāyirukka,* "to be or become pregnant." This last form reveals all the nuances of generation: what is *(uṇḍu),* is continually *(iru)* in the process of becoming (*āy* < *āku*). To be pregnant is to have (inside) something that is *becoming* in an ongoing way. Tamil is a language engineered to express processuality in various prevalent modes and forms, in the external domain of objects no less than in the internal world of thought, feeling, and awareness.

In this respect it is of interest that morphologically configured present-future tenses entered Tamil relatively late, around the mid-first millennium A.D. Prior to that, as Meenakshisundaram says, "the deep rooted tenses in Dravidian are the past and the non-past; the present and future, even when distinguished, tend to fall together."[23] V. S. Rajam has shown that in Old Tamil presentness was expressed by the compounded verbal string *ā+nil,* the first element, from *āku,* expressing an ongoing, unfinished process, while the second (from the root "to stand") halts this process long enough for us to discern a moment of present time.[24] Even today, the morphological present in Tamil is far less crisply defined than in English or German, and a primary contrast between concluded action (often with aspect marker) and ongoing process—in whatever temporal mode—still obtains.

Two last comments in this much-condensed linguistic survey. Claims by Tamil purists to the contrary notwithstanding, modern spoken

Tamil is astonishingly rich in Sanskrit loan words. Indeed, there may well be more straight Sanskrit in Tamil than in the Sanskrit-derived north Indian vernaculars. Sanskrit words tend to be Tamilized in accordance with the Tamil phonematic grid, much in the way they were already at the time of the *Tŏlkāppiyam* grammar.[25] And they may also change their meanings in the course of moving from Sanskrit to Tamil: for example, citing Muthuswamy again, in colloquial speech:

> *Ava ŏru **nitāṉattule** naṭakkaṟa polĕrukku*
> "She seems to be walking unawares."[26]

*Nitāṉam* is Sanskrit *nidhāna*—literally, placing, putting down; a hoard or treasure; also (a rare meaning we find only in the old lexicons) a place of cessation or rest.[27] Possibly this last meaning has generated the Tamil one of a dreamlike state, a lack of awareness.

We can also define specific occasions or motivations for using a full-fledged Sanskrit expression in a Tamil sentence (indeed, in a much wider sense, an author's choice of Sanskrit or Tamil always reflects the particular, respective expressive advantages of the two languages, including issues of tone, intensity, emphasis, resonance, intimacy, and so on). To illustrate but one not uncommon choice: the insertion of a Sanskrit collocation sometimes serves the purpose of powerful abstraction, slightly decontextualizing or reframing an utterance (as Latin can do in premodern English). Thus

> *avaḷ uruvaik kirakikka iraṇṭu koṇaṅkaḷ potāt' ĕṉa or arūpaccāyalil avaḷ uyir koṇṭ'iruppatāka toṉṟum.*
> "It was as if she lived as an abstract form and as if you couldn't grasp her form even from two angles."[28]

Technically, etymologically, this perfectly normal sentence is more Sanskrit than Tamil. We have *kirakikka* < Skt. *grah*, "to grasp"; *koṇaṅkaḷ*, "angles," Skt. *koṇa*, possibly originally borrowed into Sanskrit from Dravidian and now borrowed back; and the very old Sanskrit loan word in Tamil, *uruvu / uruvam* < Skt. *rūpa*, "form." But the sentence concludes with a crescendo ending in the abstraction *arūpaccāyalil*, a Tamil compound made up of Skt. *arūpa*, "formless," and *cāyal* < Skt. *chāyā*, "shadow," "shape," "beauty," "image": thus, more simply, "an abstract form." Sanskritists can see at once the rich Sanskrit layer in Tamil prose like this sentence—and also the ways that Sanskrit words and phrases have been transformed in Tamil to mean something a little different. Here the "abstract form" has become iconically abstract by being formulated in a highly conspicuous Sanskrit string.

Very similar is the following instance of pointed, emphatic Sanskrit slipped onto a Tamil phrase:

> *avarkaḷ ĕllām nāṅkaḷ atīta uṇarvukaḷoṭu irukkiṟom ĕṉpataip purintu kŏṇṭavarkaḷ.*
>
> "They all understood that we were in a state of intense emotion."[29]

Here *uṇarvukaḷ,* "emotion," "sensation," "[states of] awareness," in the plural, is modified by Skt. *atīta,* "transcendent," literally "gone beyond." Why not use a Tamil word for this meaning? But in fact *atīta is* a fine Tamil word, no less than any other, even though its Sanskrit provenance is very marked and could be said, in itself, to intensify the utterance and thus to conduce to the iconic enactment of meaning.

Of course, there are domains of experience where Sanskrit vocabulary feels natural, even inevitable: what we might term religious language, for example, is replete with Sanskrit words. A curse (*cāpam,* Skt. *śāpa*) may have a date of expiration, after which release (*vimocaṉam,* Skt. *vimocana*) from its spell becomes possible. Once again, such words, which look and sound a lot like their Sanskrit originals, are entirely Tamil, just as no one would think to declare words like "fraternity" or "equality" un-English, despite their Latin derivation.

Yet in the twentieth century there was a movement, driven by Dravidian nationalists, to de-Sanskritize spoken Tamil by replacing Sanskrit words with "pure" Tamil roots.[30] Thus the daily courtesy phrase, *saukkiyamā,* "How are you? Are you well?" derived from Skt. *saukhyam,* "happiness," "goodness," is sometimes transformed into *nalamā,* from Tamil *nalam,* "goodness"—so, "Is there goodness? Are you well?" But the purists have failed completely. One cannot get along in Tamil without Sanskrit words. They were there at the beginning, and they are there today. We will have occasion to speak further of Sanskrit-in-Tamil in the following chapters. Indeed, the long and complex relations between these two languages is a major theme throughout this book; this theme is still clearly alive and full of passion in current debates about language and culture in the Tamil world, and there is, I think, room for a historical and scholarly perspective on it. What is at stake here is not simply a historical-linguistic reading of what Tamil once was and what it is or should be today. In modern south India, Tamil has become a major criterion for collective identity, often seen now as forged in opposition to Sanskrit and an invasive north Indian culture and ideology. I will touch on these issues in the final chapter; clearly, the historical record has powerful implications for present-day politics and self-definition.

Finally, it is important to recognize that Tamil is, even today, a nonstandardized language characterized by strong diglossia or polyglossia—that is, by very marked differences between a formal literary or semiliterary register and the colloquial language of the home or street.[31] The formal register, although strongly influenced by spoken syntactical and morphological patterns, largely retains the grammaticalized, authoritative linguistic forms present from very ancient times—or, more precisely, the relatively stable morphology of literary Tamil that crystallized during the first half of the first millennium A.D. All South Asian languages that have strong literary traditions are diglossic, but the Tamil diglossia is indeed impressive, to the point that the two registers could almost be considered different languages, like, say, medieval Latin and Renaissance-period Italian—though most Tamil literati would surely reject such a comparison, being committed to a notion of extraordinary linguistic continuity in Tamil from very early times to the present day. In a sense, they are right: grammaticalized "high" Tamil, sometimes called *cĕntamiḻ*, "bright" or "beautiful" Tamil, is indeed remarkably stable over centuries, even more so than, for example, post-Paninian grammaticalized Sanskrit—though one should not exaggerate the apparent uniformity of literary Tamil.

Nor should we think of Tamil diglossia as more extreme than what we find in other south Indian languages, for example Telugu, despite the fact that Telugu (like modern Greek) fought a language war in the twentieth century that eventually produced an intermediate formal register of urban, educated speech and writing.[32] In practice, even today, Telugu is no less diglossic than Tamil; the same could be said of Malayalam and Kannada. Moreover, it is important to bear in mind that nonformal Tamil exists as an extraordinarily wide spectrum of regional and social dialects, some of them close to being mutually unintelligible. Modern Tamil prose writers often try to reproduce actual speech in their prose, and we now have whole novels written entirely in one version or another of colloquial Tamil, although it is by no means simple to capture in writing the entire range of phonological and morphological phenomena natural to speech. What we find are fascinating approximations, always, of course, based on specific dialects, such as that of Dalits in South Arcot villages in the fine novels by Imayam or of distinct, socially inflected forms of Madurai-district speech, as we see in G. Nagarajan's pioneering short stories and novellas.

We will come back to this issue at the end of our journey. In any case, we should not underestimate the unifying force of the still vibrant elevated register that serves the entire range of regional, professional, or caste-based groups, including the far-flung Tamil diaspora, and that continuously innovates by extending its lexical and syntactical resources, as one can easily see by reading the entries in the superb Cre-A dictionary that records and elucidates precisely this supple level of the modern language.

## On Beginnings

Can we propose some kind of dating for the early forms of Tamil and other Dravidian languages? Let me review some of the evidence we have. The earliest attestation of Dravidian words is in the Rig Veda (mostly but not only in the later strata of the text), that is, roughly, in the final centuries of the second millennium B.C. It was once quite common to assume that the archaic Sanskrit of the Rig Veda rested on, or had somehow absorbed, a linguistic substratum that was possibly Dravidian—this assumption being ironically in line with the modern Dravidianist myth of origins, according to which all of prehistoric India was once Dravidian in speech. Alexander Lubotsky has, however, proven decisively that the Vedic "substratum"—that is, the linguistic environment that the speakers of Vedic Sanskrit encountered as they moved southward and eastward into the subcontinent—cannot have been Dravidian; and Michael Witzel has convincingly shown (following

F. B. J. Kuiper) that there is a significant lexical level of Munda (Austroasiatic) language in the Veda, with hundreds of loan words, thus making Austroasiatic a more likely candidate for the early substratum.[33] Austroasiatic languages, linked with Mon (in Burma), Khmer (in Cambodia), and Vietnamese, have survived, in largely tribal settings, in modern India, mostly in the east: thus we find Santali and Mundari in Jharkhand, West Bengal, and Orissa, and several smaller Munda languages in southern Orissa near the border with modern Andhra Pradesh.

Dravidian lexemes—some two dozen, some of which remain controversial—do exist in Vedic and include:

*mayūra,* "peacock" (Tamil *mayil;* but perhaps originally Munda)[34]
*ulūkhala,* "mortar" (Tamil *ulakkai,* "pestle")
*phala,* "fruit" (Tamil *paḻam*)
*kāṇa,* "blind in one eye" (Tamil *kāṇ,* "to see," perhaps in a negative verbal form)
*muktā,* "pearl" (Tamil *muttu*)
*bala,* "strong" (Tamil *val-*, "strong")

A good summary of the generally accepted borrowings from Dravidian in Vedic Sanskrit has been given by Franklin Southworth,[35] who also offers additional lists of probable Indo-Aryan loans in early Dravidian and of shared lexical items of uncertain origin. Among the latter are many words that, whatever their ultimate source, appear to have entered Sanskrit via Dravidian. For example:

*lāṅgala,* "plow," attested in the Rig Veda (see Tamil *nāñcil* and *ñāñcil*); possibly from an Austroasiatic root; also possibly from Sumerian.

*agasti,* Tamil *akatti,* "West Indian pea-tree," presumably the origin of the name of the Vedic sage Agastya (likely a Dravidian root: see below)

*candana,* "sandalwood" (probably originally Dravidian: Tamil *cāntu,* "sandal tree," "sandal paste")

Similarly, we find a large number of other items relating to flora and fauna, grains, pulses, and spices—that is, words that we might expect to have made their way into Sanskrit from the linguistic environment of prehistoric or early-historic India. Tamil *vāl,* "tail," may be connected to Vedic *vāla / vāra,* though Mayrhofer rejects this etymology.[36] It is possible that the word for "orange" in many languages goes back to Tamil *naranta/nārattai* (Sanskrit *nāraṅga*).[37]

Aside from individual lexical loans, Dravidian certainly influenced Sanskrit phonology and syntax from early on. It is still an open question whether Dravidian was the source of the ubiquitous phenomenon of retroflexion in Sanskrit and the Indo-European languages of north India—that is, those consonants that we mark as *ṭ, ḍ,* and *ṇ* (among others) and that are articulated by the tongue curling backwards against the palate. Retroflexion, a hallmark of Indic speech and one of the first phenomena to strike a foreigner's ear, is already present in the Rig Veda; it is pervasive in Dravidian phonology. M. B. Emeneau, an eminent authority in ancient Indic, both Indo-Aryan and Dravidian, offers the following balanced summary of the discussion:

> The fact . . . that the later in Indo-Aryan linguistic history we go, the greater is the incidence of retroflex consonants and the further fact that most of the Dravidian languages and the proto-Dravidian itself have this type of consonant in abundance, can only lead to the conclusion that the later Indo-Aryan developments are due to a borrowing of indigenous habits through bilingualism, and to the well-grounded suspicion that even the early development of retroflexes from certain Indo-European consonant clusters results from the same historic cause.[38]

In other words, in Emeneau's view Dravidian speech is the main factor in the integration of retroflexion as phonemic in Vedic and post-Vedic Sanskrit. Other scholars, including Kuiper and Southworth, argue that Sanskrit retroflexion is largely rooted in the "certain Indo-European consonant clusters" to which Emeneau refers—and, partly as a consequence of this view, that "in the case of Sanskrit, the origin of retroflexion lies not so much in the Aryans' borrowing this trait from Dravidians in early times as in Dravidians' adapting Aryan speech to their native phonology."[39] This chapter is not the place to attempt to resolve this issue, although I think we should definitely avoid confusing "Dravidian," which is properly a linguistic term, or, for that matter, "Aryan," with ethnic or social categories. I doubt very much that there were ever "pure Vedic Aryans"[40] or "Dravidians" among the speakers of any first-millennium B.C. Indic languages. What we can say with confidence is that speakers of Vedic Sanskrit were in contact, from very ancient times, with speakers of Dravidian languages, and that the two language families profoundly influenced one another, to differential effect in accordance with geographical and cultural-historical variation throughout the subcontinent. As far as syntax goes, there is ample room for continued debate; but it is likely that the Dravidian nonfinite verbal forms (called *viṉaiyĕccam* in Tamil) shaped the usage of the Sanskrit nonfinite verbs (originally derived from inflected forms of action nouns in Vedic). This particularly salient case of possible influence from Dravidian on Sanskrit is only one of many items of syntactic assimilation, not least among them the large repertoire of morphological modality and aspect that, once one knows to look for it, can be found everywhere in classical and postclassical Sanskrit.[41]

Where did the speakers of early Dravidian languages come from, if they were not, in fact, already indigenous to India? Some have argued for the Iranian plateau as their original home, and for a link between Dravidian and the ancient Elamite language of Mesopotamia.[42] Zvelebil has reviewed the evidence for this claim, concluding that it is possibly the most likely of any of the many hypotheses that have been advanced for some genealogical relation between Dravidian and some other language family.[43] In my view, the proposed links with Elamite are tenuous in the extreme. Other scholars have situated Dravidian within the long historical movement of Neolithic pastoralists southward into India from areas to the north and west.[44] Unfortunately, we have no idea what languages these people spoke, though it is more than tempting, for many reasons, to imagine them using an early form of Dravidian (which is *not* to say that they were the purely fictive "Dravidians"). Precisely the same could be said of the attempt to associate Dravidian speech with the widespread megalithic remains of the Iron Age Deccan (second millennium B.C. to late first millennium B.C.).[45] We do not know who these people were, but there is much to commend the notion that late prehistorical south India was home to Dravidian languages, and that these languages and their oral poetry and poetics underlie, in various modes, though not without substantial contact with Indo-Aryan, the earliest literary works in Tamil and Telugu, with possible influence over early Prakrit poetry as well.[46]

Still, we have the persistent problem of identifying a plausible dating sequence for Dravidian speech. I want to avoid boring the reader with yet more fragile reconstructions based on sparse linguistic evidence. But I have to mention, at least in passing, the Dravidian, probably early Tamil, loan words in the Hebrew Bible. Most of these have been known since the mid-nineteenth century, when Christian missionaries, who were trained in biblical Hebrew, arrived in south India and began learning Tamil. A famous verse from I Kings (10.22) contains three Indic loan words describing imports to the kingdom of Solomon from a mysterious land called Ophir—possibly a port in the Persian Gulf or even on the West Indian coast, though we cannot say for sure. These items are *shenhabim,* "ivories," possibly derived from Semitic *shen,* "tooth," and Sanskrit *ibha,* "elephant," though other etymologies have been proposed; *kofim,* "monkeys," certainly derived from Sanskrit *kapi,* itself a Munda loan word in Sanskrit (like many other Sanskrit nouns beginning with the prefix *ka-* signifying the yellow-brown-gray color of monkeys and elephants);[47] and *tukkiyim,* always translated today as "parrots," as in modern Hebrew *tukki,* but originally taken from Tamil *tokai,* the male peacock's tail, thus metonymically signifying peacocks. One can, I suppose, imagine ancient Israelite mariners pointing to the splendid tail feathers and asking their Tamil-speaking colleagues what name it had.

Thus one of the three terms is clearly Dravidian, indeed a very early attestation of Dravidian, depending on when we date the compilation and redaction of the Book of Kings (mid-first millennium B.C.?).[48] *Tokai,* is not, however, the only Dravidian-based word in the Bible. We have *ahalim,* "eagle-wood," probably derived directly from Tamil *akil* rather than from the Sanskrit *aguru,* itself a loan from the Tamil (Numbers 24.8; Proverbs 7.17; Song of Songs 4.14; Psalms 45.9—the latter two instances with the feminine plural form *ahalot*). *Akil* is, we think, native to south India, and it is thus not surprising that the word was borrowed by cultures that imported this aromatic plant. *Karkom,* turmeric, curcuma (Song of Songs 4.4) is probably derived from Tamil *kūkai,* Sanskrit *kuṅkuma.* Hebrew *armon,* "palace," may be related to Tamil *araṇmaṉai,* with the same meaning, though again this etymology is only one of several possible ones. The post-biblical Hebrew word for rice, *orez*—like the words for rice we know from European languages, including Greek *oryzon*—is probably from Tamil *arici*, "unhusked rice," itself perhaps from a Munda source.[49] The Semitic linguist Chaim Rabin studied these Dravidian loan words in ancient Hebrew and suggested several others, some of them highly controversial.[50] It is, in any case, clear that trade relations between south India, the Persian Gulf, and the Levant going back at least to the middle of the first millennium B.C. brought Dravidian names for exotic products westward centuries before Tamil becomes present in the historical record as the language of inscriptions and of poetry.

On the basis of this linguistic evidence alone, we will have to conclude that speakers of Dravidian languages were in place in south India, and perhaps also farther north, in the first millennium B.C., and that there was interaction between the speakers of Vedic Sanskrit and Dravidian even earlier. But how far back does this take us? Not anywhere near the period when the prehistoric civilization of the Indus Valley, spread over a wide area in today's Pakistan and northwest India, reached its peak, around 2200 B.C. As is well known, large numbers of inscribed and beautifully illustrated seals have been recovered from Indus Valley sites such as Mohenjo Daro and Harappa; but so far no proposed decipherment of the inscriptions—and there have been many—has convinced us. Two sustained and intriguing attempts to read the seals as Dravidian, by the Finnish Indologist Asko Parpola and by a team led by the Russian Yuri Knorozov, one of the main decipherers of the Mayan script, remain highly speculative, as are the ongoing studies of the Harappan script by Iravatham Mahadevan.[51] In recent years the Vedic specialist Michael Witzel, together with Sproat and Farmer, has argued forcefully, but not entirely convincingly, that the Indus Valley inscriptions are not linguistic signs at all but rather emblematic markings like medieval heraldic insignia. In short, we cannot yet read these seal inscriptions and, in all honesty, we have no idea what language was spoken in the Indus Valley in the third millennium B.C. I, for one, doubt that it was Dravidian. We eagerly await the rebirth of Michael Ventris.

We are, at last, on firmer ground when we reach, at the latest, the second century B.C.—the moment when prehistory becomes protohistory in south India. "Real" Tamil inscriptions, written in the old script known as Tamil Brāhmī—possibly a derivative of north Indian Ashokan Brāhmī of the third century B.C.—have been discovered in several sites in the Tamil country, most of them caves inhabited by Buddhist and Jain monks. However, if the newly proposed radiometric datings for Tamil Brāhmī inscriptions discovered at Porunthal and Kodumanal turn out to be correct, we would have to push the transition to protohistory back to the fourth or even fifth century B.C.[52] There is still reason to remain a bit skeptical about these dates, which would situate early Tamil Brāhmī prior to Ashoka; we need to keep an open mind.

The second-century B.C. Buddhist and Jain inscriptions are, not surprisingly, replete with Prakrit words, since such monks undoubtedly used Prakrit for both ritual and pragmatic purposes. Consisting of laconic records of donations by patrons, these texts reveal a south Indian world saturated with north Indian linguistic and conceptual elements; there is no "pure" Tamil here (or anywhere else, for that matter). We can date the inscriptions by paleographic analysis which, while far from exact, does offer a useful point of departure. Two distinctive features of the Tamil Brāhmī script should be highlighted: first, it contains characters for phonemes proper to Tamil but unknown in north India (*ṟ, ṉ, ḻ,* and *ḷ*); second, nearly alone among Indian scripts (the other case, not fully carried through, being the Bhattiprolu inscriptions from coastal Andhra), Tamil Brāhmī marks vowelless consonants (the diacritic vowel sign being added to the pure consonant sign).[53] This is in contrast with the other Indic scripts, including classical Tamil, in which the basic consonant sign includes the inherent vowel *a*, "as God inheres in the world of forms."[54] We thus have the first hard evidence of datable Tamil from a century or so later than Ashoka's own famous inscriptions, in which he refers to the south Indian kingdoms of the Coḍa (=Coḻa), Pāṇḍiya, Satiya-puto (Satya-putra), and Kelala-puto (=Kerala-putra, later, Ceras).[55] By the mid-third century B.C., the far south of India was home to several dynastic states whose names we know well from the later, so-called Sangam poems, to be discussed below.

If we move forward to the first to second centuries A.D., we reach the sensational discoveries of Tamil-Brāhmī inscriptions of a semi-historical character at Jambai, in South Arcot District, and at Pukalur, not far from the large town of Tiruccirappalli. The Jambai inscription marks a donation by *satiya puto atiyāṉ nĕṭumāṉ añci,* that is, the Satyaputra ruler Atiya[mā]ṉ Nĕṭumāṉ Añci, possibly the hero whom we know from many references in Sangam heroic poetry. We also know from the poems about Atiyamāṉ's nemesis, Pĕrum Ceral Irumpŏṟai, who conquered the fort of Takadur and killed Atiyamāṉ with his spear. It appears at least possible, despite cogent objections by Krishnan and Tieken,[56] that Pĕrum Ceral Irumpŏṟai is to be identified with one of three kings (father, son, and grandson) mentioned in the Pukalur inscription.[57]

Whether these identifications are correct or not, you can easily understand the excitement the finds initially generated. It would be almost like coming across an autograph of Agamemnon or Hector in some Aegean site. We will come back to the still unresolved chronological issues in Chapter 2. For now, it should suffice to point out that a swelling body of epigraphical, archaeological, and numismatic evidence, some (though not all) of it in apparent harmony with what we read in the early Tamil literary sources, reveals to us a sophisticated, cultivated, proto-urban culture fully in operation on the ground in the far south by the early centuries A.D. There were small-scale polities, usually at war with one another, some of them closer than others to an even earlier, pastoralist model suited to wilderness zones. There were the major cultural centers such as the Pandya capital of Madurai and early Cera Karuvur, whose wealth came, at least in part, from large-scale rice cultivation.[58] There were Brahmins performing Vedic rites and Buddhist and Jain monks supported by sympathetic lay communities and by royal patrons. There were, we think, poets and singers and other musicians. There was brisk international trade, including the presence of Hellenistic (Roman) merchants in small outposts—probably not so different from the seventeenth-century "factories" established on the Indian coasts by the European trade companies—that left behind them rich caches of Mediterranean gold and silver coins and other items.

Classical Mediterranean sources have confirmed this last perspective. Already Megasthenes, a Selucid ambassador to the court of Candragupta Maurya in the late fourth century B.C., had heard of the distant

Pandya kingdom, ruled over by "Herakles' daughter, Pandaia."[59] By the first century A.D. an anonymous manual for seafarers, the *Periplus of the Erythrean Sea,* gives names of major ports and cities along the South Asian coast, including sites in the far south, nearly all of the latter Dravidian toponyms.[60] *Damirika,* apparently *Tamiḻakam* or the Tamil heartland, appears as a name for the southern region; the Pandya kingdom is mentioned, as is the still mysterious port of Muziris, Tamil Muciri, on the Periyaru, which archaeologists under the direction of P. J. Cherian have been searching for at the remarkable site of Pattanam in central Kerala. The *Periplus* speaks of pepper and other spices, diamonds and sapphires, tortoise shell, and other luxury items as available in plenty in southern India. Archaeological work at Arikamedu, close to Pondicherry, has brought to light first-century Roman coins, amphorae, and glass along with further Tamil-Brāhmī inscriptions on potsherds (of particular note being one of the earliest we have, probably from the first century B.C.).[61] Early Tamil poetry offers detailed descriptions of these *yavana*—Hellenistic, "Ionian"—traders and the exotic cultural world they brought with them to Damirika.

Once we have emerged into the predawn twilight of history—although the correlation between the literary and the epigraphical/archaeological sources is still more than tenuous—other kinds of evidence begin to build up rapidly, including the sorts of linguistic borrowings with which we began this section. Empirically speaking, Sanskrit-in-Tamil and Dravidian words in classical Sanskrit are numerous. Eventually a point will be reached, in medieval times, where every Sanskrit word is potentially a Tamil word, as is also the case with Sanskrit flowing into Malayalam and Telugu. But here we would do well to remind ourselves that the interpenetration of Sanskrit and Dravidian is not a simple matter of cumulation over time in some seemingly linear mode. Nothing could be farther from the truth. As Gros has aptly said in connection with the early Tamil poems, "To establish a chronology relating to the Caṅkam texts according to the proportion of Sanskrit vocabulary in them is, without a doubt, to depend on shaky reasoning based on the postulate of a progressive 'Aryanization' of Tamil and the summary idea that that process can be measured by a single formal criterion: Sanskrit vocabulary."[62] The regnant scholarly paradigm embodying this "idée sommaire" has long ago outlived its usefulness. We can do better—as, in fact, the Tamil literary tradition itself did over the past 1,200 years.

## Agastya and the Origin of Tamil Speech

So far we have been examining external testimonies to the existence of ancient Tamil—mostly because such evidence lends itself to relatively reliable dating, or at least to the useful and no doubt necessary illusion of chronological stability. But the Tamil tradition has its own persistent theory about its origins, a theory that comes with trenchant perceptions about the way this tradition viewed its defining features and its primary, sustained themes. According to the most widespread narrative, existing in several distinct variants and crystallized in canonical fashion only in the high medieval period (ca. the thirteenth century), at the very beginning of Tamil we find the figure of the maverick Vedic sage Agastya, a dwarflike but weighty scholar *(kuṟumuṉi)* who was sent south from north India and who eventually took up residence on Mount Potiyil in the Tamil country, in the Western Ghats near the southern tip of the subcontinent. Agastya is the putative author of the first Tamil grammar, the *Akattiyam,* now lost except for a few stray verses quoted in medieval commentaries;[63] in this role he effectively makes Tamil speech possible and provides a necessary framework for judging its correctness and thus ensuring its longevity.

We don't know when Agastya's name was first connected with Tamil grammar. This sage, the last and most unusual of the so-called seven Vedic sages *(saptarshi),* is already well known in the Rig Veda, which includes, among other references, a dialogue hymn between Agastya and his wife, Lopāmudrā (1.179). Late Vedic traditions and their reflexes in medieval commentary tell us he was born as a fish in a pot *(kumbha)* after two gods, Varuṇa and Mitra, shed their seed in it when they saw the ravishing dancing-girl, Urvaśī.[64] Being conceived and born from the pot, this odd sage assumed the pot's dimensions.[65] The Sanskrit epics describe the circumstances of his southward excursion: he was sent by the gods to force the Vindhya Mountains, which had risen to the zenith of the cosmos and were interfering with normal cosmic operations, to shrink back to their normal size (*Mahābhārata* 3.102). He also drank up the waters of the ocean in order to expose the demons who had taken refuge there; and he is closely associated with two particular demons, Ilvala and Vātāpi, and thus with the south Indian site of Badami (the name is derived from Vatapi), the ancient Calukya capital, in modern Karnataka.[66] Kālidāsa links Agastya with the Pandya kingdom of Madurai and its king, at whose horse sacrifice the sage officiated;[67] thus by the late fourth century, if not earlier, classical north Indian sources thought of Agastya as having a south Indian connection—indeed, he was probably pictured as a pioneer of Vedic civilization in the far south, a role he also assumed in mid-first-millennium Java. He has an astral identity as well, as the star Canopus (Arabic-Persian Suhail) in the southern sky whose appearance in the fall season marks the transformation of turbid water to a limpid state.[68] These references in Kālidāsa, incidentally, offer us a highly nontrivial point of reference in our attempt to develop a developmental sequence for early Tamil. It is as if we were glimpsing, from a vast distance, a still young political and literary culture situated in Madurai but known, at least by hearsay, to literati in the Gupta capital—a culture already attached to the emblematic name of this Vedic sage.

Agastya's very name, as we have seen, is probably Dravidian. He is mentioned in the Tamil sources beginning around the fifth and sixth centuries—in the Sangam anthology *Paripāṭal* (11.11—an astrological reference, without the explicit name of the sage), and in the preface to the long Buddhist narrative poem *Maṇimekalai,* where, at the request of King Kāntamaṉ, Agastya turns his water pot upside down and allows the Kaveri River to flow eastward through the southern land.[69] Agastya is thus the prime source of earthly benefice, the catalyst for the formation of the fertile delta that is the Tamil heartland. A little later we find numerous references to this rishi, and to his abode on Mount Potiyil, in the *Tevāram* poems sung to Śiva.[70] But the first glimmer we get of what was to become the standard view of Agastya as the foundational grammarian appears, along with closely related materials on the ancient Tamil "academies," in the old prose commentary ascribed to Nakkīraṉār (eighth or early ninth century) on the first *sūtra* of the *Grammar of Stolen Love, Iṟaiyaṉār akappŏruḷ (IA).*[71]

Note this name and the approximate dating. Why should stolen love need a grammar? But it does: *kaḷavu,* the ecstatic love consummated secretly before marriage, is a favored topic for the early Tamil poets; as a literary topos it is ruled by a large set of conventions and stages that do, indeed, comprise a grammar amenable to formalization (in the case of the *IA,* by the god Śiva himself, as we will see). This particular grammar appears at an important moment in the evolution of the tradition. The standard, though far from certain, scholarly scheme for old Tamil posits a period of some centuries, beginning around the first or second century A.D., during which the first Tamil poems we have, belonging to the so-called Sangam corpus, were composed. "Sangam" refers to three mythic literary academies at which much of this early literary activity was supposedly located. We will examine this canonical tradition shortly; it emerges, fully formed, only in the *IA* commentary—the *locus classicus* of the Sangam story even as it embodies segments, some of them very old, from earlier stages of editorial and grammatical work on or around the classical materials. Stated more simply: in the eighth and ninth centuries in the Pandya capital of Madurai, and perhaps at the Pandya court itself and under the royal aegis, a considerable body of traditional erudite lore focusing on the origins of Tamil culture—and, specifically, on the Grammar of Love—crystallized in a masterpiece of early Tamil prose attributed to the poet-scholar Nakkīraṉār. Once this version was in place, it largely shaped the views on Tamil origins in the mainstream of traditional Tamil scholarship through the high medieval period and right into modern times.[72]

We have these ancient poems, in the thousands, many of them exquisite—a signal contribution to South Asian, indeed to world, literature. And we have the conspicuous story the literary tradition tells itself about the circumstances of these poems' composition. Here, at the start of Nakkīraṉār's commentary,[73] we find Agastya mentioned as having been there at the very beginning of Tamil, in the first academy (*caṅkam* = Sangam) together with the gods Śiva, Murugan, and Kubera and 545 other members of this august body. Not only that: his book, the *Akattiyam,* was *the* book *(nūl)* for this first academy and for all the 4,449 poets who sang poems at or for it. This academy "sat" for 4,440 years in Madurai—not the present-day city but an earlier city, far to the south, that was swallowed up by the sea.[74]

But the long-lived Agastya was also a member of the second academy, which sat in a place by the eastern sea called Kapāṭapuram for 3,700 years before it, too, was swallowed by a flood. This middle academy retained the *Akattiyam* as one of its reference books, along with the *Tŏlkāppiyam*—literally, the "Old Composition," that is, the oldest surviving grammar we have today—and three other books that have been lost (*Māpurāṇam, Icainuṇukkam,* and *Pūtapurāṇam*).

Both the *Akattiyam* and the *Tŏlkāppiyam* survived the flood and served the academicians of the third Sangam, which operated for 1,850 years in "northern Madurai," the city we now know by this name. Nakkīraṉār tells us that 449 poets, including himself—the son of the accountant *(kaṇakkāyaṉār)*—sang poems for members of this academy. He then proceeds to list, for the first time in any of our sources, with slight variation in names, six of the great anthologies of Sangam poetry that we see today as containing the oldest Tamil poems we have: the 400 Long Poems (*Nĕṭuntŏkai nāṉūṟu,* which we call *Akanāṉūru*), the 400 Short Poems *(Kuṟuntŏkai nāṉūṟu)*, the 400 Poems on the *Tiṇai* Landscapes *(Naṟṟiṇai)*, the 400 Outer Poems *(Puṟanāṉūṟu)*, the 500 Very Short Poems *(Aiṅkuṟunūṟu)*, and the Ten Tens *(Patiṟṟuppattu)*. Six other works are also listed, two classed by the poetic meters they used, and the other four perhaps referring to four works included in the *Pattuppāṭṭu* (Ten Songs) anthology of longer poems.[75]

Today we speak, in the wake of the medieval commentators (especially Perāciriyar and Mayilainātar, thirteenth and fourteenth centuries), of *Eight Anthologies (Ĕṭṭuttŏkai)*, including the perhaps somewhat later *Kalittŏkai* and *Paripāṭal*,[76] and the Ten Songs, the latter being much longer and far more discursive-narrative in character than the anthology verses.[77] These works, together with the *Tŏlkāppiyam*, constitute, *stricto sensu,* what we call Sangam literature; over the centuries, they were slowly marginalized and even "lost" or forgotten before being "rediscovered," edited, and published in the late nineteenth and early twentieth centuries by scholars such as U. Ve. Caminat'aiyar, Ci. Vai. Damodaram Pillai, and A. Narayanacami Ayyar (see Chapter 7). Since the publication of these great texts and the appearance of partial translations of the anthologies into English, notably by the outstanding poet-translator A. K. Ramanujan, scholarship, sometimes intemperate, on the Sangam works has become a veritable cottage industry; what is more, these poems have to no small degree displaced attention *within* the Tamil world from the monumental literary works of the past thousand years or so to these more ancient, hence suddenly prestigious, poems. Chapter 2 of this book addresses issues of sequence, dating, and above all the meaning of these works, in particular the poetry of love. Before we return to Agastya, let me just note that there is not the slightest shred of evidence that any such literary academies ever existed (although we do know of a Jain *drāviḍa-saṅgha* [Prakrit *dāviḍa-saṅgho*] academy established in Madurai by one Vajranandi in the year 470).[78] On the other hand, the *idea* of these Tamil academies turns up in the Pandya inscriptions, roughly contemporaneous with the *IA* and its commentary, and later spread widely beyond the bounds of Tamil itself. In the well-known Larger Sinnamanur inscription, for example, we hear of a mythic Pandya king "who had the *Mahābhārata* made into Tamil and established a Sangam in Madhurāpuri [=Madurai]."[79]

The term *draviḍa-saṅghāta*, the "Tamil collection," that is, the Sangam poems, appears in Sanskrit commentaries on Daṇḍin's *Kāvyâdarśa* (1.13: Vādijaṅghala and Taruṇavacaspati);[80] and the Telugu poet Nannayya, who occupies for Telugu the same slot that Agastya does in Tamil—that of first grammarian and culture hero—may be referring to the Sangam story when he says at the start of his pathbreaking eleventh-century *Mahābhārata:*

> There are assemblies where a subtle fragrance of wisdom
> pervades the air as in pools of perfect lotus flowers,
> accessible to all, and the good lives those scholars lead
> purify and please like flowing water:
> joyfully he [Nannayya] praised them all.[81]

In short, by the last centuries of the first millennium the image of an ancient community of scholars and poets engaged in a shared literary enterprise, or of several such communities organized sequentially, attached itself to the Tamil cultural tradition seen both from within and from without. Implicit in this image is the awareness of a particular corpus of works preserved in edited anthologies and illuminated by an authoritative grammar that helps to make sense of the poets' linguistic praxis and, no less important, of the poetic norms ruling the poets' work. Here is where Agastya comes in.

## The Grammarian's Blessing and Curse

There are two main expansions of the story of Agastya as culture hero in the Tamil south;[82] each of them fixes on a critical feature needed for the complete delineation of his role, which is say that together they shape the main story of origins the Tamil tradition chose to tell itself.

The first shows us a fissure in the integrity of Tamil grammatical science. In the fullest version of the narrative, in Nacciṉārkk'iṉiyar's late-fourteenth-century commentary on the preamble to the *Tŏlkāppiyam*, the weighty dwarf sage was sent south to balance the earth, which was dangerously tilted toward the northeast because the gods and sages had all come together in the Himalaya. On his way he received the Kaveri River from the Ganges and also found his best pupil, Tŏlkāppiyaṉār, the author of the *Tŏlkāppiyam* (whose "real" name was Triṇadhūmâgni/Tiraṇatūmākkiṉiyār), the son of the famous irascible sage Jamadagni/Yamatakkiṉi. Agastya also married Lopāmudrā—whom we remember from the Vedic hymn—said to have been the sister of the sage Pulastya, but Agastya left her behind as he headed south. Accompanied by a vast retinue of potential settlers, including the Veḷir and the Aruvalar, he found his home on Mount Potiyil in the Western Ghats. From there he sent his star pupil to fetch Lopāmudrā, instructing him to keep a safe distance from her throughout the long journey. But as they were crossing the flooding Vaikai River near Madurai—almost home—Tŏlkāppiyaṉār helped his master's bride across by holding out to her a bamboo pole. This was too much for Agastya to bear: he cursed both Tŏlkāppiyaṉār and Lopāmudrā never to reach heaven, and they, understandably incensed, cursed him back. Because of Agastya's curse, Tŏlkāppiyaṉār's grammar was ignored.[83]

In medieval and early modern sources, Tŏlkāppiyaṉār is one of a formulaic set of twelve disciples of Agastya (not named in full until the mid-nineteenth century).[84] Jean-Luc Chevillard has carefully studied the various names offered at different points in the evolution of this tradition. For our purposes, the striking feature is the violent antagonism structured into the line of teaching itself and the consequent gap in transmission. The *Tŏlkāppiyam,* it seems, was not, in the eyes of the literati, a perfect record of Agastya's lost teachings. At the very starting point of grammatical science—that is, of Tamil itself—we find a fracture. Grammar, in short, as we know it, is neither consensual nor complete. A curse hovers over the whole precarious enterprise.

The fracture and the curse emerge in part from the wider cultural pragmatics of this science. Grammar, strongly allied from the start with poetic praxis, is, like poetry, a practical medium for working on the world, for better or for worse—for paralyzing or even killing your enemies, or for generating wealth, health, long life, and eventual translation to a heavenly world. We will have occasion to return to this theme, which lies at the very core of Tamil literary and musical production.

Now consider how Agastya came to be a grammarian in the first place—the second major expansion of his image in Tamil. We have the story in several important texts from Madurai, in Tamil, Sanskrit, and Telugu, about the Sangam, the famous Academy of Poets. By the fourteenth century, Nakkīraṉār's version of the Sangam story, summarized above, has developed in a surprising direction. Nakkīraṉār speaks of a big stone slab *(kalmāppalakai)* on which deliberations by the scholar-poets apparently took place.[85] We hear nothing more about this *palakai* slab until the local *purāṇa* texts that present the traditions of the Mīnâkshī-Sundareśvara temple in a fully integrated, reimagined form, notably in the Sanskrit *Hālâsya-māhātmya* ("Story of Madurai and its God," *HM*) in the late fifteenth or early sixteenth century and continuing into the much-loved Tamil classic *Tiruviḷaiyāṭaṟ purāṇam* ("Śiva's Games") by Parañcoti muṉivar (probably late sixteenth or early seventeenth century).[86] These works speak of a set of sixty-four games or amusements (*līlā, viḷaiyāṭal*) of the playful god Śiva in Madurai, a set that includes several escapades relating to the Academy of Poets and, in this context, to the First Sage, Agastya. This is the story that everyone knows today—the version of origins that, drawing from and reworking the earlier notions I have mentioned, has achieved canonical status. The Madurai *purāṇas* tell the tale as follows (I follow Parañcoti in the main, with occasional glances to his source in the *HM*).

It all began in Kasi-Varanasi, in the far north, where the creator god, Brahmā himself, was performing a series of ten horse sacrifices. At the conclusion of the rite, Brahmā went with his three wives—Sarasvatī, the goddess of speech; Sāvitrī; and Gāyatrī—to bathe in the Ganges. But on the way, Sarasvatī's attention was momentarily diverted by one of the women singers who move between heaven and earth; she stopped to listen, her heart wholly given to the music. So by the time she reached the river, her husband and her two co-wives had already bathed and come out of the water. This made her angry, and she told them how she felt. "But it's your fault," said Brahmā, now angry himself. "And because you spoke in anger, you will have to undo the mistake by undergoing forty-eight human births" *(ĕṇṇ aṟu makka'ṭoṟṟam)*.

Curses have their own grammar. Since it is the sheer linguistic articulation of the curse that shapes the reality it creates, a close examination of the utterance often offers a way out. In this case, it could well be that Brahmā really meant to say, or now reinterprets his words to mean, that Sarasvatī, acting in all-too-human a manner, deserved to be born as a "senseless" *(ĕṇṇ aṟu)* human being—but only once. It is all a matter of how you decode the poetic statement; and the double entendre, *ślesha,* that is possible here is itself a sign of the consequential, intralinguistic mechanisms at work. Everything issues from the sounds or words that will automatically take effect, although they may be subject to contrasting understandings. Sarasvatī, truly alarmed at what has happened, pleads with her husband: "I'm your wife! You want me to suffer the confusion inherent in being human?" She has chosen one reading of the ambiguous phrase in question. By now Brahmā has relented inwardly; but since the reality of the curse already exists and cannot be simply abrogated, he has to reinterpret and explain:

> Your body, my dear, consists of 51 phonemes; 48 of them, from *a* to *h,* will become 48 poets in the world. Each of these phonemes is set in motion variably by the first vowel *a,* which rides upon them, one by one, in accordance with their consonantal value; and that first *a* is God, flowing through them as our Lord of Ālavāy [=Madurai] that is the home of the three kinds of Tamil. He, too, will become a poet and, assuming this form and dwelling in the seat of the Sangam, will appear as knowledge in the heart of all 48—thus protecting the wisdom of poetry [*pulamai*].

Now we know how the Sangam poets came to the world. They were born as phonic pieces of the goddess who is Speech; once born, they studied Sanskrit *(āriyam)* as well as the other seventeen languages, achieving special proficiency and subtlety in the southern wisdom—that is, Tamil. Note that language moves from a divine dimension, where it may exist as potential utterance, to the human world of birth and appearance; more poignantly, this move is triggered when Speech is momentarily mesmerized by the nonverbal experience of music. Speech is, perhaps, a devalued or more limited form of music. Stated simply, sound itself—nonsemanticized energy—comes first. Within the articulated phonematic sequence, consonants have stable contours while vowels are in movement, as their very name in Tamil, *uyir,* "breath," tells us (in our text, they generate *iyakkam,* "movement"). This is an ancient notion in Tamil, also known in Sanskrit phonology.[87] The vowel—particularly the inherent *a* vowel within the Sanskrit syllables—"rides upon" the consonant and gives it life. Consonants interrupt the flow of sound, while vowels are perceived as continuous. The primary vowel *a* inheres in the Sanskrit phonemes just as God inhabits the externalized world; more precisely, God, or Śiva, *is* this vowel, hence also the first poet of the Sangam. As such, he exists as a certain kind of wisdom or knowledge, *pulamai*—the peculiar domain of the poet, *pulavar.*

The forty-eight phonemes, however we want to count them,[88] suit Sanskrit, not Tamil, phonology. More specifically, their appearance here provides a link to so-called Tantric (more properly classical Śaiva) notions of phonematic evolution from primeval sound to the creative world. The Sangam story, in this reworked version, belongs in a much wider cultic and philosophical spectrum linked to the creative goddess and, almost certainly, to a version (possibly a rather early version) of the Tantric stream of the Śrī-Vidyā, which took root in the Tamil country by the early second millennium. Mīnâkshī, the Madurai goddess, embodies this vision of the goddess who clothes herself in effective syllables and can be made manifest through their utterance, especially when sung or spoken by a competent *pulavar,* "poet."[89] By late medieval times, a very ancient south Indian notion of the pragmatics of poetic speech has merged with the Tantric practice of phonic magic.

The forty-eight syllables-as-poets have now taken human form, as required by Brahma's curse; they wander from country to country, always triumphing over the local poets by virtue of their poetic skill, until they eventually reach the Pandya land and its capital, Madurai. Śiva himself, the god of the city, takes the form of a learned poet and comes out to greet them. He leads them straight to his own temple and tells them to worship the god there—that is, himself. This accomplished, he disappears. The Pandya king, observing the poets' obvious depth of learning and their way of life, can now offer them a place of their own—a *Saṅga-maṇḍapam,* the "seat of the Sangam," in the northwestern section of the Sundareśvara-Śiva temple. From now on, they will be a single, defined body, the poets of the Sangam, *kaḻakattor.*

But they have a new problem. Other, older poets are jealous of their privileged position and come to contest with them. These disputes seem unending, and the Sangam poets are soon exhausted. They therefore turn to the god-poet with a somewhat surprising request: "Give us," they ask the god who spoke the first book (*muntu nūl*—of grammar? the Vedas?), "a *caṅkappalakai,* that is, a board or tablet that can serve as an instrument to weigh and measure actual, infinite, poetic wisdom." They want a tool that can serve as an empirical, objective standard, thus making contests and debates redundant. And they get it: Śiva, again dressed as a poet, appears with a square, luminous slate impregnated with mantric power, a mere two spans long, that will, however, expand infinitely to make room for each true poet to sit. The Sangam poets gratefully accept this slate and take it to their hall where, one by one, they climb onto it; and there is always enough room, the slate happily expanding "as a short text expands without limit into its commentaries."

So Nakkīraṉār's stone slab has now become a slate or board. A classical Telugu version of the story thinks it was made of conch, Skt. *śaṅkha*—another possible (unlikely) etymology for the word "Sangam."[90] Or maybe, as Parañcoti seems to suggest, the name came from the doubts, Skt. *śaṅkā,* the slate was meant to remove. The *caṅkappalakai* would then be a highly useful "doubt[-destroying] slate." In any case, this slate is, above all, a "special seat of knowledge" *(vidyā-pīṭha-vicitra)* that Śiva creates out of his own *vidyā-pīṭha*—the "seat of knowledge" that is always associated with the goddess, and that is made up of the primary *mātrikā*-phonemes and therefore bestows perfect wisdom.

The Sangam replica is apparently a smaller *vidyā-pīṭha* adorned with the generative *mātrikā*-phonemes from *a* to *ha* and square in shape, white as the autumn moon. The poets ascend it by turn as it expands to make room for them. It is this *pīṭha* that is identified as the Sangam slate, famous throughout the earth.[91]

Thus, empirical criteria of poetic excellence do exist. Only a true poet, one who himself embodies a piece of the goddess and her body of sound, can successfully mount the Sangam slate. Many stories insist on the tablet's negative potential: floating on the Golden Lotus Tank in the Madurai temple, it would unceremoniously dump untalented but pretentious poets into the water.

But what about grammar, our point of departure? How does it relate to the objectified standard represented by the tablet or slate? It turns out that grammar—in particular the grammar of poetic production—is now more necessary than ever. Sitting on their slate, the Sangam poets produce many poems, "rendering their wisdom fruitful." The state of poetry seems reasonably secure. But a difficulty of a different order entirely becomes evident:

> The compositions made by many,
> the richness of their meanings
> and the fullness of their words,
> the suggestions of something more—
> all these seemed so alike
> that the poets became confused.
>
> They could see no distinction between one poem
> and another. They started to argue:
> "You wrote that one." "This flawless poem
> is mine."
>
> The god of Madurai, the trickster
> who is both word and meaning,
> appeared again as a poet
> to bring clarity out of delusion.
>
> "Give me your compositions couched in meter
> that are so confused and so disturbing," he asked,
> and the poets gave him their texts.

He studied them—the pure words,
the connectedness of meanings—
and then gave them back, dividing
mature poems wisely into various sorts.[92]

The grateful poets ask the god to remain with them as the forty-ninth poet of the Sangam, and he agrees—fulfilling Brahma's original curse or, perhaps, blessing. The Sangam as well as the structured domain of Tamil poetry that it embodies are now complete. God himself drifts repeatedly into his role as a poet; but he is also clearly an editor and a grammarian, setting up criteria of excellence and differentiation among texts that look, superficially, alike. To be god, in south India, is to work on reality through the instrumentality of metrical sounds.

But what was the problem? Why were the poems indistinct? On one level, the late-medieval tradition seems to be remarking on the impressive unity of style and convention—the unique poetic grammar shared by *all* the poets—of Sangam literature as we know it (see Chapter 2). All these poems inhabit a world of dense semiotic similarity; distinctions of style are, in fact, largely invisible in the core anthologies. A voice internal to the tradition finds it appropriate to state this literary fact. But on a deeper level, there is the recurrent problem of a missing grammar. A somewhat earlier strand of the tradition[93] tells us that the Sangam poets were writing down their compositions (notice this emphasis on written texts) and then throwing them, day after day, in an undifferentiated heap, into the Sangam hall. Cumulating in a disorderly way, some on top, some on the bottom, the poems became *saṅkīrṇa,* "jumbled up," confused beyond recognition, of mixed types, impervious to critical evaluation. In the absence of an accepted standard of excellence, the poets began to quarrel over whose poems were better than whose; they were overcome by egoism rooted in the individual body *(śarīrâhantā),* their minds deluded. To extricate them from this depressing state, Śiva appeared; the poets begged him to separate the poems from one another and to give them back in this newly ordered mode *(pṛthak pṛthak samādāya saṅgāyâdyârpayâśu naḥ).* The god happily did just that, skillfully establishing criteria of taste: it was now possible for everyone to see clearly the flaws and merits in poems.

But Śiva also goes a step further and actually produces a text, *śāstra*, setting out these matters for the sake of the poets. The text has a name—*adhikāram*, surely a reference to the *Pŏruḷatikāram* or "meaning" section of the *Tŏlkāppiyam* grammar, on poetics. How does this authoritative work, which we still have today, function in the atmosphere of highly competitive creativity in the Madurai Sangam, where God himself is a poet among poets?

The grammar exists; poets can make their own aesthetic judgments. But no sooner have they received the authoritative book than Natkīra (=Tamil Nakkīrar), perhaps the best of the Sangam poets and certainly the most arrogant, a jealous man *(matsarī)*, turns it against its author. His own poems, declares Natkīra, are simply beyond compare; unlike the others' creations, his works contain, he says, the much admired "fifth note," a musical concept redefined and applied here to literary composition. The "fifth note" is the perfect tone sounded by the cuckoo, thus, by extension, the perfection of tonality that a gifted poet can attain.[94] Śiva takes up the challenge and sings, on the spot, even more delicately beautiful poetry, subtle in sound and meaning *(śabdârtha-komalatarān śabdān)*; but Natkīra, adamant, petulant, and pretentious, refuses to acknowledge the superiority of the god's verses and even insists that the god's poetry contains a defect *(dosha)*. Śiva, master poet of poets, "playing" with them, as usual *(tais sārdhaṃ krīḍate)*, asks his Sangam colleagues to decide between his compositions and Natkīra's. They are perfectly aware of the perfection, the overflow of sweetness *(mādhuryâtiśaya)*, in the god's poems; but, cowed by Natkīra, they remain silent. A voice from heaven has to intervene to make the final judgment, in Śiva's favor, evident to all: "Sundareśvara, god of Madurai, is the one real poet" *(eka-kavīśvara)*.[95]

Thus it is not so much the uniform nature of a shared, convention-bound poetic universe that is at issue as the inherent difficulty in evaluating degrees of beauty, of developing standards of taste. For this, one needs a grammar, not of language per se but of poetics. In the absence of such a grammar, only the god can provide answers about the relative merits of individual poems. But as soon as he produces an authoritative book, even he can be superseded; it is almost as if Natkīra were saying to him, not without reason, "I have used your book to write better poetry than you!" This claim, by the way, is repeated in a yet more insistent manner by the same arrogant Natkīra/Nakkīrar in a well-known sequel to our story. Once again he challenges Śiva, this time finding fault with a poem produced by the god; and when he pushes this stance to the limit, Śiva opens the third eye on his forehead and begins to burn his recalcitrant and pedantic rival, so that Natkīra has to jump into the Golden Lotus Tank at the temple to escape being burnt to cinders.[96]

Enter Agastya, one more time. Natkīra emerges from the water in an altered, more humble state of mind; he has also become entirely devoid of any grammatical knowledge, thus effectively unable to speak, or, even worse, to compose poems, his whole raison d'être. To remedy this flaw, Śiva summons the one person who has learned the rules of Tamil directly from God himself. This is Agastya, now ordered to teach Natkīra the science of grammar in an intensive curriculum of study clearly centering on poetics.[97]

Agastya, we recall, is the eponymous author of the first text, *Akattiyam,* the authoritative *nūl* that served the early poets of the Sangams according to the commentary—attributed to Nakkīraṉār/Natkīra himself—on the *Grammar of Stolen Love.* But how did Agastya attain the knowledge that allowed him to produce this grammar in the first place? It seems that when Agastya was sent south by the gods to balance the earth, he at first felt rather insecure about one essential matter, which he explained to Śiva:

> They say the Tamil land, where I am headed,
> is full of poetry [*tŏṭai pĕṟu tamiḻ nāṭ' ĕṉpa*].
> Everyone there has studied Tamil and has achieved
> sweet Tamil wisdom. I should be able
> to respond when asked a question.
> So kindly heal my ignorance and give me
> the book of natural, correct Tamil [*antac cĕn tamiḻ iyaṉūl*].[98]

Here is a request the god cannot refuse; he places before him the "first book" *(mutaṉūl)*, which Agastya studies thoroughly before taking up his post. We can easily imagine what this book contained—the three parts of grammar, no doubt, but especially the matter of *pŏruḷ,* poetics, widely defined, including how to structure a book, how to write a preface, and other formal features set forth in this chapter of Parañcoti's *Tiruviḷaiyāṭaṟ-purāṇam.*

Foundational knowledge is grammatical knowledge, conveyed by condensed, enigmatic *sūtras.* Even speakers of the language need these *sūtras* in order to know their own words. The first grammarian, instructed by God, is the only one capable of handing down this necessary knowledge. Yet the book or corpus that should preserve this knowledge is susceptible to vicissitudes of one kind or another; in particular, it tends to be forgotten by the person who needs it most. The Tamil land is, before all else, a land of poetry; everyone there studies Tamil wisdom as part of the collective enterprise of *poesis,* which informs and motivates the entire culture and, as such, is the theoretical basis for kingship. Grammar, as a science, exists not so much for itself, as an autonomous intellectual domain, as in Sanskrit, but in order to serve the deeper purpose of poetic praxis. Of course, Tamil grammarians were, historically, interested in linguistic problems for their own sake, like their Sanskrit counterparts; but we see in Tamil a very different configuration of grammar and its role within the structured fields of learning than what we find in Sanskrit erudition. Poetry, a pragmatic discipline, frames and validates linguistics.

Logically, in this view, grammar precedes poetry as the condition of the latter's emergence. Indeed, grammar may, in theory, precede speech itself. The great eighteenth-century intellectual Civañāṉa muṉivar says that Tamil grammar, in the form of the book named after Agastya, emerged on the same day that the language of the Tamil country emerged, apparently out of some potential space in which this language already existed as rule-bound possibility.[99] Without grammar, authorized by a primordial seer, one cannot speak; and without speech, there is no world.

The Tamils cannot do without Agastya. Even the Buddhist authors in Tamil need this Vedic sage who, they say, learned grammar from the bodhisattva Avalokiteśvara *(avalokitaṉ).*[100] We have by no means exhausted Agastya's profile in the medieval sources; but let us see, for now, if we can define the meanings he brings into focus whenever origins are discussed.

First, it is very striking that the Tamil tradition seeks to position itself, from its putative starting point, in relation to the Vedic world and to Sanskrit, and certainly not in radical opposition to the latter. Tamil and Sanskrit fuse in a rooted complementarity in the image of this figure who came south from the far north. But Agastya is no ordinary Vedic sage; he is a restless visionary, driven by wanderlust, the seventh, thus anomalous figure in the series of seven great sages. In later times, he very naturally becomes associated with esoteric practices such as alchemy, mantric Yoga, medicine, and verbal magic; and he also has an intimate link with music and dance.[101] So this foundational grammarian, the author of the all-important first book *(mutaṉūl)* from which all others are felt to derive, belongs in principle to the esoteric/expressive side of Sanskrit literary and scholarly practice.

Yet the first book is (and maybe always was) lost, as important texts have to be.[102] The survival of stray verses in the late commentaries only corroborates this critical cultural statement. Tamil grammar stands, in its own understanding of its origins, in a slightly oblique relation to the mainstream science of Pāṇini and his successors; it seeks its own authority in the suppressed Aindra grammar, which may, in fact, have somehow influenced the *Tŏlkāppiyam*.[103] And since grammar is, in India, the arena for the fiercest existential struggles, it is not surprising that the transition from Agastya's primeval grammar to the empirical, working grammar of the *Tŏlkāppiyam* is accompanied by devastating rage and a curse.

As Chevillard and William Davis have noted,[104] Agastya's cultural role in Tamil has a Śaiva coloring. In the medieval sources, it is usually Śiva who sends the little sage south and who reveals himself to him—the first to receive this benefice—in temple after temple. We should also note that his southward progression follows the overland route through the Deccan, not the better documented historical trajectory of ancient cultural transmission along the western coast.[105] It is likely that we have here the remnants of a true memory of cultural origins. We should also bear in mind the political implications of the Agastya narratives, which make this potent, magically effective grammarian the support and preceptor, almost the alter ego, of the Pandya kings in the early civilizational center at Madurai. The Tamil language itself is firmly situated there at the site of its first literary efflorescence and the grammaticalization that must, in the internal perspective of this tradition, go hand in hand with the composition of memorable poetry. The conjunction of grammar and poetry thus finds its emblem in the person of a grammarian gifted with mastery over the magic of poetic words. And yet—grammar is in itself never entirely complete. It lays down the conditions whereby it can, indeed must, be superseded by a competent poet.

This introductory chapter has offered two quite different visions of Tamil origins. One is internal to the centuries-long evolving tradition and accessible only from inside; it is motivated by powerful south Indian notions about language, grammar, poetry, and the world. The other is exogenous, an unfinished, contested synthesis of modern scholarship by Tamil and non-Tamil scholars alike, and motivated by somewhat less powerful notions about language, grammar, poetry, and the world. The reader who can hold these two visions in her mind as complementary forms of understanding may find it easier to read the rest of this book than one who feels driven to make a choice—although the choice is there to be made. In Tamil, as we shall see, in-ness and out-ness are, on principle, inextricably intertwined.

Seen from the outside, the transition from prehistory to protohistory in the Tamil land takes place around the second century B.C., possibly somewhat earlier, when the first Tamil Brāhmī inscriptions left by Buddhist and Jain monks appear. We know from the Ashokan inscriptions of the mid-third century B.C. that there were already at least four kingdoms in the far south of India: Pandyas, Ceras (Keralaputra), Cholas, and Satyaputras. Dravidian speech is, however, attested long before this—in Dravidian words and syntactic structures in Vedic Sanskrit, and in the Hebrew Bible. We do not know when Dravidian language first penetrated the subcontinent; there may be a link to the Iron Age cultures of the southern megaliths, or even to the far more ancient world of Neolithic pastoralists. Whether speakers of Dravidian were to be found in the far northwest during the heyday of the prehistoric Indus Valley civilization, in the late third millennium B.C., we cannot say;

attempts to decipher the Indus Valley seals as Dravidian have so far produced rather meager results. There is no evidence to support the idea that ancient Tamil ever existed in some pure state, isolated from Sanskrit or north Indian culture.

From within the Tamil literary tradition, fully crystallized by the early ninth century, the transition to history took place thousands of years ago, when the first academy, or Sangam, was established in southern Madurai, far to the south of today's Kanya Kumari. If we put the numbers aside, we have a strikingly coherent and convincing image of a culture driven by poetry and an ancient grammar that serves both poets and their royal patrons. Indeed, to be a king in the Pandya country is to be attuned to the effectual mantic-poetic word; grammar defines politics no less than literature and music. At the inception of south Indian civilization we find Agastya, the nonconformist Vedic grammarian, sorcerer, and lawmaker, a long-lived culture hero who can, fortunately, be called in whenever grammar is lost or forgotten. In its widest resonance, grammar thus points to the self-awareness of the tradition as a field of aesthetic production with internal mechanisms of acceptability, taste, self-transcendence, and the articulation of truth—never a random domain.

TWO

# First Budding: Tamil from the Inside

*Pallavi*

## In-ness

Let's begin with a poem, and then one more. The first is a love poem attributed to Kapilar, one of the most famous of the Sangam poets; it appears in the anthology *400 Short Poems, Kuṟuntŏkai* (38):

He comes from the hill
where a baby monkey plays in the sun,
rolling an egg laid by a wild peacock
on a rock.

Loving him
is good, my friend,

for any woman,
eyes welling with tears,
who can stand it
and not think too much

when he goes away.

Sangam love poems tend to be about separation, of varying intensity. We have already seen that there is a concept of stolen love, *kaḷavu,* a happy but transient moment when the two young lovers consummate their desire in some natural setting, before the relationship is made public knowledge and before marriage. Normally, in the grammar of love, *kaḷavu* is followed by states of acute longing and waiting; often the young man goes off in search of wealth and knowledge, leaving his beloved behind. Separation, *pirivu,* is associated with the landscape of the desert, *pālai;* and the grammarians tell us that this aspect of love is common to all other phases of the relationship.[1] Even joyful union retains an element of separation and longing as, a fortiori, do the states where there is actual physical distance between the lovers.

"Loving" here is *keṇmai,* which suggests "closeness, intimacy, friendship, relatedness," glossed by the commentators as *naṭpu,* "loving friendship." It's a good thing, no doubt, but not without pain. The speaker, who, we are told by the colophon, is addressing her girlfriend and companion, moves rapidly into a mode of ironic, even bitter, complaint. Loving is great if you can bear it and keep yourself from thinking in the long periods when the lover is absent. Good luck.

The verse is simply stated, deceptively so. The assertion of goodness *(naṉṟu)* comes just in the middle, at the start of line 4 out of 6 in the original. The lover's departure, *taṇappa,* ends the penultimate, always slightly shorter line; not thinking, *uḷḷātu,* begins the final line, a position of great emphasis in most Tamil poems. The full force of the irony hits us here, before she ends the verse by spelling out this bittersweet suffering. So we have the image taken from the natural world, followed by the affirmation of goodness, in turn followed by a sharp but understated subversion of this same affirmation. She is alone, and she can't handle it.

The colophon, an editorial addition to the poem—we don't know from when—laconically provides a context, known as *kiḷavi,* a "statement," that is, a defined moment or topic in the love scenario. "The heroine speaks to her companion about her inability to bear [the pain] when the lover keeps putting off the [promised] marriage."[2] I'll have more to say about these colophons, which also provide the poet's name. Do we really need this information in order to understand the poem? In this case, no. Anyone can understand the poem just by reading or hearing it. Scholarly study of the Sangam poems nonetheless depends to a large extent on these colophons, and much of the controversy that plagues the study of this literature is bound up with issues of their reliability and the role they should or should not play in helping us read the text.[3]

In a way, the true "punch" of this poem comes from the opening "inset"—the baby monkey rolling the peacock's egg. Such insets are ubiquitous in Sangam poetry, and the grammar explains their purpose and power with the important technical term *uḷḷuṟaiy uvamam,* literally "a comparison that inhabits the inside." *Uḷḷuṟaiy uvamam* operates alongside a complementary category known as *iṟaicci,* "suggestion."[4] The operative assumption is that natural description of this sort is, in general, far from random or innocent. The image cited by the speaker enacts a piece of her or his inner world of feeling, *akam,* which I am going to translate as "in-ness." A. K. Ramanujan beautifully called it the "inner landscape." There is nothing symbolic about such images—indeed, we would do well to put aside the word "symbolism" entirely when dealing with south India. Rather, we have a resonance, or a reflection, or a projection, or a subtle yet highly evocative correspondence between the inner domain and something that apparently exists in an outer domain, which is called *puṟam.* In-ness and out-ness, *akam* and *puṟam,* constitute a complementary set; you can't have one without the other. Full-fledged *akam* poems regularly enfold some internalized bit of *puṟam;* indeed, the presence of one of these categories within a poetic statement nominally classed in the other one is a dependable sign that the text belongs to a defined genre, such as, say, "love poetry."[5]

It is usually possible to articulate, or paraphrase, the suggestive meaning of the inset; modern commentators, like the great U. Ve. Caminat'aiyar, the first editor of *Kuṟuntŏkai,* do this regularly, and we can find intimations of such paraphrase in the medieval commentaries as well. There is always a danger in stating the suggestion too definitively; a good *uḷḷuṟaiy uvamam* sets off a dynamic, never-quite-finished buzz in the mind, leaving the reader both moved and a little uncertain about where the image might come to rest. On the other hand, it's impossible to resist the temptation to spell things out. Here is what Caminat'aiyar says about this poem: "The peacock should take care and guard its egg, but instead it leaves it alone on the rock; not only that, the baby monkey plays with it, rolling it around. Just like that, the male lover, by leaving his beloved, who deserves to be delighted by their togetherness, causes her grief. What is more, she becomes subject to the further grief of hearing the villagers gossiping about them, with the result that she is made an object of ridicule. That's the suggestion" *(kuṟippu).*[6] This is one way of stating the scenario, though not the only one.[7] I think there's a sense carried by the inset that the heroine herself and, indeed, the love between these two people are fragile, precious, precariously balanced on a rock where some further danger awaits (some unthinking creature might come along and start rolling the egg here and there). It's very common in Sangam love poems to see the male lover described, explicitly or implicitly, as heedless, even perhaps indifferent to the distress he has caused.

We could no doubt get still more out of this poem; you can see how dense it is with thought and feeling. One guiding principle, never stated as such by the grammarians, is: "Less is more." The intensity of resonance is usually in direct proportion to the economy of expression. Remember, too, that such poems were meant to be sung, not recited in the way we recite English or French or German verse today (if we even dare to let the aural dimension come through instead of just reading silently). The verse is metrical, and there are interesting and complex relations between the metrical units and the verbal-semantic ones (Tamil poetry normally *writes down* metrical units, not lexical ones; this has been the case for the past two centuries or so). The musical aspect may well have dominated the actual, live performance of such a verse, as we can learn from nineteenth-century descriptions and a few surviving early twentieth-century recordings of Tamil poetry-in-performance. Indeed, as we will see in Chapter 3, musicality as such is one of the primary defining features of the life force *(uyir)*, or of the self, of a Tamil person. The self sings—usually, in an *akam* context, of sorrow, yearning, pain.

Still, we should try to say a little more about the outer segment of this poem, which, please notice, is situated in the hills—a meaningful choice. Where, exactly, does the outside exist? Before trying to answer this question, I'd like you to see another *akam* poem, this time by the great poet Paraṇar, as translated by A. K. Ramanujan. Here is *Kuṟuntŏkai* 60, another mountain-based love poem:

> On the tall hill
> where the short-stemmed nightshade quivers,
>
> a squatting cripple
> sights a honey hive
> above,
> points to the honey,

cups his hands,
and licks his fingers:

so, too,
even if one's lover
doesn't love or care,
it still feels good
inside

just to see him
now and then.[8]

Another not-so-happy vignette (this is the moment to tell you that the mountain region, *kuṟiñci,* is supposed to be the site of fleeting but joyful stolen love, sometimes directly linked with the white nightshade flower mentioned here). The cripple turns up in other Sangam poems; he may remind us of the famous opening of Kālidāsa's Sanskrit *Raghu-vaṃśa* (1.3), where the poet compares himself to a dwarf stretching out his arms toward a fruit high on a tree that he can never reach. It's pretty clear what this inset implies in our poem; I'll say no more about that. Well, maybe one small point: Caminat'aiyar rightly notes that the cripple, although he can't actually taste the honey, still feels a certain delight *(iṉpam)* just from seeing the hive.

Indeed, this poem ends with the word *iṉite,* "something very sweet" (the last syllable is the emphatic *-e*). In Ramanujan's translation, this has become "it still feels good." Very striking is the word preceding this one, *uḷḷattukk(u),* "to / in the inside." You may remember from Chapter 1 that *uḷḷam,* "inside," "heart," "mind," comes from the root *uḷ,* "to be inside," which also gives us *uḷḷu,* "to think," a verb that turned up in the previous poem we looked at. Loving is good if the lonely beloved doesn't think—inside herself, of course—about the absent lover. The sweetness, mostly imagined by the cripple as well as by the heroine of the Paraṇar poem, happens somewhere inside. An imagined sweetness is not to be laughed at.

In fact, the explicit appearance of the inside here may tell us something more about that inner domain. The inset already gives us one picture of it; then the speaker draws out the implied comparison without mincing words. I think we can speak of a staggered in-ness, or of the inner surface of in-ness, which apparently has outer (more superficial) surfaces as well. It is worth reflecting on the composition of in-ness in Tamil poetry, indeed in ancient Tamil culture generally. As I've already said, elements of out-ness always inhabit in-ness. The medieval poets, drunk on god's presence, sometimes suggest that within the *akam* inner domain we find an infinite series of receding pairs of interlacing ins-and-outs: in-ness-containing-out-ness-subsuming-in-ness-unfolding-out-ness, and so on.[9] A seemingly outer being like the beloved, or the god, is so deeply twined into the poet's own in-ness that we soon give up on identifying any out-ness at all. The Tamil cosmos has no external boundary.

I promised you only two poems, but I think we can allow ourselves one more:

A little cormorant with his red beak,
looking for minnows to feed the pregnant mate
whom he loves, pecks in the black mud
in deep holes, filled with flowers,
on white sands where village women
have gathered vines to worship their god,
stamping on thick hare-leaf creepers

on the coast where he lives.

He's cold to me.
My love is ruined.
My helpless misery
is blossoming on all the tongues
in this ancient village.
My pain is much worse
than pain.

Clearly, a *nĕytal* poem of the coast: this is *Naṟṟiṇai* 272, attributed to Mukkal Ācāṉ Nalvĕḷḷaiyār. It seems that the beloved, in an acute state of loneliness and sorrow, is speaking to her girlfriend. The inset should speak for itself, but in case it doesn't, the rest of the poem spells it all out. In contrast with the little cormorant, devoted to his pregnant mate, the lover has turned his back on the speaker—trampled on her, one might say, like the heedless village women intent on their ritual (*paṭivam*, an interesting loan from Sanskrit *pratimā*, "image" [of a god], "penance," via Prakrit). Pain too, it seems, one of the primary features of in-ness, has a deeper inner surface, far more hurtful than the outer surface one feels at first. Like many *nĕytal* poems, this one also flits from black to white, as if the visible white surface were there only to contain the dark depths. The inset is syntactically complex, a tour de force of serially embedded images; but the statement the poem strives for is utterly simple, directly and laconically expressed, hence all the more devastating. Here, as often in the *akam* corpus, in-ness has been ravaged from without; or, given the cold outside, in-ness has been turned inward on itself, a recursive twist that exposes the pain that is greater than pain.

*Akam* and *puṟam* relate to each other in a realistic but far from mechanical mode. Within the categorical duality is hidden a deeper vision of reality that privileges in-ness as the wider, perhaps ultimately the only fully real term. A comparison that "inhabits the inside" inevitably shows us the inside at work, re-creating imaginatively or perceptually an outer chunk of the visible world that is already deeply internal to the speaker—and, as such, ripening and growing there, like any living seed. This chunk of externality must also have its own in-ness; the two domains can only be artificially kept apart. There are different ways to speak of this dynamic, organic universe; Anand Pandian, a sensitive modern anthropologist, says an external landscape is "folded in" to the interior of a person, thereby creating depth as well as a reflective space. He speaks of an organizing principle of "sympathy" binding *akam* and *puṟam* together; thus it is not so much that the outer might reflect the inner, or vice versa, but that both domains continually resonate with each other, to the point where imaginative operations operating in one of them cannot but operate, along precisely the same vectors, in the other.[10] Hence the empirical observation that things happening in the mind or heart impinge on the outside. But we are getting ahead of ourselves. We will have opportunity to think further about the meaning of in-ness and, in particular, about the grammar of in-ness, *akappŏruḷ*, the subject of the *Grammar of Stolen Love (Iṟaiyaṉār akappŏruḷ)*. Note already, however, that grammar seems, in Tamil, to be a primary aspect of the inner domain.

I want to look now at this grammar as we find it in the classical sources, particularly the ancient *Tŏlkāppiyam,* Book 3, the colophons of the *akam* poems, and the commentary on *Iṟaiyaṉār akappŏruḷ (IA)* attributed to Nakkīraṉār. The main lines of Tamil poetic grammar are well known and have been set forth many times before; I will limit myself to the simplest possible summary, to be set beside the grammar of *puṟam* poetry. We will then enter into the debate on sources and dating without, however, striving for the elusive, comprehensive resolution of the main problems. We will take another look at the *Grammar of Stolen Love* and the story it tells of its creation. Finally, with the help of the Pandya inscriptions, I will offer a possible developmental sequence for the Sangam corpus and the erudite editorial world that grew up around it.

## Tamil Landscapes

As we know from the tale of origins examined in Chapter 1, the poets of the Sangam periods shared a well-structured poetic universe ruled by intricate conventions; the full expressive force of a Sangam poem often depends on the reader's knowing where this poem seeks to situate itself in the patterned semiotic map of the Tamil country. This map is the product of what I have been calling a poetic "grammar." It includes, for both love poetry *(akam)* and war poems *(puṟam),* a differentiated set of five main "landscapes," known as a *tiṇai,* literally "category," each one named after a flower native to that natural setting. Each landscape is intimately linked to a particular phase in the prototypical narratives of falling in love and going to battle, respectively. These prototypical narratives are never articulated as such in the poems themselves; we find them in the third book of the *Tŏlkāppiyam* and in later works such as the *Grammar of Stolen Love* and the *Garland of Vĕṇpā Verses on Outer Matters* (*Puṟappŏruḷ vĕṇpā mālai* of Aiyaṉāritaṉār, perhaps ninth or tenth century) and also in the popular genre of *kovai,* which arranges its verses in accordance with the standard love narrative. Apart from the emotional tenor associated with each landscape, a dense series of typical signs or features *(karu)* is attached to each *tiṇai;* these include, according to *Tŏlkāppiyam Pŏruḷatikāram, Akattiṇai* 20, the god, food, animal, tree, bird, drum, profession, and musical instrument (with its melodic style) proper to each region. One basic principle of ancient

Tamil poetics is that the mention of any of these typical features suffices to call up in the mind of the listener or reader the landscape of which it is part, with the particular emotional quality proper to that landscape. A skilled poet can also mix features from more than one landscape *(tiṇai-mayakkam)* in order to evoke with precision complex emotional states. We will look at some examples shortly.

First, here is the plan for *akam,* reduced to its essentials:

> ***Kuṟiñci,*** the rare Strobilanthes flower that blossoms once every twelve years, marks the landscape of the high hills and mountains, where *kaḷavu,* stolen premarital love (as rare and precious as the *kuṟiñci* flower) takes place. Even today, the intermittent blossoming of the *kuṟiñci* on the mountain slopes of Kerala is a great occasion, worthy of celebration.
>
> ***Mullai,*** "jasmine," belongs to the slopes and forests of the pasture-lands. Here we find the heroine, *talaivi,* in a state of painful separation from her lover, a state defined as *iruttal,* "sitting and (patiently) waiting." Actually, most *mullai* poems do *not* convey a sense of patience.
>
> ***Nĕytal,*** the Blue Nelumbo, grows on the seacoast, where the heroine is in a state of mostly unbearable waiting and longing, *iraṅkal.*
>
> ***Pālai,*** an evergreen, signals the arid desert that the hero, *kiḻavaṉ* or *talaivaṉ,* is crossing—usually alone—in search of wealth or learning. Here separation, *pirivu* or *pirital,* is at its most intense. In some *pālai* poems, the heroine elopes with her lover, and the two of them are thus cut off from the whole world of their native villages and families. The *Tŏlkāppiyam* (*Tŏl. Pŏr. Ak.* 2 and 11) says, not quite explicitly, that *pālai* is the "middle category" *(naṭu-nilait-tiṇai)* common to all the landscapes;[11] an aspect of separation is always present in loving, even at times of intense union and communion.
>
> ***Marutam,*** the Queen's Flower, names the luxuriant landscape of the Delta. Here we find the lovers married, at last, but not very happily; they quarrel *(ūṭal),* and the husband tends to spend his nights with courtesans *(parattaiyar).* A typical *marutam* poem depicts the jealous and grumpy wife at dawn, awaiting her husband's return from his night out.

Please bear in mind that the sequence I have summarized is an extrapolation by the commentators and grammarians; the reality that we meet in the poems is not at all as neat and clear-cut. The colophons to the Sangam poems often identify the *tiṇai* and the love situation by referring to specific "themes" or "topics," *kiḷavi,* as I have mentioned. These *kiḷavi,* though immensely useful, tend at once both to illuminate and to obscure the deeper meanings of a given poem. In any case, one should notice that the whole love sequence, taken as a coherent progression, moves rapidly (and literally) downhill from the heights of passion in the mountain region through states of increasing loneliness and bitterness to the somewhat grim routinization of love in marriage, against the backdrop of the green paddy fields. The first, happy phase of stolen love passes all too quickly.[12]

And there are two other *tiṇai,* not named for flowers, and also not considered proper topics for the always anonymous noble lovers *(cāṉṟor)* of the five landscapes just mentioned. Thus we have *kaikkiḷai,* usually seen (following the commentator Iḷampūraṇar) as a one-sided love,[13] rare in the Sangam corpus but enormously important to the later poetry of devotion to the gods; and the sadly named *pĕruntiṇai* or "large category" of love that is simply mismatched and unsuitable from the beginning, with certain definite signs of this state. Lively and interesting poems belonging to these latter two categories do turn up in the anthology known as *Kalittŏkai,* usually thought to be later than the classical six *tŏkai* collections.

The drive to categorize and enumerate continues to generate further associations specific to each of the *tiṇais.* Thus poems set in *kuṟiñci,* the mountain region, tend to be set in the night hours and the cold season *(kūtir); mullai* poems of the pasturelands classically unfold in the monsoon *(kār)* and the heartbreak hour of late afternoon to early evening, when the light in the Tamil country turns into thick liquid gold; *nĕytal* poems transpire on the coast at nightfall (or, according to some commentators, at sunrise: *erpāṭu*) and in any season; *pālai,* the harsh desert, is characteristically experienced at high noon *(naṇpakal)* and the early spring; *marutam* deltaic scenarios, as we saw above, are suited to dawn *(vaikaṟai)*—and, as everyone knows, quarrels have no special season. Further refinements of these temporal and spatial settings (known as *mutal*) are also to be found—not that the poems themselves adhere mechanically to these conventions. They do not. A grammar naturally aims at filling in all the blank slots.

Once we have the complete map of this Tamil world in place with its hyper-semantic marks and signals, we find that each landscape, as

Ramanujan nicely put it, is "a whole repertoire of images—anything in it, bird or drum, tribal name or dance, may be used to symbolize and evoke a specific feeling."[14] "Evoke," I think, is more apposite than "symbolize." Taken together, the landscapes provide a somewhat abstracted picture of entirely real and familiar eco-zones in the Tamil land: the mountains of the Western Ghats, for example; the hilly pastures of northern regions bordering on today's Andhra and Karnataka; the long coastal strips; the fertile deltas of the great rivers such as the Kaveri and the Tamraparni; and the fierce drylands of today's Ramnad District in the southeastern region of the state. The *Grammar of Stolen Love,* by the way, aptly notes that areas adjacent to the mountains and the pasture-lands can become dry wilderness in some seasons (presumably in the all-too-common failure of the rains).[15] But quite apart from the realistic, loving picture of these landscapes as comprising, as a set, the Tamil region as a whole—and thus demanding poetic treatment as a complete set in a large-scale, integrative work such as *The Tale of an Anklet (Cilappatikāram),* from post-Sangam times—the *tiṇais* constitute the "inscape" screen of the Tamil mind, an inner, visionary backdrop to the whole range of emotional and perceptual experience a Tamil person might experience and a gifted Tamil poet might seek to express. As such, they remained accessible and useful, with interesting permutations, throughout the entire course of Tamil cultural history, right up to our own time.[16]

Look at a simple, precise, very well known example by a poet named Miḷaippĕruṅ Kantaṉ (*Kuṟuntŏkai* 234):

> The sun departs, the sky
> turns red, the ache
> becomes sharp. Light fades.
> The jasmine blooms.
>
> That's what everyone calls "evening"—
> and they're all wrong.
>
> When the cock crows in the wide town
> and night turns to dawn—that, too,
> is evening. Even high noon
> is evening
> for the lonely.

You don't have to think too hard to get the point of this indescribably sad poem. Whenever I read it in public, in whatever language, it's clear that no one in the audience fails to recognize himself or herself in the speaker's words. Already at the end of the second line of the original, *mullai*—the jasmine flower—appears, so we know that we are in the hilly pastures and that the emotional tone is one of "patient sitting and waiting." But how patient is the speaker? According to the colophon, she is the heroine, *kiḻatti,* talking to her girlfriend. She's in terrible pain, and the evening hour, *mālai,* the standard *mullai* moment according to the grammar of love, exacerbates her suffering. Now comes the poet's dramatic and surprising move. In a few well-chosen words, he exceeds the limits laid down for him by the grammarians and universalizes the notion of evening as the hardest time of the day. Evening is terrible, no doubt, but so is every other hour, every other minute, in the *mullai* mode, which is now reformulated, again in a universal manner, without having to resort to implied suggestion or any other conventional mark or sign: the very last word of the poem, *tuṇaiyillorke,* "for the lonely" or the "companionless," with the emphatic *-e* at the end, says it all. Typically, the poet uses the grammar of love to locate the lyrical voice in a particular inner state—a single word, "jasmine," suffices for this purpose—and then proceeds to transcend the bare rules of time and place and their proper feelings. We have already seen that poetic grammar demands just this sort of bold abrogation. No real poet thinks of rules as rules.

It looks simple, but it isn't. For a Sangam poem to come alive, the grammaticalized language of the *tiṇais* normally has to be mobilized in deft and subtle ways that set off that wobbly resonance in the listener's mind; then, often, the grammar is jettisoned, and something new happens. You need the first part of the process in order to move into the second part. Extraordinary complexity, minimally articulated, is routine, if we can use such a word for a literature so utterly inimical to routinization of any kind. And perhaps it is not entirely superfluous to note the remarkable directness of a poem like this one; whenever it was written—1,200 years ago, or 1,500, or 2,000, we can't say for sure—the centuries fall away as soon as we hear it. This poem was written for us.

So far we have seen only half of the grammar, the *akam* half. In all fairness, we can say that, as we look at the Sangam corpus as a whole, this half is weightier than the other one, the *puṟam* set of landscape categories that complement and complete the first set. Here they are:

> Parallel to *kuṟiñci,* the landscape of stolen love in the hills, we have *vĕṭci,* the cattle-raid or skirmish: another kind of stealing.
>
> Raiding is followed by *vañci,* serious preparation for battle, like the supposedly patient waiting in the *mullai* landscape.
>
> Battle itself follows in *tumpai,* corresponding to the *nĕytal* seacoast, with its agonies of separation.
>
> But there can also be a prolonged siege, *uḻiñai,* linked to the landscape of lovers' quarrels, *marutam*—perhaps, as Ramanujan suggested, another form of "denying entry."

Finally, the middle *tiṇai* common to all of the five—*pālai,* wilderness, in the *akam* mode—is interestingly correlated to *vākai,* "victory." We are dealing with heroic poetry; but even here, victory may well be dry and empty.

As for the two "extra" *tiṇai* in the domain of love, they too have their counterparts in the outer domain: the "large category" is paired with *kāñci,* the meditative theme of "instability," "transience";[17] and "one-sided love" is very appropriately linked with *pāṭāṇ,* panegyric directed to a possible patron or hero.[18] With the exception of the latter, the outer *tiṇais* are, like the inner ones, named for a characteristic plant or flower, often said to be worn by the warrior as he enters the battlefield. One particularly striking feature of the *puṟam* grammar is the inclusion, along with the "Homeric" themes of fighting, killing, and dying for the sake of glory *(pukaḻ),* of philosophical domains that may be said to subvert the standard heroic mode; and there are also many lyrical elegies. To my taste, the most beautiful by far of the *puṟam* poems belong to this last category.

As in the case of the *akam* grammar, there is no one-to-one correspondence between the normative rules of the grammarian-poeticians and the *puṟam* works as we find them in the anthologies. The poets have more than a little freedom to do as they like—or, to put the matter in some semblance of a development sequence, we might suggest that the grammar itself reflects only a partial and abstracted schematization by editors and scholars from the already existing texts. The colophons give us the names of many poets who composed in both *akam* and *puṟam* modes, clearly allied, indeed strongly intertwined and resonant with one another, within a single literary world. The deep complementarity, which we will explore more rigorously in a moment, includes structural contrasts: thus *akam* poems are spoken by or about a very few anonymous types or characters (the two lovers, the woman's girlfriend, her wet-nurse or foster mother, the hero's friend or, rarely, messenger, and the hero's concubine), while *puṟam* poems are, at least in theory, about specific, named figures and their public exploits. However, in most cases we learn the names of these heroes only from the colophons, not from the poems themselves, which tend to refer to warrior kings by formulaic royal titles that could fit any member of the relevant dynasty. It is relatively rare, though by no means unknown, to find a proper name of any sort in these poems.[19] I will return to the implications of this fact in discussing the problem of the colophons more generally, including their usefulness for dating the corpus.

There are further contrasts to be drawn: despite the typology of seasons and hours built into the official *akam* eco-map, Tamil love poems have a clear fondness for nocturnal settings, as perhaps befits their orientation toward the obscure reaches of in-ness and awareness; the war poems, however, tend to unfold in the clear light of day, or we might even say, of history. There are many exceptions to this generalization, yet by and large it seems to hold. Outer and inner constitute a necessary unity. We can, nonetheless, be more precise about this notion and, in particular, about how it works in individual poems.

Take, for example, the following poem ascribed to Pakkuṭukkai Naṉkaṇiyār (*Puṟanāṉūṟu* 194):

> In one house: the rumble of the funeral drum.
> In another house: swelling sounds
> of the cool wedding drum.
> Those who are together wear
> fine jewels.
> Those who are apart shed tears
> of sorrow.

The god who made all this
has no character.
That's for sure.
The world is not so sweet.
You who know this deeply:
see what's in store.

Hardly a typical war poem, this laconic meditation (classed by the colophon as such: *pĕruṅkāñci,* the "big" *kāñci*) brings together the two domains in intimate contrast. We don't know how or why someone died in the first house—only that the funeral drums and the wedding drums are somehow mixed together, at least in the poet's mind. Interestingly, in the medieval *puṟam* grammar this same theme, *pĕruṅkāñci,* is defined as a show of skill with weapons by seasoned warriors.[20] Maybe the funeral in question is that of a warrior who fell in battle, in which case loving and dying, in-ness and out-ness, are indeed juxtaposed. Indeed, there are many *puṟam* poems where dying moves directly from the outer to the inner mode. In any case, the mood here is grim, almost heretical; or perhaps deliberately detached, as if offering an implied recommendation to renounce the world. However, the modern commentators, following the anonymous old commentary and unwilling to contemplate so severe a vision, gloss the final statement in as positive a light as possible: "Those who know the nature of the world should know about the good actions that generate joyfulness in the home."[21]

It is not by chance that poems of philosophic reflection or weariness with the world are included in *puṟam.* A surprising number of the war poems have an elegiac, and sometimes even a radically skeptical, tone. Reading them is a bit like reading through the *Iliad* in the light of Book 24. Take one example, *Puṟanāṉūṟu (Puṟan.)* 310, by Pŏṉmuṭiyār, beautifully translated by Hart and Heifetz:

O my heart, in pain and in anguish for him to whom I used
  to bring
milk and feed it to him and when he wouldn't drink, though
  I wasn't angry,
I would threaten him with a tiny stick and he would show fear!
But now that descendant of strong men who fell in earlier days

has slain painted elephants over and over and says he does
not feel
either the wound or the arrow within it. The tuft of hair
on his head is like the mane of a horse
and his beard is still sparse as he lies now on his shield.[22]

Was this young death worth it, even for the immortal fame *(pukaḻ)* that the (nameless) warrior perhaps thought he would achieve? To be fair, we have other poems about ancient Tamil mothers who, in apparent contrast with the speaker of this poem, are even more bloodthirsty than the men.[23] We should not forget that we are dealing with a poetry of heroism, on the one hand, and generous patronage, on the other: the subject of perhaps a majority of the *puṟam* poems is the warrior king who fights off his enemies and who, sooner or later, dies in battle, though not before having lavished huge rewards on the skilled poet who sings of his exploits. Readers are referred to the complete, annotated translation of *Puṟanāṉuṟu* by Hart and Heifetz.

For present purposes, we need to look at one more example, a complex and heart-rending one taken from one of the love collections (*Kuṟuntŏkai* 272), where we can see the rich and deliberate mingling of in and out:

To touch her, that mountain girl—

like a doe, sad-eyed, gentle, cut off
by archers from the herd
in deep forest
with wild whistles and a hail of stones,
and now she stands and watches

as the brothers of my beloved
pull the long blood-stained arrowhead
shaped like *her* eyes, limned in kohl,
under her black and fragrant hair
from the living heart of the wild stag—

will I ever
touch her again?

The colophon says this poem is uttered by the *talaivaṉ* lover to his close companion—possibly (this isn't stated in the *kiḷavi*) as they are rushing back to the beloved after a period far away. But here is a case where the colophon seems less than precise. I think the poem sounds more like an internal monologue by the lover, who has his doubts about whether he can ever reunite with the girl and also, perhaps, about whether the love relationship can survive, given the evident cruelty of the girl's brothers (as U. Ve. Caminat'aiyar suggests in his reading of the verse).[24] The comparison of the grief-stricken doe and the beloved is only implicit in the Tamil—the doe is simply part of the whole brutal hunting scene, which she witnesses helplessly—but there is an explicit comparison of the young woman's red eyes, always known to be potentially lethal, with the blood-stained arrowhead pulled from the heart of the stag. Has she been crying? Is she angry? All in all, the *talaivaṉ* lover pictures her in terms of an inset saturated with violence, terror, and sorrow. Love, we remember, once the "stolen" ecstatic phase is over, is not meant to be smooth.

In fact, as one reads and rereads the poem, it's easy to forget that it's about love. Most of it is taken up with the painful inset. So one way to describe the loop-like structure of this text is to note the opening *akam* line—"To touch her, that mountain girl"—and then to focus on the *puṟam* hunting scene, in all its suggestiveness, before we return to the outer *akam* frame in the last few words. In-ness subsumes out-ness and reverts to in-ness. But this is far too simple a reading. The hunting scene is itself pregnant with hints, indeed more than hints, of *akam* experience: the doe that calls to mind the beloved, the eyes that are an exact counterpart *(māṟu)* of the hunters' weapon; the brothers who belong to the mountain girl and who may well enact something of her own dangerous nature. So we have, again, in-ness subsuming an out-ness informed by in-ness that is, it seems, an integral and necessary feature of the outer domain—and so on all the way down. There is surely no Archimedean point that the reader can ultimately reach in this world of nested, complementary, mutually dependent realities. In-ness here—we are in a love poem—moves into the outer mode, thus externalizing its outer aspect, or perhaps the outer, rather than the inner, surface of interiority.

More simply: here is a love poem in which the loneliness and terror of loving are fully exposed. Take this as a major, enduring cultural theme. We can find corresponding war poems in which the inner passion of battle is no less central. Both of the domains, *akam* and *puṟam,* are in fact more like directions or velocities of movement than static frames or definitions. *Akam* poems move from the outside inward, *puṟam* ones from the inside outward[25]—although even this statement can easily be shown to be inadequate to understanding many individual poems. The complex interweaving of these directions, perhaps the feature that best defines what we might call the early genres of Tamil and the sine qua non for the consolidation of a genre ecology in the Sangam corpus, is the single most conspicuous feature of this literature, though it was never thematized as such by the classical grammars. In later periods, as we will see, still further levels of complexity, sometimes reaching toward a dizzying conflation, became the norm.

## Back to Stolen Love

Before we address the hard problems of dating and sequence, we need to examine one more part of the tale of origins that, as we saw, appears in its complete form in the commentary on the *Grammar of Stolen Love* ascribed to Nakkīraṉār. We have looked at the role of Agastya, the founding figure and first grammarian, and at the tradition of the three primordial Sangam academies; and we have seen how the poet-cum-academician Natkīra/Nakkīrar challenged the new grammar provided by Lord Śiva, and how he failed in his attempt to out-sing, or out-do, this god.[26] But since origination is always, in southern India, a matter of repetition, the Sangam story is immediately followed by a sequel in which, as it were, the cultural tradition has to start again:

> A twelve-year famine struck the Pandya land. The king summoned the scholars of Tamil and said: "I can no longer support you. Go somewhere else. When this land again becomes a land, remember me and come back." The scholars left. After twelve years rain fell, and the king sent messengers to recall his scholars. But now it transpired that, while there were some who still knew the grammar dealing with phonology *[ĕḻutt'atikāram],* morphology *[cŏllatikāram],* and metrics *[yāpp'atikāram],* none survived who knew the third section, the grammar of meaning *[pŏruḷatikāram].*
>
> The king was stricken with grief. What use are phonology, morphology, and metrics without meaning? Do these sciences not exist in

order to serve poetic meaning? He meditated on the god in the great temple of Maturai Ālavāyil, and the latter, taking note of the king's distress, wrote down sixty *sūtras* on three copper plates that he placed behind his own image in the shrine. These *sūtras* are the text we know as the *Grammar of Stolen Love.*

The copper plates were discovered by the Brahmin temple sweeper who, moved by a divine sign, decided to sweep that day behind the image. He looked at the plates and knew at once that they were a gift of the god to the king. He didn't go home; he went to the outer gate of the palace and informed the gatekeepers, who informed the king, who summoned the Brahmin inside. The king, too, realized at once that these plates contained the missing section on meaning, given by the god. He convened the Sangam scholars and said to them, "God has seen our distress and given us the section on meaning. Take it and see what it means." They took it, mounted the big slab of the Sangam, and studied it, each offering his own interpretation of the laconic *sūtras.*

They came back to the king and informed him that they couldn't agree on a single interpretation, and that they needed a judge *[kāraṇikaṉ]* to decide which commentary was correct and which ones were wrong. But the king sent them away, saying, "You are forty-nine unequaled scholars. Where am I going to find a judge?" They returned to the Sangam slab. "God himself made these *sūtras,* didn't he?" they said. "He has to supply us with a judge." They prayed to him, and in the middle watch of the night a voice called out three times: "In this town there is a five-year-old boy named Uruttiracaṉmaṉ, son of Uppūri Kuṭikiḻār, with tender eyes and gentle hair. He is a mute, but don't underestimate him for that. Bring him to the Sangam, give him a seat, and expound the *sūtras* beneath him. When he hears a correct commentary, tears will fall from his eyes and his hair will stand on end. If he hears an incorrect explanation, nothing will happen. He is Lord Kumāra[27] himself, born here because of some curse."

They rushed to the boy's home, brought him to the Sangam, dressed him in white, with white flowers and sandal paste, and seated him on the Sangam slab. From below they expounded the *sūtras.* Nothing happened. But when Madurai Marutaṉ Iḷanākaṉār explained the text, at one or two points tears came to the boy's eyes, and his hair stood on end. Then when Nakkīraṉār, the accountant's son, spoke, at every word the boy wept, and his hair stood on end. "At last," they cried, "we have got the true commentary *[mĕyyurai].*"

> So, says the text of the commentary as we have it, there are some who say that Uruttiracaṉmaṉ, son of Uppūri Kuṭikiḻār, made the commentary to this book. But the truth is that he did not make it but only heard the correct commentary. Actually, the book made by the god of Madurai was *understood [kaṇṭu]* by Nakkīraṉār and *heard* by Kumāracuvāmi.[28]

The conclusion may come as a surprise. We've been referring to the existing commentary on the *Grammar of Stolen Love* as Nakkīraṉār's; everyone does this. But in fact the text of the commentary itself formulates matters differently. Nakkīraṉār was the one who understood, literally "saw," the right explanation, which was silently but dramatically authorized by the mute boy who was actually Lord Kumāra. The whole procedure of authentication takes place, as it must, on the boundary between the spoken word and silence. Silence is the seal, and the deep feeling that brings tears and goose bumps is the moving force. I think we would be justified in saying that the commentary we know projects itself backwards to the time of the famous poet (or poets) Nakkīrar, while its true author or authors must have lived generations later—perhaps, in fact, as many as ten generations, some three centuries, since the last paragraph of this crucial but perhaps interpolated introduction to the commentary gives us the line of transmission over ten stages, with precise names, from Nakkīraṉār to Nīlakaṇṭaṉār of Muciri on the Kerala coast.[29] This is not to say that the final link in this chain is the author of the commentary; rather, the tradition seems to assume a long process in the course of which the actual substance or meaning of the grammar—a scholastic enterprise of the first order—was committed to memory and, probably, writing, with Nakkīraṉār there as the guarantor of quality and precision from the distant starting point.

By now we know that there must be a break in the grammatical tradition; without that, it can't be real. But the story of the *IA* goes beyond our earlier example of Agastya's curse on his disciple, Tŏlkāppiyaṉār. This time we have a strong statement of what looks like historical discontinuity. There was a tradition of poetry and its accompanying grammar; that line was interrupted and had to be reconstructed, at least as far as poetics goes (if not phonology, morphology, and metrics). No attempt to come to grips with the internal logic of development in the Sangam corpus can afford to ignore this insistence on a catastrophic break or gap.

And there is more. The Pandya king in the story may well be Ukkirappĕruvaḻuti, the last king in the series of forty-nine who were connected to the third and final Sangam. This king is the last to be mentioned in the passage on the three Sangams immediately preceding the story I have just recounted. The author of the commentary on *IA* apparently thinks (without saying this in so many words) that he was the king who miraculously managed to retrieve the section on meaning. We know him from colophons to *Puṟan.* 21 and 367; also as the supposed author of *Akanāṉūṟu* 26. Even more important is the fact that the latter anthology, *Akanāṉūru,* tells us in its colophon that this same Ukkirapĕruvaḻuti was its sponsor, and that the person who actually compiled it was none other than our good friend Uruttiracaṉmaṉ, son of Uppūri Kuṭikiḻār—the one who could identify the true commentary when he heard it.[30] These identifications have been known and seen as historically suggestive for some time. At the very least, they presuppose a textual linkage between the *Akanāṉūṟu* anthology, some of the *Puṟan.* colophons, and the *IA* commentary, which sees itself as drawn backward to the time of this particular Pandya king and that particular scholar. To this linkage we will want to add another, to the fragmentary Sangam anthology, usually seen as late, known as *Paripāṭal.* For now, please try to keep in mind the two longish personal names that we're discussing.

Ukkirappĕruvaḻuti is clearly *not* the Pandya king whose exploits are repeatedly celebrated in the commentary to *IA,* which cites over three hundred verses from a work known as *Pāṇṭikkovai* (first identified as such by the great scholar M. Raghava Iyengar). There is reason to think that the hero of those verses is Arikesari Parâṅkuśa Māravarmaṉ, son of Centaṉ, who reigned in the second half of the seventh century.[31] The *Pāṇṭikkovai* verses are certainly later than the Sangam poems, as one sees at once from syntax, lexis, and style; this work is a seventh- or eighth-century collection, and its inclusion in the commentary gives us one great hook on which to hang the date of the latter. What is more, events cited in the *Pāṇṭikkovai* are also known from eighth-century Pandya inscriptions. Thus we can, it seems, posit an eighth-century or early-ninth-century date for the commentary ascribed to Nakkīraṉār on the *Grammar of Stolen Love*.

A word on the nature of this magnificent prose commentary, upon which so much depends. Without it, the god-given *sūtras* make little sense, as the story tells us. Whoever did write down the commentary had a hypertrophied pedantic and at the same time lyrical and expressive mind—an odd combination that comes through on nearly every page. On the one hand, this commentator loves to exhaust the logical possibilities that the *sūtras,* and their special vocabulary, open up. If stolen love is such a good thing, maybe other forms of stealing are positive as well? And what about the sequence of stages in the master love narrative that the text offers us? Just how many reasons can we count, and validate logically, for the hero's departure from his newly wedded wife, and why are they arranged in the list in the way they are, and what actually is meant to happen in each of them (commentary on *sūtra* 35)? For example, reason number 2 (remember we are in an idealized poetic universe) is *kāval,* "defense" (of the country). What does this entail?

> This does not mean that he will depart in order to remove suffering whenever there are sufferers; rather, he leaves his village to listen to the complaints of old people and women who cannot explain well what has happened to them, and of the lame people of the towns, the hunchbacks, the blind, the sick, and so on, in order to set things right. He leaves in order to bring the wicked to justice in the jungles, where one species terrorizes another; he leaves in order to free creatures that have been caught at the ocean front in nets of vines; he leaves to create wealth where there was none; to examine temples, town halls, rest houses,[32] and so forth; and to help families that are going downhill. Moreover, he will leave simply to show his face to the living beings under his protection, since they will rejoice in seeing him, just as an infant is happy to see its mother, and in order to display his vigor before the spies of enemy kings whenever they come: because of this, even hostile kings will pay him tribute.[33]

Now you know. None of this is ever mentioned in the Sangam poems; what we have is a somewhat playful scholastic expansion, in lucid Tamil prose, mostly formulated in the categorizing style of Indic commentary generally. You can guess what this learned author has to say about the painful subject of the hero's attraction to courtesans and dancing girls, a common theme in the poems. One can't have the prototypical lover compromising his singular attachment to his wife; on the other hand, "If people who are naturally beautiful and attractive take it specifically upon themselves to attract a man with their songs and their dances, is it even necessary to say he will be attracted?"[34] Deep down, however, he only really cares about (has *uṇarvu* for) his wife.

This author is profoundly invested in the great narrative of paradigmatic loving that he has, in effect, invented, drawing together the whole *akam* world, and big chunks of the *puṟam* domain as well, into a coherent pattern. The evocative understatement of the Sangam poems has given way to unrestrained descriptive excess, often overwhelming the reader with its profusion of details. I want to quote one long, exemplary passage to give you a taste of this moment of formalization and incipient canonization applied to the Sangam corpus; we are now apparently far from the original texts, in an erudite, Sanskrit-filled world that seeks anachronistically to impose its regularities on them. Take a deep breath:

> How does she [the heroine, *talaivi,* about to see the hero for the first time in the forest] stand there, you ask? All about her are sandalwood trees, champak trees, sweet mango trees, sweet jackfruit trees, breadfruit trees, asoka trees, caung trees, kino trees, and ipecacunaha trees. Gamboge, barbadoes pride, crocus-vines, copperleaf, delight-of-the-woods, jasmine, and Arabian jasmine combine their fragrances. Trumpetflowers, screwpine, and fresh laburnum burst open; water-thorn, purslane, and lemon flowers blossom. Bees buzz and suck nectar, and the musical cuckoo sings as the cool south breeze meanders through the grove. In the midst of this grove, which causes lonely people to feel resentment, upon a mound of rubies, she sees a kino tree brushing the sky and blooming pure gold with intoxicatingly aromatic blossoms yielding their honey as bees buzz by. At the very sight of it, she feels a swelling love. The anklets on her pretty little feet jingle as she walks, as though a marvelous flowering vine had learned how to walk, and she plucks some of those honey-filled fresh kino flowers. As she plucks them, in a jasmine bower by an emerald-bordered pool of rubies, under the rich shade of flowery fragrance, she grabs hold of a *kaṭikkurukkatti* vine. Pursuing diadems of pure gold,[35] washing gold nuggets and pushing diamonds and rubies along, a waterfall of rising

beauty falls upon a golden rock, sounding with the voice of a drum. Beetles and bees sound the lute, and the musical cuckoos sing. On a crystal seat covered with pleasant pollens, a peacock fans its beautiful feathers, as though a royal blue fan were opened, and the tender young sun tosses in its warmth. And so she stands watching that young peacock dance.

Meanwhile, the hero also comes to the cool mountainsides to hunt, with his many hundreds of thousands of young men with sharp spears. He chased after a lion that sprang up there, and left the youths who were protecting him. He ordered his charioteer to stand by with the chariot and its great horses, on the moon-like sands of a wild river bed. His warrior's anklets jangled, and he tied up his dark curly hair with a golden cord, as honeybees wedded themselves to the fragrant wreath on his head, and the aroma of his sandal paste spread through the wide grove. Holding an arrow with his killing bow, he moved like the god of love incarnate, and entered the great grove where she was. How could that be, you ask? As a yoke-pin tossed into the southern seas might drift north and fit into the pinhole of a yoke floating in the northern seas; or just as the sun with its hot rays, and the moon with its cool ones, might slip from their orbits and meet, these two will meet. And they will be all alone when they first see each other. Being alone implies that they are unaware of themselves. What does being unaware of themselves mean, you ask?[36]

Well may you ask. Questions of awareness, or the lack of it, fascinate our commentator. In this domain he demonstrates an impressive continuity with the poems he is trying to illuminate. To fall in love successfully, you don't want too much self-awareness. On the other hand, you may see the luxuriant world around you, also resonating inside you, in a hyper-aware state of ecstasy, which our learned commentator articulates without holding back, much in the style of Sanskrit prose *kāvya* as pioneered by Subandhu and Bāṇa (in the sixth and seventh centuries).

## What to Do with the Colophons

We have the Sangam poems—a corpus consisting of eight anthologies and ten longer poetic narratives,[37] as defined earlier, and to which there is a tendency in modern scholarship to append the series known as the Eighteen Minor Works (including the famous *Tirukkuṟaḷ* of Tiruvaḷḷuvar) and even, perhaps, the twin *mahā-kāvyas, The Tale of an Anklet,* and *Maṇimekalai.* We have the First (nominally the Second) Grammar, *Tŏlkāppiyam,* large parts of which are perhaps contemporaneous with the earliest Sangam poems.[38] We have the Tamil Brāhmī inscriptions, briefly described in Chapter 1, and impressive archaeological finds, including important numismatic evidence, from the first centuries A.D. We have the authoritative foundation narrative in the commentary on the first *sūtra* of the *Grammar of Stolen Love,* to which we can assign a date of approximately the eighth century (even if this introductory section to the commentary is somewhat later than the rest of it). We have the historical Pandya inscriptions of the late eighth century that fit well with some verses of the *Pāṇṭikkovai,* cited in the commentary on the *Grammar of Stolen Love.* We have ample evidence internal to the Sangam corpus in its present state that the poems underwent processes of redaction, collection, editorial commentary, and eventual canonization. What can we make of this highly heterogeneous mass of texts and data? Is there a story that we can tell ourselves that makes sense of at least most of these materials and that does not defy the few secure chronological pinpoints that we have? Much is at stake here—nothing less than the notions we can offer about the earliest creative stage in the evolution of Tamil and its culture. We thus have to enter briefly into some technical matters of direct relevance to our understanding of this formative historical moment.

In recent years, following the publication of Herman Tieken's *Kāvya in South India* in 2001, the question of when to situate the Sangam poems has been reopened, and a contentious debate, still unresolved, has gnawed away at the foundations of the regnant view that places the poems in the first two or three centuries A.D. Tieken has argued that the early dating is untenable, the evidence on which it is based being far too weak and circumstantial to support any such claims; on the basis of the Pandya inscriptions from the eighth century onward, he argues that Sangam poetry was a collective enterprise carried out at the Pandya court, under the auspices of the Pandya kings, at roughly the period of these inscriptions. He reads the Sangam poems largely in the light of

Prakrit poetry such as Hāla's *Sattasaī*—and indeed the affinities are evident, as Hart also noted long ago—and suggests (I think wrongly) that old Tamil poetry is stylistically or syntactically close to classical Sanskrit *kāvya,* and thus, again, to be dated much later than the received wisdom would have it. This chapter is not the place to engage in detail with Tieken's arguments, which unquestionably merit a dispassionate discussion; but we do need to consider the question of dating as it stands today without, I hope, exhausting the reader's patience. I'll keep things as simple as I can. Chronology is sometimes a useful diversion from real work.

I think it is fair to say that we cannot solve the dating problem definitively with the information we have available. In the highly nonprobabilistic universe of classical Tamil poetry, we are reduced to formulating logical probabilities. It is also unlikely, in my view, that traditional philological methods, including a tentative chronological ordering of layers *within* the available collections, will produce a solution. We at present know very little about the third to fifth centuries in Madurai—that is, the critical period of the protohistorical Pandyas—apart from what the colophons appended to the poems tell us; and these are, at best, as we shall see, a problematic source. New information will undoubtedly become available in coming years. The slow cumulation of epigraphic and archaeological discoveries, perhaps aided by new textual materials, may allow for a more reliable picture.

Our point of entry, which is also the link between the texts themselves and the thick tradition that grew up around them, is the information given to us by the colophons present in the surviving manuscripts. We have seen that the poems, both *akam* and *puṟam,* usually come with a laconic colophon in archaic prose that provides basic information about the context of composition: in the case of *akam,* the name of the poet and the particular situation or theme *(kiḷavi)* in the prototypical love sequence suited to the poem; in the case of *puṟam,* the names of the king, hero, or patron celebrated in the poem and of the poet who sang of his deeds—or rather, as Tieken rightly shows, of some fictive speaker inside the poem, who may or may not be identical to the poet. (It is impossible to give a single rule that will cover all cases.) We also often get a terse description of the scene that the poem describes or in which it was ostensibly sung. Ever since the first publication of the *puṟam* poems, there has been a tendency among scholars to take these colophons at face value and to assume that the information they contain is historically accurate—as if we were reading a verse directly describing a concrete, realistic situation. Whole histories of Sangam-period Tamil Nadu have been written with this implicit assumption at work.

Yet it has been clear for a long time that the colophons have to be separated from the poems they identify and contextualize. We might like to think of the colophons as an early form of editorial intervention in the corpus.[39] Tieken has convincingly shown the prevalent "fictive" character of the colophons, which thus dovetail nicely with the obvious fictions of the love themes embodied in the *akam* colophons. The Sangam texts are crafted aesthetic productions, certainly not bardic or oral in the usual sense of the words, created for an appreciative, cultivated audience, perhaps at the royal court. In many cases, as Tieken shows, the poem could not have been composed under the circumstances described in the colophon. For example, we have the wrenching lament of a warrior's widow who finds his body on the battlefield:

> I would cry out for help, but I am afraid of tigers.
> I would embrace you, but I cannot lift your broad chest.
> May evil Death, who made you suffer so,
> shiver as I do.
> Take my wrist, thick with bangles,
> and we will reach the shade of the mountain.
> Come, walk, it is very near.[40]

The woman who speaks still has her bangles around her wrists—she has only just at this moment discovered her slain husband and has not yet broken and discarded these auspicious ornaments. According to the colophon, the poet is a male bard, Vaṉpāṇar, and the *puṟam* theme situation is *mutuppālai,* a new widow's lament. Medieval commentators class this theme in the *puṟam tiṇai* of *kāñci,* the perception of transience (not specific to any landscape). It is obvious that the poet has imagined the entire scene and produced an artistic statement rich in feeling, meant for an audience of connoisseurs. A considerable number of the *puṟam* poems reveal some such pattern of projected scenarios;

the poems were clearly performed musically, and the speaker's voice within the poem—not necessarily the poet's, by any means—is what the listener hears. The colophons were perhaps conceived initially as a way of providing needed background information that the listener would need to have, much as we see today in textualized performance genres of various kinds in south India.[41] I will return to this point shortly.

Is it possible that the poet's voice and that of the speaker within the poem could, in some cases, coincide? Here is a rather crucial question, rich in implication. Tieken would answer no. But his conclusion is far too sweeping. If the information in the colophons is not factual in the historical sense but some later attempt to set out a poetic situation, then, Tieken suggests, the poems themselves must have been composed to order, as literary exercises, long after the period they purport to describe—let us say, at the eighth- or ninth-century Pandya court. But there is no reason to assume that all the colophons follow the same pattern, or that all of them are "fictive" in the narrowest sense of the word. Consider the following example, *Puṟan.* 165, classed as *pāṭāṇ,* "encomium, praise" for the famous hero Kumaṇaṉ. The *tuṟai* or theme is *paricil viṭai,* "giving permission to depart after bestowing gifts."

> There were those who aimed at living on
> in this world that doesn't live on. They won fame
> before they died. And there were wealthy men
> of exceptional goodness who lost their link
> to the paragons of the past because they had nothing
> to give to those who asked. But when I sang
> to that prince of undying renown, master of horses,
> who would give his bards restless elephants
> with flowers on their foreheads and bells ringing
> one after another on their feet, he said:
> "What's the use? To see a good singer
> go away empty-handed and unhappy
> is much worse than losing
> my whole kingdom." Then he handed me
> a sword and with it he offered me
> his head. I was happy, for nothing
> could be better than giving

oneself. Now I've come here
to tell you: I saw your unyielding
elder brother.

Look at the poem as it stands, without commentary or context. What can we infer about its *mise en scène?* The speaker is apparently addressing himself to a younger brother. The older brother is clearly one of those extraordinary heroic figures for whom generosity is an ultimate virtue, even a compulsion. Unable to offer anything of value to the singer, he gives the latter his sword and—in some obscure sense—his head. This older brother is unyielding; he has *oṭāppūṭkai,* a determination that never turns back. He deserves *pukaḻ,* undying fame. The younger brother seems to be of a lesser order, perhaps shamed by what the singer tells him. A philosophical or meditative opening offers the tantalizing hope that in an unstable world there are some things, such as selfless giving, that can survive.

A confession: even this short summary has been slightly contaminated by the account that the tradition gives of this poem. I have translated *niṉ kiḻamaiyoṉ,* the penultimate words of the poem, as "your elder brother." But *kiḻamaiyoṉ* could, in theory, be any older, authoritative relative or senior. Here the colophon steps in and helps us out. "Pĕruntalaiccāttaṉār sang this after seeing Kumaṇaṉ, who had been robbed of his kingdom by his younger brother and was exiled in the wilderness, and who gave his sword to the singer, who took it and showed it to Iḷaṅkumaṇaṉ." We are meant to understand that Iḷaṅkumaṇaṉ is that younger brother, as indeed the name suggests. In modern reimaginings of this story, the singer is sometimes said to have fashioned a fake head and to have taken it to the younger brother; the latter apparently had promised lavish rewards to anyone who could bring him his brother's head. Upon seeing the fake head, the younger brother is said to have been stricken with remorse and to have restored the kingdom to Kumaṇaṉ. Poems, uttered in the right circumstances, work magic.

These modern retellings of the story may go back to a late-medieval poet named Opp'ilāmaṇippulavar, who, so the tradition tells us, also sang to a king named Kumaṇaṉ; like his Sangam prototype, this Kumaṇaṉ also offered his head to the poet with the instruction to exchange it for a great reward (at the hands of the younger brother, Amaṇaṉ). Interestingly, five stray verses *(taṉippāṭal)* attributed to this Opp'ilāmaṇippulavar recapitulate the narrative that seems to have emerged from the colophon to *Puṟan.* 165. One of the poems actually quotes, in simplified form, lines from *Puṟan.* 164, also attributed to Pĕruntalaiccāttaṉār; the poet has sought out Kumaṇaṉ in the wilderness and begged him for help, first describing his impoverished state in heart-wrenching terms:

> My oven is overgrown with mushrooms,
> our hunger is great.
> Every time my child sucks the wizened breast
> of his mother, and no milk comes, he looks
> at her face, and she looks at my face,
> and now I'm here, looking at yours.

This is Opp'ilāmaṇippulavar quoting *Puṟan.* 164. Kumaṇaṉ can't bear to hear this and offers the poet his head.

> Great Tamil poet! You didn't come to me *then.*
> You've come only now, in great pain.
> Take this head of mine, deliver it into
> my younger brother's hand, and take its worth
> so you suffer no more.[42]

These verses, together with the lore that accompanies them in modern collections of such poems, clearly derive from the *Puṟan.* poems just mentioned along with their colophons. In other words, the late-medieval poet has imitated the Sangam-period author very precisely or, better, reinvented him and taken over his story, right down to the name of the famous king/patron Kumaṇaṉ. Incidentally, this evidence shows us that *Puṟan.* 164 and 165 were still well known, a current part of a Tamil literary education, well into the eighteenth or even early nineteenth centuries. This evidence cuts through the common belief that the Sangam corpus was truly lost or forgotten by the mid-nineteenth century (see Chapter 7).

In the *Puṟanāṉūṟu* collection, poem 165 is the last of a series of eight devoted to Kumaṇaṉ; the first six are ascribed in the colophons to a poet named Pĕruñcittiraṉār. All eight celebrate Kumaṇaṉ as the epitome of the generous giver, *vaḻḻal;* one poem, 162, was supposedly triggered when another lord, Vĕḷimāṉ, gave the singer only a miserly gift, and the singer then sought out Kumaṇaṉ, who rewarded him with the gift of an elephant. The colophons to 164 and 165, both ascribed to the poet Pĕruntalaiccāttaṉār, give us the elliptical story that later tradition must have filled out. Without the colophons, we are almost completely in the dark. In the poem I have translated, Kumaṇaṉ is not even mentioned by name.

So what are we to make of this poem, or set of poems? (Whoever arranged the poems in some order, and whoever wrote down the colophons, clearly saw these eight as constituting a set united by reference to a single patron.) Can we assume that Pĕruntalaiccāttaṉār actually sang *Puṟan.* 165 in the presence of Kumaṇaṉ's younger brother, Iḷaṅkumaṇaṉ, as the colophon states? Probably not. Probably what we have is a poem composed by someone on the theme of Pĕruntalaiccāttaṉār's visits first to Kumaṇaṉ and then, equipped with the latter's sword, to Iḷaṅkumaṇaṉ. Perhaps the story was well known. Thus, as Tieken rightly says, "The *Puṟam* colophons do not identify the poets of the poems but the persons speaking in them."[43] Note, however, that it is not impossible that the colophons, or some of them, could actually be "right"—that is, for example, that Pĕruntalaiccāttaṉār could indeed have composed *Puṟan.* 165, whether that is what he sang in the presence of Iḷaṅkumaṇaṉ or not. Nothing compels us to believe that a poem celebrating, say, a patron, dead or alive, was *not* composed by the named singer at some point during that patron's lifetime.[44]

To put the matter more simply: It seems not unlikely that at least some, perhaps many, perhaps most of the *puṟam* colophons record some sort of traditional information associated with their respective poems. It matters little whether this information is historical, that is, "factual"; we should, in general, resist the temptation to take it at face value, without further reflection. Historicity here matters less than the hard fact of a crystallized tradition that may, eventually, be dated. It is likely, as Takanobu Takahashi has argued, that the colophons were added considerably later (perhaps centuries later) than the time the poems were composed; there is some evidence that at least in some cases they were added *after* the stage of anthologization, or in tandem with it.[45]

No doubt many of the colophons *are* attempts to project backwards a possible context to suit the poem and make sense of it. That is how a complex literary tradition works. A certain corpus is assembled and eventually canonized; there are moments of redaction and organization, and other moments where commentary of one sort or another is attached to the texts. The Sangam colophons are one kind of early commentary on a corpus that had, I think, been carefully preserved and that inevitably generated comment and explanation, some of which may well go back to very early stages in the literary process. Were we to examine the other major *puṟam* anthology, *Patiṟṟuppattu,* a Cera production, we would find even more salient examples of relatively convincing information (mixed in with mythic materials) preserved in the *patikam* prefaces to each of the surviving decades of poems. There is no reason to assume that the *patikam* authors concocted such evidence, including specific names and legendary feats, even if the decade poems were not composed in the actual presence of the heroes of whom they sing.

An example from a later period of Tamil literature may be helpful here. As we will see in Chapters 3 and 4, there is evidence that what is now known as the *Tevāram*—a seven-volume set of poems ascribed to three devotional *(bhakti)* poets on the god Śiva in his many shrines scattered mostly throughout the Tamil-speaking area (also Kerala)—was edited and arranged in its present form in the course of the eleventh century in the Chola country. A strong tradition identifies the editor and redactor as Nampi Āṇṭār Nampi of Naraiyur and associates him with the Chola dynasty. This same Nampi Āṇṭār Nampi is the author of a work, the *Tiruttŏṇṭar tiruvantâti,* which builds on an earlier list in one of the *Tevāram* collections (Cuntaramūrtti Nāyaṉār's *patikam* 37) to produce a picture of the sixty-three exemplary Tamil devotees of Śiva. Nampi's text in turn served the great poet Cekkiḻār, whom we can date in the mid-twelfth century, as the basis of his monumental *Pĕriya purāṇam,* which gives both discursive narratives for the entire set of sixty-three devotees and specific contexts of composition for hundreds of the *Tevāram* poems themselves. We thus have a paradigm that might fit the Sangam corpus as well: the poems themselves are produced over a long period of time; eventually they are canonized, that is, organized in anthologies and ascribed to named poets (the poems are also identified and arranged by the musical *paṇ* or *rāga*-mode in which they are sung, and located at the temple to which each of them belongs); at a somewhat later stage in the canonization process, a body of traditional lore is compiled as narrative commentary providing context for many, if not most, of these texts. The colophons to the Sangam poems would thus belong, in one way or another, to the second stage of the process, that is, to the attempt to identify, redact, and fix the poems within a certain narrative and thematic range.

Unfortunately, this scheme is more than a little too neat. It might work for the Tamil canon of poems to the god Vishṇu, as Friedhelm Hardy showed in a brilliant study of the central figure of Nammāḻvār: the later hagiographical accounts of this poet's life clearly build on often laconic statements or hints in Nammāḻvār's texts, so we can draw a fairly straightforward developmental sequence.[46] Much the same has been shown to be the case for the large corpus of poetry composed by the Provençal troubadours.[47] But in the case of at least one of the *Tevāram* poets, Cuntaramūrtti Nāyaṉār (I am speaking here as if Cuntaramūrtti were a single person and author), the surviving corpus of poems already contains references to narrative materials that we meet in their mature form in Cekkiḻār's much later hagiographical text. In other words, it appears that the *story* of Cuntarar, as we know it from Cekkiḻār, was already known in part, at least, to the composer or composers of these poems.[48] There are very similar instances in the Sangam corpus—as if the poems themselves were already well aware of the story that the colophons record about them, as in the example of Kumaṇaṉ cited above. How are we to explain this situation?

Tieken has suggested, on the basis of the problems we have outlined, that all the Sangam poems in the major anthologies were composed to order by poets who were perfectly aware of the fictive nature of their subject *(tuṟai)* and its context. Thus eighth- or ninth-century poets at the Pandya court, in Tieken's reconstruction, deliberately composed poems with an internal speaker addressing a far more ancient hero or patron—as if a poet today were to adopt the persona of, say, Christopher Marlowe writing verses for Queen Elizabeth. But there is no need to conjure up such a scenario, with early-medieval court poets busy composing thousands of poems deliberately retrojected into the distant past, using conventional themes as well as invented materials meant to bring these ancient kings and bards to life. Is it not far more economical to imagine a process whereby the poems, many of them very old, all of them self-conscious literary efforts to begin with, survived through a slow process of recording, editorial accretion, and explication? Moreover, the relation of poem to colophon must have been, in many cases, far more intimate than any linear development could account for. There may well have been cases where the text and the colophon are, in a special sense, mutually determining—that is, cases where the poetic situation at work in the poem fits and informs the colophon long before the latter was recorded. Again, there is no need to assume that the "fictive" nature of the colophon means it is false. Quite the contrary may be the case: poem and colophon, though certainly distinct, usually share a single mental template. Fiction often offers a much closer approximation to truth than what passes for fact can give us.

It's also possible that some of the colophons are arbitrary editorial interventions long after the period of composition—that is, that well-known, ancient names were recycled by creative editors. We need to keep an open, critical mind as we investigate these materials.

But a further difficulty awaits us before we can even begin to propose a set of dates.

## Clusters of Time

Consider the following information, lucidly discussed by François Gros, among others. We have the name of a great poet, Nallantuvaṉār, probably a longer form of Antuvaṉ. Old Tamil names, by the way, have the habit of repeating, and very often we cannot say if we are speaking about one person or many persons bearing the same name. Nallantuvaṉār is said by the colophons to be the author of four strong poems in the collection *Paripāṭal,* often considered late relative to the main anthologies, and this name is also associated with an entire section in the *Kalittŏkai* anthology, also usually thought to be late.[49] This same Nallantuvaṉār is credited by the tradition with the invocatory poem in *Kalittŏkai* and with editing that entire collection.[50] The name

Nallantuvaṉār also turns up in colophons of several more poems in the large anthologies.[51]

Now we have an important poem, *Akanāṉūṟu* 59, attributed to Maturai Marutaṉ Iḷanākaṉ. If you go back to the section "Back to Stolen Love" in this chapter, to the end of the story about the recovery and explication of the *Grammar of Stolen Love*, you will see that this name belongs to one of the Sangam poet-scholars whose commentary on the laconic *sūtras* elicited a slight positive response, at a few points, from the dumb child, Uruttiracaṉmaṉ, the ultimate arbiter of correctness. Please try to keep these names in mind for another paragraph or two. As it happens, Marutaṉ Iḷanākaṉ's poem (according to the colophon) includes two lines about the mountain Paraṅkuṉṟu, near Madurai, which was "praised in song by Antuvaṉ." As Gros says, "Any reader will understand those two lines as an obvious homage to the author of *Paripāṭal* VIII,"[52] that is, Nallantuvaṉār, as the colophon of the latter says; the *Paripāṭal* poem offers lyrical descriptions of Paraṅkuṉṟu. It seems hard to believe that this cross-reference is an accident. Antuvaṉ, or Nallantuvaṉār, and Marutaṉ Iḷanākaṉ must belong together; and we know, in fact, where they meet in a wider narrative—in the introductory commentary of the *Grammar of Stolen Love,* which lists both of them among the poets of the Third and Final Sangam and which makes Marutaṉ Iḷanākaṉ the runner-up in the commentary sweepstakes at the Pandya court—seemingly that of Ukkirapĕruvaḻuti, the patron of the *Akanāṉūṟu* collection as a whole, if we are to believe the metacolophon to that anthology. You might even remember that the name of this king turns up in two colophons in *Puṟanāṉūṟu.*

Thus we have a rather striking cluster of names, present in the colophons but also in at least one poem,[53] together with fragments of a narrative binding them together. Is there a problem with this set of interlocking links? Perhaps. Until now most scholars have thought of *Akanāṉūṟu* as one of the earlier anthologies—and now we see that one of its poems appears to refer to a (later?) *Paripāṭal* poem and to the colophon attached to the latter. A coincidence? Should we isolate *Akanāṉūṟu* 59 from the rest of the anthology, or declare it a later addition to the collection (the easy way out)? Eva Wilden argues that the colophon *kiḷavis* of *Akanāṉūṟu, Kuṟuntŏkai,* and *Naṟṟiṇai* belong to a single tradition,[54] itself related in interesting ways both to parts of *Tŏlkāppiyam Pŏruḷatikāram* and to the *IA*. The three *akam* anthologies just listed may constitute the oldest core of Sangam love poetry.[55] Or do they? Is there, in fact, any meaning to such a claim? In passing, just to make matters worse, we may note that Māṅkuṭi Marutaṉ, possibly the father of Marutaṉ Iḷanākaṉ, is supposedly the author of one of the most beautiful of the Ten Songs, *Maturaikkāñci*—in theory, a second- or third-stage work in relation to the earliest anthologies. Also, the versatile Nallantuvaṉār is the reputed author of *Paripāṭal* 11, the most notorious poem in this collection because of a very precise horoscope the poet offers us. I am not competent to judge the validity of the various attempts to correlate the poem's data with historical astronomical conjunctions; I'm also skeptical about the usefulness of these results. Gros, however, is more or less satisfied with a date proposed after careful calculation by Swamikannu Pillai—that is, June 17, 634.[56] By orthodox Sangam standards, this is rather late.

It would be easy to go on multiplying examples like the one just given. Again and again we find names in the colophons that, if the early dating of the corpus were correct, and if the textual stratigraphy that we've attempted to define were somehow close to reality, should simply not be there. This corpus is astonishingly full of bewildering cross-references, made still more baffling by the frequently recurring names. I am not going to subject you to more of this dizzying play with the textual materials at our disposal. Enough is enough. It's time to ask ourselves if there is a way out of the maze.

Perhaps there is, though not in any definitive sense. I have used the term "cluster" to indicate a concentration of textual data, of the sort just mentioned, together with some elements of a relative developmental sequence. What if the large *Akanāṉūṟu* anthology—which may, of course, incorporate material from various stages in the tradition, but which is also very precisely structured, as Tieken has shown[57]—were to be seen as deeply, even intrinsically, connected to the legendary moment the *IA* commentary describes, when the great Nakkīraṉār "saw" the true meaning of the *sūtras*? But when was that moment? Clearly not in the seventh or eighth century, the period of the *Pāṇṭikkovai* hero, probably Arikesari Parâṅkuśa, who stars in the commentary in its present form. The commentary is describing a moment of crystallization in the first, mythic segment of the Pandya genealogies, as we find them in the eighth-century inscriptions and later (see below)—a moment profoundly tied to the gap or break in the literary tradition. We cannot say how many generations of transmission bridge the gap between Ukkirapĕruvaḻuti Pandya and Arikesari Parâṅkuśa. Ten? Half that number? Does it really matter? If Arikesari Parâṅkuśa is indeed to be placed in the late seventh century, then the mythic moment of recovery and initial commentary, and also of the creation of the *Akanāṉūṟu* anthology as such and, why not, of the composition of at least some of its poems, would be somewhere around the fifth or late fourth century, give or take. Other, again circumstantial evidence, would support this guess, including the boom in trade coming from the Mediterranean to south India in that period, as R. Nagaswamy has shown;[58] the extensive descriptions of Yavana traders that we find in the poems may be better suited to the fourth century than to the first or second.

The most convincing, perhaps the only real chronological "sheet anchor" that we possess, at this point, is the text of the *Pāṇṭikkovai,* cited in the *IA* commentary. There is an unmistakable divide between the language and style of this *kovai,* clearly in early-medieval Tamil and allied with other works from that period, and the language of the Sangam poems, however we define the corpus. The *Pāṇṭikkovai* has to be contemporaneous with its hero—otherwise the work makes no sense. So: late seventh century or so; maybe eighth. The Sangam poems are earlier, probably by several centuries. They are so replete with archaisms, both lexical and morphological, which we can situate within a developmental continuum from early south Dravidian, not to mention characteristic syntactical features, as to rule out the possibility that they could belong to historical Pandya times.[59] We have to work backwards from the *Pāṇṭikkovai* to a possible date.

But we have to note another possible cluster, which commands attention. What about the Tamil Brāhmī inscriptions from the first and second centuries, with the names they contain, some of them evoking names we know from the Sangam colophons and the *Patiṟṟuppattu patikams?*[60] Is it possible that Atiya[mā]ṉ Nĕṭumāṉ Añci, from the Jambai inscription, is indeed the celebrated Sangam *puṟam* hero of that name? Yes, it is definitely possible, just as it is possible that the Kŏlli Irumpuṟaiyaṉ of a first- or second-century coin is the Chera warrior king Pĕrum Ceral Irumpŏṟai, who conquered the Kolli hills and the great fort of Tagadur, as Nagaswamy has convincingly argued.[61] This coin, incidentally, and two others similar to it, are interesting in more ways than one; on two of the three we find a standing portrait of the king clearly patterned after early imperial images on Roman coins (thousands of these, from the first centuries A.D., have turned up in excavations in Karur and elsewhere in Tamil Nadu).[62] Thus we arrive at a first- or early second-century date for both coins and inscription. It's possible that this date will slip forward over time, but for now let's assume that this period could belong, in something akin to historical reality, to our heroes.

Does this mean that the *puṟam* poems must also belong to the second and third centuries? Not necessarily. Think of Homer. The Homeric poems describe a twelfth-century B.C. Mediterranean world, before the catastrophic dark age that overtook that world. But scholars are confident that the Homeric poems date from the eighth century B.C.—three hundred years or so after the events they describe. One interesting confirmation of this dating, one among many, is the existence of anachronisms in the poems—for example, the occasional reference to iron weapons in a Bronze Age setting. It might well be worth looking more closely for similar anachronisms in the Sangam poems. In any case, I don't think it's at all impossible that poets removed in time from the actual events they describe were capable of composing poems about those events (note, though, that the lyrical Sangam poems are *not* like sustained heroic epic). How far removed in time? In this case, three centuries are almost certainly too great a gap.

I'll tell you why. If we put aside, for a moment, all the technical considerations and overlapping obscurities, one indubitable fact stands out about the *puṟam* poems. They have an immediacy and freshness that ring true—true in the sense that they must have been familiar, perhaps from first-hand experience, to both the poets and their audience. It's almost impossible to imagine that a poem like the following was composed decades, or even centuries, after the event:

His legs strong and lithe,
his bravery fierce and unyielding,
my lord is like a tiger living in a cramped cave
who stretches, rises up, and sets out for his prey.
But they did not think him hard to fight against.
They rose up bellowing.
"We are best, we are the greatest."
Our enemy is young and there is much plunder."
Those foolish warriors who came with contempt
ran with dim eyes, showing their backs,
but he did not let them be killed then.
He took them to the city of their fathers,
and as their women with fine ornaments died in shame
and the clear *kiṇai* drum sounded,
there he killed them.[63]

The colophon tells us the name of the speaker, Iṭaikkuṉṟūrkiḻār, and the name of the warrior king: Neṭuñcĕḻiyaṉ, the greatest of the ancient Pandya heroes. It makes little sense, to me at least, to insist that the "real" poet was someone reimagining the words of Iṭaikkuṉṟūrkiḻār, and assuming the latter's identity, centuries after the little skirmish and its ruthless conclusion. Why not go the simple, economic route and assume that, unless proven otherwise, Iṭaikkuṉṟūrkiḻār composed this poem and sang it in some public space close to the moment he describes? He has, of course, stylized and formalized the text, as do all the poets (who are certainly capable of taking the voice or persona of someone in the dramatic situation they are describing). We are not talking about poems improvised on the battlefield or the execution ground. These are crafted, artistic works meant for performance. But listen to the vivid description, the resonant voice speaking in this poem; note the direct, personal relation between the speaker and the king ("my lord," *ĕṉṉai*); observe the sparseness of the lines, which reveal no need to explain anything or to elaborate a context—they are telling us about something we, the audience, already know. It feels as if the attack and its outcome happened only last week.[64]

Both *Puṟanāṉūṟu* and *Patiṟṟuppattu* describe a believable world populated by real people with names and, in many cases, personal funerary monuments. There is almost nothing of the often conventionalized death descriptions in the *Iliad* (though it, too, must surely preserve much archaic knowledge passed down orally). Even if the poets of the Sangam period offer us, for the most part, fictionalized, or semifictionalized, accounts—but I have tried to persuade you that not all the poems need be seen as fictional in a narrow sense—these texts reek of concrete, sensuous, often tragic, reality. By far the strongest argument, in my view, in favor of an early date for the *puṟam* poems is precisely this overwhelming atmosphere in the poems of an intimately known set of circumstances along with the typical heroic values that make those circumstances somehow bearable.

I cannot go farther than this. I see a possible cluster as early as the second and third centuries, and another, more ample and possibly more likely one in the fourth and fifth. Then there is a third, entirely historical cluster that can be located in time and place: Madurai of the eighth and ninth centuries, where the anthologies probably underwent their final codification and canonization, and where Pandya kings prided themselves on knowing and loving Tamil and on their ancestors' having had the *Mahābhārata* translated into Tamil and having established a Tamil Sangam. Tieken's vision of Sangam poetry as deeply embedded in historical Pandya Madurai, and then transferred westward to Kerala, applies not to the composition of the poems, or of most of them, but to the great cultural task of their redaction and the establishment of a canon, including the formalization of entire erudite domains crucial to the very existence of such a rich canon.[65] Ongoing work on the corpus will undoubtedly shed new light on these.

## Pandyas, Pallavas, and the Carriers of Tamil Knowledge

Let's start over, this time with our feet on the ground. Whenever the composition and redaction of the Sangam corpus took place, we can be sure it happened in a singular cultural setting, in real sites, and in specific political conditions; and it didn't just "happen"—there were particular actors involved, carriers of the tradition, probably divided into competing factions, like in all human institutions. In fact, somewhat surprisingly, we can identify some of these carriers and conjure up something of their world. I want to begin with a sketch of the political and social background before moving on to discuss the role of the ancient Tamil poet, on the one hand, and then of the masters of ancient Tamil learning, on the other.

A good introduction to the evolution of Tamil society in the first half of the first millennium A.D. is the work of R. Champakalakshmi,[66] nicely complemented by the brilliant studies of K. S. Sivathamby.[67] We can trace the slow shift from small-scale polities based largely on a mixture of pastoralism and rice and millet farming to more substantial states with a strong agrarian base and urban centers. A tension between seminomadic pastoralists and wetland rice farmers has endured in many parts of south India right up to the present day; sometimes it appears as part of a wider structural divide between mobile groups (pastoralists, traders, artisans), labeled "left-hand" castes in the indigenous vocabulary of the south, and peasant farmers and warriors, permanently settled on the land, and thus linked to the "right-hand" segment of the social order.[68] Each of these two large social configurations comes with its own moral universe: left-hand groups tend to gravitate toward universalistic, context-free values, including an ideal of self-sacrifice; right-hand groups, committed to a homeostatic order on the ground, are intimately tied to a sacrificial ideology with an inherent element of normative violence.[69] We cannot say how early this conceptual scheme came into being, but its seeds surely lie in the period we are exploring. One could tell a version of south Indian history, from the beginning, in terms of the necessary opposition and dynamic complementarity of these two social-conceptual modes.

By the middle of the millennium, two dominant state systems were in place. In the northern Tamil country, including the coastal region known as Tŏṇṭai-maṇḍalam but extending westward into the southern Deccan with its strong pastoralist presence, we find the Pallava dynasty, which always claimed, with apparent justice, to have come down from regions to the north. The Pallavas survived for some five centuries as a major political force; their capital was located at Kancipuram (not far from today's Chennai), and they were the builders of the impressive port town of Mamallapuram or Mahabalipuram, with its exquisite artistic remains. They left a large corpus of inscriptions in which we can trace a progression from Prakrit, the first language of royal donations, to Sanskrit, and then to mixed Sanskrit and Tamil.[70] As we will see in Chapter 3, the Pallavas invented the south Indian temple as we know it, that is, as a permanent edifice built in stone and serving as a focus for economic activity, including royal endowments. The Pallavas are mentioned (as Tŏṇṭaiyor, the Tamil equivalent of the Sanskrit name) in one of the *Ten Long Poems*[71] but not, it seems, in the anthologies; this striking silence about a major polity has often been taken to mean that the early Sangam poems must predate the existence of the Pallava kingdom. Arguments from silence are, however, usually weak and often wrong.

In the far south, beginning in the middle of the millennium, we find a rice-based state centered on Madurai and the Vaikai and Tamraparni river deltas—that of the Pandyas, who have concerned us for most of this chapter. This dynasty saw itself as having emerged from a much more ancient precursor state led by kings, some of whose names are familiar to us from the colophons to the Sangam poems. Fanciful reconstructions of this early dynastic history, based solely on the colophons, are easily found in the modern secondary literature for those who like such games. "Hard" history has been retrieved from the Pandya inscriptions to which I have referred. As one would expect, it includes long lists of battles and military raids, mostly with the Pallava rivals to the north and with the Chalukyas of Badami still farther north, in the western Deccan. The doyen of south Indian historians of the last generation, K. A. Nilakanta Sastri, referred to the middle centuries of the millennium as a "conflict of three empires"—thereby upgrading these three middle-level states to a rather grandiose imperial order.[72] Reconstructed dynastic lines for all three of them, not entirely uncontested, can be found at the end of his chapter on the Pallava-Pandya period in the far south.

What is certain is that the historical Pandyas fostered intense cultural activity and, more specifically, as we have already seen, actively cultivated the practices of Tamil learning and literary composition. Their self-image as patrons of the mythic Sangam comes through clearly in the foundation story preserved in the *Grammar of Stolen*

*Love.* They thought of themselves as Tamil kings, preserving a very ancient link with Tamil grammar and its first preceptor, the sage Agastya, as well as with the god Śiva, one of the founders of the dynasty and, you will recall, an accomplished Tamil poet himself. Pandya Madurai, described in loving detail in the *Maturaikkāñci,* one of the *Ten Long Poems,* boasts, along with its pearl traders and goldsmiths and judges and Brahmin sages, dancing girls *(viṟaliyar)* with chiming bracelets and bards *(pāṇar)* rewarded by the king with gifts of elephants.[73] The language of their songs is *kūṭal tamiḻ,* "the Tamil of Kūṭal," that is, Madurai, the historic font of Tamil wisdom.

It is significant that this same long paean to the Pandya capital ends with a reference to a much earlier king, Mutukuṭumi "of many sacrifices" (*pal cālai mutukuṭumi,* line 759), whom we find playing a critical role in the Velvikuti grant of the late eighth century. We know this king—his full title is Palyāka-cālai Mutukuṭumip Pĕruvaḻuti, "the Pandya who established many sacrificial sites"—from the colophons to *Puṟan.* 9 and 15; the former poem mentions Kuṭumi by name, and the latter specifically states that its hero performed many Vedic sacrificial rituals. Clearly, the Pandya genealogists had a special love for this figure. Let us take a moment to see how the Velvikuti grant uses his name for a pragmatic end.[74]

The main purpose of this important bilingual (Sanskrit and Tamil) text was to record and validate a land grant, represented as a renewal of a much more ancient grant that had lapsed. The initial Sanskrit portion offers a short list of the mythic early Pandya kings, "whose family priest was Agastya"; then the Tamil section repeats and elaborates this genealogy before telling us that a certain Naṟkŏṟṟaṉ asked and received from Palyāka Mutukuṭumi Pĕruvaḻuti a grant of land in Velvikuti village. All this happened in the distant past (relative to the present moment of the inscription); Mutukuṭumi is one of the very ancient names such as the eponymous Pandya / Budha, son of the moon, the famous Purūravas, and a series of other kings who performed feats of mythic proportions. The specific problem on the ground that requires solution has to do with the fact that a bad king called Kaḷabhra took over the earth and, among other things, took back the land grant of the village.

Now a renewed line of Pandyas, beginning with Kaṭuṅkoṉ, arose and reconquered the land. A list follows of several generations of kings who, despite continuing controversy over their precise identities and dates, are clearly historical, in the usual sense of the word.

We eventually arrive at the current king of the inscription, Nĕṭuṅcaṭaiyaṉ. One day a certain Kāmakkāṇi Naṟciṅkaṉ, chief of Koṟkai, petitions the king to restore the original land grant to the descendants of Naṟkŏṟṟaṉ, after the land had been lost in the Kaḷabhra time. The king asks that the ancient claim be authenticated, which it is—probably by a surviving written document—and he then happily confirms ownership by a group of Brahmins in the village represented by Kāmakkāṇi Naṟciṅkaṉ.[75] As Gillet has said, a certain theatricality informs this unusual inscription: "The act of presenting an ancient official document to the king may be a subterfuge to justify the regal choice of giving this land to the Brahmins, a choice which might have been contested at the time."[76] The once prevalent notion of a dark interregnum in which a mysterious dynasty of "Kalabhras" penetrated, with devastating effect, into the Tamil country now seems rather exaggerated, if not, indeed, entirely fictive.[77]

For our purposes, the main point of interest is the apparent tripartite structure of the Pandya genealogies as we find them in Velvikuti and elsewhere. (Closely parallel to the Velvikuti grant are two well-known bilingual copper-plate inscriptions from Cinnamanur with similar variants of the royal lineage).[78] In both the Sanskrit and Tamil portions of these grants, we find an opening sequence that could be called *purāṇic* and that includes snapshot biographies of the mythic early kings. Let me stress again that Mutukuṭumi, the Sangam hero, clearly belongs here. Then a transitional, protohistorical figure appears—Kaṭuṅkoṉ in the Velvikuti grant, whom we know from the beginning of the commentary on the *Grammar of Stolen Love* as the last antedeluvian king of the First Sangam (assuming this name applies to the same person), thus marking the end of the earliest mythic time. Finally we get history proper, with varying names and exploits, some of them beautifully correlated with the *Pāṇṭikkovai* verses incorporated into the above-cited commentary. Prehistory/myth proceeds into protohistory and from there to the historical light of day. As far as the authors of the eighth-century grants are concerned, the Sangam warriors, epitomized by one famous name, are nicely situated at the first stage of this progression.

You can see the implications of such a division in the recorded genealogy. To return briefly to the problem of dating: once again we find ourselves, working backwards from the eighth-century record, converging on a legendary figure who might easily be situated, together with other heroes from the mythic past, in the fourth or fifth century. In other words, we keep coming across indications that a body of traditional lore, some, indeed most of it having to do with the Sangam poems, had crystallized in something akin to its present form by the fourth or fifth century. It is this legendary material that we find, in bits and pieces, in the colophons to the poems, in the commentary to the *Grammar of Stolen Love*, in the *patikams* of *Patiṟṟuppattu*, in parts of *The Tale of an Anklet* (especially the third part, *Vañcikkāṇṭam*), and in the much later medieval commentaries on the *Tŏlkāppiyam*, some of the anthologies, and other works. I think we can conclude, tentatively, that this layer of consolidated tradition constitutes something good and true—not in the sense of brute historical facts, but in the sense that the Tamil literary tradition achieved a certain semistandardized form at that time (and probably also in large part at a place we can name—that is, historical Pandya Madurai).

This tradition commands respect. Its claims are of a different order than the mostly concocted empiricist histories that modern historians have produced with so much toil. Notice, by the way, that if we take the commentary on the *Grammar of Stolen Love* at its word, then this moment of narrative consolidation and textual redaction comes just where it should be, namely, after a gap when the grammar of poetry had been forgotten. This crucial juncture in the evolution of a collectively shared erudite tradition deserves further attention.[79] It was probably the moment when the information in the colophons was, for better or worse, codified and appended to the poems,[80] and also when the business of writing things down assumed dominance. The codified literary tradition was unquestionably a written one. By this time, the poems, too, were surely recorded in writing and not only in or on the minds of professional reciters. More on this below.

A major element in this way of telling the story has to do with the sudden visibility of carriers of the emergent literary tradition. We can see them at work in the Velvikuti and Cinnamanur inscriptions, and we know some of their names. They include people like our friend Kāmakkāṇi Naṟciṅkaṉ, chief of Korkai, though he may have been only a figurehead; more important are his revenue officers and accountants and the learned Brahmins who made the formal application to the king and who witnessed it—also the scribes such as Arikesari, son of Pāṇṭi Pĕrumpaṇaikkāraṉ, who wrote down the smaller Cinnamanur plates. In fact, a crowd of learned Brahmins was intimately drawn into the whole Velvikuti transaction and its documentation—people like Maṅgalarāja, a sweet poet and orator *(vāgmin)* as well as an accomplished Vedic scholar, who formulated the request for the grant; and, again, witnesses from the village, the engraver-recorder, and the signatories. These names emerge from the mists as real people who can be assumed to have internalized the great names, and probably some of the great texts, from the distant past; they were part of a chain of transmission going back in all likelihood to the fifth century or beyond. Some of them at least must have known about Mutukuṭumi and his Vedic rituals (did one of them come up with his name to substantiate their claim on the land?). They may well have known the poem where he is mentioned and other poems about Kumaṇaṉ and Nĕṭuñcĕḻiyaṉ and a wealth of stories about Agastya and the early history of the tradition. Whether they were based in a village or in an urban center like Madurai, such people were engaged in a long-term cultural enterprise of codification, grammaticalization, and interpretation. Notice that in the cases just noted—but almost certainly not only in such cases—these literate carriers of the tradition were Brahmins conversant, to some degree at least, with Sanskrit knowledge.

Literacy, in the present context, means graphic literacy, which is by no means the only kind of writing we know from ancient India. The Mediterranean mode of writing things down on parchment or stone was clearly privileged throughout most of Western history. But in India we find, from early on, a far more dependable way of recording texts that matter—by inscribing them on the neurons of highly trained memorizers. Huge chunks of text can be precisely transmitted by memory; and to this day we find this mode of recording and transmitting to be privileged in various south Asian contexts (for example, in the teaching of professional musicians, who tend to abhor the act of writing). The standard term for an "illiterate" in Sanskrit is *nirakṣara-kukṣi,* literally, "one who does not have the phonemes in his belly." The belly is where they belong—not on palm leaf or birch bark. Knowledge should be *kaṇṭha-stha,* on the tip of the tongue (literally, the throat).

I am not in any way trying to romanticize a notion of nongraphic literacy, but rather seek to give it its due alongside discrete forms of graphic literacy in the preservation of texts considered to be prestigious in ancient India. It is also crucial to understand that, as George Hart noted long ago,[81] the important distinction in classifying literary texts is between those that were fixed, whether in memory or in graphic form, and those that were not, such as improvised performance texts (although in India, most oral epics turn out to be, unlike the well-known Serbo-Croatian materials, fixed in an underlying, memorized text).[82] In this sense, we can state confidently that the Sangam poems were, indeed, fixed, as works of that level of complexity and sophistication nearly always are. It is true that the Sangam poems, like much later Tamil works, are often heavily formulaic (as in Homer); there was a time when scholars such as K. Kailasapathy thought that by identifying the prevalent formulae one could prove that Sangam poetry was an oral, bardic corpus, akin to what Milman Parry and Albert Lord had (wrongly) concluded about Homer.[83] We now know that Kailasapathy also erred. Sangam poems, like Sanskrit *kāvya,* were composed to be learned and remembered precisely in the form their author gave them. When exactly they were written down is a different matter—in the Tamil case, almost certainly by the fourth-to-fifth century period of redaction, at the latest. Textual variation in the Sangam corpus is, on the whole, rather limited and may reflect mostly the contribution of later copyists, although the work of Eva Wilden is revealing to us a somewhat more complicated picture. As we shall see in Chapter 3, the written artifact of the poem eventually acquired a particular importance in its own right alongside a continuing investment in the living, spoken Tamil word.

What about the other major class of carriers, that is, the poets themselves? These were clearly no longer bards, wandering with their accompanist-drummers and improvising texts as they went along. The Sangam poets—let us call them *pulavar*—were learned men and women at home in the royal courts and, we can suppose, in learned village assemblies with their Brahmin scholars.[84] Remember that grammar itself was seen as serving such poets, before all else. If we go by the colophons, there were kings who were poets themselves; and we can be sure that already in the earliest period there were cultivated people who combined the roles of poet and scholar, such as we find in much later times. What, then, defined a Tamil poet of the Sangam period? Without doubt, such a figure had technical competence within the grammaticalized realms that were of relevance to poetry. He or she may also have been peripatetic, like the hungry bards often described in the *puṟam* corpus. But there is one diagnostic feature that needs to be stressed as this section comes to an end. As hinted already in Chapter 1, a Tamil poet is a master of the effectual, life-changing word spoken or chanted aloud, however it may have been recorded.

This feature is an intrinsic part of pan–south Indian literary culture and may well go back to prehistoric roots in the ancient cultures of the Deccan. We see it in operation in many of the Sangam poems themselves, especially when a poet finds an opportunity to utter a threat or a curse. Some of the ancient poets, such as the famous Kapilar, were particularly adept in this business of coercing a stubborn or reluctant patron. Failure to do what the poet wants may activate the poet's word magic and quickly finish off the king entirely and devastate his land.[85] In short: if you happen to be a Tamil ruler, don't mess with poets.

In a later period, the poet's gift of blessing or cursing is seen as rooted in a serious science of phonetic combinations, as we will see. We have already noted how grammar fits nicely into this same pragmatic frame. Tamil has never lost, even to this day, the innate mantic potency of the spoken syllable, which also animates musical composition in the classical Carnatic system.[86] Audible speech of all kinds, but especially poetically intensified speech, acts in and on the world. The corpus of Sangam poetry provides us with the first sustained examples of this understanding of the poet's role. In this sense, Sangam poems are, indeed, "oral" in nature and use—not because they were improvised (they were not), and not because they were not recorded (they were, in one way or another), but because they were meant to be sung aloud in some public space where, with all the linguistic and cognitive complexity that informed them, they could do their work.

We might be able to say something more about such public spaces. Scholars such as Takahashi and Nagaswamy have suggested that the Sangam poems were primarily intended for dramatic performance, *kūttu*. "All the poems were presented in the form of utterance of one of the main dramatis personae."[87] *Akam* poems, you will recall, are spoken by a very limited number of active (and fictive) characters such as the two lovers, the hero's friend, and the heroine's girlfriend. Takahashi surmises that, as in the case of ancient Chinese male poets who recited courtesan poems while dressed as women, Tamil women reciters "wore young women's costumes when they recited the heroine's song, and a bit simple[r] costumes may have been enough in the case of her friend's songs."[88] Such professional performance, he thinks, was meant for a broader audience; initially, the poet may have sung his work in the presence of his patron alone. For Nagaswamy,[89] the true performance context must have been dance, in both primary modes: *akakkūttu*, the dance of in-ness, and *puṟakkūttu*, the outer dance (both terms are mentioned in the old commentary on *The Tale of an Anklet* 3.2).[90] *Akam* poems were thus dance dramas, performed with the *abhinaya* language of hand and eye gestures; *puṟam* poems were fictive productions based on historical memories.[91] Textual recitation *per se* would have accompanied bodily movement or have been integrated into it, as we find today in performance genres throughout south India.[92] There is no way to verify these tantalizing suggestions for very early poetic performance; what we can say is that *The Tale of an Anklet*, to which we turn in a moment, does offer striking images of poetry in performance within a wider range of modes and genres, including music and dance. To the erudite Brahmins whom we have identified as carriers of the consolidated literary tradition, we may want to add professional dancers and cultivated courtesans in mostly urban settings.

## Toward an Integrated Cultural World

Before taking leave of the Sangam and its mysteries, we need to focus on three works situated on its temporal periphery, if for no other reason than that two of them, the *Tirukkuṟaḷ* and *The Tale of an Anklet,* are probably the best-known Tamil literary works in the world and also among the most beloved within the Tamil region. If you travel on the city buses in Chennai, you're very likely to see posted near the driver's seat one of the pithy, gnomic couplets from *Tirukkuṟaḷ*—some useful advice about how to live your life, or some widely applicable universal truth. Something like:

> The feather of a peacock will break the axle
> of an overloaded cart. (48.5)

Or:

> Friendship with someone whose actions don't match his words
> hurts even in your dreams. (82.9)

Or:

> Sharing your food and caring for all that breathes
> are at the top of all wise lists. (33.2)

What you won't see on the Chennai buses is a *kuṟaḷ* couplet from the third, and by far the most beautiful, section of this book, the generous, wry, and inventive exploration of erotic love in light of the grammar of in-ness.

The *Tirukkuṟaḷ* was, for obvious reasons, highly popular with Christian missionaries who came to south India in the colonial period (although they didn't care much for section 3). Some of them also translated the collection, or parts of it, into English, usually badly. They liked to think that the reputed author, Tiruvaḷḷuvar, was even influenced by early Christianity, perhaps via Alexandrian or Syrian Christians who may have made their way to Mylapore. Sentimental moralism is not, however, the key to the book's vast popularity, which surely reflects, even before the contents of the couplets are addressed, the miracle of linguistic compression in musical, metrical form. All verses are in the challenging *vĕṇpā* meter, with four feet in the first line and three in the second[93]—so that, in general, the statement builds down to a slightly syncopated end, leaving the listener with both the satisfaction of a proverb-like simplicity and an ongoing resonance in the silence following upon the words. Even someone who knows no Tamil can, I think, hear the bewitching music of such a verse. Let's try:

> *nattampol keṭum uḷat'ākum cākkāṭum/*
> *vittakarkk' allāl aritu//*

In P. S. Sundaram's deft translation:

> It is only the wise who can convert
> Loss into gain, and death into life.[94]

A nice thought, made much more than "nice" by the way it is stated. More literally, it reads: "Like gain, loss, and death that is something alive— / Except for the wise, this is a hard thing." Note the way the two sets of opposites are stated initially and then left dangling until the second line supplies a predicate and creates closure. You can see the four metrical feet in the first line and the three in the second, ending in the almost anticlimactic *aritu,* "a hard thing." A metrical scan would look like this (_ marks a single long beat, = a bisyllabic beat):

> _ _ _ / _ _ / = _ _ / _ _ _ /
> _ = / _ _ / = _ /

If you try to say the syllables out loud, you can hear the slow, somewhat heavy beat of the first line, ending in the ominous, three-beat *cākkāṭum,* "death," and then the tripping, lighter, somewhat hopeful conclusion. Each metrical foot (x) is linked to the following one (y) by strict rules regulating the length of the opening syllable of y (this is called *tŏṭai,* "connection," and is specific to each meter or set of meters); I won't try to spell these out here. You should, however, attend to the head rhyme, very typical of south Indian meters, called *ĕtukai* in Tamil (*dvitīyâkṣarânuprāsa* in Sanskrit): *nattam* at the start of line 1 thus rhymes with *vitta-* at the start of line 2 (the second phoneme carrying the rhyme in both cases). As a rule, Tamil much prefers such head rhymes to line-final rhyme, though the latter is not unknown. Often, semantic emphasis or contrast emerges from the head rhyme: in our case, "gain" resonates to good effect with "wise." All in all, each such couplet is a musical, phonoaesthetic triumph. You can easily become addicted to the *vĕṇpā* rhythm, both to its versatile opening and its abbreviated, subtle closure. Try reading the lines aloud another few times.

Are we, then, to assume that the putative author of the *Tirukkuṟaḷ* was a metrical wizard who produced one marvel after another over 1,330 verses? I doubt it. Indeed, I am somewhat skeptical about the unitary nature of the book altogether, despite the traditional view reflected in the many medieval commentaries on it (the most authoritative among them being by Parimelaḻakar, probably in the late thirteenth or early fourteenth century).[95] I tend to think of it as a collection, thematically organized, of *kuṟaḷ* verses that deal, first, with ethics and practical wisdom, widely defined—what came to be known as *nīti* in later times—and then with the favorite Tamil theme of loving and its vicissitudes.[96] Since we have dealt in this chapter with the grammar of inness, it makes sense to expand our discussion a little to see how this topic was treated in the *Tirukkuṟaḷ*. First, however, we need a moment, again, to consider dating and the canon.

As mentioned earlier, this book is part of the larger set of the *Eighteen Minor Works,* usually thought to come after the Sangam period proper. That would mean, in my view, that we would want to place Tiruvaḷḷuvar (as a collective persona) in the middle of the first millennium, or somewhat later. The linguistic evidence is, as usual, critical. We do not see in this work the archaic features of the Tamil of Sangam anthologies; and we do find elements, both lexical and morphological, that are first attested in the Pallava-Pandya period, or even later, including the relatively young nominal plural forms in *-kaḷ*.[97] Yet the *Tirukkuṟaḷ* definitely found a place within the classical Tamil canon as the first, most visible item in the *Eighteen Minor Works,* its popularity clearly attested by a heterogeneous collection of fifty-three panegyric verses on it called the *Tiruvaḷḷuva-mālai,* perhaps from Chola times. Moreover, we should recall that Tamil had an objective mechanics of canonization. The widespread popular story about Tiruvaḷḷuvar's birth and literary career, *Tiruvaḷḷuvar carittiram,*[98] says that when this low-caste (or even out-caste) poet sought the authorization of the Madurai Sangam for his book, the academicians told him to place the palm-leaf manuscript on the renowned Sangam plank floating in the Golden Lotus Tank of the temple. He did so, and the plank at once contracted itself to the size of the manuscript, unceremoniously hurling the forty-nine great poet-scholars who usually sat there into the water. The

*Tirukkuṟaḷ* thus triumphed over all other Tamil books and ever since has been clearly "in."

This same popular account interestingly identifies the poet as the son of a Brahmin father, Bhagavān, and a Dalit mother, Ātiyāḷ (the two names constitute a gloss on the opening couplet of the text). Abandoned at birth, the baby was rescued and nursed by a weaver *(vaḷḷuvaṉ)* from Mayilapur (Mylapore in Chennai), then later adopted by a Veḷāḷa farmer. The standard iconography makes him an honest weaver—a bona fide left-hand artisan with a pedigree well suited to a book of universalistic textures and context-free values. But he is also seen, not by chance, as a magically potent Siddha Yogi and exorcist, befriended by the great Śaiva Siddha Tirumūlar; when he died, birds who pecked at his body were turned to gold. This association with esoteric Yoga, sorcery, and alchemy also suits the left-hand environment; but it is tempered by the poet's biological and / or metaphysical links to both Brahmin and Dalit communities as well as to merchants, in the form of his close friend and disciple Elelasiṃha, and, however briefly, to right-hand peasant-farmers. Like his book, Tiruvaḷḷuvar thus effectively belongs to everyone, though, as Blackburn has shown in a thorough study, his Paraiya-Dalit nature is integral to the thick web of stories woven around him in both premodern and modern times.[99]

Because of several statements in the opening chapters of *Tirukkuṟaḷ*, including the benediction-like first decade, there is a widespread scholarly view that the author was a Jain. In this case, too, the left-hand orientation of the work is preserved; the historic constituency of the Jains (and of the Buddhists) was largely urban and mercantile. Whatever the original framing of this work, its author appears in the Tamil imagination as an iconoclast and a social rebel. At the same time, he is an exemplary householder, with a highly idealized, perfectly submissive wife, Vācuki (who bears the name of a great serpent; nothing in the Vaḷḷuvar story is entirely normative). The first two large sections of the *Tirukkuṟaḷ—Aṟattuppāl,* on *dharma,* and *Pŏruṭpāl,* on fortune (including political science)—have negative things to say about courtesans (a whole chapter, 92, is devoted to denouncing such women); one couplet (91.1) also says that only a fool is in love with his wife. On the other hand, love, per se, is celebrated:

When breath and bones come together, they create
life lived with love. (8.3)

The third section of the book, *Kāmattuppāl,* on desire, takes us through a paradigmatic love sequence in dramatic monologues. With some effort, one can almost squeeze this sequence into the standard narrative offered by the commentary on the *Grammar of Stolen Love,* or by the *kovai* genre, which arranges its verses according to a straightforward developmental (mostly devolutionary) set of moments and phases. The great medieval commentators on the *Tirukkuṟaḷ* do their best to make the *Kāmattuppāl* intelligible in terms of the classical categories, including the *tiṇai* landscapes; Parimelaḻakar, writing in the Vaishṇava, highly Sanskritized environment of Kancipuram, also finds a way to graft the two primary Tamil love modes, *kaḷavu* ("stolen" premarital union) and *kaṟpu* (wedded life), onto the prevalent Sanskrit division of erotic love, *śṛṅgāra,* into enjoyment/union, *sambhoga,* and love-in-separation, *vipralambha.*[100] Parimelaḻakar regards the first seven decade chapters as exemplifying stolen love and the remaining thirteen as expressing the many subheadings of separation, the hallmark of wedded life.

This is by no means the only way to analyze the thematic progression built into these chapters; other commentators had their own ways of arranging them. The artificial nature of all such schemes points to the irregular and irreducible nature of the whole section on love, which does, indeed, tell some sort of composite and more or less continuous story—from the life-changing moment when the two very young lovers first set eyes on each other (109) to the playful but still painful quarrels and fits of sulking *(ūṭal)* that characterize love-making in marriage, at its best (the final three chapters). In fact, we would do better, as some modern readers have recognized, to think of this section more as a collection of vignettes and witty *aperçus* than as an orderly series governed by a single narrative logic; the old *akam* template, though not absent, is there only to serve the crafted individual couplets, as we would anyway expect from the poetic form that has been chosen. Everything depends on these singular, nonrepeatable moments in the lives of two lovers; in this sense, the *Tirukkuṟaḷ* verses on love are remarkably reminiscent of the sixteenth- and seventeenth-century genre of *padams* by the Telugu poets Annamayya and Kṣetrayya and the Tamil Muttuttāṇṭavar, among others.

It goes without saying that many of the couplets are delightful, even ravishing. (There has been an inane academic discussion about whether this book is even worthy of being called poetry;[101] the section on love alone would suffice to put any doubts to rest. Once again, I recommend giving up on a strict notion of unified composition by a single author.) Look, for example, at 111.10:

> Whenever we learn, we see that we don't know.
> Each time I make love to her, I want more.

It's the comparison—the vast open space of ignorance—that gives this verse its punch. The thought is, as usual in this work, a general and universal one. Yet this love is still utterly Tamil, rooted in the south Indian vocabulary and conventions, as one sees from the verse immediately preceding this one:

> Fighting, making up, making love—these
> are the true fruits of love.

Remember that *ūṭal,* the lovers' quarrel, is the main marker of the *marutam* landscape, proper to married life. Sometimes *ūṭal* is paired with *kūṭal,* "uniting," a rhyming complementary set. In 111.9, however, we have a full triptych: *ūṭal, uṇartal* (making up after a quarrel), and then *puṇartal,* love-making. One shouldn't give up on the middle moment, which may be the sweetest of all.

Above all, we find in these chapters the endlessly inventive exploration of the modes of separation, as in the classic *akam* poems and their grammars. The entire rich menu tends to collapse into infinitely condensed mini-statements, so sharp they can take your breath away:

> If you're *not* leaving, speak to me.
> Speak of your speedy return
> to those who will still be alive. (116.1)[102]

And since there is a strong, justified tendency to portray Tiruvaḷḷuvar as a householder keen on affirming the joys of worldly life, I'd like to cite verse 131.6, reminiscent of Rumi, one of many that celebrate a wide range of human experience without excluding the darker, hurtful sides. Back to sulking:

> Without anger and squabbles, love
> is a fruit either too ripe or raw.

And then we have the no-win situations like the following:

> If I tell her I love her more than anyone, she asks:
> "Which anyone?" (132.4)

I'm going to resist the temptation to go on quoting couplets. The reader is warmly advised to find his own favorites in translations such as P. S. Sundaram's or the beautiful French one by François Gros.

At some point beyond the Sangam period proper,[103] two closely linked, large-scale lyrical narratives—usually wrongly called epics—were created: *The Tale of an Anklet, Cilappatikāram,* by Iḷaṅkovaṭikaḷ, and its twin masterpiece, *Maṇimekalai,* by Cāttaṉār. Both are works of conscious integration, drawing together the disparate fragments of early Tamil culture and reframing their grammars in the service of this comprehensive vision. The first tells the story of Kovalaṉ, a merchant from Pukār on the eastern coast, and his wife, Kaṇṇaki, the true heroine of the work. Kovalaṉ falls in love with a dancing girl, Mātavi, and spends all his fortune on her until, one evening on the seashore, he hears her sing songs in the *akam* mode of longing, like those we saw earlier in this chapter. He takes them literally, utterly disregarding their conventional expressive grammar; he thinks Mātavi is singing about some other lover—that her exquisite songs are all "a pack of specious lies" *(māyappŏyp pala kūṭṭu māyattāḷ).*[104] So he leaves her and returns, penniless, to his wife, who welcomes him back and offers him her remaining capital—the two golden anklets she wears around her feet. They set off southward toward Madurai, to begin life anew. Here disaster strikes. As Kovalaṉ enters the city, carrying one of the anklets, he is seen by a treacherous goldsmith who has stolen an anklet belonging to the Pandya queen. The goldsmith sees his opportunity and rushes to inform the king that the stolen anklet has turned up in the hands of the thief. The king hastily, without thinking further, orders his men to kill this thief and bring the anklet back—and so they do.

Kaṇṇaki, waiting outside the city among the shepherds for her husband to return, hears the news of his death. She has had an ominous dream. Now she rushes into the city, in grief and rage, and confronts the king; she has the remaining anklet, with inset jewels, in her hand, and she proves to the king that he has made a grievous error—the queen's anklet had pearls, but no jewels, inside it. When the Pandya realizes what he has done, he collapses in self-loathing and dies.

By now Kaṇṇaki has been transformed from a gentle, devoted wife to a furious goddess. She wrests off her left breast and casts it at the city of Madurai, which is at once consumed in flames. Still raging, she heads west toward the mountains. There she is seen—a divine apparition, ascending to heaven, with the gods beside her, together with her slain husband—by the Kuṟavar hunters who live in these hills. They report what they have seen to the Cera king, who sets off on a campaign to bring a stone from the Himalayas to his Kerala capital; this stone will be carved in the image of Kaṇṇaki, the true wife (Pattiṉi), and installed in the temple that is still very much alive today—the famous Bhagavatī shrine to the Goddess of One Breast, *ŏṟṟaimulaicci,* in Kodungalur. The Cera raid on the north and the installation of the goddess icon in her shrine forms the subject of the third book of *The Tale of an Anklet,* the *Vañcikkāṇṭam;* although for some time it was fashionable among scholars to claim that this third section was a later addition, and that the first two books—*Pukārkkāṇṭam* and *Maturaikkāṇṭam,* ending with the death of the king and the burning of the city—together comprised the true, tragic *Tale,* today we can see that the third book is utterly integral to the work as a whole. Indeed, it is, in a sense, the true point of the story. This is a work about the creation, from outside as well as inside, of a fierce royal goddess and about the establishment of her temple and its modes of worship.[105]

*The Tale of an Anklet* fits a pattern still widely generative in Kerala, particularly in north Malabar: we call such stories and their associated rituals *Tĕyyam;* very often they are based on outrage, violent death, and unthinkable injustice leading to the actualization of a divine identity.[106]

The *Cilappatikāram* is a classic *Tĕyyam* narrative in the form not of popular song, *pāṭṭu,* such as we find today (in Malayalam), but of a highly crafted, exquisitely polished literary composition, enlivened by the whole range of ancient Tamil poetry and story. The core narrative, moreover, is linked not only to Kerala and the west coast but also, clearly, to the city of Madurai and its great goddess Mīnâkṣī, "Fish-Eyes," who, according to the Madurai *purāṇa*s, was born not with two but with three breasts—as if the breast that Kaṇṇaki lost had reappeared on this seemingly androgynous deity.[107] We don't have time to explore this connection more deeply, but it is important to note that the Kaṇṇaki-Mīnâkṣī mythology lives on in Tamil oral epic (the *Kovalaṉ-katai* and its various elaborations), as well as in the active cult of the goddess Pattini in Sri Lanka.[108]

If we stay with the *Tale* as we have it today and try to understand its inner logic and its aesthetic program, we might want to begin with the *patikam* preface that was added to this work, probably at a somewhat later period, in an attempt to frame and to explain its primary themes. This *patikam* explicitly names three such themes: (1) for kings who do wrong, *dharma* is death; (2) noble people perform worship for the famous goddess Pattiṉi; and (3) ancient deeds come back to us and activate whatever happens (*patikam,* lines 55–57). The literary tradition clearly chose to interpret the book along these lines, which are, indeed, well suited to its narrative. We have a work about kingship, its dangers, and the consequences of royal error; about the emergence into public worship of a great goddess; and about the forces set into movement by our own actions, whose consequences we may well not be able to avoid. Some scholars like to translate the relevant Tamil term, *ūḻviṉai* as "fate;" others prefer *karma,* undoubtedly a possible equivalent.[109] For myself, I think there is nothing fatalistic about *ūḻviṉai* in the *Tale.* The notion of consequential deeds does appear at critical moments such as the end of Canto 9, when Kovalaṉ leaves Mātavi and comes back to Kaṇṇaki, and in the climactic Canto 16, when Kovalaṉ is executed, "struck by his inevitable karma"[110] (*ūḻviṉai*—just as the Pandya king dies because of *his* karma). But at no point does this term imply a mechanistic law operating blindly. The characters make their choices, and pay the price; they cannot escape the complex causal chain that they themselves have largely shaped, although, as in the *Mahābhārata,* particular moments and events tend to be highly overdetermined. An entire chapter, 23, takes the causal sequence back to Kovalaṉ's former birth, when he himself rashly killed an innocent man whom he mistook for a spy; Nīli, the dead man's wife—another Tamil goddess-in-evolution—cursed her husband's killer to suffer, one day, the same fate he did. The business of unraveling such sequences fascinates the reputed author of our text, Iḷankovaṭikaḷ. At the same time, we can observe an interesting tension between the second and third themes defined by the *patikam:* the operation of personal causality cannot explain the deeper, mostly unthinkable process by which an effective goddess is brought into being.

We know the name, or title, of the *Tale*'s author only from the *patikam* preface; but the author, still unnamed, speaks of himself in the final canto through the mouth of a possessed woman, Tevantikai. In her clairvoyant state she addresses him and tells his story: he was the younger brother of the famous Cera king Cĕṅkuṭṭuvaṉ (whom we recognize from the *Patiṟṟuppattu*); when an astrologer or soothsayer predicted that this younger brother would become the next king, he—"Iḷaṅko," the "young prince"—at once renounced the throne and the world. Hence, one assumes, his honorific title, *Aṭikaḷ,* an ascetic or devotee.[111] In precisely this same context, in Canto 30, we are told that Kayavāku (=Gajabāhu), the king of Lanka surrounded by the sea, was present and also worshipped the newly installed goddess.[112] For a long time, this reference, known by the grandiose title of the "Gajabāhu synchronism," was thought to provide a firm date both to the *Tale* and, beyond this, to Sangam literature generally. Gajabāhu I ruled in Sri Lanka from 171 to 193 A.D.; hence, it was argued, he must have been a contemporary of Cĕṅkuṭṭuvaṉ and, if we believe the story in Canto 30, of Iḷankovaṭikaḷ as well. But far too much has been made of this slender wisp of evidence, if indeed it can be called evidence. And who is to say that some old memory of Gajabāhu has not surfaced in a much later work? As Zvelebil has said, and I have also argued from a rather different standpoint, there is no reason to assume that late material is "necessarily unauthentic."[113] Probably the most we can say (with R. Nagaswamy) is that it is possible that the *Tale* was composed at a point when a memory of Gajabāhu had not yet disappeared. We will have to look for better ways to situate the *Tale* and its twin work within the continuum of Tamil poetry.

Here the *patikam* to the *Tale,* together with a similar *patikam* prefaced to the *Maṇimekalai,* is of real interest. The preface to *Maṇimekalai* gives us, along with a synopsis of the story, the name of its author—Maturai Kūlavāṇikkaṉ Cāttaṉ, the merchant (probably a grain merchant) Cāttaṉ of Madurai. The name Cāttaṉār is familiar to us from the Sangam colophons (to some twenty poems); we have no way of knowing how many poets bore it. More interesting is the *patikam* to the *Tale,* where it turns out that Iḷaṅko learned the whole story of Kaṇṇaki and Kovalaṉ (including the previous lives of both these persons) from this grain merchant Cāttaṉār, who asked Iḷaṅko to compose a poetic narrative about it. How did Cāttaṉār know the details of the story? As it happens, he was resting, possibly sleeping, inside the temple of Śiva in Madurai at the time of the great conflagration, right after Kaṇṇaki had torn off her breast, when the goddess of Madurai herself appeared to Kaṇṇaki/Pattiṉi and told her about her previous birth and its tragic karmic conditioning. Did Cāttanār literally dream up the whole story? Maybe. If he did, the dream would be the best guarantee that the *Tale* is true. The intertwined prefaces also tell us about the first audiences for these twin texts; the two authors serve as each other's interlocutors and listeners even before the two great works assume their final form. Cāttaṉār, for his part, provides the necessary trigger for Iḷaṅko's poetic enterprise.

We might, then, think of both works, as the Tamil tradition seems to think of them, as having crystallized in a gruesome moment of fiery destruction, at night, while one already existing goddess addresses another goddess-coming-into-being and is overheard by a somnolent poet. Moreover, they tell what is, in effect, a single story. For *Maṇimekalai* is the direct sequel to the *Tale*—the story of Kovalaṉ and Mātavi's daughter, Maṇimekalai, named for the great goddess of the sea, Maṇimekhalā, who will eventually flood the city of Pukār/Kāvirippūmpaṭṭiṉam in a watery apocalypse precisely complementing the fiery one in Madurai. Maṇimekalai is brought up to be a courtesan like her mother, but her instincts are all opposed to this role; she wants to renounce the world and eventually does so as a Buddhist nun.

The *Maṇimekalai* is thus the surviving pearl of a once extensive Tamil Buddhist literature. It, too, has a tragic love story, for the prince, Utayakumaraṉ, is in love with the nun-to-be and dies, through another terrible misperception, because of this unrequited passion. You can see even from this brief abstract the tremendous resonance this second text has with the *Tale;* I, for one, sometimes prefer it, on aesthetic grounds, to the much better known work of Iḷaṅko.[114] The intertextuality built into *Maṇimekalai* also includes a direct quotation from the *Tirukkuṟaḷ*—at 22.59–62, the words of "a poet without lies" *(pŏyyil pulavaṉ)*—and there is an oral story that explains this citation. Cāttaṉār's epithet is *cīttalai,* "Pus-head," because whenever he heard bad poetry, he would scratch his head with his stylus, causing a wound that became infected. (There's a lot of bad poetry out there.) Only when he heard the *Tirukkuṟaḷ* was he satisfied to the point where he could leave the wound alone, and at last it healed. Once again, the tradition offers us an objective standard for excellence in the form of this poet's perfect pitch.

Together, the two long poems give us a rich picture of the Tamil country seen as a composite, complex conceptual unit. In particular, a panoramic social landscape emerges from the two texts, as their heroes wander through the cities and villages, the forests and deserts, of southern India. There are merchants—who effectively set the tone—as well as princes and kings, Brahmin sages and Jain and Buddhist ascetics, pastoralists, farmers, hunters and gatherers, courtesans, musicians, bull fighters, warriors. The *Tale* was clearly composed with this unifying vision in mind; its final words, in the *nūṟkaṭṭurai* epilogue, list the elements that have been brought together in this book:

> Here ends the *Cilappatikāram.* It ends, in truth,
> With the story of *Maṇimekalai.* Like a mirror
> Reflecting the far hills, it reflects the essence
> Of the cool Tamil country, enclosed by the Kumari
> And Vēṅkaṭam, and by the eastern and western seas.
> It comprises the five landscapes of pure and impure Tamil
> Where live gods and humans following their duty
> And practicing virtue, wealth, and love.

Its noble language expresses in perfect rhythm
Good sense, the themes of love and war,
Exquisite songs, the lute, musical mode, chants,
Drama, acts and scenes, dances
That conform to the established rules of the vari
Round dance and cētam, put in simple and perfect Tamil.[115]

The grammar is fully present, narrativized, enacted: we have the five landscapes, the domains of *akam* and *puṟam,* the literary and performance ecology (with an emphasis on dance), but also the three goals of the human being, *puruṣârtha,* as in Sanskrit (virtue, wealth, and love). The intrinsic relation between the *Tale* and *Maṇimekalai* is also directly stated. "Noble language" is, more literally, "words united with phonemes and the meaning that arises from within them" *(ĕḻuttŏṭu puṇarnta cŏll akatt' ĕḻu pŏruḷ)*—thus the three parts of grammar, phonology, morphology, and meaning, with the highly nontrivial statement that meaning arises from inside *(akattu),* possibly from the inner surface of the inseparable bond between sound and the word that triggers it. De Saussure would have approved. An entire world has been exfoliated in language, from the inside, moving outward, just as Kaṇṇaki moves from the inner space of the home to the open wilderness and finally to the public domain of the temple—but the latter, too, is, in the end, another exemplar of in-ness, as we will soon see. Everything that moves through language carries something of the interior. And not just any language: this is the tongue of the "cool Tamil country" in both its elevated grammatical form *(cĕntamiḻ)* and its colloquial varieties *(kŏṭuntamiḻ),* and this language is "simple and perfect," a natural, organic force *(iyaṟkai)* that brings lucid knowledge into awareness *(tĕriyuṟu vakaiyāl).* Here, at the very end of the *Tale,* is one more meaning of the word "Tamil"—clarity, lucidity, flowing from the very nature of this special language. We will encounter this idea again.

This chapter has brought us deep into historical time. We have glimpsed the life of two great kingdoms, that of the Pallavas in the north and that of the Pandyas in the far south; the latter state rightly saw itself as the font of Tamil poetry and learning. In the second half of the first millennium, Tamil poetry was clearly a going concern, with a classical literature organized in anthologies and other works, redacted, illuminated by commentaries, and ordered by an authoritative grammar. The elaborate discursive commentary to the *Grammar of Stolen Love* shows us a mature tradition, replete with a powerful myth of origins and clearly familiar with much of the classical canon. It also incorporates the exemplary poems of the *Pāṇṭikkovai* that have the merit of anchoring the date of Sangam poetry some two centuries, at least, before these verses (the latter must belong to the late seventh or early eighth centuries). A consolidated, stable, continually evolving literary tradition must have been in place by the fourth and fifth centuries. Eighth-century Pandya inscriptions show us something of what the carriers of that tradition must have looked like: erudite, literate (orally and / or graphically), articulate in Tamil and Sanskrit, endowed with a highly trained memory, mostly Brahmin. Some were poets themselves, thus, like their Sangam predecessors, capable of impinging via musical and metrical sounds on the world ostensibly outside.

This crystallizing Tamil literary tradition was, in its own terms, highly autonomous and self-regulating, but not in the sense of being remote from Sanskrit sources or influences; there is no such dichotomy in any of our sources. As Emmanuel Francis has shown, Pallava-period inscriptions are primarily in Sanskrit but also reveal strong Tamil elements, including Tamil verse forms and *biruda* royal titles—so that we can definitely speak, by this period, of "political Tamil" (that is, royal panegyric), a relatively early form of what Sheldon Pollock has called vernacularization, involving local inflections of the Sanskrit cosmopolitan models.[116] Perhaps this is not the best way to state the matter. Pallava and Pandya political Tamil was largely standardized, universalized, and at the same time an integral variant of pan-Indian political discourse; thus "the Pallavas played a decisive role in making the Tamil country part of the Sanskrit cosmopolis."[117] Were it not to reinstate the false dichotomy, I would be tempted to say that Pallava and Pandya patronage of Tamil poets and scribes played a decisive role in making the emergent Sanskrit cosmopolis an organic part of evolving cosmopolitan

Tamil.[118] Certainly, by the time of *The Tale of an Anklet* and the *Maṇimekalai,* the Tamil region was seen as culturally unified, a distinctive though diverse eco-domain with its own internal logic and favored themes and with a temporal depth of many centuries, and a huge literary canon, to work with. As we will see in Chapter 3, it was also a region experimenting with highly original metaphysical intuitions and engaged in creating new institutions to embody them.

THREE

# Second Budding: The Musical Self

## *Anupallavi*

### Breath and Life

"Self" is a big word. To find a Tamil equivalent for this enigmatic notion is also no simple task. There are many words for "heart," "mind," even "me-ness"—words that change over long periods of time and begin to take on new meanings in accordance with evolving models of the person and her inner constitution. These words function in complicated ways in relation to the innermost core of the Tamil being, which our texts call *uyir* or *āvi,* "the breath of life" or, in a slight expansion and abstraction, "aliveness."[1]

Look, for example, at *Tiruviruttam* 4 by the great poet Nammāḻvār (eighth or ninth century):

My lonely heart was lost
once before—to *his*
great bird.

Soon this heart will be lost again
to his cool and fragrant basil.

We, in any case,
are without it.

As for you, frigid wind
poisoned with basil from his crown
after he savored the nipples
of the false and angry demoness,

is it natural that you steal inside
to freeze our very breath?

At first reading, a *Tiruviruttam* verse often looks puzzling, disorienting: who is speaking, and to whom? Who is the *he/his* the speaker refers to? Even without knowing the answer to these questions, the poem should, I think, work on the reader's heart or mind (I'm not sure which organ in a Western sensibility is appropriate). All of us know what it feels like to lose a heart. We can also identify with the sense of something inside us that is freezing or paralyzing our aliveness.

One gets used to these poems. They belong to the *akam,* "in-ness," category; like in so many of the Sangam models, this poem is put in the mouth of a woman longing for her absent lover. But we are in a new period, a radically different cultural configuration, which has altered the old *akam* paradigm and molded it to another expressive purpose. The absent lover is now the god Vishṇu, and the speaker, longing for him, with his usual attributes—the eagle Garuda he rides upon, the basil he wears, and a mythic memory of the time he, as a baby, killed the demoness Pūtanā by sucking her life out of her breasts—gives oblique voice to the hopeless yearning the devotee feels for this god, whom he can never "have" or even fully know. Not that these poems are allegorical: later Vaishṇava commentators tried to read them as if they were, but that effort belongs to a period of commentary and rationalization, not entirely unlike what happened with the Sangam poems, as we have seen. Taken by themselves, the *Tiruviruttam* poems create a poetic or aesthetic world suffused by the classical grammar we have studied, within which the worshiper can somehow find his or her way. That world is autonomous, largely resistant to philosophical paraphrase.[2]

Let's go back to the despairing beloved. She is, technically, speaking to the north wind, probably on a wintry night. She's not only alone and restless but also cold, inside and out. It's not fair. She wants him, and he won't come. Two pieces of her in-ness have been affected: her heart, *nĕñcam,* has disappeared (*he* took it, probably forever); and her breath, *āvi,* is being frozen *(paṉippu),* from the root *paṉi*—to be bedewed, to flow out, be shed; to tremble, quake, shiver with cold; to be in pain; to spring forth, as tears; or, in the causative form, which we find here, to cause to tremble, to cause to suffer, or, interestingly, to beat, as a drum.[3] Archana Venkatesan nicely translates: "my life shivers:/Is this your nature?"[4] All of the above meanings are appropriate to *āvi* or *uyir*, a fragile, delicate inner being that in its natural mode tends to the liquid, to states of flowing movement, to welling up as tears, to feeling and perceiving in a continuously shifting and evolving way, also to shaking and quaking and feeling pain, and perhaps to moaning or beating like a drum struck, or a string plucked, by a musician. In general, *āvi*, the rhythmic breath of life, quivers and sings. But it can also, it seems, be slowed down to the freezing point, where the person can no longer feel his or her own breath.

Love can do that. Now read verse 6 of this same powerful text:

> Sinuous vine bearing darts
> deadlier than arrows and bent bows,
> she is Death, lurking in ambush
> to strike down with love
>
> this slayer of demons as he comes riding
> his swift bird.
>
> And you: look at her, look
> to your own lives
> inside this world.

You who? We can't be sure. It seems that the male lover is speaking about his beloved, whose eyes, as everyone knows, are more lethal than any earthly weapon, even lethal enough to strike down the great god himself as he arrives on his swift bird. Despite everything, for once she (that is, *we*) has (have) the upper hand. Here the self-contained poetic universe of in-ness momentarily fuses the *akam* lover and the "real" beloved, the god riding his swift bird. Such sudden overlaps are not uncommon in this book.[5] The threat to the god and lover is the direct outcome of the woman's own feelings of passionate love,[6] and this danger is then universalized: whoever the audience is, they are warned to care for their own lives, *uyir*. The *uyir* inhabits the inner zone of this world (the final word of the poem) in an all-too-precarious manner. Breath could depart at any moment. Indeed, the poem is meant, I think, to take our breath away.

The *uyir* goes in and out, following a mysterious, utterly unconscious cycle of its own. Such is our life, literally conceived; but also the life of the god. When he breathes out, the world is born; each time he breathes in, he reabsorbs that world within himself. These processes happen every second. The world is continually externalized, reconfigured and simultaneously taken apart, drawn back into the recesses of Vishṇu's being.[7] In the early Tamil devotional poems, such as Nammāḻvār's *Tiruviruttam* and *Tiruvāymŏḻi* or their Śaiva parallels in the *Tevāram*, a powerful isomorphism characterizes the business of breathing on the universal, cosmic level—the rhythm of god's out- and in-breaths—and on the individual, human level. We breathe as he breathes, and to similar, if somewhat more minor, effect. The tracks are really one. What is more, both he and we breathe in accordance with an internally active expressive drive. The *uyir* always speaks the self (that word again). Even better, it seeks to sing. Observe *Tiruviruttam* 48:

> A worm sliding with its soft body
> through an open wound—
> what does it know of this world?
> What have I learned
> of the poem that Tirumāl,[8] in his guile,
> utters to himself
> through me?
> Some would say it's like
> the clicks of a gecko,
> as old as old can be.

Let's say the poet is speaking to us directly here and describing his sense of how he makes a poem. Actually, it isn't the author who makes it. The god is using him to speak,[9] or rather sing, to (and about) himself. The poet is an instrument in the hands of a clever deity, who apparently wants, or needs, this inner conversation to be heard outside himself, as it were—in metrical, musical form. Does the poet have any agency in this strange transaction? Maybe a little. Does the poem or song have intelligible meaning? Perhaps. From ancient times (here the verse offers a correct historical snapshot) Tamil people have interpreted the clicks and squeaks of the gecko *(palli)* as revealing the future to those who can read them. This future, always specific to a person, preexists and can be decoded. Poetry, too, then, is a kind of divination. One should not, perhaps, rush to chop up a poetic line into discrete syllables and meaning-bearing words.

The *uyir* sings, willy-nilly. Not coincidentally, it does so in Tamil. I keep using the pronoun "it," but there is a problem here. Tamil nouns and pronouns come in two classes: *uyar-tiṇai,* the "high category" (the same word, *tiṇai,* that serves to denote the Sangam landscapes) of living, conscious beings such as humans, gods, and Nāga serpents, and *aḵṟiṇai,* a "non"-category that can include objects, lower forms of being, but also something like the breath of life that eludes categorization altogether. By its very definition, *uyir* is alive and cannot but be alive until it stops moving or dies. Even then, it stops only in the sense that it no longer goes in and out of a particular body or bodies; the breath flows out of such a body only in order to merge into the wider level of breathing before re-embodying itself in some new being.

Thus in Kamban's Tamil *Rāmāyaṇa,* a Chola-period work (probably twelfth century), the rushing river—ostensibly the Sarayu in Ayodhya, but in fact a transparent description of the Kaveri in the Tamil heartland—with which the book opens, is

> like living breath that fills and empties
> body after body (1.1.20)[10]

Filling and emptying comprise the in-breath and the out-breath, thus the dissolution and remaking of the world. Such is the rhythm of the *uyir* as music, an unstoppable river. To describe this process as a rhythmic beat is to do away with any primitive dualism. Breath and body are not two dichotomous entities, nothing like spiritual substance wedded to inert matter; they are more like the drum and the drummer, an intimate interdependent pair. When Rāma comes back to his empty hut in the forest after Rāvaṇa has kidnapped Sītā, he, Rāma, is like "the *uyir* that has been separated from its containing body *(kūṭu)* and has come in search of it, but cannot find it" (3.8.158). Sītā once held the god's *uyir* inside her; now this *uyir* has nowhere to go. It is lost in the world and, a little paradoxically, itself empty in the absence of the singular being that should claim it and contain it. Without Sītā, Rāma can no longer breathe; breath itself has dispersed in uncontainable sorrow.

It is the *uyir* that can love, always in a tangible and sensual way. When Rāma and Sītā first see each other in Mithila, before they are married, they become

> one breath of life
> in two different bodies (1.10.38)

Thus the *uyir* is always unitary, even if it flows in and out of an endlessly fragmented series of distinct bodies; this underlying unity is what two lovers naturally feel, though others, too, can touch it and know it at least in fleeting moments. The breath of any single individual is the medium of his or her connectivity to another person, intimately known, but also to all other persons and to the profoundly interconnected cosmos as a whole. Again, it is this awareness of connectivity—always a matter of deeper self-knowledge and awareness—that sets in motion the need to speak or sing. Movement is continuous: thus in phonology *uyir* is the technical term for a vowel, unbroken, unblocked, as opposed to *mĕy,* "body," "consonant," which momentarily stops the flow of breath and sound. As we have seen, the primary graphemes in the Tamil script mark consonants with an inherent *a*-vowel, a continuous breath inhering in the phoneme and in its sign just as God dwells in the world.[11]

There is unconscious bodily delight, a kind of tasting, just in breathing in and out. We never find in early Tamil devotional poems any hint that the inner, sensual nature of the *uyir* is meant to be suppressed, even if the five senses, and the giddy mental apparatus of any living person, are sometimes, often, seen as traps, distractions, false starts. The poet may seek to pry the *uyir* free from such constraints. In general, however, probably the most conspicuous feature of Tamil devotional religion is its full-bodied affirmation of sense and feeling as the *sādhana,* "the means or path," to whatever soteriological goal is sought—god, enhanced freedom, a wider awareness, continued (painful) loving in birth after birth. Here we find a contrast with the classical world of Yoga, which is suspicious of, indeed downright hostile to, sensual input and everyday mentation. In Tamil, passionate feeling and the knowledge commensurate with it *(uṇarvu),* usually, though by no means always, an intuitive, nonanalytical mode, is what we have to work with—a primary attribute of the *uyir.*[12] More generally, the *uyir* in its continuous movement carries or embodies awareness itself.[13]

## "Brickless, timberless, metalless, mortarless"

How and when did this happen? The conventional wisdom says that Tamil *bhakti,* the devotional religion that underlies the vast networks of temples, stone images, and daily domestic ritual, is first seen, in relatively mild form, in the supposedly late Sangam collection known as *Paripāṭal,* mentioned in Chapter 2. Here there are, indeed, long poems to two main deities, Tirumāl and Cevveḷ. Some like to say that these are Tamil gods who were identified with, or merged into, the north Indian Sanskrit deities Krishṇa/Vishṇu and Skanda, the son of Śiva and Pārvatī, respectively. Such statements appear to me to be without meaning. We can, however, say that the tone of the *Paripāṭal* hymns is relatively restrained, and even slightly impersonal, when compared to the new genres that emerged sometime in the mid- to late- first millennium in two parallel streams, one focused on Śiva, the other on Vishṇu. The former is the subject of the *Tevāram* poems attributed to three major poets—the child gnostic Tiruñāṉacampantar, the older man Tirunāvukkaracu cuvāmikaḷ or Appar, and the "harsh devotee" Cuntarar—together with a fourth, Māṇikkavācakar, and a fifth, who is actually perhaps the first, the woman or demoness Kāraikkālammaiyār, the Lady from Karaikkal. The Vishṇu poets are known as Āḻvārs, "those who plumb the depths"; they comprise a series of twelve, including one woman, Āṇṭāḷ, and the surpassing poet of this entire set, Nammāḻvār, whose *Tiruviruttam* is quoted above.

These complementary bodies of hymns developed in relation to specific temple sites; the vast majority of the poems are localized at a particular shrine, whose external setting, highly individualized deity, and idiosyncratic features of iconography and/or ritual, are usually mentioned or hinted at by the poet. In some sense, these poets wove the hundreds of shrines together into a single, self-reinforcing set in each of the two streams; they celebrated the local deity in his singularity while also asserting his wider, pan-Indian, indeed cosmic, identity.

Again, there is no need to think in terms of a tension between these two modes of conceptualizing the god, although in somewhat later times the radical localization of the deity in a particular image (the *arcâvatāra*) at a specific shrine did exercise the theologians, since it seemed possibly to compromise this deity's universal presence and context-free attributes. Seen in the experiential perspective of the local villagers or pilgrims moving from one site to the next, each such embodiment is complete, the universal resonance of god's presence being a direct function of his particularity in nature and local context. One lives in a temple village with a god who is nearby, accessible, in a way integral to the social and kinship structures in place there, so that in coming to see him one is, in effect, visiting a local king who may also be nearly an intimately known relative, and no less divine or whole for that.

The temples themselves, as fixed edifices, built with a particular preference for stone, are apparently an invention of the Pallava period (roughly mid-third to eighth century) and soon came to serve as a focus for royal interest and patronage. They were constructed at first, probably for centuries, out of perishable materials such as wood and thatch. The transition to stone temples can be clearly seen at the great Pallava site of Mahabalipuram, just south of Chennai, where the first carved monoliths and free-standing structures still imitate precisely the shape of earlier wooden shrines with their sloping thatched roofs. By the early seventh century, the great Pallava polymath king Mahendravarman I (600–630) can boast of having made a shrine that was "brickless, timberless, metalless, and mortarless"—and meant to last.[14] The king is referred to here by his telling title, *Vicitra-citta,* a man "of restless (or many-faceted) mind." He certainly knew that he was creating something new.

Historians, notably Nicholas Dirks, have convincingly argued that Pallava kingship shifted its primary orientation and reconceived the basis of its authority in the course of its first few centuries.[15] An early pride in the performance of Vedic sacrificial rituals, including, at least according to the royal rhetoric, the enormously expensive and demanding Horse Sacrifice *(aśva-medha),* gave way to a drive toward patronage and endowment, *dāna.* We recognize from the inscriptions both individual or family (often Brahmin) recipients and early collective and institutional beneficiaries, including the rock-cut or free-standing stone temples that stand in marked contrast to the inherently mobile Vedic cult. We know for certain that some of the new stone temples from this period housed deities to whom the *bhakti* poets sang their prayers, sometimes apparently close to the time of construction. If we wish to believe the hagiographies later recorded for these poets, they had complex, sometimes adversarial relations with the royal courts. Already at this early period, a major axiom of south Indian kingship was already operative: as a rule, the royal donor needed the institutional recipient of his gift more than the latter needed the king. South Indian kingship was then, and has remained to this day even within the new game of democratic politics, a precarious business in need of continuous renegotiation in relation to the true sources of its authority. Among the latter, in premodern times, temples and Brahmins came first.

We will go deeper into this equation in Chapter 4. For now, I'd like briefly to examine further the intense tonality of the Tamil *bhakti* poems, arguably the single most powerful contribution of Tamil south India to pan-Indian civilization. South Indian tradition correctly saw this form of worship as its own invention: in the Sanskrit *Bhāgavata-māhātmya,* undoubtedly a south Indian text entirely rooted in a Tamil milieu and prefaced to the equally south Indian *Bhāgavata-purāṇa* (perhaps eighth century), *bhakti* "herself" says she was born in the Tamil *(draviḍa)* land.[16] The *Bhāgavata-purāṇa* tells us that devotion to Lord Vāsudeva/Vishṇu developed among the Tamils *(draviḷeṣu),* who drink the waters of the Tamraparni, the Kritamala, the Kaveri, and the western Mahanad Rivers;[17] it is not by chance that this passage mentions the Tamraparṇi, in the far south, first. The earliest Vaishṇava-Āḻvār poets, on the other hand, claim to have found the god in northern Tamil Nadu, at Kovalur (modern Koyilur) or Gopapuram. Or rather, to be precise, *he* found *them:* on a rainy night, Pŏykai Āḻvār found refuge on a small porch (*iṭaikaḻi,* Skt. *dehalī*) near the shrine in this village; then Pūtatt'āḻvār arrived and squeezed himself in, only to be followed by Peyāḻvār. The porch was by this point so crowded that the three poet-saints had to spend the night standing, but soon they felt that yet another presence was taking up what little space was left. This "extra," invisible person was the god Vishṇu himself, as the three poets, examining themselves with the inner light of knowledge, came to understand. They then burst into Tamil song, the most ancient, very moving texts in the Śrīvaishṇava Tamil canon. Vishṇu at Kovalur is Dehalīśa, "Lord of the Porch."[18]

The Tamil Śaiva image of origins is bound up with the poetess Kāraikkālammaiyār, in theory the first to worship Śiva in the Tamil mode of personal prayer. We know the tradition thinks she came first because Tiruñāṉacampantar, the boy gnostic, first of the *Tevāram* poets, refused to set foot in the shrines she had visited; he visited them upside down, walking on his head. Icons of the Lady from Karaikkal show her as a rather scary skeletal figure with cymbals in her hand—for she is the musician accompanying Śiva's famous Dance of Ecstasy. She lost the flesh on her body at her own request (addressed to the god) when her husband, terrified of her power, refused to live with her: thus she refers to herself as Kāraikkālpey, the "demoness from Karaikkal." It is of some importance that both the Śaiva and Vaishnava textual collections put a *pey* or *bhūta*—a prowling, hungry demon or ghoul—at the moment of inspired beginnings.

Read the opening of the *Poem of Amazement (Aṟputat tiruvantāti)* by the Lady from Karaikkal:

> No sooner was I born, no sooner did I
> learn to speak, than yearning overcame me
> and I came to your golden-red feet,
> oh great god of all gods
> with your luminous black neck.
> How soon will sorrow
> cease?

You can see the words of this verse inscribed around the narrow opening of the small shrine to the Lord of the *Puṉṉai* Grove, *Puṉṉai-vaṉa-nātar,* in the famous Mylapore temple in Chennai. If you stand nearby on any day, you'll see pilgrims, mainly women, circumambulating this sub-shrine situated at an oblique angle to the main sanctum of the Lord of the Peacock and his wife, Kaṟpaka Valli, Vine of the

Wish-giving Tree. It has always seemed to me that the moving words of Kāraikkālammaiyār were one reason for the special attention the Lord of the Puṉṉai Grove receives.

There's no way to miss the personal voice. The poem is autobiographical, thus singular, irreducible, a matter of memory—indeed, of the speaker's first memory, when yearning, *kātal,* was already working its magic inside her. Hardly more than a baby, she already took refuge at Śiva's feet. Not that this move put the longing to rest. Far from it. Unsatisfied longing is the very definition of coming to the god, giving oneself to him, living with him inside oneself. We already hear the characteristic note of Tamil metaphysical poetry: an ineluctable sorrow permeates awareness. The poet cannot bear it, even though it is the dependable mark of her *kātal.* She is impatient. She has a question for Śiva. When, exactly, will the ache subside? "When"—*ĕññāṉṟu*—comes at the critical opening of the final line; the restlessness, the agony, overwhelm the verse, drowning out the measured statement with which it began. It's almost a scream: "Tell me when! How many minutes from now?" She can't wait any longer. Love is like that, as everyone knows.

She is perfectly aware who this god is, who they say he is, what stories they tell about him, but actually none of this matters much:

> They say he's the one in the sky.
> They say he's king of the gods.
> They say he's this place.
> The wise one. The one whose neck
> grew dark with poison.[19]
> But I say: he's the one
> in my heart. (6)

What happens in the heart, in the inner, *akam* domain, is what counts—far more than anything a person might happen to know or think. *Karuttu,* "thought," is not, in itself, highly valued, though the poetess says she can tell us how to fix it or upgrade it quickly (73). She has, in fact, used her own thinking apparatus to good effect:

> I thought one thought.
> I decided one thing.
> There is one thing I've locked

in my heart.
Only one. The lord with Gaṅgā
and the bright moon in his hair
and flames flashing
in his hand: I just want
to be his. (11)

She's in love. She's unsatisfied. She's counting the seconds. She knows her heart. No one can tell her what to do. No external source, no sacred text, no ritual, no pious platitudes, can have any effect. She is breathing this god in, minute by minute, and she sings.

Let's juxtapose this passionate, hallucinatory vision of Śiva with a statement by Kārikālammaiyār's Vaishṇava counterpart, Āṇṭāḷ:

Dark clouds ready for the season of rains
chant the name of the lord of Venkatam
  who is valiant in battle.
Tell him, like the lovely leaves that fall in the season of rains
I waste away through the long endless years
waiting for the day when he finally sends word.

This is *Nācciyār Tirumŏḻi* 8.8, beautifully translated by Archana Venkatesan.[20] The speaker—Āṇṭāḷ herself, or an assumed persona; it hardly matters—is no less impatient than the Lady of Karaikkal. "Long endless years" have passed, possibly in the course of a single night, each moment as long as an age; meanwhile, the clouds are singing God's name. The speaker thinks that her lover will "finally" send word, but we may be skeptical about this happy dream. In fact, she knows it may well not happen, and she's more than a little angry:

I melt. I fray. But he doesn't care
if I live or die.
If that stealthy thief, that duplicitous Govardhana
should even glance at me
I shall pluck these useless breasts of mine
from their roots
I will fling them at his chest
and stop the fire scorching me.[21]

She won't be the first Tamil woman we've met who tears off a breast and throws it at someone or something. Frustrated, in despair, she's all fire. She's melting, fraying. Take this as emblematic of the Tamil god-intoxicated singer. She or he is coming apart. The harmonious synergy of *uyir* and bones that we learned about in the *Tirukkuṟaḷ* has given way to a state of terminal self-fragmentation. Loving hurts.

Fragmentation of this order is often glossed by the poets as a hardening, an encrustation that substitutes a metallic, lifeless exterior for the gentle, flowing innerness in which knowledge, especially self-knowledge, might be possible. Thus the Śaiva poet Māṇikkavācakar tells us in another autobiographical verse:

You came into me
as I was lying alone
inside my deeds,
and you stayed there
as if to say, "*I* am
the end of deeds."
That's how you introduced
yourself and took me
to be yours. But I,
a puppet made of iron,
don't sing to you,
don't dance,
don't shout or wail.
Even my breath fails
to fall away.
Oh you who came first,
is that fair?
You who are both first
and last: I'm still becoming
me, and I don't know
how this will end.[22]

This poet is famous, and beloved, for his self-deprecating candor and for the intensity of feeling he conveys throughout the *Tiruvācakam*.[23] This particular verse shows us what might be seen as the standard sequence: the god enters his poet and remains hidden within him or her, but after the initial shock and discovery, the poet loses contact; he or she is a "puppet of iron," devoid of true feeling, locked into himself or herself, unable to find the living part inside. Even his breath, *āvi*—the liquid core self—lacks the grace to faint, to lapse into unconsciousness or weakness *(āvi coreṉ)*. It is this everyday existential failure that makes the poet describe himself in the very next verse as a demon or ghoul, *pey*, like the Lady from Karaikkal. At the same time, this state of extreme fracture and frustration is the very definition of what it is to be human—that is, of the unfinished business of becoming oneself, which is thus also the ground for some hoped-for future wholeness. This business of self-becoming as loosening an internal harshness, or as a gradual meltdown, takes place wherever one goes, but it finds the local stone temple a particularly conducive arena for experiment.

Those who want to read more of the Tamil *bhakti* poets can now easily find annotated translations. Anyone who visits a Tamil temple is likely to hear a pilgrim gently singing these very poems as he or she comes within sight of the image of a god or goddess. When you see the deity, you might feel the familiar, unappeasable longing, tearing at your very breath, disrupting "normal" metabolic processes, driving you to the limit of sensation and thought; and at the same time, you might feel blocked, disconnected, lost in the stony surface of self. These two modes tend to coincide. This may be the moment to tell you that this enormous corpus of unruly, passionate poetry—duly codified, canonized, and integrated into temple rituals, as we shall see—seems to have played, historically, a homeostatic role in medieval Tamil Nadu. Contrary to what one sometimes still reads in secondary works about the Tamil *bhakti* corpus, there is almost nothing antinomian about it. It's true that it served in both Śaiva and Vaishṇava tracks to cement the solidarity of a new community of devotees, overriding to some degree the normative hierarchies that were in place. But these poems are full of praise for the Veda, for Brahmins, for Sanskrit erudition and orthodox rituals (they are also, very frequently in the Śaiva case and sometimes also in the Vaishṇava *prabandham* canon, full of scorn for Buddhists and Jains, who are clearly outside the bounds).[24] Throughout the formative centuries in which Tamil devotionalism invented itself, attracted royal patronage, and built its major institutional sites, it clearly provided a conceptual and metaphysical basis for the mainstream social order. Real antinomianism, with a devotional tinge, comes into Tamil much later, as we will see in Chapter 7.

For our purposes, it is important to note that these powerful new currents clothed themselves in Tamil and developed an ideology—perhaps too heavy a word—about the role of their mother tongue in the emerging cultural dispensation. Āṇṭāḷ, whom we have just quoted, says in the final verse of her *Tiruppāvai* that she (she calls herself Kotai / Godā) has spoken thirty verses of a garland in Sangam Tamil *(caṅkat tamiḻ mālai muppatum)*. A hint of classicism? We're not sure when Āṇṭāḷ lived—possibly the ninth century—but it is clear that the Sangam story was current in the age of the canonical singers of Tamil devotion. It is mentioned in the *Tevāram* poems, notably in a particularly elaborate reference in a verse by Appar (6.76.3):

> He [Śiva] became a gifted poet, mounted the Sangam [plank],
> and bestowed the purse of gold on Tarumi.

The story of Śiva as a Sangam poet—the author of *Kuṟuntŏkai* 2 who quarreled with the president of the academy, Nakkīrar, for the sake of a poor Brahmin, Tarumi[25]—was thus known to Appar or to whoever sang this song in his name.

Apart from isolated citations like these, we find throughout the early *bhakti* corpus praise for Tamil as the medium for connecting to god. Especially important in this respect are the final, signatory verses of the decades *(patikams)*, known as the *Tirukkaṭaikkāppu* or "closing of the doors," which regularly mention the critical role of Tamil. For example:

> These ten verses in cool Tamil
> in metrical song
> by Ñāṉacampantan of Kāḻi[26]
> with its fragrant groves—
> it is certain that all dark chains
> will fall away from those
> who can sing them.[27]

The poet is very aware, and proud of the fact, that he is singing in "cool Tamil." He also tells us that his poems are in metrical form *(cantam)*—and, indeed, the huge *Tevāram* corpus is, among other things, an arena for complex metrical experiments. There is a slight dissonance between this fact—the clearly crafted, poetically rich form of the Tamil *bhakti* poems—and the culturally privileged image of the devotional poet as singing spontaneously, without erudition or premeditation, from the depths of his or her heart.[28] The language of the *bhakti* poems is markedly different from that of the Sangam works; in general, it is far more accessible than the latter, a medium intended to be intelligible to any audience, in the mother tongue. Again and again we hear praise for Tamil: Cuntaramūrtti tells us that he "came, saw, and sang these ten verses in fine Tamil set to resounding sweet music" (67.11); that "we can escape [death and rebirth] by worshiping the lord of Tiruppurampayam in fine Tamil meter" (35.10); that he utters "rich Tamil verses" (30.11), or a "Tamil garland, cooling to the heart" (29.10); that he has "defined the way to serve" because he can sing good Tamil (18.10); that he sings verses in Tamil "that does not lie" (13.11). What is more, he is sure that the god, Śiva, is himself "the meaning *(pŏruḷ)* you grant to poets" (4.5). Śiva is a poet and, at the same time, the substance of any good poem.

There are easily hundreds of such references to Tamil in the *bhakti* canon. Is there an implied opposition here to another kind of language—Sanskrit, for example? Perhaps there is. The new community of devotees is united by the mother tongue and, I think, by the particular nuances of intimacy that only a living mother tongue can offer. But it seems likely that these poets were also reacting against the somewhat forbidding language of Tamil *kāvya,* for example in the great Jaina work by Tiruttakkatevar, the *Cīvaka cintāmaṇi,* "Jīvaka the Wishing-Stone," with its heterodox axiology.[29] Most of the compositions we find in the *Tevāram* and the Vaishṇava canon, *Divya-prabandham* or "Splendid Collection," ostensibly aim at being understood, despite what is often a daunting conceptual complexity and subtlety in the content of the verses.

The Vaishṇava works, incidentally, exported the Tamil language to regions far beyond the Tamil land, in particular to Andhra, where large parts of the *prabandham* came into daily use in temple worship and acquired a status, both for their message and as musical, mantric, or phono-aesthetic exemplars, not unlike that of, say, the Arabic Qur'an in the wider, non-Arabic-speaking Islamic world. In this respect, Tamil Vaishṇava devotion established one form of cosmopolitan Tamil. To this day, the most beautiful printed editions of the *prabandham* are in Tamil recorded in Telugu script, with Telugu commentary. Telugu poets sometimes refer to these poems by the general term *pallāṇḍu*, after the Tamil title of Pĕriyāḻvār's famous *Tiruppaḷḷāṇṭu* (epitomizing what was in effect a musical genre).[30] Similarly, Āṇṭāḷ's *Tiruppāvai*, together with its Śaiva counterpart, the *Tiruvĕmpāvai* of Māṇikkavācakar, and parts of the *Tevāram*, made its way to the temples of Thailand, a still more exotic linguistic milieu than Andhra or other parts of south India.[31] Thus, as often happens, what began as a set of texts deliberately addressing and giving voice to native speakers became, once fixed as a canon, a major, though not the only, vehicle for the spread of the language far beyond the geographical range of those speakers. (In fact, the Tamil Śrīvaishṇava tradition itself had a strong tradition that Tamil would spread throughout the world.)[32] Integral to this process was what might be called the talismanic role of Tamil within new ritual contexts. As we shall see, that role has its roots in the Tamil *bhakti* corpus itself and is closely linked to the process of writing down these texts.

## Inscribing (1): The Visible Word

I have spoken of canonization with reference to the Sangam poems and the exegetical materials attached to them, probably through a long process of accretion. We have good reason to believe that these poems (including their necessary grammars) became canonical in at least one critical sense—namely, that they eventually formed the basis for a Tamil education and served as a reference point for an entire evolving world of Tamil erudition, over many centuries, probably from late Pallava-Pandya times and into the Chola and post-Chola periods. We have also seen how the Tamil tradition itself thematized this fact of canonization and offered narrative meditations on the way the process unfolded. The Sangam corpus taken as a whole also became bound up with notions of cultural continuity and self-definition for the community of Tamil speakers, as we can see both in the rich post-Chola commentaries on these texts[33] and in occasional external sources such as the fifteenth- or sixteenth-century Kerala grammar, *Līlā-tilakam,* which cites the *Eight Anthologies* and the *Ten Long Poems* as specific to the non-Malayalam-speaking parts of the far south.[34] We will return to these materials.

In one respect, however, the Sangam texts elude a strong notion of canon (or, better, of what should probably be called "foundational" works): they do not appear to conform, in later usage, to a "principle of charity," that is, to ongoing, sometimes quite desperate attempts to read them as necessarily true even under the radically changed conditions of subsequent generations. As Halbertal has formulated this principle with reference to a very different textual corpus: "The degree of canonicity of a text corresponds to the amount of charity it receives in its interpretation. The more canonical a text, the more generous its treatment."[35] Although the Sangam poetic grammar was, indeed, extended and defended over centuries as a template for literary production, the Sangam poems themselves seem not to have inspired assertions that they contain an immutable truth.

The case of the Tamil *bhakti* canon is, however, rather different. Here, too, we have thematized accounts of how these poems were standardized, organized, and recorded. The process began, clearly, in late Pallava-Pandya times and accelerated in the early Chola (ninth and tenth) centuries. The two streams, Śaiva and Vaishṇava, adopted different models to describe the initial stages of producing a canon. As we might by now expect, both models insist on a break in the textual tradition; the corpus has to be lost, forgotten, and then recovered, in part or in full, if it is to count as authoritative, just as we saw in the case of the ancient Tamil grammars. We need to examine these accounts carefully if we wish to understand how Tamil encoded the business of canonization and the process of what we might call "scriptualization" that formed a necessary element in it.[36] I will argue that a deep, culture-specific model of Tamil textuality underlies the ex post facto narratives we have about this process and, what is more important, the living, ritualized performance contexts that emerged in its course.

Both accounts reveal a formative—though in a sense somewhat superficial—tension between a privileged notion of "pure" oral composition and the sometimes reluctant recognition that the canonical texts had to be recorded graphically, in several possible modes. These understandings of canonization and transmission remained in force for well over a millennium. To some extent they survived even into the colonial period and beyond. I want to trace the evolution of such primary reflexive images of textuality in Tamil; to do so we will have to exceed the boundaries of the early "rhapsodic" period of Tamil *bhakti,* when patterns of transmission and collection were first established, and examine the later stages in this process. By Chola times, vivid depictions of the formation of the two canons had clearly crystallized around a more ancient historical core.

The Śrīvaishṇava model is the more radical one. Here we find Nammāḻvār's *Tiruvāymŏḻi* ("True Speech" = Veda) as the central text, augmented by the same poet's *Tiruviruttam,* which we have quoted, and two other, shorter texts, the *Tiruvāciriyam* (seven verses) and the *Pĕriya tiruvantāti.* Together these four works are seen by the tradition as commensurate with—in fact, as superseding on several counts—the four Sanskrit Vedas.[37] Nammaḻvar has thus supplied us with a Tamil Veda, classed as a visionary literary composition, *prabandha,* anchored in a trans-empirical source that eventually came to be seen as defining the boundaries of true Tamil speech.[38]

Nammāḻvār composed these poems, so we are told, in a state of meditative joyfulness. Born in the village of Kurukur, Alvartirunagari in today's Tamil Nadu, already as a newborn baby he crawled around Vishṇu's temple and came to rest under a tamarind tree outside it. He never nursed at his mother's breast, never opened his eyes, and never uttered a single syllable; he remained absorbed in contemplation of the god. After sixteen years he composed the thousand verses of the *Tiruvāymŏḻi* and its accompanying texts; or rather, these perfect poems poured out of him, apparently inaudibly, but definitely spontaneously, without premeditation or poetic polishing. A Brahmin from Kolur in the Pandya land, named Maturakavi or the "Sweet Poet," was touring the shrines of Vishṇu throughout India when, in the far north, he saw a great light shining from the direction of the south. He followed this light all the way back to Kurukur, where he found Nammāḻvār sitting in silence under the tree. Maturakavi asked a riddle:

> *If that which is small is born in the belly of that which is dead,*
> *what will it eat? Where will it rest?*

Now the poet-Yogi answered, still in the enigmatic mode:

> *It will eat that, and there it will rest.*[39]

One can go far with this riddle, which models the composition of the complete person—the tiny divine element mysteriously hidden in lifeless matter. The answer, too, with its indexical pronouns and unspecified adverb, is well worth contemplating. Apparently, Maturakavi understood it. In any case, Nammāḻvār then proceeded to recite the entire fourfold set of his compositions so that Maturakavi could learn them by heart. We are nowhere told that Maturakavi wrote anything down. He did, however, supposedly set the poems to music, which is to say that he made their inherent, latent musicality audible, and he also set up an image of Nammāḻvār, made of wood, metal, and stone, right there, under the tree—in effect a concrete and visible form of the Tamil language itself that now held within it the meaning of the Veda.[40]

Here is the nascent canon in the process of formation: oral composition followed by recitation, memorization, musical textualization, and tangible embodiment in an image of the language itself that has generated these texts. Maturakavi is said to have taken the next step as well. He brings the image to the major temple of Srirangam, where already a festival—the *Adhyayanotsava* or Festival of Recitation—has been put in place for the annual performance of the entire *Tiruvāymŏḻi* together with the Vedas.[41] Now, during the ten days of the festival, the Sanskrit Veda is recited by day while Maturakavi *enacts* the Tamil Veda by night, singing the verses and at the same time articulating them through the language of hand and eye gestures, *abhinaya*.[42] From this point on, the canon exists, and not only in the minds of those who may have memorized it as a whole. It has been inscribed: not on palm leaf, not in stone, but in the far more durable and reliable medium of movement and gesture in space. *Abhinaya* is perhaps the most prestigious, also the most effective, medium of recording a south Indian text.

And for some years, all is well with the corpus. Then, inevitably, it is forgotten, and the festival with it. Some generations go by. A learned sage—not a poet!—named Nāthamuni happens to hear some verses of the lost works of Nammāḻvār from the lips of pilgrims on their way to Kurukur. The verses catch his attention; he wants to hear more. He goes to Kurukur and cannot find Nammāḻvār there (the image, we recall, has migrated to Srirangam). Under the direction of a devotee known as Parāṅkuśadāsa, he sings to a mental image of Maturakavi, the reciter / compiler of Nammāḻvār's works. Now Nammāḻvār and Maturakavi both become present and teach Nāthamuni the entire body of works. At this point Nāthamuni assumes an editorial role. He adds to Nammāḻvār's poems the compositions of the other eleven Āḻvārs, arranging them in the form we know today: the Tamil Śrīvaishṇava canon, *Nālāyira divya-prabandham,* outwardly, at least, is complete. But where, in what media or forms, does it really exist?

We can be sure that by the time of Nāthamuni—late ninth or early tenth century, according to the scholarly consensus—these poems were committed to writing. No less important to their survival, however, was the fact that, as the tradition tells us, Nāthamuni revived the *Adhyayanotsava* at Srirangam and taught the Araiyar ritual performers the mode of musical recitation of the entire corpus along with the *abhinaya,* just as Maturakavi had imagined it into being. This mode of performance became institutionalized in what is today known as *araiyar cevai,* "the Araiyars' service," which includes all three traditional elements of Tamil, *muttamiḻ:*[43] music, *icai,* in the form of divine singing, *devagāna;* drama, *nāṭakam,* in the language of gestures, *abhinaya-rūpa;* and natural discourse, *iyal,* that is, the integration of commentary into the text, *vyākhyāna-rūpa.*[44] The Araiyar singers of the Tamil Veda are masters of all three modes and the prime carriers of this rich series of texts from generation to generation.

None of this happened without the intervention of the political order: the Chola king is said to have been involved in Nāthamuni's revival of the performance and to have appointed a gifted woman singer to take part in it.[45] The setting is now the great stone temple, with its daily and intermittent ritual order; recitation of the Tamil Veda becomes an intrinsic part of that order. One can, no doubt, think of this result as the "integration into 'orthodox,' Brahmin, and Sanskritic Vaiṣṇavism"[46] of a corpus that was originally non-Brahmin, local, and entirely Tamil. I'd prefer to speak of scriptualization in a universal, cosmopolitan idiom that requires meticulous editing and recording of a now standardized canon in both graphic and dramatic (gestural, ritualized) forms.

It is important to stress that in the case of these Vaishṇava materials the corpus is believed to have survived in its entirety, thanks to its repeated revelation and recitation by Nammāḻvār (first to Maturakavi, then together with the latter to Nāthamuni after the amnesia-induced hiatus). It was lost and regained in toto—a highly unusual eventuality in south India. Still, one can see that even inscription of the sort we have been discussing comes together with a sense of precariousness or potential loss. The *Tiruvāymŏḻi* exists in its author's mind; it can be actualized by teaching, and later by repeated performance; but its atemporal prototype, like the image of Nammāḻvār first erected under the tamarind tree at Kurukur, like the Tamil language that it incorporates and defines, is independent of the vagaries inherent in any transmission. In some sense, the astonishing ritual performance during festival times of *araiyar cevai* is an attempt to reconstitute this nearly inaudible, though by nature musical, original. A breathtaking beauty attaches to this attempt—one can see snippets on YouTube[47]—in which the performer also appears to reassemble within himself the ardent personae of the first poet-singer and subsequent reciters and to reveal the open-ended love story of the poet (or poetess)[48] and the god. In doing so, he makes the words of the Āḻvār not merely audible but also visible. Here is scriptualization in its classic south Indian form. Only when one *sees* the charged and potent sound does it truly exist in this sensual, human world. Still, at the very core of the now public canon there remains an inaudible, primordial, ultimately noninscribable text.

*Araiyar cevai* follows a standard sequence in each of the three main Vishṇu temples where it is performed.[49] In Alvartirunagari, it takes the poet, Nammāḻvār, through a ten-day process that includes, along with the recitation of the whole of his *Tiruvāymŏḻi*, a divination using pearls, *muttukkuṟi*; a moment of severe crisis and quarreling between Vishṇu and the goddess, *praṇaya-kalakotsavam*, ultimately mediated by Nammāḻvār himself; and, at the final climax, the poet's *moksha*, "release," classed as melting into the god. Throughout, the performance of the canon generates delight, *anubhavam*. We have to keep this express goal in mind as a primary aesthetic drive: poetry is intimately and naturally tied to pleasure, here intensified many times over into a shared sensual joyfulness available to the god no less than to his singers and devotees. At Srivilliputtur, where the poetess Āṇṭāḷ lived, *araiyar cevai* ultimately leads to the complete union of this woman-and-goddess with Vishṇu. Note that in both sites the author of the poems is himself or herself present as a living image, who listens to the recitation and also takes part in it in ritually powerful ways. The author is inside his or her text, though his/her existence is not limited to this embedded state. One could also say that he or she bursts out from the text into the collective dimension of its ritual performance.

For a sustained and nuanced treatment of the *araiyar cevai*, the reader is referred to Archana Venkatesan's insightful work, in which we also find central analytical features specific to the textuality in operation here. Let me try to list, without further elaboration, what I see as the main features of this deep Tamil form of scripturalization, whose early stages belong to the late Pallava-Pandya period though the main parameters probably go back much farther in time.

1. The text is fixed: secondarily, in writing on palm leaf or stone, but first and foremost in the mind of the specialist who performs it in voice and bodily movement, *abhinaya*. It is not subject to improvisation in the sense of textual variation, but it *is* amenable to compression and expansion, nonlinear bunching or acceleration, and elaborate forms of emphasis and intensification. Linear, unbroken recitation/performance exists along with the selective reorganization of the performed text.[50]
2. Sound, the primary medium of recording, exists in several distinct but overlapping modes: as an utterance inaudible and whole; as audible only as presemanticized music; as audible in semanticized text, in multiple polyphonic or criss-crossing statements, and thus as both grammaticalized and transgrammatical utterance, and, with special emphasis, as visual syllables.

3. The performer is not the poet, not a second author (as in *purāṇic* recitation) creating the text in performance,[51] but he speaks for, and sometimes *as,* the author, who inhabits the deeper reaches of his or her text. The performer takes us, his listeners, through the stages the poet repeatedly undergoes in moving toward freedom; thus theosis, self-divinization—a to-and-fro rhythm internal to text and to its singer—is one available metaphysical end. The poet is present (in the form of his or her icon) during the performance. Given the above, it is not surprising that in the devotional mode the performer also, at times, sings in the voice of the god or gods: "In these moments, he is as much speaking *as* them as *for* them, acting as the mediator."[52] One could also say that the performer, like the god he addresses and whose voice he sometimes embodies, is creating or re-creating a living world, as if riding the *uyir* and its rhythmic breathing that will hold this world together from within.[53] The survivability of such a text in its fixed form depends upon its continuous re-creation of itself and its space-infused world. What is more, in the course of performing *araiyar cevai* the Araiyar himself becomes a "conduit" for the enjoyment, *anubhava,* that is the express goal of the ritual for all concerned, including the deity; the ritual itself thus becomes an *anubhava-grantha,* an "enjoyment text" or a visible poem, *drishṭi-kāvya.*[54] The boundaries of text, performer, and performance easily overlap.
4. Commentary is integral to the text. (In *araiyar cevai* the commentary is what is most natural, *iyal,* to textual discourse.) Here we would do well to forget, as much as possible, the Mediterranean models of textual accretion and expansion, with the "original" work continually subject to historically later explications. Such a model may work, at times, in some southern Indian contexts, but we should at least consider alternative textualities in which what is classed as commentary actually precedes the condensed fixity of the text-for-performance or is at least coeval with its emergence. In *araiyar cevai,* so-called Maṇipravāḷam (mixed Tamil and Sanskrit) commentaries[55] on the *Tiruvāymŏḻi* are a third level of performance, after the initial musical recitation and its partial enactment in *abhinaya;* but somewhat parallel performance genres, such as the Sanskrit

drama of Kerala, *Kūḍiyāṭṭam,* assume, I think, the preexistence of expansion and explication relative to the text waiting, as it were, to be expanded and explicated.

5. Dramatic narrativization—a full-body enactment rich in movement—goes hand in hand with musical-metrical recitation. Let me repeat: here is where we find the text primarily fixed, enacted in visible space. Canonization is not complete before the *abhinaya,* with its narrative rituals, is in place. Sounds, syllables, words—all are inscribed not so much in ink-borne graphemes as in the performer's body and in visible space. The canon is at home in this space. Recall that perhaps our best guess about the performance mode of Sangam poetry fits this model precisely.[56] Not until roughly the fourteenth century do we find fixed Tamil literary texts that are entirely discursive, based on conventional forms of writing, and intended for individual reading, either aloud or in silence. Before that time, the deep textual model we are exploring applies to most literary genres.
6. Poetry is for pleasure and delight, and the telos of grammar, broadly conceived, is to generate poetry as a dependable source of pleasure. One needs a body to feel a poem. Performance literally incorporates the sounds and words.[57] Such pleasure, moreover, may be activated by exceeding the terms of any normative grammar—by emptying out the given forms and then filling them up again, in play (we have seen that a similar movement may apply to grammar itself). An experimental quality is not foreign to this process: poetry is a laboratory not only for metrical and musical experimentation, but also, indeed primarily, for existential experiment. Filling and emptying may be the fundamental process of making and remaking a text worth preserving.
7. More generally: poetry is less expressive, in the modern romantic sense, than effectual. It works on whatever outer reality it may encounter, but also directly on various levels of in-ness: self-awareness (in the performer, in the listener or spectator, in the deity), intuitive knowing *(uṇarvu),* temporal experience, complex emotions, and, most fundamental of all, the continuous rhythm of the *uyir* moving out and in, usually saturated with some form of longing. The template

of in-ness that we saw in Sangam love poetry has clearly shaped the radical, organic in-ness of the *uyir* seeking, desperately, for "its" god. (It is worth noting that at the *Adhyayanotsava,* Vedic recitation is a daylight—one might say a *puṟam*—event, while recitation of the Tamil *prabandham* takes place largely in a classic *akam* nightscape.) Is the *uyir* then conscious? Yes, increasingly so, and always insofar as it is aware of its longing. Poetry addresses, and probably redresses, the ache of the *uyir* in movement. Poetry effects a change in internal state; it is set up to induce such change, to enhance aliveness (or, as we saw, some version of freedom). It is never merely descriptive. To the extent that poetry follows the *akam* logic, it also puts in question the inner-outer division per se, privileging in-ness as the deeper source of what is experienced as out-ness, as we have seen.

8. Enactment, one of the three primary aspects of textualized performance, is normally reenactment. Here the ritual sequence rings remarkable changes on all who are present: poet, performer, listener, god.[58] Not by chance, divination is a natural part of this progression. The future may well become present long before its predictable place in sequence. Thus poetry is theurgy, or condensed cosmology, a nonlinear evolution in time and space.
9. Deep textuality of this kind tends toward what we might call, following Sheldon Pollock, a cosmopolitan modality—that is, a universalizing statement of cultural identity. In this respect, Tamil offers a cosmopolitan alternative to "political Sanskrit." We can understand why Nammāḻvār's text became a boundary marker for Tamil language and for the cultures that live and grow in Tamil. The Nammāḻvār text shows us the deep textual model at its fullest. It will take another half a millennium for Tamil to develop a strong contrastive model in which the poet speaks autonomously, discursively, assuming responsibility for his particular, idiosyncratic vision—in short, as an author in a new sense. We will explore this shift in Chapter 6.
10. Finally, for all the powerful musicality and effectual, mantic process at work in a Tamil poem such as Nammāḻvār's, the textual reembodiment of such a poem always includes silent spaces: there are statements that neither the god nor the poet can utter. The performer

> sometimes physically occupies a middle zone where such unspoken thoughts and feelings can arise; he may move back and forth between the male and female parts of the divinity, negotiating movement that will reunite them, just as he continually negotiates the distance between the author of the poem and his or her audience and topic.[59] These thick lacunae—often the expressive core of the text—deserve attention.

All of this is, in varying degrees, distinctive for Tamil as a language and for Tamil poetry as a literary tradition. Neighboring south Indian cultures have their own textual models, in some but not all ways very close to the Tamil one. The spectrum of classical Sanskrit textualities is at least one step removed. It is of some importance that what I am calling the deepest textuality comes to its fullest expression in Tamil Śrīvaishṇavism and in the surpassingly creative voice of its greatest poet toward the end of the first millennium. Here we find a practical guide, or an implicit protocol, for reading a Tamil poem.

## Inscribing (2): Instrument, Talisman, Trigger

The Tamil Śaivas followed a more familiar course. Already within the *Tevāram* corpus itself we find significant compilations of traditional knowledge relevant to these texts—notably *patikam* 39 of Cuntaramūrtti, the *Tiruttŏṇṭattŏkai,* listing the whole series of sixty-three exemplary devotees of Śiva; and also, again in Cuntaramūrtti's collection, three decades (12, 31, and 47) that enumerate famous shrines of Śiva in the Tamil orbit.[60] The process of formalization of relevant knowledge and incipient scriptualization begins in the later strata of the canon-to-be itself. But the tradition states explicitly that knowledge of the *Tevāram* was lost, except for a stray verse that by chance came to the attention of a Chola king, Rājarāja.[61] He wanted to hear more and found his way to a young Brahmin boy, Nampi Āṇṭār Nampi, an Ādiśaiva priest at the temple of Tirunaraiyur, who had succeeded by dint of sheer devotion in making the image of the god Gaṇapati there physically devour the offerings of bananas made to him. The boy asked the god if he knew where the *Tevāram* poems could be found. Gaṇapati, very amenable to communication with this young devotee, informed him and the king that the texts were kept in a room, sealed shut with the hands of the three *Tevāram* poets themselves, in the temple of the dancing Śiva at Cidambaram.

The king rushed to Cidambaram. But the temple priests, the Dīkshitars, informed him that the door to the locked chamber could be opened only if all three of the original poets came there in person. Rājarāja had a festival performed; the icons of the three poets were carried in procession around the shrine. Such icons are never representational; they *are* the presence they embody. So when the poets' images were brought together before the sealed door, it opened of its own accord. Inside were thousands of palm leaves inscribed with the *Tevāram* poems. They were cleaned with oil, but it quickly became evident that nearly all of them had been ruined beyond recovery.

Fortunately, a legible remnant did survive: 384 decades of the original 16,000 composed by Tiruñāṉacampantar; 310 decades of Appar's 49,000; and 100 out of 38,000 by Cuntarar. The king had these poems edited and collected in seven volumes, the first seven *tirumuṟai* of the Tamil Śaiva canon; and he also found a female descendant of the musician, Tirunīlakaṇṭa Yāḻppāṇar, who had first set these poems to music. With the help of this woman, who knew something of the ancient mode of singing, the system of musical *paṇs*—the old Tamil word for what is now called *rāga*—was restored, for a while. We know virtually nothing of this system today.[62]

Such is the story, a classic example of the vulnerability inherent in written transmission. The Śaivas have no figure to set beside the Vaishṇava Maturakavi, who is said to have received and preserved Nammāḻvār's corpus in its entirety.[63] Palm-leaf manuscripts are all too fragile: insects (the notorious white ants) eat holes in them, and the black ink rubbed into the scratch marks made on the dried leaves with a metal stylus tends to dry up and disappear, as anyone who works with such manuscripts knows all too well. Even if we put aside the inflated numbers in the story just cited and take account of the metaphysical necessity that the precious text be lost and only partially regained, we need to recognize the realistic element in this story of long-term preservation. In the very long history of Tamil literature, many texts have truly been lost forever.[64] No one should ever rely on a merely written text.

Yet inscribing the text on palm leaf has a value of its own, and the written record sometimes serves purposes that transcend the immediate issue of making a copy. Scriptualization in Tamil, from the middle of the first millennium onward, naturally includes graphic inscription on palm leaf, copper plate, or stone. One should keep in mind that such graphic records remained dependent on oral performance, as in the case of the *araiyar cevai* mentioned above. For the Tamil Śaivas, this task was entrusted to a caste of *Tevāram* reciters, *otuvār,* already mentioned in the Chola inscriptions and still highly active today. And while the *otuvār* do not enact the *Tevāram* texts with *abhinaya* gestures, they do traditionally perform them in what is now called *viruttam* style: they are free to extract phrases from the text, detaching them from the metrical line, repeating them many times, thereby illuminating syntax and emphasis. In short, they *play* the text, taking it apart and putting it back together in what is in effect a musical commentary on its meanings.[65] *Viruttam* recitation in this mode became standard for most oral performances of Tamil poetry, as one can hear from the few recordings we have from the early twentieth century. Memorization and oral recitation are necessary conditions for such performance.

Yet there are pragmatic results that only the silent written text can achieve. Many stories about the Tamil *bhakti* poets focus on this point. Tiruñāṉacampantar challenged his Jain rivals in Maturai to a contest in the presence of the hunchbacked king Kūṉ Pāṇṭiyaṉ: the Jains would inscribe a palm leaf with a written text, and Campantar would do the same; they would then cast these leaves into the Vaikai River; if one of them floated upstream, against the current, that would be the sign of victory. The stakes were high: if Campantar won, the king would have the Jains impaled. The Jains wrote two words on their leaf: *atti nātti* (Sanskrit *asti nâsti*), "exists/does not exist"—a hint of their doctrine that "it is possible to predicate the truth of a proposition and its negation at one and the same time" *(syādastināsti).*[66] The Śaiva boy saint sang a complex, passionate poem in twelve verses, not specific to any given shrine (the *Tirupācuram* beginning *vāḻka antaṇar,* 3.54 in our editions), and had it recorded *(varaintu)* on what must have been a rather capacious palm leaf. The Jain leaf was rapidly carried downstream to the sea; Campantar's leaf floated upstream. The king was healed of his hunchback and stood erect (this in response to a phrase in the first verse of poem: "May the king rise high," (*ventaṉum oṅkuka*); poetry works wonders. The defeated Jains were executed.[67] Truth, in this case, is not open to doubt or to logical paradox; and the validity of the Śaiva truth is visibly demonstrated, first and primarily, by its written embodiment and, second, by the immediate effect of the words uttered orally by the poet. Graphic form has its own not inconsiderable powers.

Similarly, a single verse of Nammāḻvār's *Tiruvāymŏḻi,* inscribed on palm leaf, is placed (like Tiruvaḷḷuvar's *Tirukkuṟaḷ*)[68] on the famous Sangam plank, which accepts it after submerging all its usual inhabitants, the great Sangam poets, in the water of the Golden Lotus Tank.[69] When these learned poets arrive, sputtering, on the shore and read the written verse, they understand that this poem "containing the god's feet" left no room for them, with all their learning—and, moreover, that their learning was not worth one one-hundredth of the divine wisdom that Nammāḻvār possessed, intuitively, without ever having been taught Veda or *śāstra,* at birth. Again, it is the written text that can achieve singular results. This idea is extraordinarily long-lived in south India. The magical potency of a pregnant set of letters—assumed to correspond precisely to an individual's *hasta-rekha,* the subtle lines on the human thumb—underlies the still prevalent practice of *Nāḍijyoshyam* or divination from palm leaves, a speciality of the Vaittisvarankoyil temple in the eastern Kaveri delta.

Classical Tamil is replete with instances where a (usually concise) text written on palm leaf plays a critical and entirely positive role. Like in medieval Japan and in Java, and also in Sanskrit dramas, Tamil lovers are prone to leaving written messages, personal, urgent, sometimes anguished, for each other to find. Kāntaruvatattai, forlorn wife of Cīvakaṉ, the restless hero of the romantic Jain *kāvya Cīvakacintāmaṇi,* sends a relatively long message to her husband—seven verses inscribed on a single palm leaf—in a tone at once plaintive and ironic. She describes the suffering of her lonely co-wife, Kuṇamālai, in the following lovely poem:

> "Don't be sad," says her pet parrot. "He'll be back
> tomorrow." "Good," she says, "but this 'tomorrow'
> you're talking about—is it soon or far away?"
> The parrot laughs.[70]

What lover could bear this sort of blackmail? Elsewhere in the same work, Cīvakaṉ's friend receives from a beautiful young spy a secret warning to spirit Cīvakaṉ away to safety; the text is inscribed on a palm leaf rolled up and hidden in a slender container inside the petals of a water lily.[71] The whole process of such unspoken communication can also be turned into an elaborate metaphor: the dancing girl Aṉaṅkamālai performs on a stage that is actually "the minds of men"; she writes *with her eyes alone* a palm-leaf message for her lover, who is in the audience, telling him how she is withering away in longing, and she leaves this message in the care of her girlfriend, that is, her knowing smile.[72] We are not so remote in this case from the mode of communicating and recording in air or open space that we have discussed; but it is writing nonetheless, with the eyes serving as the *olai* leaf (and also, perhaps, as the stylus), as in the *abhinaya* of a virtuoso actor or reciter.

Thus, in marked contrast with the prevalent early north Indian understanding of writing as a rather low-grade, even polluting business,[73] very remote from the process of actually composing a text, in the Tamil tradition the scribe is often a prestigious, even divine figure. We have already seen one major example of this notion, from our period, in the commentary to the *Grammar of Stolen Love*, where Śiva himself records the lost *sūtras* on copper plates that are hidden in the Maturai temple.[74] The same image recurs in later, retrospective visions of the Śaiva *bhakti* poet Māṇikkavācakar (perhaps ninth century), as we learn from his lyrical "biography," the *Tiruvātavūraṭikaḷ purāṇam* of Kaṭavuḷ māmuṉivar (ca. fifteenth century).

Here we are told that the aged poet was living simply in Cidambaram—"no searching, no confusion, no special clarity, no misery, no exultation." One day Lord Śiva himself came, dressed as a Brahmin, with an empty palm-leaf book in his hands, and stood before him. The god told his poet that he wanted to record the Tamil poems of the

*Tiruvācakam,* and the latter began to sing them, melting inside. "As he sang, the Dancing God took a palm leaf in his hand and wrote it all down, very precisely. When it was finished, God, overflowing with feeling, said: 'Now you must compose a *kovai* anthology to Śiva, who has the woman within him, to free the world of sorrow.' "

So he did, with Śiva seated there, recording the four hundred verses as they came from the poet's mouth. These are the coded love poems we know today as *Tirukkovaiyār,* in the eighth book of the Tamil Śaiva canon. When the recitation ended, Śiva disappeared together with the palm leaves that he had inscribed with a stylus, afterwards smearing dark ink over the letters to make them stand out clearly *(maikkāppu).* But since he wanted to reveal the poet's vision to the world, this god—as in that other time—hid the book on the threshold[75] of the Inner Space, the *ciṟṟampalam,* in the temple, where the Brahmin priest found it and brought it to the people of the town. There was a first public reading, *araṅkeṟṟam,* concluding with the colophon that stated that Śiva, Lord of the Inner Space, had written down this manuscript at the dictation of the noble Vātavūraṉ (=Māṇikkavācakar). "The people listened with their hairs standing on end. "[76]

So we have a book, *puttakam,* inscribed on dried palm leaves bound together with strings that pass through holes pierced on either end of the leaves; and there is even a colophon telling the listener the name of the scribe—God himself—as well as that of the inspired author, who dictated both of these long works orally. That is how a Tamil book should be composed, at least in this period.[77] In this case, the scribe is also the true subject of the book, although the poet doesn't know this.

A certain tension resides in this model of literary production: the tradition, rightly, will not relinquish the primacy of the oral word, but it also recognizes, indeed strongly affirms, the necessity of recording that word in graphic form, thus creating an object that is itself the focus of worship, celebration, and—just as in the case of the *Grammar of Stolen Love*—somewhat ambiguous explication. For the *Tirukkovaiyār,* at least, is not truly amenable to linear paraphrase; each of its four hundred verses offers us the dizzying back-and-forth movement that we saw in Nammāḻvār's *Tiruviruttam,* at the start of this chapter. The good citizens of Cidambaram in the end seek out the poet and ask him to help them understand his surpassing text; and Māṇikkavācakar leads them to the temple, points to the image of the god, and says: "The meaning of this string of Tamil poems—is He." The poet then enters the sanctum and disappears into the god. That is what "meaning" means.

We are poised at the very moment of canonization and concomitant scriptualization, and the god has been co-opted into the business of fixing the text that sings to him about himself. Apparently, even a deity can't be sure that he'll remember the whole text; a fortiori, human transmission will henceforth rely on inscription of one kind or another. To be more precise: transmission is, at this point, a matter of inscription and oral—musical—performance. The palm leaves themselves are no more than a silent witness to the living text, which requires a human voice. The Śaiva reciters, unlike their Vaishṇava Araiyar counterparts, are not in themselves playing out a transformative movement of theosis. They do, nonetheless, take the text apart and recompose it, thereby integrating a half-articulated commentary into its recitation. Performance in this mode makes the human mind into a medium of inscription. It is hard to say which of the copies—the graphic scripting on palm leaves (or later printed book) or the memorized text—is a backup for the other.

I want to conclude this section with a much later story that takes up the theme of graphic textualization in Tamil and spells out the pragmatic, or talismanic, force of the written word. Here we observe the decisive moment of conversion in the life of an antinomian, nonconformist Siddha poet known as Paṭṭiṉattār, a paradigm of extreme (and sudden) renunciation and a fierce opponent of all forms of normative social and family life. As such, he belongs in a wider historical movement, perhaps beginning in the early fifteenth century, which we will briefly discuss in Chapter 7. For present purposes, we are concerned mainly with the role of a written text as metaphysical trigger in his mythical story.

Paṭṭiṉattār was a wealthy merchant—actually, an incarnation of the banker-god Kubera—born in Kaverippattinam and originally named Śvetâraṇyar or Tiruvĕṇkāṭar (after the god of the great temple of Tiruvenkatu). Śiva himself took the form of a baby born to a poor but profoundly devoted couple who, directed by the god in a dream, gave the child for adoption to the wealthy merchant; the latter compensated them with the child's weight in gold. The boy, named Marutavāṇar, the name of the god at the major shrine of Tiruvitaimarutur in the central Kaveri delta, grew up in this merchant's home and, when he came of age, set off by boat on a trading expedition together with several comrades. Śvetâraṇyar, the father, waited impatiently and anxiously for the return of his beloved son. But when the boy's boat put into port, the father discovered that his son had brought back nothing but paddy husks *(taviṭu).* Angry, he took the young man home and locked him in a room; then he went out to cast the paddy husks to the wind. As he did so, he saw them turn into gold and precious gems.

Śvetâraṇyar hurried home only to discover that his son was gone, having left behind, in his mother's hands, a locked metal box to be given to his father. The father opened it: inside there was a needle without an eye and a single palm leaf on which was written one metrical line, the opening of a poem: *kāt'aṟṟav ūciyum vārātu kāṇ kaṭai vaḻikke,* "Not even a needle without an eye will come with you on your final way." That was enough: the father understood. At once he renounced all wealth and family ties and set off on a life of mendicancy, meditation, and miracles (much of it spent at Tiruviṭaimarutur).[78]

Could the eyeless needle alone have sufficed to make the existential shift? Apparently not, though it is an eloquent enough image of blockage and waste. Its message has to be spelled out in words—written words. (Some versions of the story say that the palm leaf with the line of text was wrapped in a rag and left with Paṭṭiṉattār's wife by a beggar—no needle this time.) It seems the words have to be not merely heard—though in somewhat similar cases, overhearing a meaningful poem at the proper moment can do the trick[79]—but actually seen in their graphic form, black on yellowed leaf. By this point, the graphic device may have superseded, indeed rendered redundant, the inspired oral text, for all its alliteration and powerful rhythm. Paṭṭiṉattār, a merchant working with recorded accounts, has graphic literacy and is highly susceptible to the power of writing; he apparently reads the critical line silently, to himself, and the change that comes over him also takes place in some unspoken, but not invisible, dimension. The poetic works ascribed to him, however, after his immediate act of self-liberation, are still seen as metrical oral productions in the first instance—and indeed, they live on today largely in that mode of memorized and recited text.

This late-medieval example nicely articulates several of the main components of Tamil textuality that have emerged from our discussion. Oral composition remains a privileged mode, endowed even with a certain moral primacy and an intrinsic connection to existential in-ness; thus Paṭṭiṉattār's surviving, enormously popular poems are, *by definition,* improvised and oral in origin. Yet in the case of truly inspired works, products of the full-throated, musical *uyir,* inscription is also necessary and eventually moves the corpus toward canonization. Moreover, in the present case the impetus to textual expression, or to the revitalized awareness that will seek such expression, is itself a starkly visible, graphic text paired with a concrete, evocative object embedded in the still incomplete poem. Or we could say that the needle and line of verse are embedded in each other. The graphic text has its own magic, as in the case of Tiruñāṉacampantar's inscribed palm leaf and in a host of early-modern examples.[80] In any case, the instrumental and pragmatic force of poetry, never obviated by sheer lyricism, works in all available tracks—in oral recitation, first and foremost, but also in talismanic inscription, in texts recorded by a god, and in the most resilient and enduring mode of inscribing through gestures in open space. An element of ambivalence continues, however, to haunt the written text, even the modern printed book meant for silent reading.

## North and South

Before we conclude this chapter, we need to examine in more detail the nature of intellectual and artistic life at the Pallava court, especially in relation to the role the Tamil language assumed in that life. What did Tamil mean to Pallava culture, including the political order and its institutions? We have seen that the contemporaneous Pandya state to the far south nurtured an ideology of patronizing Tamil and its literature. Does the Pallava period in northern Tamil Nadu offer a contrast to this self-conscious sponsorship of Tamil?

Not really. As Emmanuel Francis has shown, the Pallava inscriptional record amply documents a royal interest in Tamil as a medium of self-assertion functioning side by side with the pan-Indian political idiom couched in Sanskrit.[81] The Tamil *bhakti* poets are linked by tradition with both the Pallava and the Pandya courts, and in a moment we will discuss the relatively late (ninth-century) Pallava royal text in Tamil, the *Nantikkalampakam,* which we can put side by side with the *Pāṇṭikkovai,* discussed at some length in Chapter 2. Nonetheless, the Pallavas had, in certain specific senses, a northern orientation: they saw themselves as having arrived in the Tamil country from somewhere to the north, and for much of their history their ties to the larger polities of the northeastern Deccan, such as the Vishṇukundin state in the Godavari-Krishna doab, remained strong.[82] Pallava genealogies identify the dynastic founder as the *Mahābhārata* Brahmin hero Aśvatthāman, wandering the world forever because of a curse; his union with a Nāginī princess is the moment of origin, probably hinted at in the great royal relief at Mahabalipuram known either as "Arjuna's Penance" or the "Descent of the Ganges" (see below).[83] We might go so far as to posit a northern, Deccani model of Tamil kingship alongside the southern, Pandya type.

What does "north" signify in middle-period Tamil? It is, for one thing, the source and first home of the northern language, *vaṭa mŏḻi,* that is, Sanskrit, as opposed to the southern language, *tĕṉ mŏḻi,* Tamil. Each of the two tongues had its own expressive advantages, which a poet or the author of an inscription could choose from; we have seen that historically they formed a complementary unity, not without a certain tension.[84] We could also say that in the Tamil world north and south, that is, Sanskrit and Tamil, necessarily constitute and inform each other in a single interlocking conceptual core that includes context-sensitive vectors of contrast.[85] In general, the north is only rarely, to my knowledge, devalued in premodern Tamil, even if a special love for and affinity with the southern pole comes through at times in second-millennium Tamil, particularly in the Śrīvaishṇava commentaries.[86] The latter also occasionally give voice to a special fondness for the north: thus the fact that Vishṇu-Raṅganātha, the lord of Srirangam, reclines facing south is said to reflect an act of divine grace for northerners—since Vishṇu's back has a supernal beauty and is turned toward people living north of Srirangam.[87] We might also distinguish between "north" (Venkatam and beyond it the area of the Vaṭukar and its northern speech, that is, Andhra) and "deep north" (for example, the sites of Krishṇa's childhood in Braj / Mathurā, or the sacred geography of the Himalayas), just as Tamil distinguishes between the "deep south" (for example, the original Madurai, now under the sea) and the south as we more or less recognize it today, beginning at the Venkatam ridge. Thus historic Madurai—perhaps the archetypal southern cultural site—is, as we have seen, called "northern Madurai" by the commentary on the *Grammar of Stolen Love.*

By the time of Mahendravarman I (end of the sixth century and the first three decades of the seventh), at the latest, the Pallava royal court was a site of tremendous creative activity couched largely in Sanskrit. The polymath king himself composed two Sanskrit farces, the *Matta-vilāsa* and the *Bhagavad-ajjuka.*[88] Mahendravarman's successor, Narasiṃha Mahāmalla (630–ca. 688), was probably the inspiration for and patron of the great relief at Mahabalipuram, which, as Rabe has cogently argued, may well have been conceived as a visual counterpart to the poetic device of *śleṣa*—the simultaneous unfolding of two distinct but mutually superimposed texts couched in the same sequence of sounds.[89] We should see as natural the close relations, to the point of shared expressive techniques, between sculptors (and no doubt painters) and learned poets and scholars under the patronage of royal connoisseurs such as the seventh-century Pallava kings. We know, for example that Daṇḍin, arguably the greatest intellectual of the Pallava period and the author of literary masterpieces in Sanskrit and of the outstanding textbook of Sanskrit poetics, the *Kāvyâdarśa* or *Mirror of Poetry,* visited Mahabalipuram toward the end of the seventh century at the invitation of Lalitâlaya, the head of the atelier of sculptors at this site. In the course of their tour, they visit the royal palace (probably of Narasiṃha II Rājasiṃha) as well as an image of reclining Vishṇu whose arm had been broken off, only to be reattached seamlessly by the master sculptor (perhaps at what is today known as the Shore Temple). Daṇḍin has left us a rare, first-person description of this outing in his *Avanti-sundarī-kathā,* which gives a good sense of the creative ambience at the Pallava court at this time (although Daṇḍin tells us that sculpture had in fact declined since the days of Lalitâlaya's father,

Mandhātar, portrayed as a genius capable of creating a mechanical man who could speak at least a single sentence (apparently in Sanskrit: "I'm hungry!").[90]

It is, I think, telling that Daṇḍin, a native Tamil speaker, chose to compose his work on poetics in Sanskrit, the cosmopolitan language accessible to scholars throughout India and beyond—and indeed, the *Kāvyâdarśa* became one of India's bestsellers, known throughout Asia and eventually translated / adapted into Tamil (*Taṇṭiyalaṅkāram,* possibly twelfth century), Tibetan, and other languages. The Pallava court was clearly open to the pan-Indian world of erudition and artistic production couched in Sanskrit and also eager to contribute to that world. Conspicuous in the Pallava-period inscriptional record are references to institutions of higher learning in the Vedic sciences (*ghaṭikā, vidyā-sthānam*), for example in the major urban center of Kacci or Kancipuram (possibly going back to the fourth century or even earlier), and also at smaller sites scattered throughout the northern Tamil country. The Kancipuram *ghaṭikā* attracted royal patronage and support.[91]

Burton Stein has suggested a social-structural logic underlying the cosmopolitan ethos of the Pallavas at their height. He sees the Pallava-Pandya period as a critical time of institutional innovation, when non-Brahmin peasant farmers established an enduring "alliance" with Brahmins, including learned masters of the Sanskrit tradition, throughout the "riverine tracks of the southern Tamil plain."[92] One sees the active presence of Brahmins in the village assemblies, which begin to appear in epigraphic records at this time: recall the Brahmin carriers of the tradition whom we met, by name, in the Pandya Velvikuti grant. *Brahmedeyas*—that is, land grants, free of tax, by kings or local chiefs to Brahmins versed in the Veda—become common in mid-to-late Pallava times and reveal precisely the sort of Brahmin–non-Brahmin alliance that Stein found so compelling.[93] Stein argues partly on the basis of what seems to him to be a strange lacuna—the absence of a stratum of Ksatriya warriors, with its own political and social tradition, distinct from that of peasant farmers.[94] The reason, he thinks, for this "failure of a Kshatriya tradition to emerge in medieval South India" was the "entrenched secular power of Brahmans."[95] That is one way to put it, although it is far from clear that Kshatriyas as such—as kingly warriors organized in discrete kinship networks and defined as a specific social category or class *(varṇa)*—ever existed anywhere in premodern India. But Stein was right to stress the notion of *brahma-kṣatra*—polities formed around Brahmin royal dynasties and infused by Brahmin and Sanskrit ideologies—as germane to the Pallava state model; as we saw, these kings claimed descent from the epic warrior-Brahmin, Aśvatthāman. We find more than one model of *brahma-kṣatra* in the medieval south, the most far-reaching being situated in Kerala; but the Pallava paradigm is early, indeed foundational, and reflects the profound symbiosis of Sanskrit and Tamil in the cultural life of the court as well as in the agrarian regime of the countryside.

It is possible that Pallava courtly culture saw a gradual intensification of Tamil literary and scholarly activity in the last century or century and a half of the dynasty; we also see an increase in inscriptional "political Tamil" in the early eighth and ninth centuries—famously in the long narrative of a complex political transition engraved on the walls of the Vaikuṇṭhapĕrumāḷ temple in Kancipuram (ca. 800). These inscriptions accompany the sculpted reliefs that illustrate their content (the coronation of Nandi II)[96]—another striking instance of the interweaving of artistic and verbal arts. The emblematic Pallava-period courtly poem in Tamil is the mid-ninth-century *Nantikkalampakam* ("Nandi's Collection," mentioned above), of anonymous authorship, on Nandi III.[97] This exquisite collection of poems in diverse Tamil meters and genres, often blending together the *akam* and *puṟam* modes just as we find in the *kovai* poems and the *Tiruviruttam* (see above), praises the Pallava king as *tŏṇṭai ventaṉ*, "king of the Tontai region," and *mallai aṅ kāṉal mutalvaṉ*, "lord of Mallai [=our Mahabalipuram] on the sea," among other epithets. He is also a reimagined exemplar of the ancient Sangam lover and hero and a scholar who has "gone to the limit of the ancient books" *(tŏllai nūl varampu muḻutu kaṇṭāṉ)*, presumably Tamil texts and their grammars.[98] Perhaps this royal role was at first slightly less axiomatic in northern Tamil Nadu than it was in the Pandya court in Madurai, but by the mid-ninth century one can hardly distinguish the Pallava kings from the Pandyas in this respect. As Francis says of the *Nantikkalampakam*, "the vocabulary [of royal panegyric] is mostly Tamil and the metre is the profoundly Tamil *āciriyappā,* which is the principal metre of *Puṟanāṉūṟu.*"[99] It is possible, though not certain, that this same king was the sponsor of the Tamil *Mahābhārata* composed by Pĕruntevaṉār, who may even be the same person credited with invocation verses to five of the Sangam anthologies;[100] if this is the case, the Pandyas cannot claim any monopoly over the classical Tamil corpus. Tradition says that the author of the *kalampakam* prophesied that whoever heard the hundredth verse of this work would die; the king ordered him to sing it at any cost and was burnt to ashes as the poet recited the final verse. It is certainly possible, and at moments perhaps even necessary, to die for good poetry.

One element particularly characteristic of the northern, Pallava paradigm should be stressed before we leave this chapter. It is in Pallava reliefs, notably at Mahabalipuram, that we find the first portrait sculptures in south India. No one who looks closely at these carvings can fail to notice their striking individuality: there is almost nothing conventional or abstracted about them. They are royal portraits, as we know from the inscriptions identifying them: for example, the wonderful images of King Siṃhavishṇu and his two wives, in the Ādivarāha cave at Mahabalipuram, have a breathtaking clarity and expressive force.[101] We are looking at real persons portrayed by artists concerned with capturing their individual vitality. Many centuries will pass before we find, in Nāyaka-period Tamil Nadu, portraits of similar power and idiosyncratic taste.[102] One might attempt to establish a relation between this visual medium and the personal voice for which Tamil *bhakti* poetry is allegedly famous. "Allegedly" because much of the canonical corpus is, in its own way, heavily patterned, although we have indeed heard a markedly personal note already in the poems of Kāraikkālammaiyār. At least two of the early Vaishṇava poets can clearly be seen as strongly, even radically, individualized in style and content: Tirumaṅkaiyāḻvār and the surpassingly eloquent Nammāḻvār. At least in these two cases, but to some extent also in many other canonical works in both Śaiva and Vaishṇava streams, the irreducible intimacy of speaking in one's mother tongue clearly informs the poet's voice; and this intimate expressivity is itself repeatedly thematized in these poets' works.

A concluding word about Nammāḻvār and what we might call the southern, Pandya paradigm. We have already seen something of the strong interpenetration of the political and literary spheres at the Pandya court: Tamil poetry, and Tamil science, are from the start, in the eyes of the southern tradition, cultivated by these Tamil kings. The political and literary elites of southern Tamil Nadu were clearly intertwined, and the accomplished poet-scholar was no less of a courtly, political figure than the Pandya kings were known for being, of ethical necessity, connoisseurs of Tamil. Nammāḻvār's personal names (as opposed to his standard title)—Māraṉ and Parâṅkuśaṉ, both recurring regularly in the Vaishṇava sources—were drawn from the political domain, as R. Nagaswamy has shown in several essays. He was probably named after the Pandya king Arikesari Parâṅkuśa Māravarmaṉ, the heroic figure we encountered in the panegyric verses of the *Pāṇṭikkovai.*[103] In all likelihood, the poet namesake of this famous king thus belongs to a generation or so after the royal exemplar and can be placed in the mid-eighth century.

Like other Tamil *bhakti* poets, Nammāḻvār shares the official Pandya ideology, if one may call it that, of celebrating and nurturing the Tamil language. Look, for example, at the following well-known verse:

> "Māl! Great magician, master of tricks!"
> That's how Caṭakopaṉ [Nammāḻvār] cried out
> to him in mad delight, moved
> by His maddening mercy, in a thousand verses,
> including the ten stanzas of this poem.
> Those who can perform them, praised as they are
> by those who speak and sing and love
> in Tamil sweet as milk,
> know no sorrow.[104]

The Śrīvaishṇava commentators like to identify each of the three categories mentioned here—speakers, singers, lovers[105]—with particular individuals (thus the first three Āḻvārs, Tiruppāṇāḻvār, and Pĕriyāḻvār, respectively, according to the *Īṭu* commentary).[106] But it seems that anyone who speaks Tamil, and especially anyone who can sing in Tamil, enjoys the promise of an end to suffering. It is no small thing to be born into this milky tongue—in itself a privileged form of the god's "maddening mercy" *(māl aruḷ)*. In the eyes of a great Tamil poet, natural Tamil speech may, indeed, be this god's greatest gift to human beings.

Perhaps Tamil is God's own language. To the innate musicality of Tamil *(icaittamiḻ)* one can now add the crystallized tradition of Tamil musical science, an achievement of this same period, as we know from a highly detailed, erudite Grantha inscription from Kudimiyanmalai (perhaps seventh century), in the shatter zone between the Pallava and Pandya kingdoms.[107] The *bhakti* poets composed their works to be sung in the ramified modal system of *paṇs.* As we have seen, the living, breathing *uyir* sings even before "it" speaks of its longing.

South Indian *bhakti,* as we find it the rich repertoire of the Śaiva and Vaishṇava poets in the second half of the first millennium, is probably the single greatest contribution of the Tamil country to pan-Indian civilization. The new model of intensely emotional and sensual devotion to the god in his local home eventually spread throughout the entire subcontinent, where to this day it constitutes the mainstream religious experience of hundreds of millions. There were earlier forms of *bhakti*—notably the rather cold *bhakti-yoga* of the *Bhagavad-gītā,* where devotion to an abstract deity comes with a program of overcoming sensory, cognitive, and emotional experience. The contrast with the full-blooded, temple-based Tamil modes of encountering god is a stark one, though strong elements of classical Yoga and, of course, of Upaniṣadic metaphysics found their way into the *bhakti* corpora in Tamil almost from the start. The poets seek the god with their whole being, at the core of which is the rhythmic movement of the breath, *uyir,* as it enters and exits the person in harmony with the breathing of the world.

In the Pallava-Pandya period, two Tamil Vedas, one Śaiva, the second Vaishṇava, took shape and moved toward assuming canonical form, a process that would be completed only in Chola times. This same period witnessed the invention of the most beautiful of all south Indian scripts, Pallava Grantha, which we see in many stone inscriptions. The sheer beauty of this writing system may have influenced the shift, in this period, toward graphic recording of the great texts; writing assumed a set of roles that were not merely, or perhaps even primarily, functional as textual memory, but were rather effectual, talismanic, and meaningful in their own right. Probably most effective of all in fixing the great canonical texts were forms of writing not on palm leaf, copper plate, or stone but in visible, empty space and in bodily gesture. Such modes of preservation were possibly important to the classical Sangam corpus no less than to the Tamil *bhakti* canons. A deep axiology of textual performance, characteristically Tamil, came to maturity at this juncture.

In terms of political and social dynamics, a northern oriented, highly Sanskritic state centered on Kancipuram and the Tondai plain complemented the southern kingdom of Pandya Madurai with its Tamil-centric ideology. Powerful literary works in Tamil appeared a little later in the Pallava north than in the Pandya south, though we should not forget a great narrative poem such as the *Pĕrumpāṇāṟṟuppaṭai,* from the *Ten Songs,* with its vision of urban Kanci. The north-south distinction should not be taken too far: both states spoke Tamil, sang Tamil, engraved Tamil on copper and stone, wrote it down on palm leaf and, through the language of gesture, in uncluttered space; both saw themselves as inhabiting a Tamil cultural ecology not exclusive of other linguistic presences. At least two classical poetic grammars—one, by Daṇḍin, now achieving definitive formulation in Sanskrit, probably in Kancipuram, the other inherited directly from the Sangam stratum—were in place by the eighth century; both were poised to enrich themselves further, partly through mutual infusion, in the explosion of literature and erudite science during the high Chola centuries.

FOUR

# The Imperial Moment, Truth, and Sound

## *Caraṇam* 1

### Horizons

Around the year 850, a warrior family calling themselves by the ancient heroic name Chola conquered the tiny town of Tanjavur in the delta of the Kaveri River. Over the next several generations they went on to establish a state that claimed to exert authority—not a synonym for control—over most of southern India and that sent off large-scale military and naval raids to Sri Lanka and Srivijaya in distant Southeast Asia. Was this Chola state an empire? It depends on what we mean by the term. A protracted debate in recent historiographical literature has so far not resolved the issue.

One thing, however, is certain: the Cholas were happy to use Tamil as an official state language, along with Sanskrit; and they, or the poets they patronized, created a courtly milieu in which several of the great Tamil masterpieces were composed. Tamil is now, explicitly, the language of kings and gods. There is no question about its prominent status in Chola inscriptions, where the Sanskrit-Tamil symbiosis we have seen in the Pallava and Pandya epigraphs continues to operate even as the Tamil component in Chola epigraphy extends its range and roles. Tamil is also, by this period, a transregional language, appearing in inscriptions in the Andhra delta, in the western Deccan, in Sri Lanka, and as far afield as Burma, Thailand, Sumatra, and even China.[1] This impressive geographical range of the language is not coterminous with the geographical extent of the Chola state; nor does it simply reflect the Cholas' diplomatic and military adventures abroad. It would be more faithful to our sources to think in terms of a vast linguistic expansion, also in the literary and learned domains, motivated by deep cultural, intellectual, and economic currents and following in the wake of the wide-ranging carriers of this language and its traditions as they explored the limits of their world.

Look, for example, at the following itinerary, which we know from Chinese sources. In ca. 1012, Rājarāja Chola (whom the Chinese refer to as Lots'a Lots'a), or more probably his son, Rājendra, sent a delegation of fifty-two courtiers, led by four senior ministers, to the Song ruler Cheng Tsung. The party traveled from Tanjavur to the major Chola port of Nākai (Nagapattinam) and thence, in a leisurely fashion, to Sri Lanka, at the time at least partly under Chola rule; then to Rammanadesam (Tam. Arumanam) in Burma, and on to Kadāram on the northern Malay peninsula and to some part of the Srivijaya kingdom (either in Sumatra or in one of the Srivijaya satellite port cities of Southeast Asia),[2] before arriving, after just over three years en route, in the mercantile metropolis of Quanzhou in southern China. The leader of the Tamil contingent, "Choli" or "Chola Samudran" (following a possible Chinese transliteration of the Tamil name), died in southern China; the emperor is said to have sent an official to offer a libation at the grave.[3] The Cholas presented the emperor with classic south Indian specialties: pearls, ivory, spices, and medicinal herbs. Although we sadly lack a Tamil source for this journey, such as Choli Samudra's diary, we can easily imagine these south Indian travelers—probably pious Śaivas who performed daily rituals and prayers at sea and on land—encountering a somewhat baffling, exotic civilization after long wanderings among the somewhat more familiar peoples of Southeast Asia.[4] At every port of call they would have found Tamil-speaking merchants such as the "Five Hundred" *(ainnūṟṟavar)* Cheṭṭis (also referred to as *nakarattār*) who turn up in an inscription from 1088 in Sumatra—among others scattered widely throughout this region.[5] By the eleventh century, a rich Tamil diaspora had come into existence, with an assortment of imported schoolmasters, ritualists, shipbuilders, cloth merchants, and temple masons. Toward the end of the Chola period, in the mid- to late thirteenth century, we find a Tamil temple, possibly dedicated to the god Kadalīśvara, in the same southern Chinese port of Quanzhou (recently studied in depth by Risha Lee);[6] a bilingual Tamil-Chinese inscription here gives us the date of dedication and the somewhat mangled name of the deity. Chinese-speaking Tamilians, or Tamil-speaking Chinese merchants, must have rubbed shoulders in Quanzhou with speakers of Arabic, Khmer, and Old Javanese, among many other languages. It is thus only logical that in later Malay traditions, such as *Sejara Melayu* from fifteenth-century Malacca, the official genealogy of the Malacca sultans incorporated not only Alexander the Great and the kings of Srivijaya but also the conquering Chola emperors.[7]

Concomitant with these Tamil outposts dotting the shores of the Indian Ocean was the emergence of a substantial Southeast Asian presence, material and symbolic, in the Nagapattinam port town on the Coromandel Coast. A famous Buddhist *vihāra* was established there by the Srivijaya / Śailendra king, Māravijayottuṅgavarma, in the name of his father, Cūḷāmaṇivarma; the Buddhist shrine was endowed ca. 1006 by Rājarāja Chola with the income of the village of Anaimangalam and freed from taxes *(paḷḷiccantam)*. The grant was reconfirmed by Rājarāja's son Rājendra. We have a formulaic picture of the multicultural, multireligious, and undoubtedly polyglot reality of early Chola Nagapattinam in the Larger Leyden Copper Plates, which give details of this grant: the city (called Nāgī-pattana in the Sanskrit portion of the text) is "delightful [on account of] many a temple, rest-house, water-shed, and pleasure garden and brilliant with arrays of various kinds of mansions."[8]

We also hear of a "Chinese Pagoda," a three-storied brick tower constructed, according to Chinese sources, in 1267 and possibly connected to the *vihāra,* which survived in this town until the mid-nineteenth century.[9] Chola times were, in some respects, happier than modern colonial reality: the "Chinese Pagoda" was torn down in 1867 under orders of the governor and its bricks recycled to build a Christian missionary school.

In short, we have firm evidence of an impressive web of bilateral, sometimes trilateral, relations, on several levels, between the Chola south and various parts of Southeast Asia. Rulers from Burma and Cambodia sent embassies to the Chola court (the Burmese king Kyanzittha in the late eleventh century claimed to have converted the "Choli prince" to Buddhism by a personal letter inscribed on golden leaves). Tamil was probably heard in the vast complex of Angkor Wat, whose builder, Suryavarman II, gifted a precious stone to Kulottunga I (1114).[10] Tamil merchants traded throughout Southeast Asia in textiles, a Chola speciality; Chola-style bronze sculptures from the eleventh century, including some modified to suit local taste, have come to light in northern Sumatra. Thus by the turn of the first millennium Tamil had clearly become an international language, used by merchants and bankers, Buddhist monks, and, we can surmise, expatriate literati, among others.

It was also truly an imperial language in Sri Lanka, first raided intermittently by the early Cholas and then far more aggressively by Rājarāja, who is said to have destroyed the capital of Anuradhapura and to have plundered the *vihāras* (Chola times were not so enlightened after all). Rājendra I (ca. 1012–1044) consolidated his father's military gains on the island and nominally assimilated at least parts of the north as a province of the Chola state (under the administrative title *Mummuṭi-coḻa-maṇḍalam*), establishing a new capital at Polonnaruwa, where we can still see two splendid Chola temples, complete with inscriptions in Tamil.[11] Only in the last quarter of the eleventh century were the Tamil conquerors forced by the Sinhalese king Vijayabāhu I to begin to withdraw. Tamil merchant networks like the Five Hundred mentioned above were also active in Sri Lanka, probably displacing their Sinhalese counterparts, the *vaṇigrāmayan,* during the Chola conquest.[12] More important was the lasting cultural and linguistic impact of Tamil on Sri Lankan history; a very ancient Tamil community settled in the far north of the island was further entrenched by the centuries of Chola invasions and has survived, with its own distinctive Tamil dialect and sparkling cultural production in Tamil, up to today, through the tragic events of our own generation.

The early Chola state system was continually extending the limits of its power, both horizontally, in military campaigns throughout south India and beyond, and vertically, in long-term processes of increasing protobureaucratic penetration of the core agrarian heartland of the Kaveri delta, as scholars such as James Heitzman and Noboru Karashima have shown us.[13] The rich epigraphical records allow us to detect a gradual institutional movement, relatively pronounced from the eleventh century on, away from largely arbitrational sovereignty over the local agrarian regime, based on riverine rice cultivation, toward more centralized, rationalized, and managerial control of local resources. In this, the Chola state seems to have been an exception to the far more widespread south Indian political pattern of permanent systemic oscillation between periods of centralizing efforts aimed at some version of hierarchical integration and other periods of reversion to effective rule by local, more or less autonomous, upwardly mobile elites.[14] Something akin to the latter phase of local self-assertion and relative political independence can be seen in the Chola shatter zones, such as the present-day South Arcot District, somewhat removed from the Kaveri heartland.[15] Somewhat paradoxically, the ascendance of a more heavily bureaucratic system bound to the political center coincides, in the Chola case, with dynastic decline and eventual demise. Heitzman sees as one cause of this process the predominant mechanisms of endowment and alienation of fertile lands, mostly to temples or to Brahmin settlements, by the local peasant elite, who in this way managed to limit or elude taxation by the royal center and to redirect control of resources to local authorities.[16] This process coincided, not by chance, with a pronounced rise in, or formalization of, private property rights throughout the core Chola domain in the twelfth and thirteenth centuries.

The expansive Chola world, extending over much of the Deccan and also well beyond peninsular India, naturally generated its own characteristic, bold, stylistic idiom. Most conspicuous in this respect are the hundreds of Chola temples that grace the green landscape of the Kaveri heartland; many of these temples record traditions, occasionally embodying a refashioned historical memory, about a founding figure or major patron from the Chola family. We will visit these temples shortly. But we can hear the new language in all the major courtly works, in the thousands of Chola temple inscriptions, in the linguistic and ethical textures of the emblematic temple poet Kamban, in the newly crystallized universe of erudite discourse in Tamil, Prakrit, and Sanskrit, and in the cultural monuments of the heterodox (Buddhist and Jain) communities. To sample this idiom in practice in the hope of formulating, inductively, its major themes and concepts, we begin with the classical courtly poems dedicated to the Chola kings. We will also want to see what the Tamil literary tradition has to say about their authors.

## Display

We have a plethora of official Chola genealogies. They turn up in inscriptions such as the detailed Kanyakumari text, with its Sanskrit preamble, of Vīrarājendra Chola (1063–1069),[17] among others, and in many of the literary works produced at the Chola court or on its periphery: Cayaṅkŏṇṭār's *Kaliṅkattupparaṇi* ("War on Kalinga"), on Kulottuṅga I and his military campaign in Orissa ca. 1110; the processionals *(Mūvar ulā)* by Ŏṭṭakkūttar on three major monarchs; and Kamban's Tamil *Rāmāyaṇa.* There are intriguing differences among these attempts to provide an ancient pedigree for the Chola rulers; but all of them share a heightened vision of imperial origins and, in general, the same tripartite structure that we have seen in the Pandya Veḷvikkuṭi grant—mythic *(purāṇic)* origins, protohistorical legendary names, and then dynastic history proper.[18]

The royal genealogy is framed by high drama in Cayaṅkŏṇṭār's book, whose royal patron, Kulottuṅga I, is said to have rewarded his poet by rolling a golden coconut down the aisle to his feet after each verse was recited. The main protagonists of the work are the hungry demons, *pey,* who are hoping against hope that the Chola king will attack his Kalinga enemies on the eastern coast and provide these demons with a delectable dinner of fresh corpses.[19] The entire royal lineage is related by a senior demon, *mutupey,* who should know what he's talking about, to the gruesome goddess Kāḷi and her retinue of ghouls. In case you are worried, I can tell you that the demons do get the feast they wanted. It also turns out that demons, like human beings, have castes and other differential identities: there are Brahmin ghouls who beg (in Sanskrit) for a taste of battlefield sambar, and highly intelligent Buddhist ghouls who get sambar made specially with human brains, and Jain ghouls who carefully strain their soup to be sure there are no hairs in it (verses 565–67). A similarly grisly context is famously described by the twelfth-century Chola court poet Ŏṭṭakkūttar, who, like Cayaṅkŏṇṭār, wrote a *paraṇi* war poem, the *Takka-yākap-paraṇi,* "The War on Daksha's Sacrifice," on the purāṇic theme of Śiva's destructive raid on his father-in-law Daksha's sacrificial rite. We will return to this text. One might note in this context the persistent, somehow privileged demon's-eye perspective on Tamil history and culture; recall that both Śaiva and Vaishṇava *bhakti* currents claim to have originated in poetry composed by demon-like devotees (Kāraikkāl Pey/ Kāraikkālammaiyār; Peyāḻvār and Pūtatt'āḻvār). In Tamil as in Telugu, demons have an inborn affinity with poetry.

For a taste of Chola kingship in action, we can have a quick look at Ŏṭṭakkūttar's processional poems, which belong to the emergent genre of *ulā.*[20] The template, defined by the *pāṭṭ'iyal* handbooks first codified in Chola times and by the eleventh-century (Chola-period) commentator on the *Tŏlkāppiyam,* Iḷampūraṇar,[21] shows us the royal hero riding his great elephant through the streets of the capital while seven classes of women, ranging in age from five years to forty, are overcome by passion for this unattainable lover. Indeed, in general, the king moves, impassive and unresponsive, through the ecstatic scenes unfolding in the streets.[22] *Ulā* poems begin with a synoptic version of the royal genealogy, then situate the king in time and space; he also must be brought into explicit relation with the great gods, especially the Chola family deity of the Dancing Śiva at Cidambaram.[23] The Chola monarch begins his day by worshiping this god. He is then shown himself in a mirror[24]—the first reflective moment in a long series designed by the poet precisely to show this king his own reflected self. Like the mirrors invariably fixed in place in sight of the deity in the great Tamil temples, the *ulā* generates in its subject a necessary self-awareness as well as a sense of his capacity to make an entire world through reciprocal, oblique, yet intimate relations with his people.[25] The Chola court poets crafted a courtly Tamil idiom, distinct from previous styles—in effect, another polished mirror—to serve this goal.

Observe the culmination of the procession described in the *Vikkiramacoḻaṉ ulā,* when the king finally passes by the fully mature, sexually experienced *periḷampĕṇ* (supposedly thirty-two to forty years old). I cite the translation by Blake Wentworth:

At the time when the strong, pungent toddy flows
to the tips of the young palm spathes, and the runoff hums
with bees,

A maid poured some off and filled a palm-leaf cup,
she wiped off the bee-swarmed froth, then offered it to her[26]
with praises,

She glanced at it, her mind in pain, flicked away a drop with her
sharp nail,
and drank it down, then collapsed in the arms of her maids,

And in the drunkenness that followed, the best of the best of
Manu's line
came to her, offering a dream suited to her lust,

Ecstasy was in that dream, but also the hunger to make love,
they arose together, each striving to drive the other off,

She sees her own reflection at her side
cast on a high wall of shining, pristine crystal,

The bright girdle of fine coral wrapped around her loins becomes
her only dress,
her blouse falls away as her arms grow lean. . . .

In her dream she saw these things, and took them as real life,
gushing with happiness as she tried to tell everyone,

But for this woman whose garland was fragrant with nectar,
swarming with bees,
the true joy that suffused her mind turned into a lie,

Under a parasol decked with garlands, wide open to give shade,
the terrible rutting elephant of Jayatuṅga approached,

"I am ruined!" cried the woman with sweet honey words when
she saw this,
"All that happened was nothing but liquor, I took my dream for
real life!"[27]

Wentworth has lucidly worked out the implications of such erotic scenes, and he correctly notes that "Oṭṭakkūttar is at his best when he delves into the twists of consciousness provoked by the king's presence."[28]

But the king's own consciousness is also, it seems, very much at stake: the royal patron is the first listener to the poem, which was certainly recited at court. Note that the woman in question also has to see her own reflection, just as the king sees his. The two images may exist in the same autonomous domain, a new form of *akam* in-ness, heavy with dream, unfolding within the *puṟam* procession outside. Perhaps most striking in this vignette is its philosophical conclusion: "I took my dream for real life!" It is, for a moment, as if *puṟam* had conquered *akam*. Chola court poetry, for all its lyricism and complex figurative effects, offers us perhaps the most realistic works we have from the first thousand years or so of Tamil literature.

As the *ulā* unfolds, the contrapuntal movement of delusion and awakening slowly becomes the rhythm of the royal procession, perhaps the rhythm of Chola kingship itself. Within the poem, the Chola inhabits a world of luxurious excess—the lush world of the delta—and here he acts in an imperial mode, holding oceans and mountains in place, keeping the seasons on course in their natural order, and, of course, conquering his many foes. He is as beautiful, indeed as perfect, as only a universal emperor can be. There is something intoxicating, ecstatic, in conjuring up his presence. He is also, clearly, a Tamil king, with a taste for poetry inherited honestly from his great predecessors such as Koccĕṅkaṭcoḻaṉ, who (as we know also from the other Chola genealogies) was gifted a great Tamil war poem, the *Kaḷavaḻi-nāṟpatu* or "Forty Verses on the Battlefield Spoils," by the poet Pŏykai.[29]

This kingly fondness for Tamil is focused here on the new courtly style. The *ulā* is usually, in effect, a single sentence produced by intricate, sequential subordinate clauses, with head-rhyming couplets stacked in loops and a strong tendency to use syncopated rhythms. Linguists call such complex sentences hypotactic; the various clauses that constitute them are formally linked in hierarchical patterns and differentiated morphologically from the main sentence with its finite verb (which in the *ulā* usually comes at the very end of the text). Thus just after the section I have cited, couplet 342, the last one, finally releases the listener or hearer from the syntactic suspense that has built up over the previous 341 couplets; we learn that, after all that has been said, all that has happened to the king en route, "the generous Chola, Uttuṅka-tuṅkan, went (*pontāṉ*) in procession on his furious elephant that strikes down his foes." Or perhaps, this being the end, the king, like the poem, now "went away."[30]

Ŏṭṭakkūttar's three great *ulās* might best be seen as radical experiments by a metrically adept, professional court poet intent on capturing, or rather modeling, this ethos in ornate, hypotactic Tamil. Their closest counterparts are the high-Chola bronzes with their bold and delicate images of male and female beauty. Ŏṭṭakkūttar, carving not in metal but in words, won for himself a place of honor in the Tamil literary canon, as we can see from a large body of stray verses and traditional stories about him and his relations with the Chola kings and other poets they patronized. A beautiful stanza appearing in the Tamil version of Daṇḍin's grammar of figures, *Taṇṭiyalaṅkāram* (178), says that:

> Among those things that offer pleasure,
> that strike your ear and stick in your mind,
> we count, one, a glance from the eye
> of a beautiful woman, flowers in her hair,
> and, two, the perfect poems of Kūttan who comes
> from Malari.[31]

But most of these same stories in which Ŏṭṭakkūttar figures prominently also appear to demote him slightly in comparison with his great rivals, especially Kamban and Pukaḻentip Pulavar (historically, a poet who lived some two centuries after Ŏṭṭakkūttar); sometimes Ŏṭṭakkūttar himself is made to voice severe self-doubt. In a supposed contest between him and Kamban set up by the Chola king in order to produce a Tamil *Rāmāyaṇa,* Ŏṭṭakkūttar worked steadily, in his earnest fashion, while Kamban, by far the greater poet, whiled away his time with courtesans. After some months had gone by, the king called the two poets in for an update, to see how far they had progressed in their work. The assiduous Ŏṭṭakkūttar had by then completed five books of the epic and was well into the sixth. Kamban, who had not thought up even a single verse, claimed to be no less far along, at the section when Rāma builds a bridge to Lanka. In proof of this claim, Kamban improvised seventy exquisite poems (one of them has an unusual lexical usage that the goddess Sarasvatī herself has to be called in to authenticate).

Disheartened, Ŏṭṭakkūttar somehow managed to finish the whole work but then tore it to shreds in the presence of Kamban, who salvaged only Ŏṭṭakkūttar's final book, the *Uttara-kāṇḍa.* We still have this surviving fragment, attributed, probably wrongly, to Ŏṭṭakkūttar; few bother to read it anymore.[32]

The judgment of the literary tradition deserves respect. One striking feature of Tamil literary culture as a whole is that, in contrast with the world of classical Telugu, for example, and to some extent also with classical Sanskrit, most of the truly great poetic masterpieces in middle-period Tamil were produced outside the main royal courts. This is not to say that the Chola court was in any sense barren of literary excitement. I have already mentioned the *paraṇi* poet Cayaṅkŏṇṭār in the late eleventh century; and in the twelfth century we find a supposed court poet, Cekkiḻār, commissioned by Aṉapāyaṉ (probably Kulottuṅga II) to compose the monumental hagiography of the sixty-three Śaiva saints, the *Tiruttŏṇṭarpurāṇam* or *Pĕriya Purāṇam,* "the Great *Purāṇa,*" a magnificent text by any standard. Yet even this work, in which the author praises his royal patron explicitly (1.8), was apparently composed mostly in the Cidambaram temple; the king had to take himself to this major shrine for the first public recitation *(araṅkeṟṟam)* of the work. Thus even this indispensable poem, intricately linked to the royal center, is really at home in the temple context, and Cekkiḻār, like Kamban, was primarily a temple poet, faithful in tone, style, and conception to this type.

Still, Ŏṭṭakkūttar does show us one critical, highly innovative feature of Chola-period Tamil. He is the first major cultural figure to reveal to us a still somewhat inchoate world of Tantric or Śākta metaphysics, focused on the goddess, already coloring, though not yet dominating, the *bhakti* mainstream religiosity. Ŏṭṭakkūttar's greatest work is the outlandish war poem on Daksha's sacrifice, the *Takkayākap-paraṇi,* in the *paraṇi* genre I have already mentioned. Like the *Kaliṅkattupparaṇi,* this grisly poem is, literally, a feast for demons, with a demon narrator and the goddess Kāḷi as listener. Ŏṭṭakkūttar was clearly a devotee of this goddess; and the medieval commentary on his work is one of the first full-fledged Tamil Tantric texts, still relatively unstudied. Here again the Tamil tradition has something to say.

The story is that Ŏṭṭakkūttar was himself from the "left-hand" weaver community *(cĕṅkuntar),* and that the weavers came to him and begged him to produce a long poem about them and their history; but the poet at first refused, saying that it would not be right for a member of this group to praise his fellow weavers. True praise should be disinterested, from someone who comes from outside. When the weavers insisted nonetheless, Ŏṭṭakkūttar told them he would only create such a work if they proved their courage by cutting off their heads—he needed at least seventy such heads, of first-born sons, before he would begin—and he explained to them how only such acts of heroic self-sacrifice merited a powerful poem such as he, and only he, could compose. The weavers complied with this condition, and soon seventy heads, still bleeding, were carried in baskets and dumped at the poet's door. He asked the weavers to take them where they belonged, at the entrance to the royal palace. Now the king was horrified and alarmed; he summoned Ŏṭṭakkūttar and asked him what he thought he was doing: "What kind of play *(kūttu)* is this?" The poet asked him to be patient. He piled up the severed heads, took his seat on top of the pile, and, sitting in the lotus posture, produced, extempore, the *Īṭṭiyĕḻupatu,* "Seventy Verses on the Spear" (undoubtedly a later work that has nothing to do with this particular poet). As the poem reached its conclusion, the poet prayed to the goddess Sarasvatī to reattach the severed heads to their bodies so that these weavers, too, could hear the verses he had sung about them. Why else should they need to come back to life? A poet's vanity has no limit. The goddess happily agreed to do this, and thus the poet got his name: "Kūttar the Reattacher (of heads to bodies)."[33]

The traditional narrative, crystallized in a period long after that of the imperial Cholas, speaks its own kind of truth. Ŏṭṭakkūttar does truly belong to the world of hungry goddesses (here even the usually gentle and pacific Sarasvatī has joined them); and his poem on Daksha's sacrifice is among the darkest, and most lurid and melodramatic, in the long history of Tamil war poetry. It shows us an incipient Tantric riptide coursing through the courtly Chola world, with its royal rituals and its obsession with temple worship. If we stick to the story, then we see how a refined court poet is transformed over time into a new kind of author, who indeed appears in the post-Chola times—the practicing Tantric sorcerer-magician. It is also worth noting the poet's affinity with the left-hand segment of society, the relatively mobile artisans, merchants, and weavers with their own system of values. Tamil poetry and erudition were never limited to kings, warriors, high-caste peasant farmers, or Brahmins, as we have already seen in relation to Tiruvaḷḷuvar and his *Tirukkuṟaḷ*. At least one vision of Tamil cultural production seeks to attach the creative impulse itself to a left-hand ritual of self-sacrifice and an impressive pile of freshly severed heads.

## Temples and Tamil Prose

On the one hand, the great Chola kings were heavily invested in displays of power, as we have seen in the courtly processionals; their court poets were the prime instruments of this public effort to create a visibly compelling kingship endowed with the accoutrements of aesthetic pretension. As in earlier times in the far south, kings and poets were bound together in relations of asymmetrical dependence, with the poets usually enjoying the upper hand. The particular forms of knowledge we have called "grammar" were central to this relationship and continued to evolve and to generate new texts. On the other hand, the predominant expressive arena for the royal presence, and for regal action, was undoubtedly provided by the great temples, organized in sets and networks scattered throughout the Chola domain with a particular concentration in the Kaveri delta. By far the most characteristic mode in which we encounter these kings is in donating land or movable luxury goods to temples or in confirming similar donations by others, whether members of the royal family and its wider entourage or local peasant landowners, merchants, and nobles. It would be no exaggeration to say that the political act par excellence in Chola-period Tamil Nadu was temple endowment, accompanied by temple worship and, in certain emblematic cases, by royal intervention in the process of canonizing temple-oriented Tamil poems.

As I have said, nearly all great Tamil temples have a tradition about a Chola king who came there and set in place major components of the ritual and metaphysical order. Most of these traditions clearly originated as retrospective inventions in post-Chola times: thus at Tiruvarur, the monkey-faced Chola king Mucukunda installed the god Tyāgarāja with appropriate rites and festivities after correctly selecting him, in Indra's heaven, from a series of seven identical bronze images.[34] At Cidambaram the king is Hiraṇyavarman, who was cured of leprosy by worshiping at the Śivaganga tank inside the walls of the shrine; Hermann Kulke has argued that this story, prominent in the *Cidambaramāhātmya* and later *purāṇas* from this major site, reflects a political reality of the late eleventh century, when Kulottuṅga I, born in the Eastern Ganga line in the Godavari-Krishna delta, came to assume the Chola throne in the far south.[35] If he is right, this is a rare case of a historical figure working his way into local *purāṇic* myth even within his own lifetime. In any case, it was normative that an important shrine, renovated or expanded by order of the Chola family, should inscribe this historical memory in its account of ritual origins.

When the Chola kings sometimes tell us in the preambles to their inscriptions that they are the first servants of the deity, we would do well to believe them. They are naturally happy to record their military feats, which made them "famous through all livable space" (*ĕṇ ṭicai pukaḻ tara,* in the formula we find in the inscriptions), as well as their acts of almost unthinkable largesse, spelled out at often tedious length. But the primary source of the prestige they claim is the direct benefice of the god, a visible effect of their ritual precedence.[36] One competes for proximity to the deity and for a prominent place in his service. In this sense, the king is indeed the first competitor and thus the "first servant." As George Spencer has shown,[37] the Chola kings, ostensibly the most powerful in the entire history of south India up to early-modern (Vijayanagara) times, slowly and tenuously shored up their position by following in the wake of the gods and utilizing the pilgrimage patterns oriented to the latter as prime goals for endowment. They also created dense transactional networks around each of the great temples, drawing into this inherently political arena the peasant villages with their assemblies, pastoralists living off their herds, soldiers, courtiers, Brahmins, ritualists, artisans, accountants, washermen, dancing girls, tailors, watchmen, and other service workers—all of whom contributed to the temple economy and lived to no small degree off its fruits. The most lucid model of this kind of transactional network has been worked out by James Heitzman, who also nicely differentiates between the various subregional eco-landscapes involved, each with its distinctive relation to the political capital.[38]

The most impressive, though not the most typical, example is Rājarāja Chola's Brihadīśvara Temple in Tanjavur. Some fifty-five major inscriptions cover the walls of this great shrine, built toward the end of Rājarāja's life with the clear intention of doing everything on as grand a scale as was humanly possible. And indeed this temple is one of the wonders of the world, with its central *vimāna* tower reaching a height of sixty-six meters and crowned with a single stone weighing sixty tons. The temple as a whole was constructed of some sixty thousand tons of granite and sandstone in an effort, stretching over five to seven years, that required the active conscription of the entire social spectrum in the delta; the inscriptions describe in precise detail the vast number of functionaries—around a thousand, including four hundred dancing girls[39]—appointed for a lifetime of service to this god. We can see Rājarāja himself in the magnificent painted murals, skillfully photographed and recomposed by modern technology,[40] that line the circumambulatory passage around the god's *liṅga*. If our identifications of the images are correct, the king stands erect and alert but somewhat dwarfed by his Brahmin guru and / or court poet Karuvūrttevar.[41] This temple was clearly Rājarāja's personal monument, and the god naturally came to be known by the king's name, Rājarājeśvara or Rājarājapureśvara, as we see from the poet Ŏṭṭakkūttar's casual reference to Śiva with the latter title in his *Takka-yākap-paraṇi*—as if "Lord of Rājarāja's Town" was the self-evident way to address Lord Śiva in Tamil, even in a generalized mythic setting.[42]

It takes a slight imaginative leap for us to understand the Chola kings' burning compulsion to build and endow temples. Even if we put aside the earlier, clearly inappropriate model of Chola polity as a variation on the absolutist state of seventeenth-century Europe,[43] we still have to contend with our notion of power as derived from, and primarily expressed in, brute control and a centralized amassing of resources. No one would doubt that south Indian kings were also eager to maximize these two components of state building, often through the kind of episodic but large-scale military raids mentioned earlier.[44] But power is never simply a given; it comes from somewhere and waxes or wanes in accordance with culturally determined metaphysical notions. I have argued elsewhere that a vector of renunciation, genuine or assumed, in varying degrees and intensities, was active in all premodern political formations in south India.[45] Here the royal road to power proceeds via a landscape of generous donations and an oddly luxurious abstinence, informed by personal love for the deity in his or her always local incarnations.

In the course of carrying out temple endowments, the Chola kings, or their literate staff and employees, in effect reinvented Tamil prose. Unlike the mellifluous, lush prose of Nakkīraṉār's commentary on the *Grammar of Stolen Love,* the great Chola temple inscriptions show us what we could call "quotidian prose," often existing side-by-side in the same text with Sanskrit *praśasti* (genealogy and panegyric) and with eulogistic Tamil *mĕykkīrti,* "true praise" (always in verse), focused on martial achievement. *Mĕykkīrti* became a recognized poetic genre in the Chola-period handbooks, the *pāṭṭ'iyal,* as Francis has shown.[46] Bilingual inscriptions are common—Sanskrit *praśasti* joined with *mĕykkīrti* and then the transactional details in quotidian prose. Sometimes the Sanskrit and Tamil portions repeat and reflect each other.[47]

These texts have their own style, a novelty in the history of Tamil. Philological analyses, beginning with the careful introduction by V. Venkayya to volume 2 of *South Indian Inscriptions* (1913) and the Tanjavur Brihadīśvara inscriptions, have emphasized some peculiarities of this official language; they include distinctive lexical choices and grammatical usages sanctioned by the medieval grammars such as *Naṉṉūl* and, in particular, the Buddhist *Vīracoḻiyam*[48] but rare in literary Tamil. One also sees considerable orthographic variation—including the nonstandardized use of characters from the old Grantha script for Sanskrit words, which abound here—various archaic linguistic elements, phonological idiosyncrasies, and dialectical features such as medial palatalized dental clusters, as in modern colloquial speech.[49] Indeed, colloquial language could be said to haunt the formal language of the inscriptions, especially in syntax, in marked contrast with the convoluted courtly poetic idiom.

Apart from these particularities, of great interest to historical linguists, one senses at once the expressive force of the new prose and its ability to convey precise information with great lucidity, as in a legal document. There is no space to demonstrate in detail; we will return to the issue of prose when we reach early-modern times. For now, we need to keep it in mind as another achievement of the Chola literati whose fate was linked to both court and temple.[50]

## Kamban's View of Truth

These two domains, though profoundly intertwined in ways I have mentioned, remained distinct. The Chola king was never a god, as his palace was no temple; only much later, in Nāyaka times, from the sixteenth century on, did the two realms begin to coincide.[51] We can thus identify literati of the court as differentiated from those primarily linked with the temples, the latter group, in general, privileged over the former in the eyes of the literary tradition, especially as it developed in the medieval mutts, the prestigious academies of Tamil erudition and instruction. We saw that even Cekkiḻār, a court poet responsive to royal commissions, supposedly crossed the line and composed his great work in the Cidambaram shrine. But the finest example we have in this period of an early temple poet is that of Kamban, whom many, myself included, would crown as the most gifted of all Tamil authors. To be precise: Kamban tells us, every thousandth verse or so, that he was patronized by one Caṭaiyaṉ or Caṭaiyappaṉ of Tiruvenneynallur—probably a wealthy local noble. But this connection is not enough to make Kamban a court poet: his entire poetic endeavor is addressed to the god, Vishṇu-Rāma, and this deity's devotees. The tradition identifies Kamban as an *uvaccaṉ*, a non-Brahmin priest, probably at a temple for the goddess Kāḷi. We are also told that after his competition with Ŏṭṭakkūttar to produce a Tamil *Rāmāyaṇa*, which Kamban won by improvising a verse from a point toward the climax of the long story,[52] he had to rush to complete the whole work, some 10,000 verses—and this he did in a mere two weeks at the temple in Tiruvorriyur,[53] writing day and night, with the goddess Kāḷi herself holding up flaming torches for him in the dark.

Kamban belongs to the Chola heartland, specifically to the temple site of Teraḻuntur, where his image is carved on the inner wall of the *gopuram* and local tradition claims him as its own. We think, on the basis of very fragmentary evidence and, more to the point, because of his stylistic indebtedness to predecessors such as Nammāḻvār and the Jain poet Tiruttakkatevar (see below, "The Inner Borders"), that he may have lived during the twelfth century. For our purposes, the central point is Kamban's unique gift of articulating, as none before him, the great themes of Chola-period Tamil civilization. Among these one might list the mysteries and tensions of kingship and of power, which we touched on above; a deep exploration of the south Indian person as a complex entity, rife with intuitive feeling and knowing *(uṇarvu),* structured around the *uyir* and driven by an urge to self-knowledge; and the meaning and pragmatics of beauty, including the distinctive wonders of the classic south Indian landscapes, strikingly developed in a departure from the Sangam poetic grammar. There is no space to explore these here. Instead, I want to concentrate on a theme close to our concern with the Tamil language and its vicissitudes over time, as well as with perspectives on language generally, internal to the Tamil erudite and literary traditions. Kamban is clearly fascinated with the properties of speech as a vehicle for truth, especially truth of a special kind. He is also interested in expressive silence.

This question of true speech *(vāymŏḻi)*[54] is a Chola-period obsession. Nammāḻvār's central work, the *Tiruvāymŏḻi,* proudly bears this word as its title. True speech is not, of course, disconnected from ideas about gods and goddesses, in particular an embodied god like Rāma, more or less at home in the human world, or a village goddess heavily invested in Tamil poetry. One might think that truth is a universal concept not in need of further, local characterization. There is truth and there is untruth, and the difference between them is, we could imagine, clear in every culture. But in fact the notion of truth or truthfulness is *always* culturally determined. The Greeks called truth *aletheia,* a "nonforgetting" or "noninattention," and linked it with unveiling, penetrating past the shimmering surface. Tamil conceptions of truth are quite different. They are, above all, dependent on ideas about the autonomy and integrity of the spoken, audible (musical) word that, once uttered, will always live out its life in the world independent of the speaker's will. Thus truth is connected to sound—specifically, to the phonemes of the Tamil language—and what sound can do in, or to, a world that is itself made up of sonic forces, inaudible quivers, subtle buzzes. This set of ideas is also, of course, tied to the realms of poetry and grammar.

This theme is most powerfully stated and restated in Kamban's Book II, the *Ayodhyā-kāṇḍa,* where Lord Rāma, on the eve of his coronation, is sent off to the wilderness for fourteen years by his father, Daśaratha, complying with the demand of Queen Kaikeyī. (Incidentally, Rāma knows Tamil, perhaps as his mother tongue, as we shall see.) Long ago, at a critical moment, Daśaratha had promised Kaikeyī two boons, to be actualized at her convenience. She has waited many long years, and now she activates the gift; she wants her own son, Bharata, crowned instead of Rāma, and she wants Rāma to be sent away. Daśaratha feels he has to agree, though in doing so he will die.

We will have a look at three short passages, rich enough, I hope, to give you some sense of Kamban's conceptual world as well as of his poetic textures and techniques. Although the story came to Kamban from Vālmīki's Sanskrit *Rāmāyaṇa,* it assumes the contours of a Tamil story, suffused by a south Indian metaphysics of effective speech. Consider how Kamban handles the critical moment just after Kaikeyī asks her husband to grant the boons. Daśaratha is in shock; his family priest, Vasishṭha, is present, trying to comfort and encourage him. At this critical moment, words and their eerie power loom large in everyone's mind:

> As the venom in the words of the woman
> who was poison in spate abated slightly,
> the king spoke the name of the son he loved
> and breathed again.
>
> Vasistha saw it and said, "Master! Put aside
> this great sorrow. The prince will rule this land
> in the pride of manhood. What obstacle can intervene?
> She who spoke those inglorious words will herself
> give him the crown. If this one black as a raincloud[55]
> were to refuse it and go away, would we go on living?
> Suffer no more."

The king looked at the sage. "Master," he said,
"before I die, heavy with unthinkable deeds,
make *him* wear the great crown,
make him stop thinking of the wilderness,
and save me from the shame
*that rests in my words.*"

The sage looked straight at the fierce woman
who had done the hateful deed. "Now," he said,
"golden lady, won't you give back the kingdom
to your son who is the breath of life to all of us,
above all to your husband who holds fast
to Manu's way, and thus win a good and holy name,
free from blame?"

He spoke, who had cut off karma at the root,
and she wept, gasping for breath, as she said,
"If the king swerves from truth, I will have no desire
to go on breathing or living in this world. To ensure
that my word does not turn to a lie,
I will die."[56]

We can deduce from the final, agonizing verse a rough definition of truth, *mĕy* (in this case; but truth in Tamil is also *mĕymai, vāymŏḻi,* and *uṇmai,* from the root *uḷ,* "to exist," discussed in Chapter 1). Kaikeyī has been speaking; she is the immediate cause of the whole disaster, a form of poison or death itself. Yet Kaikeyī is also weeping. She will get what she thought she wanted; ostensibly, she should be satisfied, even happy. Why, then, these sobs and tears? "If the king swerves from truth, I will have no desire to live on in this world." Her husband, whom she has effectively destroyed—and she knows it, even before the sage Vasishṭha tells her so explicitly—has uttered words that have the unerring force of truth. If he swerves from these words, if he takes them back, if he finds some excuse (as Vasishṭha is begging him to do, offering one rationalization after another), then she, Kaikeyī, will have no option except to die in order to preserve *her* truth, to keep it from becoming a lie. It's a zero-sum game: either she or Daśaratha will have to go. Truth has a potentially tragic tinge to it, once it has been spoken. Kaikeyī says this in the strongest possible way in Tamil, a double negation (litotes): literally, "I cannot not die." Two no's are, in Sanskrit and Tamil, much more than a single yes.

Interestingly, this last verse makes the connection between truth—that is, true speech—and the breath of life, *uyir*. Any impairment of the former will immediately impinge on the latter. The two are, in a way, one. Both have an inner quality and a regular and necessary rhythm: *uyir*, the unitary, godly force that moves in and out of all bodies and that also lives and breathes on the level of the cosmos itself, will be fatally compromised if *mĕy*, that inner truthfulness inherent in any spoken word, is blocked, prevented from moving or flowing or dancing in its natural sequence and direction. The sound that has been uttered aloud sets in play an entire field of energies and potential events. You can't take the sound back, you can't withdraw it into the zone of preart-iculate latency, you can't cross it or shape it or channel it at your will. You have to live it out, with its consequences.

This notion of irreversible, consequential utterance is not, of course, limited to Tamil and other south Indian languages, though it does assume a particular prominence there. Sanskrit, too, knows of speech acts that generate transformative processes that cannot be halted; usually such acts are classed as curses or blessings, and the appropriate verb is Sanskrit *śap*—to take an oath, to speak in heightened ways, to impinge verbally upon the world. The verb made its way into Tamil, too. Curses, however, can be, and indeed usually are, modified post factum. Kamban's concept of consequential language is of a different order. Any truly uttered set of sounds must enact their meaning. In fact, "meaning" may be the least of it. Truth language is, at base, not propositional in the usual sense.[57] It is something lived; something touched by the extraordinary. Hence the enormous danger attendant upon someone who denies his or her true speech.

In the corresponding passage in Vālmīki's Sanskrit *Rāmāyaṇa* (2.17–23), Daśaratha's irreversible promise to Kaikeyī is also linked to truth, *satya*, including the notion of keeping one's word; also to what Rāma himself calls *daivo bhāvaḥ* or *kṛtânta* (22.15–16), a fateful mode of existence built into the very operation of the cosmos. Words and sounds are a fundamental aspect of this dimension of fatedness, which also extends to what could be called "character," that is, one's personal responsibility for what one says and does. But the south Indian notion of audible sound as a force almost independent of intention has a more focused and specific sense that turns up in the medieval grammars, as we will see. Tamil words often hover over the boundary of life and death.

Thus when Rāma's mother, Kausalyā, arrives at the palace and takes in the grim scene we have just observed, she quickly realizes that a devastating and irreparable word has been uttered:

> She knew: It was all the doing
> of the other wife. The king had granted her wishes,
> but his heart couldn't take it. She wanted to comfort him
> by saying, "He'll come back"—but she hesitated
> at the thought that the king would break his word.
>
> *She said to him, suffering as he suffered: "Great one,*
> *if you fail to hold fast to unerring truth, your greatness,*
> *that no one can deny, will turn to disgrace. If you are weakened*
> *by love that can't face separation from your son, the world*
> *won't approve."*
>
> In agony good Kausalyā thought: "Our son won't
> not go, and the king can't not die." Tormented
> by what could happen to the king's good name, she couldn't
> ask him to hold back the prince. She groaned in pain.
>
> Listening to her words, the king understood. "Our son,
> celebrated in words, will not wed
> the earth. He will certainly leave
> for the wilderness." Grief overwhelmed him,
> and he cried: "Come help me, heavy with deeds,
> Oh my son, Oh my friend. Why won't you come?"[58]

We can see how everyone who is caught up in this dark moment is struggling with the notion of truth and its cost—truth both in the transparent sense of acting out a promise, not slipping away from the commitment that the spoken word implies, but also in a deeper, less obvious meaning. Truth is "unerring" *(taḷḷā nilai cāṉ mĕymmai).* It is Kausalyā's son who will be leaving for the wilderness, but she recognizes that the king has to keep his word; the opposite of truthfulness, in this sense, is *iḻivu,* "disgrace," a concept that belongs most naturally to the ancient world of heroic values in which fame, *pukaḻ,* ranks first. Rāma, too, is "celebrated in words" *(urai cāl),* as a hero should be; were he not to fulfill his father's command, his fame, and thus his very existence, would be vitiated. We are clearly still dealing with the oral, audible, spoken or sung word that is, by definition, beyond proof or disproof. Such a word, which has issued out of a prearticulate zone and now exists as an object of sorts in the world, has a life of its own.

In fact, it would be fair to say that such a word, *urai, cŏl,* is the object par excellence in this Tamil world. It is words that create externality and, as a result, objective reality; the metaphysics and poetics of true speech are here, as elsewhere in south India, entirely objective. A medieval Tamil poetics is *not* about subjective experience but about hard facts—word facts, let us call them (rather like Sanskrit *padârtha,* "object," literally the meaning of a word). Such objects are always linked to in-ness—that is, to the interiority of the speaker—in overdetermined ways. The ancient poetic grammar of in-ness has thus evolved to the point where it can incorporate a strong language-oriented aspect.

There is a temporal dimension to this kind of language. A spoken word like Daśaratha's to Kaikeyī holds a deep future within it even though it belongs to a fast-receding past. That future preexists by virtue of its articulation, though it is susceptible to diversion or distortion. We also note a profound correspondence between the spoken syllable, especially in its primary or presemantic musicality, and the rest of continuously emergent reality. Once again let me stress that such a syllable is a fact within the field of forces that is our life.

To repeat: you cannot negate the linguistic force already set loose in the world, with or without the speaker's intention. Not to carry through on such an utterance is to lie, in an incorrigible sense touching on the very aliveness of the speaker, on his or her inner core, the *uyir.* The catastrophe that follows upon lying thus reflects a notion of language as a domain where nothing accidental can occur. The syllable lives and breathes, like the breath of life that keeps the cosmos in motion. To interfere with that internal rhythm is to invite entropic forces into the heart of what, or who, is real and, like anything real, alive. A linguistic metaphysics of this kind is present to some degree in all the south Indian cultures and the literatures they produced; it exists in Tamil from the earliest strata we have, and we shall see that it dominates the Chola *pāṭṭ'iyal* handbooks. Earlier we witnessed the vast power vested in a good Tamil poet who speaks or sings his verses aloud.[59]

The question of speaking comes up again, with a slight twist, a little farther along in the text. Rāma's brother, Lakṣmaṇa, is infuriated when he hears the news; he wants to kill Kaikeyī and her son, Bharata, now supposedly the king to be. Rāma holds him back:

> "Brother, will your rage subside only after
> you go to war against our younger brother,
> who lives the good way that holds madness at bay,
> or after you've triumphed over our one father,
> whom great ones praise, or after conquering
> the woman who gave us birth?"
>
> He [Rāma] knew what to say;[60] he was good with words.
> His brother said: "I've borne words spoken
> by our enemies. Weary, I bear two tall rocks
> you can call my arms. I was born to bear
> this quiver and this bound bow. What use, now,
> is my fury?"
>
> "To take the kingdom against the word of our father
> who spoke only good words, who cared for me
> and raised me, can't be right. And what advantage
> is there for you in acting against *my* word?"
> Thus spoke the man who had gone to the end
> of southern speech[61] and learned the northern wisdom
> to its limit.[62]

Note the emphasis here on "me," "*my* word": it is Rāma's own speech, together with the words he got from his father, that are at stake. A highly personal quality attaches itself to the notion of Rama's verbal truth, and to the possibility of going against or beyond it. Indeed, this question of "going beyond" *(kaṭantu)* is critical here; clearly, it is not some kind of technical transgression but something deeply related to the very core of the person who speaks. Rāma could, in theory, go against or beyond his word, and Lakshmaṇa could also cross Rāma's word, which would, in effect, mean crossing his own words—but we already know what the cost of this act would be. Not by chance, in Rāma's case, we are talking about Tamil words, which seem, however, to be informed by northern wisdom. Rāma is a native speaker of Tamil.

To understand the deeper reaches of Kamban's understanding of truth-in-language, we would have to consider his fascination with laconic utterance, ellipsis, and silence—the latter seen as yet another, pregnant kind of speech, indeed perhaps the truest, most expressive, emotionally complex speech of all, *vāymŏḻi.* For now, sadly, I will have to leave this statement itself as an ellipsis.

What have we learned about the idea of truth in Chola-period Tamil Nadu? Here is a brief summary, derived from the passages we have just read but strongly resonant with our earlier discussions of in-ness, grammar, and the role of *uyir* in fashioning a person. Truth is, first and foremost, aural, audible, and musical; also largely noncognitive or supra-epistemic, a personal, individual matter, not readily generalized, linked to the interior and to breath. It is something that is made through speech, not merely revealed or discovered, but it is capable of being vitiated by its opposite, a lie. Truth is thus, at times, existentially fragile, dependent upon further decisions, acts, and words. It is, above all, a human business and, as such, close to the god. In Rāma's case, possibly amenable to being generalized, truly true speech apparently takes place (only) in Tamil.

## The Inner Borders: Jains and Buddhists

When the time came for the first public recitation *(araṅkeṟṟam)* of Kamban's *Rāmāyaṇa,* so the tradition tells us, and the major Vishṇu temple of Srirangam was chosen for the venue, the priests at the temple had some objections: "If the poem was in Sanskrit, we'd have no cause for concern; but as it is in Tamil, we cannot pronounce upon your competence." Another problem they raised was the presence of the few scattered verses in praise of Kamban's patron, Caṭaiyappaṉ; this looked like the sin of *nara-stuti,* praising a human being rather than the god. (We see here the categorical quandary mentioned above: Kamban is an early temple poet who nonetheless was supported by a local patron.)

The Srirangam priests demanded that the poet provide them with written consent *(kaiyŏppam)* to the planned event on the part of groups from a wide spectrum of Tamil society: courtesans, artisans, the Śaiva Dīkshitar priests of Cidambaram, the kings of the Tamil country and far beyond it, the poet's own extended family (embodied by his son, Ampikāpati), and the learned Jains in the village of Tirunarunkontai. The Jains raised some fussy objections to parts of Kamban's work; the poet answered these skillfully. They then wanted to know if the Jains, too, were mentioned in the book. Kamban recited verse 6.27.56, describing the gods' ecstasy at the death of Rāvaṇa's son, Indrajit, in battle:

> When the finest archer of all perished in battle, the gods
> were overjoyed: "The rule of this King of Lanka
> won't last!" They stripped off their fine clothes and shouted
> like an assembly of gods worshiped by those who vowed
> never to kill.[63]

Digambara Jains are "clothed only by sky," thus a useful image at this moment of rejoicing. Although the story probably belongs to the late-medieval period, its vision of an integrated social world gathering around a great work of Tamil poetry is well suited to the ethos of Chola times. It is of some importance that this social spectrum includes representatives of the heterodox communities, despite the highly negative image these groups, primarily Jains and Buddhists, assume in canonical Tamil *bhakti* works. Tamil devotional religion rendered the boundaries between Vedic and anti-Vedic currents in the far south crisp and heavy with consequence; Tamil Śaivism, in particular, assumed a proselytizing stance appropriate to the burning, exclusive vision of its founding personae—one of whom, Appar, is supposed to have chosen Śiva over the Jain path recommended by his sister. But we know that the Jains maintained a conspicuous profile within the Tamil world, and that they were, above all, associated with deep learning and the transmission of precious texts. A Chola-period poet with universalist ambition could not ignore them.

The Jains were also strongly linked with Tamil literary and scholarly production. They made conspicuous contributions to certain scholarly domains, such as metrics *(yāppu)*, lexicography, and grammar.[64] That is one way to put it; we would perhaps do better to speak in terms of a generalized cultural ecology in which Jains and Buddhists were natural and integral players, no doubt with their own agendas and collective identity issues, and certainly with their own vision of what constitutes a Tamil tree of knowledge.

Along with the prominent Jain scholars of Tamil, we have Tamil Jain poets of the first order, with a dense concentration of literary activity in the early Chola period. One major narrative work, the *Vaḷaiyāpati,* has been lost (the great Chola court poet, Ŏṭṭakkūttar, is supposed to have been fond of it). Two others should be mentioned: Tolāmŏḻittevar composed the massive and largely unstudied *Cūḷāmaṇi,* "Crest-Jewel," with an imaginative *Märchen*-like plot, perhaps in the mid-to-late tenth century; and, from roughly the same time, there is a strange blend of narrative and philosophy, the *Nīlakeci,* in which a famous Tamil demoness is eventually converted to Jain-style nonviolence.[65] But the true masterpiece of Jain Tamil is the long narrative *kāvya* by Tiruttakkatevar, the *Cīvaka-cintāmaṇi,* "Jīvaka the Wishing-Stone," which may well have served as a poetic model for both Kamban and Cekkiḻār; there is reason to date it, too, in the early- or middle-Chola time.

"Jīvaka the Wishing-Stone" tells the story of its irresistible, much-married hero Cīvakan (Jīvaka),[66] who falls in love with and quickly makes love to every beautiful woman he encounters over 3,145 exquisitely crafted verses. The plot is derived from earlier Jain sources in Sanskrit and Prakrit, though the text as we have it is saturated with the Tamil milieu, and a particular Tamil literary dialect, of the late first millennium—more specifically, with the culture of a south Indian urban and mercantile setting.[67] We can read it as one of the most trenchant testimonies we have to rapid Chola-period urbanization and its links to international sea trade—this despite the somewhat superficial courtly setting of the story, which belongs, first and foremost, to the literary stratum we call *kathā,* "story." *Kathā,* a pan-Indian generic classification, reveals a world of racy narratives that mostly take place in towns and cities and involve practical, earthy, multilingual heroes such as merchants, artisans, and artists, including (above all) polished courtesans.[68] The presence of such alluring women in this urban setting, and in the text, is striking; there is a tradition that 445 of the verses were composed by a poetess named Kantiyār, and indeed the final verses of the work tell us that Tiruttakkatevar was the author of only 2,700 of the poems in this text.[69] The book contains perhaps the finest verbal articulations of musical experience as well as some of the most lyrical descriptions of love-making in all of Tamil literature—and thus offers a corrective to prevalent scholarly views of the Jain ethos as austerely ascetic. Even when Cīvakaṉ finally gives up on life in the world and gives himself to the pursuit of release, the poet describes this moment as his wedding with Miss Freedom *(kevala maṭantai),* followed by an ecstatic honeymoon (*iṉpakkaṭaliṉuṇ mūḻkiṉāṉe,* verse 3117). Not for nothing does the Tamil tradition call this work *Maṇanūl,* "the book of weddings."

I'd like to give you a taste of the imaginative-artistic life in one of the Chola cities—say, the great port of Nakapattinam, mentioned earlier—before we move on to somewhat more technical issues raised by this long poem, which, as hinted above, is at least a half-sister of Kamban's *Rāmāyaṇa.* Let us go to a concert. A merchant named Cītattaṉ has come back from a perilous sea voyage (in which his ship was, in fact—or rather, in apparent fact—swallowed by the ocean) with a beautiful young woman, Kāntaruvatattai, daughter of the king of the celestial Vidyādhara musicians and magicians. She is to be married to whoever can defeat her in a music contest. Many suitors try their luck and fail; Kāntaruvatattai has a consummate command of the veena. Now it is our hero Cīvakaṉ's turn to sing and play. Trees and rocks melt as they hear the notes of his veena; gods and human beings faint in wonder. Looking straight at the young woman, clearly aiming his song at her heart, Cīvakaṉ sings three captivating verses, ostensibly spoken by the girl friend of the beloved in mild reproach of the hero and with the aim of preventing him from going away:[70]

Need I say  
that when lightning roars in the rain,  
a little snake shivers in fear?  
Need I say  
that she, breasts chafing

under strings of gold, is sick
with lightning and with rain?

Need I say that when rain pours from cloud,
a waterfall rumbles on the hill?
Need I say that when she sees
a waterfall on the hill,
her heart breaks, hungry for you?

Need I say that when it rains,
jasmine blossoms in the forest
like stars in the sky?
Need I say that she grieves,
her hair flowing with honey,
when she sees the forest in bloom? (724–26)

These verses share the formal grammar of the Sangam *akam* poems, with their standard *dramatis personae:* the hero, the heroine, her girlfriend, and the active and expressive natural world attuned to the heroine's inner state. Yet how different these poems are, how comparatively straightforward, barely resonant with suggestion but precise in their observation and their laconic description of the world and its seasons. The words may well be secondary to the music, which we can no longer hear; but still we can understand Cīvakaṉ's message, though it is couched in a female voice—a message of longing and pain, including the pain that inheres in beauty, but also the promise of flowering and maturing. Kāntaruvatattai understands it well. The words and the melody, she thinks, are like a hawk and its shadow (730); she knows she has been defeated, and now she takes up her veena and sings in response, this time in the voice of the desperate beloved herself:

My breasts, covered with jewels shaped like leaves,
and my brow, a bent bow, are pallid with love.
The waterfall on the hill gleams like a sword.
Tell me, my sweet-spoken friend: can *he*
fail to see? (732)

And so on, repeating, like Cīvakaṉ's song, the basic image over three verses. The waterfall cuts through her like a sword, like the haunting music: can't he see that she is his? Can he still contemplate going away?

The answer is yes. Cīvakaṉ is always going away, always moving on to the next beguiling beauty. And for all the rich eroticism of the text, there is often a tinge of Jain melancholy, as when Kāntaruvatattai's father, sending her off by sea to the contest that will produce a husband for her, tells her sorrowing mother:

*muṉivarum poka pūmip poka'muṭṭātu pĕṟṟum*
*taṉiyavarāki vāḻtal cātuyar ataṉiṉ illai*
*kaṉipaṭu kiḷaviyar taṅkatalar kavaṉiṟ ṟuñciṟ*
*paṉiyiru vicumpiṟ ṟevar pāṉmayiṟṟ' ĕṉṟu cŏṉṉāṉ*

Even if they enjoy the pleasures
of our almost immortal world,[71]
young women with soft, sweet voices
still suffer loneliness and the pain of dying.
There's no other way.
If they sleep twined into their lovers,
they'll at least share the happiness
of gods high in the cool sky. (553)

The father continues: "Who can avert his (or her) lot?" (*pāṉmai yār vilakkukiṟpār,* 554). Suffering is structured into existence, even in the worlds of superhuman species; in the end, everyone dies, with the same dread and suffering. There are, no doubt, those sages and ascetics who give themselves to the strict practices that may provide freedom from this given template; as we saw, Cīvakaṉ himself will eventually join them. But in the meantime—so the girl's father says, with a gentle humaneness—there is every reason to seek even the transient comfort and joy that sexual love can offer. This Tamil Jainism seems capacious enough to contain both the pathos of universal sorrow and the embodied passion that, in theory—but apparently only in theory—nurtures and intensifies that sorrow. This complex, moving tone is sustained throughout the three thousand musical verses of the *Cintāmaṇi.*

Clearly, something significant has shifted in the mainstream ethos of Tamil poetry. We find ourselves in a distinct, novel aesthetic world built up of the now prevalent metrical-poetic form of elastic *viruttam* verses. *Viruttam,* as we have seen, can accommodate many meters, including experimental rhythmic lines, sung in accordance with the personal choices and emphases of the performer. Tiruttakkatevar did not invent *viruttam* recitation, but he extended its use and stretched its expressive capacities to hitherto unknown heights. In this, he both helped create a new, rival Tamil canon, as we shall see, and opened a path for later large-scale Tamil narrative poetry in general. He also produced a template for the early Tamil poetic encyclopedia: his immense *kāvya* offers its listeners or readers large chunks of erudite discourse crystallizing at this period in a range of fields—practical wisdom *(nīti)*, a hallmark of the proto-urban *kathā* style; philosophical debate; erotics; and an astonishing series of technical domains, each with its own vocabulary, specific to nautical navigation and shipbuilding, urban architecture, specialized aspects of painting and music (including the crafting of musical instruments), the art and techniques of writing, and warfare, among many others.

For a modern reader, even someone as adept as the work's first editor, U. Ve. Caminat'aiyar, there are constant lexical challenges in this book; Caminat'aiyar tells us in his autobiography that he had to seek out the Tamil-speaking Jains of Kumbhakonam in order to understand the language of the text.[72] Moreover, the nonstandard (community-based) dialect is only one aspect of Tiruttakkatevar's idiosyncratic Tamil; archaic and exotic morphology, evident everywhere in this work, is yet another marker of its distinctiveness and of the flexible rules of high literary Tamil in Chola times.

Of particular relevance to this level of a reorganized cultural ecology is the story that has come down to us about the relation of "Jīvaka the Wishing-Stone" to the older Sangam world with its inherited poetic grammar. Caminat'aiyar tells us the story, garnered orally from Jain Tamils in the second half of the nineteenth century, as follows:

> Tiruttakkatevar, born in the Chola lineage, was educated as a young boy in classical Tamil literature and grammar as well as in Sanskrit and Jain texts. He took the vow of renunciation and found a teacher, with whom he came to Madurai in the Pandya country. There he was allowed by his teacher to attend literary discussions in the Sangam; he became close to these great poets.
>
> After some time they said to him: "No Jain poet has ever written a book in praise of sexual love." He said: "It's not because they don't

know about this subject, but only because they find the topic unpalatable." "In that case," the poets said to him, "*you* should write such a book."

The young man returned to his teacher to ask permission. The teacher put him to a test: seeing a running jackal, the teacher asked his student to produce a short work about jackals. Tiruttakkatevar at once improvised the fifty-one-verse text known as the *Jackal Poem, Nari-viruttam,*[73] highlighting themes of bodily impermanence and the instability of wealth. Now the teacher, certain that his pupil was properly oriented toward renunciation, commanded him to accept the Sangam poets' commission and to compose a book about Cīvakaṉ. The teacher also composed an invocation verse for the start of the long poem; but when he heard Tiruttakkatevar's own verse of blessing, the teacher asked that the latter stand first, and that *his* poem come second.

Tiruttakkatevar composed the *Cīvaka-cintāmaṇi* in eight days and brought it to his teacher who, astonished by its beauty, added the colophon verse (3143) and sent the author to recite his book in the presence of the Sangam poets at the court of the Pandya king. They liked it, and the king praised it, too.

But among the poets there were some who had doubts. How could a man who had renounced the world in his youth describe sexual passion so deftly? He must have had some personal experience of "minor ecstasy" *[ciṟṟ'iṉpam].* Tiruttakkatevar had a ball of iron heated in flames; he swore an oath—"If I renounced the world as a young boy, may this not burn me"—then took the heated iron in his hand and touched his tongue to it, without pain. The doubters asked forgiveness for their mistake. Tiruttakkatevar took leave of the Sangam and returned to his teacher.[74]

The story situates the poet within the long tradition of Indian works on erotics; thus Vātsyāyana, the author of the *Kāma-sūtra,* tells us at the end of his book that the entire effort of composing it was only an exercise in Yoga and self-control. The Tamil Jains found a similar tension in the "Wishing-Stone" between "great" and "minor" ecstasy. But for our purposes, the more interesting point follows from the attempt, or need, to bring this poet and his book within the purview of the Madurai Sangam and its royal patron. A nominally heterodox stream of Tamil art and learning is retrospectively validated by the two primary institutions of authority within Tamil letters—the respected community of scholar-poets and the Madurai court and its connoisseur king. The Jain origin story about this great book requires that kind of formal authorization; at the same time, it clearly suggests that Tiruttakkatevar has changed Tamil poetry from within, at once infiltrating the ancient canon and altering its modes and rules. And while this popular story is undoubtedly an ex post facto rationalization and expressive commentary on the text, the same thrust toward expansion and conceptual revision of the classical canon can be seen in Jain Tamil texts such as the *Neminātham* grammar and the commentary on the fundamental textbook of metrics, *Yāpp'aruṅkalam,* both belonging to this period.

We also see it clearly in the important Chola-period Buddhist Tamil grammar, *Vīracoḻiyam,* by Puttamittiraṉ, lucidly and subtly analyzed by Anne Monius. The *Vīracoḻiyam,* probably dated to the reign of its eponymous king, Vīrarājendra (1063–1070),[75] is usually seen as the first fully Sanskritized Tamil grammar—a thoroughgoing exercise in reformulating the primary definitional and derivational procedures of grammar to match the categories and methods of the Sanskrit Pāṇiniyan school. Not only does it summarize phonology and morphology in the light of Sanskrit technical terms and, more important, conceptual modes,[76] but it also explicitly tells us that its analysis of poetic figures and styles—a hypertrophied topic within this grammar—follows the method of Daṇḍin, the Pallava-period author of the foundational Sanskrit work, *Kāvyâdarśa* (discussed in Chapter 3, "North and South").[77]

Poetics thus breaks out of the ancient framework laid down in the *Tŏlkāppiyam* and the *Grammar of Stolen Love* and, among other innovations, reorients itself toward an analytical definition of major figures in Daṇḍin's now widely accepted style. Such an analysis effectively supersedes the old fascination with the five landscapes and their associated phases in the parallel domains of love and war; as Monius rightly states, it also points the way toward the full Tamil version of Daṇḍin's book, the *Taṇṭiyalaṅkāram,* probably completed in the mid-twelfth century.[78] In other words, the very subject matter of poetics has now been radically altered; a new way of understanding poetry is taking over the Tamil literary world, with tremendous consequences for the later history of this science—although the old south Indian notion that grammar exists largely in order to serve poets and their audience is still intact. As we will see in Chapter 5, the *Vīracoḻiyam* is also the first Tamil text to define the emergent stylistic and literary category known as Maṇi-pravāla, "Ruby and Coral," a profound mixing of Sanskrit and Tamil both in technical and far-reaching aesthetic ways.[79]

It is tempting to characterize this maverick grammatical text, so conspicuously at odds with the earlier traditions of Tamil grammar, as embodying a vector of consistent "Sanskritization," that is, as integrating a richly elaborated domain of Sanskrit erudition into Tamil scientific discourse. In a certain sense, this way of stating things is correct. But it is also a little misleading, insofar as it feeds into the misguided notion that some relatively autonomous, indigenous Tamil system of grammar and poetics, largely free from Sanskrit influences, was now coming under the sway of northern, hence foreign, theories. We have to keep in mind that Sanskrit is present in Tamil from the start, as the mature tale of origins itself tells us,[80] and as we can see at once from the earliest grammars and the body of literature they address. The very term "Sanskritization" drives us toward an unnecessary, stark dualism, itself foreign to the Tamil tradition, with implications of mutual exclusivity; it also reduces our descriptive capacity to impoverished notions of influence and assimilation.

This is not to say that relations between the two languages remained constant or stable in either practice or theory; they clearly did not, as we will see in Chapter 5. But the paradigm recently formulated by Andrew Ollett for the complex history of Sanskrit and Prakrit, in its various crystallized linguistic-literary forms,[81] holds true for the premodern multilingual south Indian system as well: Tamil (*tĕṉmŏḻi,* the southern language) and Sanskrit (*vaṭamŏḻi,* the northern language, or *āriyam,* as the commentators call it) constitute a set in which each language largely and intrinsically defines the other, each both contrasting with and complementing the other; the terms included in this dyadic set are mutually constitutive, "closely related to each other but contrasted across a number of dimensions."[82] Only such a perspective allows us to begin to chart the true intricacies of a single history and to define critical moments of change, including those times when highly specific Sanskrit contents, usually derived from a single text or textual corpus, were deliberately assimilated into the Tamil tradition. Such moments are sometimes referred to as a "second wave of Sanskritization,"[83] assuming an earlier, formative "wave" going back to Sangam times; this terminology makes sense if we think of discrete contents borrowed by Tamil science from known Sanskrit models and adapted to normative Tamil discourse.

The early-to-middle Chola period was clearly a moment of far-reaching systemic change. We have approached the problem of defining this change by looking at what happened to the literary canon—in particular, at the Jains' extension of the existing classical canon and at the revision of poetic norms in the Buddhist grammar of Puttamittiraṉ. Another way to state the matter is to observe the sudden proliferation of several competing canons of Tamil literature.[84] In Chapter 3 we saw how the two major bodies of Tamil *bhakti* poems, the Śaiva and Vaishṇava versions of a Tamil Veda and the later texts generated by and appended to such works, indeed underwent a process of canonization in Chola times; the key figures who traditionally embody this process are Nampi Āṇṭār Nampi and Nāthamuni, respectively.[85] We have also seen how the Sangam corpus achieved near-canonical form, including early editorial practices and initial commentary, by the end of the Pallava-Pandya period. In all three cases, we find the dense saturation with meaning and authority that typically goes with a crystallized canon, though with differential emphases. But we can now observe how the very idea of a canonical corpus becomes a focus for rival visions closely linked with distinctive communities. Later, the same kind of competition, extension, and effective recanonization will occur with the appearance of an Islamic literary corpus in Tamil.

In any case, both Jain and Buddhist commentators in Chola times clearly redraw the boundaries between what is inside and outside the canon. In effect, we now have not three but at least four rival canons, if we think of the Jain and Buddhist commentators as sharing a somewhat wider vision than that of their mainstream rivals. In this respect, the Tamil Jains must have derived their breadth of vision from a more general, pan-Indian Jain tendency toward a skeptical inclusivity, which required "taking different points of view into consideration," as Gary Tubb has shown.[86]

But the canon is only one, somewhat circumscribed, site in which the new intellectual currents come clearly into view. There are more powerful ways of addressing the transformation at the imperial moment in the Tamil country. We are now in a better position to understand what a word like "imperial" might really mean.

## The New Cultural Ecology

Why "imperial?" There is, of course, the Chola state, expanding rapidly in the early period, contracting and eventually disintegrating by the mid-thirteenth century. It would be a mistake to tie the fortunes of the Tamil language too closely to those of this state, although, as we have seen, the Chola kings and administrators did greatly extend the use of Tamil prose, and sometimes of poetry as well, in their inscriptions. Moreover, political conquest and maritime adventures unquestionably enhanced the cultural presence of Tamil in places far outside the Tamil country, especially in Sri Lanka and peninsular Southeast Asia.

But the deeper meaning of a word like "imperial" has to do with expansion of a different order. What we now observe is the emergence and self-definition of many distinctive arenas for Tamil cultural production, each with potentially universalist claims or pretensions, often in intense rivalry with one another and carried by competing elites. Intrinsic to such claims is the active presence of Sanskrit within Tamil, or even of literary Tamil as itself *saṃskrita,* in the sense of cultivated speech and creative composition of a certain intensity and power and endowed with a trans-local cachet.

This supra-local range of the language and its expressive forms—or the tremendous intensification of those forms to the point where Tamil can serve a universalist ethos—is at the heart of the new imperial program. It includes, indeed depends upon, features such as bold regrammaticalization, as in the case of the *Vīracoḻiyam* and the *Nemināthaṃ;* a revolution in taste; the appearance of heterogeneous canons, as noted above; and a restructuring of the cultural ecology as a whole. The boundaries of the Tamil social order have widened: Buddhists, Jains, Śaivas, Vaishṇavas, elite courtiers and village priests, deep-sea merchants, urbane courtesans, wandering shamans, proto-Tantric mystics—all these use the currency of elite Tamil to press their claims. At the same time, the geographic sphere within which Tamil functions as a powerful expressive medium is continuously expanding. We saw that Nannayya, the founding figure of Telugu poetry, working in the Andhra delta in the mid-eleventh century at the Eastern Calukya court, seems to see the Tamil Sangam corpus as a possible precedent for the poetic universe he is creating;[87] Pālkuṟiki Somanātha, a century later, actually composes in Tamil, Kannada, Marathi, and Sanskrit, as well as his main language, Telugu, within the compass of a single work;[88] and the narrative traditions of Tamil Śaiva religion found new homes, and new uses, throughout the Deccan, in the iconoclastic works of Telugu and Kannada poets. We will study the special case of Tamil in Kerala in Chapter 5.

These processes are bound up with the theme of vernacularization and regionalization, powerfully stated by Sheldon Pollock in his already classic work.[89] As Pollock himself notes, Tamil occupies a somewhat exotic position in relation to the India-wide movement toward the formation of vernacular literatures at the end of the first millennium A.D. and in the early centuries of the second.[90] The Tamil claim to venerable antiquity and the staggering richness of its first-millennium sources, along with the early, deep-rooted grammaticalization of the literary tradition, suggest that the creation of a strong regional culture self-consciously rooted in Tamil speech preceded by some centuries, at least, the wave of vernacularization that swept over other parts of south India. But Chola times did witness a process of elevating or extending "a long-standing regional literary language to translocal status," as Monius has shown us with reference to the *Vīracoḻiyam*.[91] Implicit in this process is a conception of Tamil as entirely commensurate with Sanskrit, including the whole of Sanskrit erudition, now fully active *within* the Tamil world of letters. For the *Vīracoḻiyam* author, "True Tamil is the Tamil that corresponds entirely to the linguistic and poetic frameworks of Pāṇini and Daṇḍin."[92] It is of some importance that such claims emerge initially within the heterodox traditions, with their marked universalistic orientation. But imperial Tamil, in the senses I have tried to define, is an achievement that cuts across sectarian, social, political, and geographical borders without suppressing the tensions among rival elites. A new, rather inclusive cultural ecosystem has come into being. Tamil has become a world language.

Look again at the newly emergent literary canons, especially those linked to both Buddhist and Jain literati. If we read the commentators, such as the Jain Kuṇacākarar on the textbook of metrics, *Yāpp'aruṅkala-kārikai*, or the Jain author of the *Virutti* on *Yāpp'aruṅkalam*, or the Buddhist Pĕruntevaṉār on *Vīracoḻiyam*, we see a shared pattern of wide-ranging citation from sources used to exemplify the rules of the parent text. These commentaries have been deeply studied by Anne Monius and Jennifer Steele Clare; both note the unusual scope of the exemplary verses, which are extracted not only from the hard-core classics of Sangam-period Tamil but also from the *Eighteen Minor Works* (most of them on the margins of the conventional canon), Sanskrit or Sanskrit-derived texts such as Daṇḍin's poetics, sectarian narrative poems such as the (lost) Buddhist *Kuṇṭalakeci*, the Jain *Cūḷāmaṇi*, and the *Cīvaka-cintāmaṇi*, moralistic or pragmatic how-to-live poetry from books such as *Tirukkuṟaḷ* and *Nālāṭiyār*, rare Śaiva texts, the Sanskrit epics or Tamil versions of them, and other texts of greater or lesser obscurity in the eyes of the mainstream tradition.[93] Pĕruntevaṉār himself also cites Amitacākarar, the author of the *Yāpp'aruṅkalam* and the *Yāpp'aruṅkalakārikai*, as well as the *Virutti* commentary on the former work.[94] Sectarian authors seem to be aware of one another and to have a similarly capacious library at their disposal.

Virtually everything that we have seen in this chapter points to a restructured and reconceived relation between the Tamil poet and Tamil audiences. Royal patrons are still prominent members of such audiences, but the new poetry presumes a much wider set of listeners or readers: Jain and Buddhist literati, whether monks or laymen (in the Tamil country or beyond it in Sri Lanka and the western Deccan); erudite craftsmen like the weavers and shipbuilders and architects we have seen at work; the composers, recorders, and consumers of stone and copper-plate inscriptions; Brahmin intellectuals both inside and outside the royal centers; theoreticians and grammarians of various rival traditions, well aware of the complex, multilingual currents now at work in the world of Tamil letters; and, without doubt, "floating" connoisseurs who may not fit easily into any such categories but who have access to the particular powers of Tamil speech, especially poetic utterance. This last group may be the most important for what lies in store. We have to assume that such connoisseurs have expectations that correspond to newly crystallizing forms of poetic praxis.

The most consequential point has to do with a revised aesthetic universe evolving organically in the course of the Chola centuries. Tamil literary expressivity now means something quite different from what we find in the earlier, classical corpus. Utterly new techniques of suggestion and, in particular, of figuration, clearly linked to the penetrating analysis of literary figures by Daṇḍin that has now made its way into Tamil, push aside, to some extent, the well-worn methods of the past. As usual, the poets are far ahead of the literary theorists; but theory, too, slowly begins to change. For example, there are striking instances where fragments of naturalistic vignettes from classical Sangam poems—where they originally served as elements in the suggestive "inscapes," *uḷḷuṟaiy uvamam*[95]—are extracted from their textual settings and combined to create a new poem, with the addition of a final line by the later poet-compiler. This technique, known as "mixing of lines" *(pāta-mayakku),* is perhaps a graphic equivalent to the oral practice we know as *samasyāpūraṇam,* often the creation of a new poem by cumulating lines from three or four poets around a single line or topic set by the patron.[96] Clare offers one remarkable example from the *Yāpp'aruṅkala Virutti.*[97] Naturalistic description, *svabhāvokti* or *taṉmaiyaṇi*—a very powerful, indeed fundamental, figure in its own right, perhaps inherent in all other ornaments—emerges as a defining feature of the new literary economy.[98]

This preference for the natural and real appears, not by coincidence, in the context of the commentators' concerns with complex metrical and phono-aesthetic effects. There is an intrinsic relation between these parallel vectors and also, historically speaking, a link with the ancient but still active tradition of Prakrit poetry. But there is also another, more powerful principle at work. On the one hand, the old grammar of *akam* and *puṟam* continued to generate new attempts at synthesis; thus we have Aiyaṉāritaṉār's *Puṟappŏruḷ vĕṇpā mālai* (possibly a ninth-century work), an exhaustive, updated compendium of "outer" themes together with illustrative verses that diverges to some extent from the

*Tŏlkāppiyam* conventions. On the other hand, we find a set of creative handbooks aimed at mapping the contours of literary practice on the basis of a new structural logic: these works are known collectively as *pāṭṭ'iyal,* "On the Nature of Poetry," and the earliest of them, the *Paṉṉiru pāṭṭ'iyal* and the *Vĕṇpā pāṭṭ'iyal* or *Vaccaṇantimālai* (by the Jain scholar Kuṇavīra Paṇṭitar), seem to belong to the Chola period. They have been studied by Clare, who notes their thorough cataloguing of Tamil genres, seen as such for the first time, according to meters, stanzaic or multi-stanzaic forms, and thematic contents. These new genres, the prototypes for what will come to be known as *prabandham* or *ciṟṟ'ilakkiyam,* "short literary works," are overwhelmingly focused on praise for the author's patron, whether human or divine.[99] However, the manifold textures of praise do not exhaust the expressive potential of these new forms, as we will see.

A significant part of the new governing logic of composition has to do with a principle of phono-pragmatics, with its associated metaphysical, or existential, phonology. Sounds—the syllables of Tamil speech—are meaningful not only in simple, or not-so-simple, referential ways. Compounded into words, sounds do have meanings, including, as we know, nonexplicit, indirect, suggestive meanings. But sounds also work on the world in entirely practical ways. They can bring blessing, auspiciousness, health, and wealth to a patron; they can also kill him or reduce him to sickness and poverty. There is, moreover, a science of phonic combinations that allows a sensitive poet to achieve such effects deliberately. A poet, as we have seen, has the ability to bless or to curse. (A little later he also becomes endowed with the useful auxiliary faculty of omniscience.)

By arranging the phonemes of a poetic line in a particular order, including their corresponding rhythmic and metrical characteristics, the poet releases sonic forces into the world. Once released—like the words of truth, *vāymŏḻi,* we saw in Kamban's *Rāmāyaṇa*—they work their magic; in principle, they can never be recalled. An entire aesthetic program is built up around these concepts, which are certainly ancient ones in south India, though never explicitly formulated in Tamil until the early second millennium A.D. They can be linked to the Vedic pragmatics of mantras; in another, probably more telling sense, they reflect a Tantric metaphysical and ritual cosmos that is more and more present within the Tamil cultural world.[100] Even more striking, however, is the prevalence of such theories of phono-pragmatic poetry throughout all the major south Indian literatures, perhaps most notably in Telugu and the handbooks of the Andhra poeticians of the fourteenth and fifteenth centuries, but also in Kannada and Malayalam.[101]

To speak of grammar is now also to take account of this new science of effective syllables. The *pāṭṭ'iyal* works deal in detail with these materials under the rubric of *pŏruttam,* "fitness," "correspondence"—that is, the corresponding effects of specific syllables, especially in the opening *(maṅgala)* words of a text, on the fate and nature of the poet's patron and, no less, on the poet's mastery of his or her medium.[102] Syllables thus have origins *(piṟappu)* in a certain divinity or divine realm. They are, so the texts say, like food, either ambrosial and beneficent or poisonous and lethal. They have differential effects on patrons of different genders, ages, and social positions. They are intimately linked with astral powers, with temporal rhythms, with sheer aesthetic experiences, with land and landscape and region—in short, with the entire organic web of a living, breathing cosmos on which the energy of even a single phoneme has an impact. A poet needs to know the whole range of such active forces; if he or she does have this particular kind of knowledge, then the divine realm, or even a palpable and effective divine identity, are not out of reach.

The poet's responsibility for what happens to his patron as a direct result of singing a poem is now immense. Thus the syllables *a, i, u, ĕ, ka, ca, ta, pa, na, ma,* and *va,* if used at the start of a verse or a long poem, are ambrosial, life-giving, replete with blessing.[103] In contrast, *ā, o,* the half-vowels *y, r,* and *l,* prosodic lengthening *(aḷavu),* and the rare fricative *āytam* when used in the patron's name, in initial position, are potentially fatal, or at the very least can set off fits of shaking.[104] Relations of friendship, indifference, or hatred between poet and patron, or perhaps even beyond this axis, can be determined by specific initial letters. And so on. The rules, seen as empirically based and put to concrete use by great poets from ancient times onward, have an astonishingly high resolution and a ramified complexity of application.

This is the stuff of poetry. It informed poetic production in Tamil, also in south Indian Sanskrit, Telugu, Kannada, and Malayalam, for the past thousand years, in different degrees of attention and commitment. It is implicit in the notion of the poet's enduring, autonomous truth. It inheres in the musicality that shapes every Tamil poem. It molds the image of the late-medieval Tamil poet and makes sense of that poet's multilingual range and cultural environment. It of course presumes and requires oral recitation: poetry has to be heard if it is to work its sorcery. There will always be other, more conventionally thematic drives in a poetic work; one cannot reduce poetry to a sonic calculus, a cosmo-phonetics to be manipulated by the skilled artist. But the incantational qualities of Tamil poetry should never be forgotten or set aside. They survive even into today's supposedly "secular" literary production. The cultural continuities between late-Chola times and our own generation are far more impressive than we usually recognize.

In practice, *pŏruttam*, "correspondence," though empirical and scientific, is never a mechanical set of equations and combinations. The governing principle is far more flexible and subtle than its bare rules of operation might suggest. Sound, especially when channeled, calibrated, and amplified by a Tamil poet, is capable of transforming many potential contexts ranging from the blessing that should open a work-in-recitation to a wide range of physical responses to the sung words on the part of the listener, and beyond that to what we might call intrapsychic or cognitive processes set in play by the marriage of sound and meaning. All such contexts of usage and performance are linked to a notion of truth. From the time of the *pāṭṭ'iyals* onward, a vast expressive range has opened up for the trained poet and his or her audience; also for the theoretician interested in studying these complex effects.

One sees at once how the ecosystem has rearranged itself around a field of newly defined genres, altered social or institutional settings (notably, diverse forms of personal patronage), and a wide metaphysical vision with pragmatic implications. Within the new order, we find a series of shifts in taste as well as in poetic theory. There is also room for experimentation with form and many formal features, as we will see in Chapter 5. And there is one further consequence of the process I have just described. The *pŏruttam* poetics ascribe and assume a critical cultural role for Tamil itself, including its phonemic and phonic structure, as world-creating, potentially world-changing, and thus godlike in its very nature. The syllables of Tamil are in no way less potent than those of Sanskrit, including mantric Sanskrit. The *pŏruttam* rules relate to Tamil but harmonize well with similar analytical lists for Sanskrit, such as we find in Viśveśvara's *Camatkāra-candrikā*, "Moonlight of Wonder" (late-fourteenth-century Telangana), and, somewhat later, for Telugu (Appakavi, seventeenth century). Particular identifications of phonic triggers and practical effects may vary among these works, but the underlying unity of purpose is evident. From this point onward, it is but a short step to thinking of Tamil as a living being, in fact a god or goddess.

Two of the grammatical books I have mentioned—the metrical treatise, *Yāpp'aruṅkala-kārikai* of Amitacākarar and the Buddhist grammar, *Vīracoḻiyam*—address the rules they are presenting to an internal listener, a beautiful young woman with long dark hair, golden bangles, and a mellifluous voice. Who is this enticing lady? Some think that she is an embodiment of the *kārikai* form of prescriptive (metrically fixed) verses itself; *kārikai,* in fact, means "young woman."[105] Others, such as Anne Monius, believe that the unnamed beauty is the Tamil language, as some of her epithets would indeed suggest: she is "divine speech" or "pure speech" (*temŏḻiye, tūmŏḻiye*) as well as a "lady of cool speech" *(paṉi-mŏḻiye).*[106] Perhaps the true and natural audience for a grammar is the grammaticalized language itself (herself). At the very least, this mysterious person is certainly a speaker of fine Tamil, as is the Chola king under whose rule the *Vīracoḻiyam* was composed.[107] A Tamil king should, indeed, have mastered Tamil no less than his royal realm. We have already seen that in Pandya-Pallava times the king, almost by definition, is a connoisseur of Tamil poetry, especially in the historic center of Tamil culture, the city of Madurai. The long imperial moment solidifies this bond between the political sphere and the musical and literary world even as pride in Tamil and a collective image of its unique beauty crystallize in explicit statements, both in poetry and in science. Tamil-ness, we could say, an idea rooted in linguistic reality and cultivated taste, has become an enduring cultural theme.

From roughly the mid-ninth to the mid-thirteenth century, the Tamil land and much of south India beyond it were incorporated within the large-scale polity of the Chola kingdom. Whether we understand the Chola state as a relatively loose configuration of localized alliances or as an increasingly centralized, bureaucratized, and regularized system—or perhaps as some mixture of these two ideal types—it is certain that under the Chola kings the Tamil language burst out of its original boundaries and became a cosmopolitan medium spoken in far-flung diaspora communities, from Sri Lanka to southern China. At the same time, in conjunction with this geographical expansion, Tamil became an "imperial" language in other ways, such as in its social and sectarian reach, in its self-understanding as a universal tongue easily on a par with Sanskrit, and in its ever-richer self-awareness as a heterogeneous tradition with competing canons and far-reaching metagrammatical features. To some extent, this imperial identity was linked to the deep internalization of Sanskritic erudite, especially grammatical and aesthetic-poetic, norms. Tamil and Sanskrit in south India are by now two magnetic poles within a single field of force. With the appearance of the new handbooks of genre-cum-poetics and the emergence of penetrating, sparkling commentaries on major works of grammar, including metrics, Tamil arts were effectively regrammaticized even as literary taste was radically revised.

These processes unfolded both within and beyond the royal court. Great poets such as Ŏṭṭakkūttar and Cayaṅkŏṇṭār celebrated the victories of their kings in a newly fashioned idiom of imaginative praise. The Chola kings also appear in traditional accounts as closely tied to Tamil literary production; Rājarāja Chola is credited by later authors with the recovery of the lost Śaiva *bhakti* corpus, while Vīrarājendra Chola lent his name to the Buddhist grammar, *Vīracoḻiyam.* The court and its attached literati charged with formulating inscriptions and having them inscribed on copper or stone generated Tamil prose of a new level of complexity, even as they extended the use of inscriptional Tamil to include the literary mode of *mĕykkīrtti,* that is, heroic panegyric.

But much happened outside the court or on its periphery: Cekkiḻār and Kamban are traditionally linked to temples; Ŏṭṭakkūttar sings not only of successive Chola kings but also, in his best work, of the goddess

Kāḷi in a proto-Tantric style. We should note that by late-Chola times temple goddesses were assuming a visibility adumbrating their primary cultural role in the centuries to come. It is not enough to judge their presence on the basis of the literary works alone; think of the great bronzes of Pārvatī and Bhadrakāḷi produced in the Kaveri delta during the tenth to thirteenth century, at the same time that master poets such as Tiruttakkatevar and Kamban were composing their long, encyclopedic texts.

Such works are profoundly concerned with language—with how truth, *vāymŏḻi,* can be embodied in words; with the suggestiveness of silence; with the intimate interweaving of Tamil and Sanskrit and the meaning of this deep-rooted amalgam; and with the incantational, effective character of Tamil phonemes when spoken or sung. Once these elements were in place within an expanding cultural and linguistic universe—a universe in which Tamilness itself was now a major theme to be explored—they were there to stay. A vast horizon had opened up, one shaped not by the imperial reach of the Chola armies and the high courtly culture of Tanjavur, but by the universalistic and cosmopolitan imperium of Tamil letters.

FIVE

# Republic of Syllables

## *Caraṇam* 2

### Who Knows Tamil?

Meet Black Cloud, Kāḷamekappulavar, a poet who never writes anything down except for the occasional urgent message hastily inscribed, in verse, on palm leaf and sent off to a patron or rival. At the moment, we find him hanging in a net bag, *uṟi,* at the center of what is called a *yamakaṇṭam,* a death trap. Black Cloud himself has configured the death trap to maximize danger to himself. A square pit has been dug, sixteen feet deep. At each of the corners there is an iron pillar capped by an iron frame, with another such frame perched in the middle to hold up the net bag. Underneath, in the pit, there is a blazing fire of tamarind logs. On the fire an iron cauldron is boiling with oil, bdellium, lac, wax, sulfur, and frankincense. At each of the four corners of the pit stands a raging elephant driven by a mahout; the elephants' trunks are connected to chains that are fastened to glistening, finely sharpened knives tightly tied to the poet's body (four pressing against his neck, four ringing his waist). The poet is dangling upside down in the net contraption. All around him stand sixty-four learned poets and their leader, a somewhat arrogant poet named Atimaturakavi, "Super Sweet." All of these poets take turns posing challenges (*camicai,* Skt. *samasyā*) to Black Cloud: "Sing a *vĕṇpā* verse naming all the avatars of Vishṇu" or "Compose a verse showing the equivalence of rainbows, Vishṇu, and betel leaf" or "Compare a lemon to a snake" or various demands for complicated metrical and phono-semantic tricks. Suspended over the flames, the poet has to improvise a Tamil poem on the spot, in a split second, to the satisfaction of the questioner. If there is even a slight slip in the answer—in meter or phonology or content—the questioner has only to signal with his eyes to one (or more) of the mahouts, who will plunge his pointed goad into the thick neck of the elephant, which will then jerk at the chains controlling the knives that will cut through the poet's neck and waist, leaving the severed pieces of his body to fall through the net into the boiling pot.

All this is taking place in Tirumalairayan pattinam on the east coast, not far from Nagapattinam, where the local king has patronized Super Sweet and his entourage—until the moment that Black Cloud turned up and heaped scorn on them, comparing such poets *(kavi)* to illiterate monkeys (*kavi,* from Skt. *kapi*). The homophony, as usual, is not coincidental. Black Cloud is an *ācu-kavi,* an extempore poet. He can, so he says, improvise four hundred, five hundred, even a thousand flawless Tamil verses in half an hour; better still, he can do this while holding his breath. Not for nothing is he called Black Cloud. Poems gush from his mouth like a cloudburst. He is a master of all the fancy new genres, and he knows all the Tamil poems of the past, some of which he effortlessly recycles, in ironic ways, in his own verses. He can do anything with words, and his specialty is scorn or insult, *vacai.* As we saw in Chapter 4, insults coming from a poet as adept as Black Cloud are never without tangible results.

Why is he so eager for the ordeal he has planned in detail? He shares with his rival the view that only in this way can truth or falsehood be revealed in total clarity within a single moment.[1] What is meant by truth? By now we should know. It is the audible sequence of Tamil syllables uttered by a competent poet situated on the cutting edge between life and death. Failure to pass such a test counts as falsehood. Metrical precision is of the essence. Any misuse of the life-or-death-dealing sounds will be fatal. Within these terms of reference, the ordeal is a compelling game. Black Cloud is having fun. Never mind that what he thinks of as "oral" poetry—engraved only on his listeners' neurons or, in exceptional cases, through gestures drawn in open space—is a far cry from what the word "oral" once meant in Tamil. These poems are complex, ornate, sophisticated, and erudite, and they require an audience no less learned than their author if they are to be understood and enjoyed. Enjoyment remains a worthy, perhaps the most worthy, goal.

Let's play with this poet for a moment or two. "Give us a *vĕṇpā* poem about a mountain that shakes when a fly buzzes nearby." "Only a mountain?" asks Black Cloud. "Why not the whole universe?" Out pours the poem:

*vāraṇaṅkaḷ ĕṭṭu' maka-meruvuṅ kaṭalum*
*tāraṇiyu' ninṟu calittaṉav āl—nāraṇaṉaip*
*pāṇvāy iṭaicci paru mattiṉāl aṭitta*
*puṇvāyil ī mŏytta potu*

*Vĕṇpā* is a notoriously difficult meter, but the verse has a light, simple texture and is immediately intelligible—in fact, it feels and sounds almost inevitable, as if it had been waiting somewhere inside the poet for the right moment to emerge. This "as if" clause is perhaps not so remote from what Black Cloud thinks himself. He is, on the one hand, self-confident to a point beyond any normal human sense of talent. On the other hand, he thinks this gift of his comes from a direct and unbreakable connection with the goddess Sarasvatī or with her alter ego, the Goddess of All Universes, Akhilâṇḍa Nāyakī, from the poet's home temple of Tiruvanaikka on an island in the Kaveri River across from the town of Trichy. This goddess speaks through her chosen vehicle in chaste and witty Tamil, clearly her mother tongue. Conveniently, he is, as a result, omniscient.

Here is what the verse above "means":

The eight elephants that stand at the cardinal points,
great Mount Meru, the oceans,
the Earth herself—all teetered and tottered
when a fly came buzzing
into the wound left on Vishṇu's body

by the cowherdess with her musical voice

when she struck him
with the thick churning rod.

Vishṇu as the baby Krishṇa liked to steal butter on the sly; his foster mother, Yaśodā, once caught him at it and hit him with the rod she was using to churn milk. The blow left a wound. The mere touch of a fly in the wound was enough to cause the child to shiver, and the world, which is entirely him and his, shudders with him. If there were time and space, we could further unravel the sonic marvels of the Tamil, including the all-important alliterative repetitions and the particular, necessary tension caused by the caesura at the end of the second line of the original.

"Draw in the lines of comparison between a mirror and a king:"

*yāvarukkum rañcaṉai cĕyti yāvarukkum avvavarāyp*
*pāvaṉaiyāyt tīt' akalap pārttalāl—evum*
*ĕtiriyait taṉṉ uḷḷākkiy eṟṟa racattāl*
*catir uṟalāl āṭiyaracām*

Pleasing to all.
Shows anyone
what they imagine to be there.
Takes in and holds,
or holds down,
whatever is reflected,
whatever comes against him.
Bounded by mercury
or by beauty.
Kings and mirrors
mirror one another.[2]

Naturally, this verse has to be bitextual, an example of the simultaneous embrace, *śleṣha,* of two distinct registers of reference.[3] The same sound bites are amenable to two distinct interpretations, one suited to kings, the other to mirrors; the phonetic convergence establishes the comparison, an intimate one in this case. The mirror caches whatever it reflects, an infinite repository; it's not impossible that these images emerge initially from the mirror's own depths. Perspectivism rules the relation: both kings and mirrors serve as surfaces for the varying projections, or imaginings—note the key term *pāvaṉai / bhāvanā*—of whoever looks at or into them. And so on. Pretty good for a spur-of-the-moment Tamil poem.[4]

I think it would be a good idea to look at one of the more technical challenges that Black Cloud faces. He is asked to produce a verse with the separate syllables *nā, nī, nū, and ne;* and to make things still harder, the vowelless consonants *m, l, r,* and *n* should appear in reverse order as the final sounds of these four syllables respectively. (This second, almost lunatic condition is voluntarily added by Black Cloud himself for a reason, as we shall see.) The verse states:

*araiyiṉ muṭiyil aṇi mārpi' ṉĕñcil*
*tĕrivaiyiṭatt' amarntāṉ cevai—puraiy aṟave*
*māṉār viḻiyīr malaraṇav oṟṟ' īrākum*
*āṉālā' nā nī nū ne*

On the waist.
On the head.
On his beautiful breast.
On his throat.

Lovely lady with eyes like a doe's:

If *m-l-r-ṇ* come at the end,
in reverse order, then these four—
*nā-nī-ṇū-ne—*
will nicely serve the lord
who holds a woman in half his body.[5]

That should be clear enough. The poet even has enough space left over for a long vocative to some anonymous listener (start of line 3 in the Tamil). Everything is compressed into a riddle-like format—and indeed, this verse is just that, a riddle, posed by the poet to whoever might like to unravel it. All the information is stated simply, barely encoded. The supposed questioner has been rendered superfluous. If you follow the poet's orders, then you will get the following four words: *nāṇ,* "a string or belt"; *nīr,* "water" (here the river Ganges); *nūl,* the sacred thread draped across the chest; and *nem,* "poison," also "love/ambrosia." Each of these attributes is to be found on the body of Lord Śiva—and the order follows the opening line of the poem. To make the riddle just a little more teasing, there is the unconventional meaning of "throat" for *nĕñcu,* normally "heart." Why not challenge the decipherer lexically as well as phonetically and metrically? There are a few other minor surprises thrown in for good measure, but I think we can make do with this elegant, phono-geometrical solution.

As Dan Pagis has shown us, once a literary riddle is solved, the package of riddle-cum-resolution becomes a new poem in its own right.[6] Suppose you, the reader, haven't fully followed the technical explanation of the previous paragraph. It doesn't matter. Is the poem not rather lovely nonetheless? It has a gently tantalizing, rather surreal quality, as perhaps suits a verse speaking about god. The two ladies, one outside the poem (listening to it), the second inside it and, even further inside, merged in with the god as the left half of his body, seem to converse across the phonematic barrier in the middle. A Tamil reader is likely to be ravished by the simple music of the concluding four syllables. Such verses are well known in Sanskrit and other Indian languages.[7] Once embedded in a narrative like the one we started with, they tend to deepen their expressive force. Such is surely the case here, although the final form of this story is a late-medieval or early-modern concoction. Nonetheless, the story explicates hints lurking in what lies at its core—that is, the text of the many verses it cites. The true poet—learned, entirely immersed in Tamil, the very embodiment of Tamil erudition and the power of Tamil speech, but also playful, inventive, continuously experimenting with what he has been given—offers himself, that is, Tamilness itself, as the stake in a game of incalculable consequence. The goal of this chapter is to understand both game and outcome. I shouldn't have to tell you that Black Cloud triumphs over his rivals; and it is of interest that he ends by cursing the city of Tirumalairayan pattinam to become a wasteland, as, of course, it does.[8]

We find ourselves in a new cultural-linguistic order, one in which the horizon has dramatically expanded even as the domains of practical politics have shrunk to merely local proportions. When the slow disintegration of the Chola state eventually reached its formal endpoint in the early thirteenth century, it is unlikely that anyone in the Tamil country noticed. Recall the Heitzman paradox: greater bureaucratization and centralization (eleventh and twelfth centuries) generated ever greater endowment and alienation of local resources, above all land, by local landowners, thereby undermining one of the core components of imperial power.[9] By the mid-twelfth century, the Chola imperium was limited almost entirely to the Tamil land alone. Within a few decades more, it died.

Severe fragmentation followed, along with violent military excursions from the Pandya south, the shatter zones to the southeast, and the distant north. In the period 1310–1311, the famous commander Malik Kafur, from the Delhi sultanate, raided as far south as Madurai, returning to his master, 'Ala al-Din Khilji, with vast riches stripped from temples and palaces throughout south India. More far-reaching in effect, by far, were the first incursions of Telugu warriors from the emerging state system of Vijayanagara in the west-central Deccan. They reached the northern Tamil country in the middle of the fourteenth century, under Kumāra Kampana; it was soon clear that they had come to stay. With them, but also independently of military fortunes, came waves of Telugu-speaking black-soil (cotton) farmers, who settled mostly in the far south of the Tamil country in the basin of the Tamraparni River.[10] Telugu speech, present from ancient times in the border zones of northern Tamil Nadu, now became a natural presence throughout the southern region. You can still hear it today in Tirunelveli District—a distinct dialect with archaic features preserved in relative isolation from the evolving fate of Telugu in Andhra and Telangana, somewhat like the Rabelaisian French of Quebec in relation to today's standardized urban French. We will come back to the role of Telugu in the new cultural order of Tamil Nadu.

The Vijayanagara warrior-kings slowly reconfigured the social order of the far south. Hitherto marginal social groups rose to power and eventually founded the small-scale states we call Nāyaka.[11] The institution of the managerial, heavily politicized academies of Tamil learning—the *maṭha* or mutt—sometimes patronized by these kings, assumed a dominant role in temple economies, particularly in the heartland of the Kaveri delta. Such mutts would soon become the mainstay of Tamil literary and erudite production—poetry and science now enriching one another within the lives and careers of the same great scholar-poets. The mutts, and the temples they controlled, came to supply the primary audiences for Tamil from the middle of the second millennium until late-colonial times.

Black Cloud, with whom we began this chapter, belongs to the second half of the fifteenth century, when Vijayanagara power in the Tamil country was already relatively secure. This statement should not, however, imply that life—for peasants, merchants, artisans, local kings, or poets—was in any way stable. Along with the more or less incessant warfare that characterized the post-Chola centuries, there were periods of famine and epidemic (right up to colonial times); extortion of tax/tribute was severe enough to cause the flight of agriculturists and artisans; and bandit raiders from the Maṟava and Kaḷḷar communities, known to us from very ancient times but now organized in small predatory protostates with a precarious agricultural base, became central players in the emerging political order of the south and, in consequence, worthy of literary attention as well.[12] This was the age of the military adventurer intent on desultory conquest, rampage, and, over time, the creation of a personal and/or dynastic power base dependent on access to cash and coteries of warrior followers. There is no evident correlation between such unsettled conditions and the newly configured cultural order; but fragmented polity did translate into heightened mobility among the great literati who, like Kāḷamekam, were on the move in an unending search for new patrons. Tamil literary tradition, inscribed in later (seventeenth- or eighteenth-century) synthetic works such as the *Tamil nāvalar caritai,* "Lives of the Tamil Poets," reflects this reality of restless movement, more pervasive than at any time after the early Sangam centuries.

Three primary vectors now constitute the paradigm of the successful Tamil savant-cum-poet. We have touched on the first—the mantic prowess of the nominally oral poet, master of the science of syllables, normally improvising lone verses defined as *cittirai* (Skt. *citra*), that is, "flashy" or "wondrous" poetry, rich in sophisticated wordplay, effectual in pragmatic contexts, and capable of being not merely heard but also clearly seen. (This visible dimension of the spoken world is explored in Chapter 6.) Black Cloud embodies this ethos for the early post-Chola centuries, though he is also the author of longer, discursive works such as the *Tiruvānāikkā ulā* in the formalized genre of the *ulā* processional. Second, Tamil itself, including its innate Sanskrit component, has, like Sanskrit more generally in India, become ruggedly hyperglossic: in its grammaticalized mode, which now includes a slightly deceptive normativism, Tamil is, for many, a fully divine being, far more than "merely" a multilayered medium of communication.[13] It is more than *a* language—

more like a surpassing super-idiom that naturally generates an expansive range of innovative analytical features, including both the potential for a strong classicizing reaction[14] and a tendency toward hyper-reflexive experimentation in domains such as figuration and genre ecology. Third, Tamil is now operating within a self-conscious polyglossic reality, so that it is always one (overriding, privileged) member of at least a triad. Thus our poet, Black Cloud, shows us a very young girl (*petai,* perhaps seven or eight years old) in the streets of Tiruvanaikka who murmurs easily in Sanskrit (actually citing Sanskrit books, *vaṭa nūl*), Prakrit *(pirakirutar),* and Tamil (*pāṭai/bhāṣā,* the vernacular).[15] This set, which follows a venerable South Asian notion that there are always three main languages *(bhāṣā-traya),* is one natural option for situating Tamil within its wider context—though not, by any means, the only such option. Soon Telugu will assume its place as a member of such a series, either displacing Prakrit or triggering an expansion of the set to, say, four, and later eight, necessary courtly tongues.

Who, then, really knows Tamil? The mantic poet, for one. The skilled grammarian and/or commentator (or, alternatively, the erudite courtly scholar-poet), for two. The goddess Tamil herself, for three. We have looked briefly at the first. Let us turn now to the second and third.

## Classicism: Perāciriyar and the New Poetics

If Black Cloud shows us the new, pragmatic Tamil poet-wizard of the post-Chola centuries in action, the great commentator Perāciriyar, probably belonging to the thirteenth century, exemplifies the conservative polymath committed to defining, defending, and explicating the classical Tamil past. Perāciriyar, one of the early masters of Tamil prose, belongs to a series of outstanding commentators on the *Tŏlkāppiyam* and other ancient works. The earliest among them, Iḷampūraṇar, was active during the high Chola period; Aṭiyārkkunallār and Ceṉāvaraiyar may have been roughly contemporaneous with Perāciriyar, while Nacciṉārkk'iṉiyar, the most comprehensive and versatile of the medieval literati, may have appeared a century or so later. We are clearly dealing with a stage of systematizing and clarifying grammatical knowledge in relation to the canonical Sangam and early post-Sangam corpus and its poetic theories, but also in relation to prevalent Sanskrit grammatical discourse; in the case of Perāciriyar, literary taste itself must have appeared threatened by the new poetic grammars we have mentioned, with their long lists of innovative genres. Thus we find ourselves faced with a classicist backlash, a certain sign that something radically new has taken over the world of Tamil letters. In this classicizing moment, Perāciriyar's voice is the most eloquent, as Jennifer Steele Clare has recently shown in a profound study.[16] In certain ways, however, reflective post-Chola Tamil classicism, like similar movements in other literary histories, turns out to be riddled with ambiguity and paradox.

Perāciriyar commented on four sections of the third book of the *Tŏlkāppiyam,* the *Pŏruḷ-atikāram,* dealing with poetics (and also, possibly, on Māṇikkavācakar's *Tirukkovaiyār*). He is the first to mention both the major meta-collections, *Tŏkai* (=*Ĕṭṭuttŏkai,* the Eight Anthologies), and *Pāṭṭu* (=*Pattuppāṭṭu,* the Ten Long Songs).[17] In his eyes, these collections constitute the prestigious canon, which stands in marked contrast to the poetry written in his own time. He knows about the latter, including the new poetic genres, some of whose names he lists; these are, he says, *miṟaikkavi,* "crooked poems"—probably a Tamilization of the Sanskrit term *vakrokti,* the "crooked" utterance that defines the poetic endeavor in Sanskrit poetics (notably in the work of the creative theoretician Kuntaka). He knows that the new poetry has a link to mantric usage *(mantira-vakai),* as we saw in Chapter 4; but such reality-molding verses are, for Perāciriyar, useless *(vāḷātu)* and, in any case, outside the tradition—*marapu,* a key word for this commentator—of *akam* poetry with its five landscapes.[18] One can, he acknowledges, write a grammar for such new forms—he was no doubt aware of the *pāṭṭ'iyal* works we have mentioned—but "even if [one] creates a grammar . . . and others make poetry based on these rules, one can't say that these are [legitimate] grammatical rules because there is no limit to them."[19] Here is an argument worth taking seriously: for Perāciriyar, grammar exists as a finite set of rules enshrined in the authoritative First Book *(mutaṉūl);* he is haunted by the specter of a limitless domain of rules generated by modern grammarians on the basis of their own inventiveness, or of unconstrained empirical observation (possibly the greater threat). The same unsettling specter is on hand when Perāciriyar observes the proliferation of poetic meters, including multiple subdivisions of the ancient categories that give the impression of infinity.

Similarly, rules that are anchored in the usages of other languages *(piṟa-pāṭai)* are irrelevant to the *marapu* of Tamil poetic composition *(tamiḻccĕyuḷ)*.[20] Perāciriyar is operating, like all Tamil scholars, in a multilingual environment; not only Sanskrit and its erudite sciences but also, we can be certain, other south Indian languages were present, in varying intensity, in his native literary culture. Within this environment, he defines what is meant by *marapu:* "Tradition means making poetry while adhering to usage *(vaḻakku)* as befits the refined culture *(nākarīkam)* of particular people in a particular time and place."[21] This pregnant statement deftly formulates the classicist program. Perāciriyar is interested in Tamil. He cares about the great classics of Tamil literature, and he is committed to what we might call the first wave of grammaticalization in Tamil and the lines of transmission from ancient times to the present; not surprisingly, Agastya, the First Grammarian, figures largely here. It is good to have clear derivation of authority from teacher to pupil, or from the First Book to other books that "follow the way" *(vaḻi nūl)*. It is always possible that later works somehow go wrong *(citaiyum)* and introduce errors; a good grammarian like Perāciriyar will do what he can to correct them. The *Tŏlkāppiyam* itself gives an impressive typology of such possible perversions of correct practice; they include both formal sins of commission and aesthetic-poetic divergences from good taste. For Perāciriyar, Sangam poetry is the gold standard, and the First Grammar delimits and defines his practical field of operation.

But if we read this commentary carefully, a striking complexity emerges. True, Tamil has its own tradition, which has a clear specificity, indeed singularity, and marked prestige. True, modern developments—including the expansive literary milieu of works such as the *Virutti* commentary on the *Yāpp'aruṅkalam* grammar of metrics[22]—seem to Perāciriyar to threaten this great edifice. A conservative classicism, defensive in tone, colors much of what this scholar says. But he also recognizes the inherent variability of what he calls "tradition"—its dependence on temporal and spatial contexts, the critical role of good usage, *vaḻakku,* and, above all, the enveloping order of taste rooted in a refined cultural setting, *nākarīkam.* He chooses a telling Sanskrit term to express this viewpoint. What does refinement mean for this scholar?

We can be certain of one thing: it does *not* mean that Sanskrit is in any way foreign to the world of good Tamil, or that Tamil learning can be opposed to Sanskrit learning. Indeed, the key concept of *vaḻakku*—linguistic usage and its concomitant poetic effects—is itself drawn, directly or indirectly, from the Sanskrit grammarians' notion of the *śishṭa,* the cultivated speaker of Sanskrit who serves as a model for good usage.[23] Perāciriyar calls such exemplary models "noble" or "cultivated" *(uyarntor, cāṉṟor),* which means that they are educated *(uyarntor aṟivāṉ amainta cāṉṟor),* like Brahmins, as he says.[24] Tamil-speaking Brahmins count no less than others. Such people also provide a standard for colloquial speech, which Perāciriyar, like other grammarians, naturally recognizes as proper to diglossic Tamil. Real people *(ulakattar)* speak the language; among them, the noble ones speak best. Such statements are meant to be empirical and irrefutable. Note that, as Clare has said, there is no hint in Perāciriyar that Tamil is by nature divine or in any sense other than a human thing.[25]

Yet a problem arises here: let's say that actual speech changes over time (Perāciriyar gives examples of Sangam words that have changed their meanings or gone out of use); does this mean we need a new grammar in each new period?[26] Definitely not. The First Book, by definition, can never become outmoded. All subsequent grammars derive their standard of correctness from the first. There is thus no need for books from other languages *(piṟa pāṭai nūl).*

Putting the matter in this way does not actually defuse the tension that pervades this whole discussion. A strong normativism may choose to set aside even glaring evidence of nonnormative or innovative realities. We can see where the tension is coming from: the erudite world of the thirteenth century had expanded far beyond the limits of what Perāciriyar might have considered "classical grammar." It is that very expansion that, in my eyes, reconstitutes the singularity of Tamil—by this time a far more supple and porous medium than in earlier periods, with new notions about sounds and words and new models of the skilled poet or scholar. Strong continuities with the classical past are also part of the singular fate of a language experimenting with radical forms and themes, in effect reinventing itself in relation both to its inherited grammars and to a more modern poetics.

Perāciriyar is by no means alone in his commitment to the classical past and its literary and grammatical canon. His contemporary, Nāṟkavirāca Nampi, produced what became the standard textbook of *akam* conventions, exemplified, according to the old commentary on this work, by a *kovai* composition of the same period, the *Tañcaivāṇaṉ kovai* of Pŏyyāmŏḻippulavar, "the poet who never lies." A later tradition tells us that Pŏyyāmŏḻippulavar was himself given to classicizing efforts: he is said to have tried, and failed, to revive the ancient Madurai Sangam by recruiting a skeptical Pāṇḍya king to this goal. (The poet did, however, succeed in making the stone images of the Sangam poets nod their heads when they heard his poems.) The point worth noting, however, is that both Nāṟkavirācaṉ's poetic grammar and, still more clearly, the *kovai* that is linked to it are no longer capable of being subsumed by their classical *akam* prototypes. As we have seen, *kovai* works are, by definition, built around a structure of complementary subjects[27]—the hero of the literary love-drama and the god or patron to whom the poem is sung—and thus well outside the limits of Sangam-style *akam* compositions.[28] So what does a word like "classicism" mean in thirteenth-century Tamil Nadu? It must point to a tendency, most strongly represented by Perāciriyar, toward a theoretical ideal that is, first, anachronistic and inevitably compromised in contemporaneous practice and, second, systemically linked to the dominant, modernizing mainstream. Tamil poets went on writing *akam* poems right up to our own generation, as we shall see—there is still no end in sight—but they wrote and write them in ways utterly distinct from any truly classical style.

More broadly, one could say that classicizing tendencies in medieval Tamil rest on an awareness, shared across the literary and erudite spectrum, of the still active presence of the classical tradition and its poetic grammar. Thus, for example, the great Vaishṇava commentator Pĕriyavāccāṉ Piḷḷai (late thirteenth century) tells us that the Tamils *(tamiḻar)* speak of a division of the southern landscape (*nāṉilam,* from Nammāḻvār's *Tiruviruttam* 26) into five (categories), and that the

Āḻvārs, too, follow this concept.[29] The Tamils are, in the eyes of this Tamil speaker, a discrete, collective entity (contrasting with a wider group, such as Vaishṇavas?) with its own literary corpus. The transmission of the Sangam corpus and the narratives surrounding it have been fully studied now by Eva Wilden, who notes the unique role of the seminal Chola-period work known as *Kallāṭam,* which she correctly characterizes as "strongly revivalist."[30] The temptation to some form of classicism, stubborn or moderate, whether theorized as such or not, is a staple element in Tamil literary culture over the last thousand years.

All the great post-Chola grammarian-commentators, while committed to the templates established by the prestigious First Book, are involved in an ongoing, multidirectional, subtle negotiation with the ramified tradition of Sanskrit grammar, a negotiation constrained by the salient differences in structure and grammatical logic of the two languages. Powerful concepts and methods from Sanskrit *vyākaraṇa* are assimilated to the Tamil system,[31] not without some squeezing and abstracting. This effort, which Jean-Luc Chevillard has called a "second wave of Sanskritization,"[32] would accelerate in the late-medieval and early-modern periods, where we find works such as Cuppiramaṇiya Dīkshitar's *Pirayoka-vivekam* (seventeenth century), which tries to view both Tamil and Sanskrit grammars as parts of a single system with shared origins. However, the early post-Chola prose commentators reveal, along with clear awareness of Pāṇinian categories and methods, an uneven sense of the autonomy and specificity of Tamil grammatical science, with its ancient roots; and we must certainly agree with Vincenzo Vergiani that "the complexity of this scenario should not be underestimated."[33] As Vergiani says, we can only guess at the social, religious, and institutional matrices that shaped these Tamil grammarians' thought.[34] Notions of influence and borrowing, in any case, are not rich enough to characterize the true dynamic of intellectual exchange and innovation in this period. Mutatis mutandis, the same statement applies to the literary-cultural domain.

A good example of the "modernizing mainstream" of thirteenth-century poetry is Pukaḻentip Pulavar, one of the most beloved poets in the entire history of Tamil literature. Later literary tradition places Pukaḻenti at the Chola court, together with the prototypical court poet,

Ŏṭṭakkūttar. The tradition must be wrong, but the comparison between these two figures is indeed illuminating. Unlike the professional Chola court poet, and also unlike the potent word wizards like Black Cloud, Pukaḻenti is given to erudite experimentation, particularly in the realm of figuration. He is probably the first to work out the reflexive potential linked to Daṇḍin's pioneering analysis of major (Sanskrit) figures. Daṇḍin, let us recall, belongs to the Pallava court and the late seventh and early eighth centuries;[35] his *Mirror of Poetry* was skillfully adapted into Tamil—the so-called *Taṇṭiyalaṅkāram*—in high Chola times and came to serve as the standard work on figures *(aṇi)* serving nearly all subsequent Tamil poets.[36] The great Chola poets, including Kamban, Cayaṅkŏṇṭār, and Ŏṭṭakkūttar, had already put Daṇḍin-like figuration into practice, whether or not they actually knew the *Taṇṭiyalaṅkāram* specifically—and in this respect they mark a significant point of departure from much earlier Tamil poetry.

But figuration alone, in the Daṇḍin analytical mode, is only part of the revolution in taste that concerns us. Daṇḍin, in his Tamil transforms and applications, represents a dramatic change in literary orientation. Even apart from the pragmatic and effectual aims that we saw in Chapter 4, poetry now deals in a sustained and deliberate intensification of reality—a "thickening" of experience and perception in which complex figuration plays a major, though by no means the only, part. This direction will eventually lead to the almost unimaginably "thick" narrative *mahākāvya*s of late-medieval or early-modern times.[37] A certain inward turn within poetic speech is one sign of the newly crystallizing art. Already by the time we come to Pukaḻenti, what we have called the "northern paradigm"—in which cosmopolitan, pan-Indian erudition, recorded and elaborated in Sanskrit, is fully at home in Tamil literary art—has begun to generate second-order, playful experiments. There was no way back from this truly radical development in the actual practice of composing poetry, whether of the improvised "oral" type we saw in Black Cloud or in the long discursive works and the so-called Short Genres, *ciṟṟ'ilakkiyam*, that together delimited the major fields of verbal art.

Let me show you what I mean, and how this powerful change was identified and understood by the Tamil literary tradition, especially in the inherently intertextual mode of reflection embodied in a rich stratum of post facto narratives and orally transmitted floating verses, *taṉippāṭal* or *cāṭu*. We will look at three verses from Pukaḻenti's *Naḷavĕṇpā* (all three, of course, in the *vĕṇpā* meter for which this poet was famous: he is the "Tiger of *Vĕṇpā*," *vĕṇpāppuli*).[38] The long poem (405 crafted verses) retells the story of Nala and Damayantī, the two most famous lovers in all of South Asian literature. Early on, an eloquent and prescient goose is caught by King Nala in his garden; the goose will go on to ensure that Nala and Damayantī, though separated by vast distances, fall in love with one another. First, however, Nala has to calm down his captive, who is naturally a little shaken by what has happened:

*añcaṉ maṭavaṉamey uṉ ṟaṉ aṇi naṭaiyum*
*vañciyaṉaiyār maṇi naṭaiyum—viñciyatu*
*kāṇap piṭittatu kāṇ ĕṉṟāṉ kaḷi vaṇṭu*
*māṇap piṭitta tār maṉ//* (29)

"Don't be afraid," said the king,
his garland thick with happy bees.
"I've caught you only to explore the question
of whether your charming way of walking
or the enchanting way women walk,
swaying like vines,
is best."

A scientific experiment, no more than that: the goose understands and relaxes. Possibly the goose, clearly fluent in Tamil, is also curious about this question. For women, axiomatically, in medieval Tamil as in Sanskrit, walk as if imitating the lilting rhythm of geese as they waddle on land; all women are, by definition, *haṃsa-gati*, "goose-walkers." But a king who likes poetry might well want to find out once and for all just who is imitating whom. In Śrīharṣa's *Naiṣadhīya*, the goose in question is said to study and mimic Damayantī's beautiful gait, even though Damayantī is as much a goose-walker as any other young beauty.[39] That is one possible variation or extension of the conventional simile. In our example from Pukaḻenti, we have the figure "doubt," *sandeha*, but also a reflexive reworking of what is called *vyatireka*, "excelling," that is, when the subject of the comparison (here, a beautiful woman) outdoes the standard object of comparison (in this case, the gait of the goose). But the *vĕṇpā* verse does not give us a straightforward *vyatireka;* rather, the poet bends the figure back on itself, as if to examine it in a skeptical light, at the same time throwing in the added figurative consideration that women (whose waists are thin to the breaking point and whose breasts are always full and heavy) sway on their feet like vines when they walk. A good listener to such a verse will immediately perceive this witty, intricate twist and—like the goose, listening to the king from inside the poem—will surely smile.

Here is the new mode at work. We have the pan-Indian poetic convention, nicely defined by Daṇḍin; a set of possible intertextual examples of playful extension of the figure; and a little burst of pleasure when the Tamil poet's inventive twist becomes clear. This is figuration reframed in a second-order or third-order perspective—an everyday, continuous process in works like the *Naḷa-vĕṇpā.* A new poetic grammar, in line with the analytical method of the Sanskrit poetician, has taken hold. To see the difference from earlier Tamil poetry, the reader is invited to read any poem, selected at random, from Chapters 2 and 3.

We're looking at a simple point focusing on a basic, now prevalent, indeed ubiquitous technique that eventually achieves effects of breathtaking complexity—for example, in seventeenth-century works such as the *Pirapu-liṅka-līlai* of Tuṟaimaṅkalam Civappirakāca cuvāmikaḷ and nineteenth-century compositions such as Tiricirapuram Mīṉāṭcicuntaram Piḷḷai's local *purāṇas.* Without the deep assimilation of the pan-Indian theory and praxis of figuration, such effects would not have become part of the available repertoire of accomplished Tamil poets. We know the Tamil poet can wreak havoc on the world, killing his enemies or rivals and reviving them at will, blessing his patrons, causing rain to fall, and so on. Now we see that he or she can also work wonders inside the mind of a listener. These two pragmatic modes are, in fact, much closer to each other than we might think; indeed, a major figure such as Black Cloud can easily encompass both of them. The two modes may, however, differ in their final aims. Pukaḻenti, and many like him, are profoundly engaged throughout in generating pleasure.

Note that we are witnessing much more than a simple fusion of Sanskrit and Tamil poetic practices. Even to state the matter in such terms is to reduce its meaning and to distort its history. Pukaḻenti writes exquisite Tamil verses in a uniquely Tamil meter; the semantics, the suggestive resonances, and the pragmatics of such verses are informed or molded by poetic conventions and an analytical typology of figures first fully formulated in Sanskrit (by a Tamil-speaking theoretician) but no less natural in Tamil (or Telugu or Malayalam or Hindi). The analytical style is itself translated into a standard Tamil handbook in which language-specific phono-aesthetic devices occupy a prominent place.[40] A mutually constitutive pair of language clusters that we call, largely for the sake of convenience, "Tamil" and "Sanskrit" produce by every subsequent poetic utterance a third literary-linguistic domain with its own rules and ethos, its evident integrity, and a fundamental hyper-reflexivity that is couched in terms proper only to this third level, which we now call "Tamil" (it is, after all, articulated in an intensified, enriched Tamil). The triad is the minimal unit of reflexive experimentation of this sort.

Observe the ease with which the poet exhibits his mastery. Axiomatically, Damayantī has a tiny waist. No surprise in that. But the goose, introducing to Nala his future wife (whom the goose has seen in the course of his wanderings), wants to make sure Nala knows just how tiny and fragile this particular waist must be:

*ĕṉṟu' nuṭaṅkum iṭaiy ĕṉpav eḻ ulakum*
*niṉṟa kavikai niḻal vente—oṉṟi*
*aṟukāṟ ciṟu paṟavaiy añ ciṟakāl vīcum*
*ciṟukāṟṟukk' āṟṟātu teyntu/* (36)

It—I mean her waist—
is always on the point of breaking,
Oh great king whose parasol gives shade
to all seven worlds! This waist
of hers will be worn away
and might even collapse
under a slight breath of air
if a lonely bee nearby
flaps one fine wing.

The figure is *uyarvuvaṇi,* Sanskrit *atiśayokti*—"hyperbole," one of the four most basic figures for the early Sanskrit poeticians. But again, the poetic convention has been delightfully extended and freshly exemplified. Now it is Nala's turn to smile. Along with the playful figure there is a no less impressive figure of sound in the final line: *ciṟukāṟṟukk' āṟṟātu,* with musical chiming of *kāṟṟu* (echoing *kāṟ-* in the third line) that makes for strong emphasis (the waist literally "can't bear" the "slight breath of air"). I'm not sure, by the way, that bees can flap only one wing, as the critical verb *oṉṟi* after the hiatus suggests.

One last example, to clarify the contrast between the old courtly poetics and the new experimental and reflexive literary style. Damayantī is suffering intense love-sickness for her absent lover. It is night, and her girlfriends have, it seems, been trying to distract her, and cool her down, by pointing to the star-filled sky:

> *cĕpp'ilaṅ kŏṅkaimīr tiṅkaṭ cuṭarpaṭṭuk*
> *kŏppuḷaṅ kŏṇṭa kuḷirvāṉai—ippŏḻutu*
> *mīnpŏtintu niṉṟa vicump' ĕṉpat' ĕṉkŏlo*
> *teṉpŏtinta vāyāṟ ṟĕrintu* (102)
>
> Look, my friends with breasts round as burnished
> copper pots: the cool sky, scorched by the moon,
> is breaking out in blisters—and still,
> though you should know better,
> you insist on honeyed phrases like
> "a firmament filled with stars"?

Damayantī looks up at the stars and sees only infinite heat blisters, like what she feels on her own overheated body. She must be quite certain of this perception, for she somewhat caustically berates her companions for insisting on what can only be, in her view, a poor euphemism and a cliché, that business about night and stars. Ardent desire has transfigured, or rather distorted, Damayantī's perception; as a result, the figure[41] she is articulating is intensified to the point of incipient madness—as, perhaps, a really good flight of fancy should be. The world, inside the heroine and out, has turned hostile, tormenting, and entirely surreal. She sees it as it is. She thinks everyone should see it as it is.

Or does she? Despite its compressed quality and its rather painful point of suspension in the middle, before the hyphen, the verse has a certain lightness about it. Anyone can see the deliberately ironic exaggeration. Probably even Damayantī feels it at some level. Stars are stars. The moon is not hot but normally cool. Doubt is built into the poem in its concluding verb, *tĕrintu,* "though you should know better." So should she. This is highly sophisticated poetry, and every syllable counts. Apart from all this, the style is musical but strangely choppy, perhaps mimicking the agitation in Damayantī's mind.

They say that Ŏṭṭakkūttar, hearing this verse in the course of Pukaḻenti's first oral recitation *(araṅkeṟṟam)* of the entire *Naḷavĕṇpā* in the Chola court, was outraged and immediately objected: "The notion of blisters in the sky is a proper hyperbole" (this much he grants his rival, though probably misidentifying the figure), "but if you are mentioning blisters, should they not also be oozing pus?" A deft deflation of the heightened mood: both the figure and the heroine who is made to speak it are insane—as, no doubt, by implication, is the poet as well. But Pukaḻenti recovers at once. "No pus, but there is a slight liquid excretion that you can see when mist or dew falls from the sky (at dawn)."[42]

This rather typical exchange exposes the silliness of the figure even as it reenergizes its spin—in effect parodying an already latent self-parody built into the verse in the hyper-reflexive mode we have seen at work in the new style. Several further examples of the two poets' arguments are recorded. Eventually, Pukaḻenti can take the petty criticisms no more and decides to kill his rival. With a heavy stone in hand, he slips at night into Ŏṭṭakkūttar's house. Ŏṭṭakkūttar, in despair over his own obviously inferior talent, has taken to his bed. "Even if I hang upside down in penance for the rest of my life, I'll never be able to sing poetry like Pukaḻenti." Ŏṭṭakkūttar's wife tries to get her husband up to have something to eat. He refuses. She presses further: if not rice, let him at least swallow a little milk and sugar. Ŏṭṭakkūttar, annoyed by the wife's insistence, says (in Tamil verse, apparently the only way he can speak): "No milk, no fruit, no honey, no sugar. For that matter, even if you squeeze all the supernal sweetness out of Pukaḻenti's verses in the *Naḷavĕṇpā,* I still won't swallow it." Pukaḻenti overhears this verse and understands: his rival actually *likes* his poems! He throws away the rock and emerges to embrace Ŏṭṭakkūttar, to the latter's confusion and dismay.[43]

There is sweetness beyond measure in the *Naḷavĕṇpā,* as in all the new Tamil poetry. Sometimes it is too sweet—on the verge of the artificial and the ludicrous, maybe even the hallucinatory. The verse itself points to this aspect. The figure turns inward and examines itself, thereby triggering a story. As usual when poetry is involved, a life-and-death struggle is going on. What the story reveals is the clash between two aesthetic models, each with its distinctive audience. Though Pukaḻenti himself was something of a court poet patronized by a small-scale chieftain, Cantiraṉ Cuvarkki, whom Pukaḻenti mentions occasionally, he is operating in a different world than that of the great Chola kings and their praise poets. His work bears the signs of the post-Chola revolution in taste and technique—not so much the word-magic of the oral improviser, though that may also be present, but the inward-directed, self-referential, complex play of figuration in both meaning and sound and the ever more sophisticated and ingenious metrical games in which sound and meaning are played out. A new audience of cognoscenti has emerged. The story I have told, of unknown date, shows us both the transformation that has taken place and the inevitable conservative reaction to the new aesthetic. It also leaves no doubt as to which side emerged on top.

## Maṇi-pravāḷam, Rubies and Coral: Once More, Sanskrit and Tamil

The deep interpenetration of Sanskrit and Tamil in the erudite styles we have been exploring did not go without sporadic protest, on the one hand, and explicit theorization, on the other. Both languages existed, in the far south, inside each other, as we have seen. To the extent that they could be somehow disentangled, at least in theory, a scholar or poet might choose, for his own expressive reasons, to compose in either Tamil or Sanskrit. Over time, this choice became more crystallized, meaningful, and easy.[44]

Nostalgic voices could sometimes cling to an image, or a fantasy, of a simpler, non-Sanskritized Tamil—an image that is itself a somewhat new-fangled product of the hybrid linguistic reality we have been exploring. We hear such voices with particular force in the works of the Śrīvaishṇava commentators on the "Tamil Veda," that is, the canonical *Nālāyira-divya-prabandham* containing the poems of the Tamil Āḻvārs. These commentators often wrote in what is called Maṇi-pravāḷam, "Rubies and Coral"—a language in its own right in which Tamil and Sanskrit have come together in a sometimes dissonant but always powerfully symbiotic mix. Before we examine this mixed language in its several forms, let us look at some well-known examples of the nostalgia I have just mentioned:

> One time when Vaṅkipurattu Nampi [a direct disciple of the great philosopher Rāmânuja, who must have taught in Tamil through he wrote in Sanskrit] wanted to serve Pĕrumāḷ/Vishṇu, he went and stood among some cowherd women [*iṭaiccikaḷ*]. His [fellow student Mutali-] Āṇṭāṉ saw this and asked him: "This whole group of Śrīvaishṇavas are right here, so why go and stand close to those cowherd girls?" Said Vaṅkipurattu Nampi: "It's true we have a little cleverness [*virakam* < *viraku;* but *virakam* is also Skt. *viraha,* "longing"]. But though they are simple, ignorant people [*ŏṉṟum aṟiyāta kŏccaikaḷ*]—or *because* they are simple—the bountiful love of the lord flows directly to them as water comes rushing through a channel from a high place to a low place. That's why I joined them."
>
> Āṇṭāṉ then asked: "So what did they say, and what did your Highness say?" Nampi replied: "They said, 'Please drink this milk. Eat this fruit. Put on the golden thread. Live a hundred years. Wear this well-woven set of cloths.' As for me, I said, in Sanskrit: *vijayasva vijayī bhava,* 'Be victorious, Hail!'" Āṇṭāṉ concluded: "Even though you went there, you couldn't get rid of that coarse Sanskrit [*muruṭṭu saṃskṛtam viṭṭīr illaiye*]! Wherever we are, we are who we are [*ĕṅkey iruntālum nām nām*]. So come be with us."[45]

The Tamil cowherds naturally speak to God in a simple, clear, musical Tamil—a prayer that is really a set of intimate blessings-cum-imperatives. Their speech has a rare one-to-one correspondence between sign and meaning that, by implication, Sanskrit can never achieve. The learned master, by contrast, can't free himself from his "coarse" Sanskrit, with its concomitant sense of distance, awe, and a certain pretense of control. Erudition itself only gets in his way. The conclusion drawn by his learned colleague is devastating, a statement relevant both to the experience of speaking in a mother tongue and to the psychological consequences of too much book learning: "We are who we are." Then comes the request: this being the case, Nampi might as well "come be with us"—if anyway he'll be thinking and speaking in Sanskrit. The contrast between the two language registers is stark and enduring, though this entire passage thematizing the distinction is composed in a strong bilingual amalgam, typical of a prevalent narrative level of Tamil Maṇipravāḷam. This level is now, as it were, the upper, prestigious speech register for this community. Still, for Nampi, and for the Vaishṇava commentators who report the incident, nothing can replace the immediacy of Tamil as the preferred medium for connecting to reality.

This anecdote is important precisely because Śrīvaishṇava Tamil is in many ways a language of its own—or, better, a rich dialectical range of diverse, rule-bound language forms. We could say that for these commentators Tamil was sometimes privileged in situations of contrast or tension that reflect both a far-reaching interdependence and an irreducible, necessary complementarity of two apparently discrete linguistic domains. In this respect the commentators drew on the canonical poets' evident love for Tamil—especially spoken Tamil—as we saw in Chapter 3.

Very similar to our story is the following oral verse attributed to the poetess Auvaiyār on the occasion of her visit to the famous Vishṇu temple of Tirukkurukur, in the far south:

> Five, four, three,
> and the one, beyond all knowledge,
> that flows through them all—
>
> it belongs
> in a distant tongue
> in this temple of Kurukur,
> or so they say,
>
> but as for me, it's all there
> in my mother tongue.[46]

There are five natural elements, four goals of human life (desire, profit, righteousness, and release), three great gods (Vishṇu, Śiva, Brahma), and, pervading them all, true "being" *(pŏruḷ)* that is the reality of the god in this temple. This true "being" actually *belongs to* Tamil *(tāymŏḻiyatu)*; that is, it has an innate connection to this mother language—a rare and probably rather late occurrence of this term—as if the condensed stuff of existence, or of meaning (all this is *pŏruḷ*) could emerge only, in all its fullness, in the Tamil language. It is possible that all of us feel something like this about our mother tongue. The self, if there is such a being, speaks in the first, most intimate sounds we have known.

This little poem, though deceptively slight in appearance, has an additional level of meaning. Tirukurukur was the home of the central Śrīvaishṇava poet Nammāḻvār, author of the core of the "Tamil Veda." It was at this site that Nammāḻvār first sang his famous text of a thousand perfect verses, the *Tiruvāymŏḻi;* and it was here that the text was recovered from oblivion by Nāthamuni. So Auvaiyar, in self-consciously praising Tamil as the medium of true understanding, is also restating the claim to ultimate value—precision, lyricism, musicality—implicit in the very notion of a Tamil Veda. In fact, Auvaiyar's verse goes even beyond the standard Vaishṇava assertion that Tamil and Sanskrit constitute, together, a "Double Revelation" (*ubhaya-vedânta*; note that this crucial term is in Sanskrit). For the itinerant poetess, as this authorless, floating verse *(taṉippāṭal)* conceives her, even Lord Vishṇu himself is but one of the three great deities, while dense reality itself, the true subject of the poem, is, by definition, a Tamil affair.

One rather rare instance of outright, even lethal, hostility to Sanskrit comes from the commentaries on the *Tŏlkāppiyam* by Perāciriyar and Nacciṉārkk'iṉiyar (thirteenth and fourteenth centuries).[47] Perāciriyar gives the more extended version of the story, woven around two pregnant verses; Nacciṉārkk'iṉiyar offers a little more information about the context in which they were uttered. The story survived, slightly transformed, into the much later (eighteenth-century) *Tamiḻ-nāvalar-caritai.*[48] It is cited in relation to the grammatical *sūtra* (*Tŏl. Pŏruḷ. Cĕy.* 178) defining mantra as a literary-pragmatic genre: it is the secret (or Vedic? *maṟai*) speech used in oaths *(āṇai)* by people with a full command of language *(niṟai mŏḻi māntar).*[49] We by now know what this means; Tamil words, or bare syllables, used by a competent speaker-poet, can change the world. Thus Perāciriyar speaks specifically of poems that are "Tamil mantras" and that are said to belong to a now-lost genre called *aṅkatam,* mentioned elsewhere in the *Tŏlkāppiyam* as being couched in the *vĕṇpā* meter (*Tŏl. Pŏruḷ. Cĕy.* 75 and 114). The story exemplifies this genre in the two relevant verses.

They are attributed to Nakkīrar—a potent name very familiar to us.[50] The precise details of the story are a little opaque, but it seems that a potter (Kuyakkoṭaṉ) sitting at the locked southern entrance to the Madurai temple asserted, in Nakkīrar's presence, that Sanskrit *(āriyam)* was good *(naṉṟu)* and Tamil was bad *(tītu).*[51] Nakkīrar, a Brahmin, cursed the potter to die for this pronouncement; the Tamil verse that carried the curse ends in the Sanskrit mantric syllables *cuvākā* (from Skt. *svāhā*), which, of course, along with the Tamil words of the verse, worked like magic. Onlookers begged the poet to revive the poor Sanskrit-loving potter, and Nakkīrar did so with another verse calling on the First Grammarian, Agastya, on Potiyil Mountain, and ending in the same effective syllables—and the potter revived.[52] It is perhaps not by chance that the story associates Sanskrit with the left-hand caste of potters and, by implication, with their universalistic values; and it is of interest that the defender of Tamil is a Brahmin. However we may wish to read this story, it is evident that it reflects the linguistic practices that had emerged in the Chola-period *pāṭṭ'iyals,* with their notion of effectual combinations of syllables; if there was any doubt that Tamil could hold its own with Sanskrit in this respect, the commentators cite this vignette to put it to rest.

Let me say again that by this period Tamil—as a primary medium of learning and of literary creativity in the far south—exists within a vibrant multilingual reality. Srilata Raman has called attention to an isolated verse *(taṉiyaṉ),* of uncertain date, prefixed to Kamban's *Rāmāyaṇa:*

*vaṭakalai tĕṉkalai vaṭukku kaṉṉaṭam*
*iṭam uḷa pāṭai yāt' ŏṉṟiṉ āyiṉum*
*tiṭam uḷa raku-kulatt' irāmaṉ taṉ katai*
*aṭaivuṭan keṭpavar amarar āvare*

Sanskrit, belonging to the north,
Tamil, of the south,
Telugu and Kannada—
it doesn't matter in which language
the story of brave Rāma is told,
whoever hears it with attention
becomes a god.[53]

One might have thought that a verse introducing the Tamil *Rāmāyaṇa* would emphasize the Tamilness of this work. Instead, we have a nonchalant acknowledgment of the presence of Tamil's sister languages, and of course of Sanskrit, within the wider cultural sphere that generated Kamban's text.

Sanskrit and Tamil are here *vaṭakalai* and *tĕṉkalai,* the northern and southern "parts" or "sciences" or "words"—the same terms that eventually came to signify two distinct streams within Tamil Śrī-vaishṇavism, each with its theological and ritual particularities and its social and institutional moorings.[54] There is a tendency in the secondary literature to retroject this division, familiar from more modern times, into the thirteenth century and to identify emblematic foundational figures: the great poet-theologian Vedânta Deśika (ca. 1268–1370) for the Sanskritic north, and Piḷḷai Lokâcārya (b. 1205?) or his later successor and commentator, Maṇavāḷa Māmuṉi (1370–1443) for the south. This view is clearly anachronistic. It is, however, the case that the southern Śrīvaishṇavas developed a special love for Tamil and, in particular, for the Tamil Veda, that is, Nammāḻvār's *Tiruvāymŏḻi*—and we see in works such as the *Ācārya-hridayam* of Aḻakiya Maṇavāḷap Pĕrumāḷ Nāyaṉār (thirteenth century), with its massive Tamil commentary by Maṇavāḷa Māmuṉi, the claim that the Tamil Veda is far superior to Sanskrit works such as the classical *purāṇas* and the two epics. Part of the argument underlying this claim is a universalistic and egalitarian ideology of salvation as accessible to any and all devotees of Vishṇu (including any and all Tamil speakers), unlike the apparently exclusivist and hierarchical world of Sanskritic Brahminism.[55]

It is, however, easy to overstate the sectarian tension, including its linguistic ramifications, in premodern Tamil Nadu, as, I think, Friedhelm Hardy did in his study of the *Ācārya-hridayam:*

> The *Ācārya-hṛdayam* and the material collected around it suggest that we are dealing with very powerful decentralizing forces. In different regions of the subcontinent, religion resorts to the vernacular, moulding and often justifying it as a new, and more relevant means of expression. A literature is created which becomes explicitly, or more through implicit attitudes, regarded as "revelation." This itself is seen as a conscious rejection of Sanskrit, the symbol of traditional modes of Vedic orthodoxy and orthopraxis. [56]

Hardy calls this process "de-Sanskritization," a counterpart to the notion of an integrative, upward-oriented "Sanskritization" that goes back to the anthropologist M. N. Srinivas, among others.[57] But this axis of Sanskritization and de-Sanskritization is mostly illusory, and it masks the complex dynamic of Sanskrit-in-Tamil and Tamil-in-Sanskrit that we see no less in the Śrīvaishṇava sectarian works than in the post-Chola-period Tamil poets and grammarians. I don't want to belabor this point further.[58] One telling sign, however, lies in the very language in which the *Ācārya-hridayam* and its extensive "Tamil" commentary by Maṇavāḷa Māmuṉi are couched: for this is a version, or dialect, of the "hybridic" language continuum that we call Maṇi-pravāḷam, mentioned at the start of this section. It is time for us to examine analytically this unusual linguistic creation.

Maṇi-pravāḷam was sometimes seen by those who spoke and wrote it in the far south as a language in its own right, based on Tamil, even though the first articulated grammatical definition of it in Tamil, in the Buddhist *Vīracoḻiyam,* relates to it as a linguistic-literary *style:* when Sanskrit and Tamil phonemes are mixed together, that is called *viraviyal;* when Sanskrit and Tamil words are mixed, that is *maṇi-pravāḷam.*[59] As Anne Monius has noted, the style in question is apparently meant to operate in poetry, although in the case of Tamil the overwhelming majority of Maṇi-pravāḷam works are in prose—in particular, the Śrīvaishṇava and Jain commentaries (but see below). The *Vīracoḻiyam* did not invent the term, which first appears in a ninth-century north Indian Jain work (describing a mix of Sanskrit and Prakrit) and is also noted by Abhinavagupta (ca. 1000, in his commentary on the *Nāṭyaśāstra*) as a style prevalent in south India and comprising an interweaving of Sanskrit and the vernacular *(deśa-bhāṣā).*[60] Despite the existence of two excellent scholarly studies of Śrīvaishṇava Maṇi-pravāḷam,[61] much confusion about what we mean by the name still colors modern discussions.

This is largely because Maṇi-pravāḷam is not by any means a single, homogeneous phenomenon. All the south Indian literary languages have absorbed huge lexical borrowings from Sanskrit—and sometimes this feature in itself is erroneously thought of as constituting a kind of Maṇipravāḷam. K. K. A. Venkatachari nicely says: "Mere mixture of Saṃskṛt words and Kannaḍa words cannot be called Maṇipravāḷa, because, if one were to do so, the whole of Kannaḍa literature should be called Maṇipravāḷa."[62] One could say exactly the same thing about Telugu and Malayalam literature, and Tamil, too, would fit in, noting only that the statistical incidence of borrowing from Sanskrit rises steeply over time in the medieval literature.[63] Just to clarify this point: we have many classical Telugu verses that are, lexically speaking, entirely or almost entirely Sanskrit (sometimes with Telugu grammatical endings added to the Sanskrit noun or compound); but such verses are still in Telugu and should be seen as Telugu—a miracle of transmutation has turned the Sanskrit phrasing into something that can only be a true Telugu style.[64] Malayalam offers us an important variation on this pattern, as we will see in a moment.

Śrīvaishṇava Tamil Maṇi-pravāḷam, as I have said, offers us a range of dialectical or idiolectical features.[65] Very often the reader senses that he or she is encountering a richly colloquial style, undoubtedly reflecting the context of oral teaching and textual exegesis.[66] We can also definitely assume a relation between written Śrīvaishṇava Maṇi-pravāḷam and characteristic dialectical features of spoken Śrīvaishṇava Brahmin Tamil, with its heavy influx of Sanskrit words.[67] In some authors—for example, Aḷakiya Maṇavāḷap Pĕrumāḷ Nāyaṉār in his *Aruḷiccĕyalrahasyam*[68]—there is a somewhat surprising, and rather beautiful, conjunction of recorded colloquial idiomatic speech and high-flown technical terms in Sanskrit, including long Sanskrit compounds (the latter being a diagnostic feature of Tamil Maṇipravāḷam style generally). Quotations from canonical Sanskrit and Tamil works account for some degree of the linguistic mixture that dominates the commentaries. Beyond such rather mechanical indicators, however, we can note differential stylistic and grammatical features, such as the degree to which Sanskrit words are Tamilized according to standard Tamil morpho-phonemic practice and, even more to the point, the inflection of Sanskrit either with proper Sanskrit nominal and verbal endings or with Tamil suffixes. Sanskrit-derived denominative verbs in Tamil, sometimes phonologically Tamilized, are another common marker. Graphically, this kind of prose tends to insert southern Sanskrit (Grantha) characters for Sanskrit phonemes within the putatively Tamil sentence or, in many manuscripts and modern printed editions, to write the entire text in Telugu script, which can easily accommodate both Tamil and Sanskrit phonology (with the addition of the Tamil character for the distinctive Tamil sound, retroflex *ḻ*).[69] Note the painless transition from Tamil to Telugu script among literati of the medieval period in the far south.

Still, given this considerable variation and the cultural and historical settings that determined the highly personal linguistic usage of individual commentators, we are left with a question. What exactly makes a highly Sanskritized Tamil verse or sentence into Maṇipravāḷam? Sheer statistical counts of Sanskrit lexemes are, as we have seen, not sufficient; it is, in fact, of little interest to quantify "Sanskritization" of this sort in the styles of various authors. Some use many Sanskrit words—just as modern Tamil speakers commonly sprinkle their sentences with borrowed English words—and some use fewer. So what? We need a grammatical criterion or set of criteria; and the one work that offers us a rigorous definition and set of empirical rules and observations is the anonymous grammar from Kerala known as *Līlā-tilakam (LT)* (datable, roughly, to sometime between the late fourteenth and sixteenth centuries).[70] *Līlā-tilakam* presents the reader (in Sanskrit *sūtras* and Sanskrit prose commentary) with a grammatical description of Maṇipravāḷam, seen as a distinctive linguistic amalgam of Sanskrit and the local language of Kerala, *bhāṣā,* which the author, for historical-cultural reasons, also refers to as "Tamil." To understand why he does so, we need to outline the special role of Tamil in Kerala and in Malayalam language and literature.

Historically, Tamil was spoken and written in Kerala alongside Sanskrit and early forms of Malayalam. The two languages, Tamil and Malayalam, must have separated by the mid-first millennium,[71] but they remained very close in many ways (one might wonder when they stopped being mutually intelligible); Tamil literature flourished in Kerala from the beginning—whenever that was—and was always a prestigious component of Kerala culture.[72] What is more, despite the increasing distance between the two linguistic traditions, speakers of proto-Malayalam thought of themselves as speaking Tamil, or a kind of Tamil, well into late-medieval or possibly even early-modern times.[73] On the other hand, the *Līlā-tilakam,* the first grammar to address the complex linguistic situation in Kerala, invests considerable effort in differentiating this Kerala "Tamil" from the language spoken in the nearby Chola and Pandya countries. All this points to an unusual cultural configuration in which *bhāṣā,* the spoken language of Kerala, whatever one might have called it, functioned as a mother tongue alongside two highly prestigious and authoritative "father tongues"—Sanskrit and Tamil. This triangular pattern molded Kerala culture in far-reaching ways and differed markedly from the dyadic Sanskrit-Tamil symbiosis that we have been studying.

The *LT* has a clear program: it seeks to define—phonologically, morphologically, lexically, and also aesthetically—the distinctive literary dialect it calls Maṇi-pravāḷam, exemplified by poetic works unique to Kerala; in doing so, it needs to specify major dialectical features and to lay down criteria for excluding the neighboring forms of "Tamil" just mentioned. The Chola, Kerala, and Pandya languages are seen here as "*dramiḍa* speech"—that is, as Tamil, understood in a wide sense as a set of related but discrete dialects. The *LT* records a view to the effect that the Karṇāṭândhras—that is, Kannada and Telugu speakers—were also "Dramiḍas," only to reject this view (surely based on an awareness that Kannada and Telugu are also somehow close to Tamil and Malayalam) because the former two languages are too different *(vilakṣaṇa)* from the language of the Tamil Veda—that is, Nammāḻvār's *Tiruvāymŏli,* now a litmus test for cultural-linguistic identity. And there is also another diagnostic criterion of difference: Telugu and Kannada, says the *LT,* do not share the "Dravidian" phonological features that the two southern languages have: the short vowels *ĕ* and *ŏ* (though in fact, both Telugu and Kannada do have them!); the special retroflex and alveolar phonemes *l̲, ḷ, r̲,* and *n̲;* and the absence of Sanskrit sibilants, voiced and aspirated stops, and the vocalic *r̥/r̥̄*. There is a *dramiḍa-saṅghāta,* a Dravidian phonological system serving to indicate where *dramiḍa* speech can be found.[74]

The terms "Dravidian" and "Tamil" in the *LT* require further explanation.[75] For the moment, without lingering over technical grammatical issues,[76] we can list four defining features of Maṇi-pravāḷam as formulated by this unusually perceptive text:

1. "Real" Maṇi-pravāḷam should have at least some Sanskrit nouns declined with the proper Sanskrit case endings, alongside Sanskrit nouns that have been "Malayalamized" *(bhāṣī-kr̥ta)* both phonologically and by being declined with Malayalam nominal endings. The lack of the former is enough to disqualify what is today called *Nambyār-tamil̲* from being Maṇi-pravāḷam. The example is a telling one. In the Kūṭiyāṭṭam performance tradition of Sanskrit dramas, in the play known as "The Ring" (*Aṅgulīyâṅkam*=Act VI of Śaktibhadra's play, *Āścarya-cūḍāmaṇi*), there are crucial moments when a Nambyār drummer enters the stage and recites a précis of the narrative in an archaic form of Malayalam, still referred to as Tamil. This Nambyār-Tamil has quite a lot of Sanskrit as well as some Tamil verbal endings (unlike standard Malayalam); it does not, however, have Sanskrit nouns with their Sanskrit case markers. The *LT* knows about this particular form of "Tamil," spoken, it says, by drummers *(mārdaṅgika)*[77]—knows, also, that this dialect is very remote from the literary dialect the *LT* wants to grammaticalize. Again, we note the prestigious presence of Tamil within medieval Malayalam cultural forms.
2. Malayalam words and Malayalam verbal roots can be inflected as if in Sanskrit in Maṇi-pravāḷam literary compositions *(sandarbha).* Such words and roots are thus literally Sanskritized *(saṃskr̥tī-kr̥tā).* For example, we have Malayalam *kŏṅka,* "breast," which we see declined in a verse as if it were a Sanskrit feminine noun in the instrumental case: *kŏṅkayā.*[78] Similarly, we have weirdly conspicuous

Sanskrit verbs from Malayalam roots: *pokkāṃ cakre,* "made go," a periphrastic perfect from Malayalam *pokkuka,* "to move," or the present participle *keḻantī,* "weeping," from Malayalam *keḻuka.*[79] All such usages have a somewhat playful quality about them; one hears them even today in the Malayalam of the Vidūṣaka clown in Kūṭiyāṭṭam performances.[80] They illustrate an unspoken principle: every Sanskrit word in the vast lexicon of the language is potentially a Malayalam word, and Malayalam can, if it wants, radically Sanskritize lexical items by morphological means. This latter technique is of a different order entirely than simple lexical borrowings and thus constitutes, one might say, a far more telling criterion of the literary dialect than any statistical count of such loans. (It also goes far beyond the extremely common tendency in Tamil Maṇi-pravāḷam to produce Tamil verbal forms from Sanskrit roots.)

3. "Hybridization" on the level of literary usage entails hybridic grammaticalization. The author of the *LT* seeks to authorize his rules by reference to both the Sanskrit and the Tamil grammatical systems; both grammars have contributed generative rules of operation to this attempt to formalize a grammar of Maṇi-pravāḷam. More on this in a moment. This doubling of authoritative precedent and modes of analysis is a diagnostic feature of this kind of Maṇi-pravāḷam. Sometimes it works in surprising ways, as Freeman has shown with reference to *sandhi* rules.[81] Stated as a general trend: the powerful prestige of Sanskrit and Sanskrit grammar can be channeled into sustained efforts to justify prevalent Malayalam usage—as Pollock's template of vernacularization would indeed lead us to expect. Tamil grammatical precedent is also conscripted to authorize current Malayalam norms.
4. Much the same could be said of the *LT*'s poetic theory, which is rooted in Sanskrit poetics, especially the work of the great Kashmiri theoretician Ruyyaka (twelfth century), but ends up underpinning a unique Malayalam-centered aesthetics. The dominant language of the final chapters of the *LT,* which are focused on poetics, is the familiar set of concepts from classical Sanskrit theory: suggested meaning *(vyaṅgya),* said to be the very life *(jīvitam)* of Maṇi-pravāḷam;

*rasa* or "flavor" in its standard categories; figuration (*alaṅkāra);* and so on. But one should not be misled by this assimilation of normative terms. The primary criterion of "Maṇi-pravāḷam-ness" is an aesthetic one, evident in the many literary examples the author quotes and in the large-scale early Malayalam works that he must have known well. This corpus, as he in fact tells us, achieves singular aesthetic effects. There is a particular flavor that arises from hearing such poems, with their natural blending of Malayalam and Sanskrit—and here, if we look more deeply, we can easily see that the very notion of hybridization is undermined by the praxis the *LT* author describes and by the way he articulates its cognitive and emotional power.

Put simply: Kerala Maṇi-pravāḷam is not a separate language at all. It is early literary Malayalam (known, in medieval Kerala, as "Tamil"). The Sanskrit active within it is an integral and intimate part of its very character, like Sanskrit in Tamil Maṇi-pravāḷam or normative Sanskrit-in-Telugu. Listen to how, in a critical passage early on, our author formulates the inner dynamic of this literature:

> The conjunction of *bhāṣā* [that is, Malayalam/Tamil] and Sanskrit, though difficult [*saṅkaṭa-vyavahāra*], is not at all impossible. . . . The Sanskrit part should be like *bhāṣā*—mellifluous and familiar. The *bhāṣā* should be mainly what high-caste people speak. Then the combination will work. It is called Maṇi-pravāḷam, "rubies and coral," in order to express the excellence of its composition [*sauṣṭhavam*]. If you string rubies and coral together on a single string, because they share a single color [or classification], a unity appears—unlike a string of rubies and pearls, or coral and sapphire. That is how the combination of *bhāṣā* and Sanskrit should be—without any jarring perception [*vaiṣamyam*]. Moreover, in such a unified composition, one should not even notice that there is Sanskrit. It should be seen and heard as a *bhāṣā* text.[82]

In other words, good Maṇi-pravāḷam is good (proto-)Malayalam and should be experienced as such. This point is driven home by subsequent discussions illustrated by concrete examples. One can hardly exaggerate the importance of the above statement. Note the sociolinguistic aspect of the description, a stable element in the *LT*: the kind of *bhāṣā* relevant for poetry derives from the speech of the higher castes; low-caste speech, we learn later, is remarkably close to Pāṇḍya Tamil.[83]

Taken together, and amplified by reference to a relatively small set of further grammatical and poetic issues, these features delimit the scope of Maṇi-pravāḷam in the sense the *LT* author uses the word, namely, for the literary form of Malayalam that developed in medieval Kerala and that is represented by a large corpus of classical poetic works. He knows that the language of this corpus is specific to it and, indeed, unique. However, the author of the *LT* also knows that there are many other kinds of linguistic hybrids in South India, all of which might ostensibly be called Maṇi-pravāḷam as well (thus the imagined opponent, *pūrva-pakṣin,* in the scholastic debate recorded in our text). The opponent also suggests repeatedly that words that come from, or are prevalent in, for example, the Pāṇḍya language can easily enter into Kerala Maṇi-pravāḷam, thus possibly creating new hybridic modes. In fact, wherever one looks, one sees such hybrids—there is Sanskrit in the Chola and Pāṇḍya languages, and Kannada and Telugu and even Kodagu loans or close cognates in *Kerala-bhāṣā,* and Sanskrit in Prakrit, and in Kannada, and in Telugu; even Tamil words turn up, so he says, in Kālidāsā's Sanskrit *Raghu-vaṃśa.* So why draw the line so severely, and why insist on the particularity of Kerala Maṇi-pravāḷam?

It is a complex discussion, not atypical of such debates on language and categorical cultural identity in this period in various South Asian regional traditions.[84] The imaginary opponent is right to point to rich linguistic amalgams, made up of words and grammatical forms of varying provenance, all the way down. But the answer that is offered is, in my view, persuasive. Lexical mixing alone, says the *LT* author as *siddhântin,* stating his own conclusion, doesn't matter very much when it comes to characterizing his target language. Maṇi-pravāḷam, like any other language, has its own natural integrity and a particular systemic structure *(vyavasthā).* Word-borrowings, including words attested in the grammars and dictionaries of other, rival languages—above all, in this case, the grammars and dictionaries, indeed also the classical literature, of neighboring (Pandya and Chola) Tamil—in no way erode that integrity. Identifying the provenance and derivation of a given word is irrelevant to the question of classification and cannot compete with the facts of linguistic usage, *vyavahāra,* an indisputable criterion for what belongs to any given language. There will be similarities in words and usages—Kerala "Tamil" and Pāṇḍya or Chola Tamil have a great many such affinities—but similarity, *sādṛśya,* does not mean that one language owns, or for that matter infiltrates, another.[85] "No language ever truly enters into another language—because that would destroy the overriding principle of a language-specific systematicity."[86] Kerala Maṇi-pravāḷam works by combining Sanskrit and the local Kerala language—"Tamil"—in specific and perfectly describable ways.

Throughout this long passage, we see that the author is deeply familiar with the technical literature of the Tamil grammarians, from the *Tŏlkāppiyam* and its commentators to the Chola-period grammars such as *Naṉṉūl* and the metrical handbook *Yāpp'aruṅkalakkārikai.* He also knows about Sangam literature and mentions by name the two super-anthologies, *Ĕṭṭuttŏkai* and *Pattuppāṭṭu.* He is familiar with somewhat arcane and archaic grammatical forms in Tamil as they appear in the classical corpus. At the same time, he knows Pāṇinīyan grammar and manipulates its procedures and categories very deftly.[87] A subtle negotiation is going on, as Freeman has said: "Caught between the two macrocultural spheres of Tamil and Sanskrit . . . our text deployed a complex analytic that allowed it to play both these linguistic cultures off against each other . . . by extolling its own hybrid artifact over other literary manufactures."[88] Momentarily pushed by his imagined opponent into a corner, the author admits that he, too, has classed the Keralas as Tamils, since both are part of the wider category of Dramiḍa speech *(dramiḍatva).* But, he says, only an idiot would think that this means that the two languages are one.[89]

For our purposes in this chapter, it is important to see that Tamil functions in the *LT* on two interlocking levels, as Freeman has shown.[90] The author, clearly haunted by the overwhelming presence of Tamil and its ancient sources, both literary and erudite, in close geographical proximity to but also within Kerala, thinks of Tamil as a translocal, indeed transregional—one might well say cosmopolitan—language. On this overarching level, Tamil wields authority by virtue both of its far-reaching, sophisticated grammar, in the widest sense of the word, and of its sustained historical and political impact on Kerala and other parts of south India. On another level, Tamil is a rich dialectical spectrum within which Kerala Tamil, that is, Malayalam, finds its place alongside its close neighbors, Chola and Pāṇḍya Tamil. Here Kerala Tamil is on a par with other dialects and reveals its own irreducible linguistic integrity. Both levels allow for the description of Tamil as "Dramiḍa," a capacious linguistic (not ethnic) category, evidently subject to contestation in the author's time. Kerala Tamil thus has affinities with varying cultural configurations of the far south of the subcontinent. Ultimately, both levels serve the author's primary purpose of defining and authorizing, so to speak, the unique sensibility that informs Kerala Maṇi-pravāḷam literature.

One could state the matter in another way, in line with the theme of vernacularization that, following Pollock, we have already visited several times. The *LT,* driven by the agenda I have just formulated, was composed in Sanskrit and deftly uses Sanskrit categories to make its point. It thus bears witness to the continued vitality of Sanskrit as both an intellectual and an artistic medium in medieval Kerala; and it is hardly alone in this, since Kerala generated one of the largest and most powerful literary and erudite corpora in Sanskrit of the second millennium. But we can also view the *LT* as an extreme case of successful vernacularization, precisely because of its heavy Sanskritic orientation—since it ends up affirming, through Sanskrit, the singular expressivity of Kerala Tamil and its poetry and even reflects a certain translocal range for this art, embracing Travancore in the far south of Kerala as well as the central Kerala heartland, and even beyond.[91]

In this sense, the *LT* reminds us of the Tamil Buddhist grammar, *Vīracoḻiyam,* from a somewhat earlier period.[92] The *Vīracoḻiyam,* as we saw, adopts Sanskritic norms in order to provide a basis for the transregional cosmopolitan claims of Tamil. This kind of intellectual program may well have been standard fare for early-second-millennium south Indian intellectuals. But the very definition of a cosmopolitan idiom—a linguistic affair with strong social and political implications—requires, at least in India, a diffusion of the top-down integrative aspect into multiple local variants. Not a supervening uniformity, and not classicizing standardization, but relatively autonomous sets of diglossic or, better, heteroglossic dialectical variation define the cosmopolitan in this historical setting. One could draw out an interesting contrast, not without elements that run parallel to the South Asian case, with the fate of Latin during the Carolingian Renaissance in the West (from the end of the eighth century on). As Leonhardt has shown, this imperial Latin, with its renewed normative claims and state-sponsored regrammaticalization, functioned entirely in the context of a burgeoning multilingualism, as Sanskrit did in India.[93]

For now, before moving on, we might allow ourselves to imagine the unusually perceptive and sensitive person who composed the *LT*. He—almost certainly a man, possibly a Chakyar performer of Maṇi-pravāḷam texts and/or some form of Kūṭiyāṭṭam, or at least a connoisseur of such performances[94]—was obviously highly trained in the traditional sciences. We can see him reading the *Tŏlkāppiyam* in Tamil and Ruyyaka in Sanskrit, perhaps also the new texts in logic arriving from the northeast, in his home somewhere in rural Travancore. Did he travel to Madurai, or beyond, to parts of the southern Deccan? He must have heard both Telugu and Kannada speech, and he would have spoken both fluent Tamil and a scholar's Sanskrit along with his native Malayalam. He was a linguist, at once empirical and theoretical in approach (often in ways we would think of as highly "modern")—something more than a traditional grammarian. We know he was passionate about early Malayalam poetry in live performance (there is almost no evidence from before the late sixteenth century of silent reading by a lone individual in south India), and we can see the intellectual goal he formulated for himself. A bold, wide-angle perspective informs every page of his book. Here is one image we can hold in mind, among others, of the versatile south Indian intellectual on the cusp of modern times.

The differences between the Kerala Maṇi-pravāḷam of the *LT* and the far less formalized Tamil Maṇi-pravāḷam, in its various types and intensities, should now be clear. Interestingly, Tamil also eventually generated Maṇi-pravāḷam poetry that conforms, more or less, to the strict definitions of the *LT*. We have a large-scale poetic work by Viśvanātha Sūri, from the late-eighteenth century and the village of Kalamur in northern Tamil Nadu (North Arcot District), which bears the name *Virāṭa-parva-maṇi-pravāḷa-mañjarī*, that is, a Maṇi-pravāḷam retelling of the *Virāta-parvan* from the Sanskrit epic.[95] Here we find in every verse fully inflected chunks of Sanskrit—with Sanskrit endings—along with lyrical Tamil (but without Tamil-derived denominative verbs in Sanskrit, one particular feature of the *LT*, as we have seen). For example:

> *teṉuṭaṉ* ***tava dadāmi*** *pāyasaṃ*
> *kūṟuṭaṉ* ***kim api khaṇḍaśarkarām/***
> *vā nĕṭum pŏḻutu* ***kiṃ vilīyase***
> *nāṉ ĕṭam tarukiṟeṉ* ***tavâsitum*** (2.114)

> I'll give you milk [*pāyasam*] with honey
> and some chunks of sugarcane.
> Why do you keep hiding from me, for so long?
> Come sit with me: I'll make room.

This is the rogue Kīcaka pleading with Draupadī, disguised as the hairdresser Sairandhrī. I have highlighted in bold the sweet chunks of pure Sanskrit, including the inflected present-tense forms and an infinitive. As a verse, there's nothing very exciting here; its charm lies precisely in the way the Tamil and Sanskrit flow easily and naturally together. Often, as in this case, the verses are set in the lyrical Sanskrit meters, and occasionally there are other linguistic features of interest, including colloquial Tamil forms. I won't explore the language of this text any further now.

One stylistic feature, however, needs to be noted; the author articulates it himself in one of the introductory verses to his poem:

> *muttukkaḷālum* ***iva*** *nal pavaḷaṅkaḷālum*
> *kottuk kalanta tamiḻāl* ***api saṃskṛtena/***
> *ĕttikkilum* ***bhavatu hāra-lateva baddhā***
> *puttiku'* ***mat-kṛtir iyaṃ sudṛśāṃ vibhūṣā//*** (1.11)

> A fine necklace strung with coral and pearls,
> in Tamil and also in Sanskrit,
> such is my poem: may it adorn
> the hearts and minds of those
> keen of sight
> throughout the world.

The keen of sight, *sudṛś,* could also be beautiful women with their pearls. And the pearls are, it seems, the point of this verse (in *vasanta-*

*tilakā* meter), deliberately inserted by Viśvanātha to replace the rubies of Kerala Maṇi-pravāḷam. As we saw, the *LT* explicitly rejects the idea of a combination of coral and pearls, which do not share the same "color" or texture. But for the Tamil Maṇi-pravāḷam poet, the contrast is the key to the strange and quite wonderful beauty of this work. Here Sanskrit and Tamil complement each other perfectly, creating a seamless whole, but they remain sufficiently distinct—especially given the inflected forms of Sanskrit within a Tamil verse—to tease or tantalize the reader. Note, too, the cosmopolitan claim this verse presents: the whole world might well find delight in this subtle mix. In this respect, Viśvanātha goes beyond even the *LT* author in imagining a potential audience for his strings of coral and pearl.

## Tamil as Goddess: Milk and Moonlight

Maṇi-pravāḷam, as a distinct linguistic idiom, whether in Tamil or Malayalam, self-consciously illuminates and demarcates the relations between Tamil and Sanskrit within a relatively wide range of literary as well as colloquial styles. A work like the *LT* thematizes these relations and offers a new grammar, informed by both Tamil and Sanskrit grammatical systems, of one salient expressive style. There is, however, something a little artificial about this endeavor when seen within the larger cultural-linguistic universe of late-medieval south India. The very notion of a mixture of rubies and coral requires us to abstract both the Sanskrit and Tamil components, as if they were fully autonomous and capable of being isolated from each other, before recombining them in a single, ultimately quite homogeneous necklace or string, as the *LT* tells us. For the author of the *LT,* rubies and coral merge, not quite seamlessly but nonetheless in deep phonic and semantic harmony, into a single language, which we need not hesitate to call "Malayalam." Paradoxically, the presence of "extreme" Sanskrit forms—Sanskrit morphemes conspicuously, even outlandishly, inserted into the flow of a vernacular verse or sentence—only serves to confirm, or indeed intensify, the specific vernacular identity of the resulting mixed style.

No living south Indian language in this period offered its speakers and singers such entirely abstract and isolated linguistic organisms. In the Tamil case generally, as we have seen, both Tamil and Sanskrit were somehow internal to each other and, on another level, understood as interdependent members of an integral conceptual set. Within such a set, the very meaning of the word "Sanskrit" was far from fixed—shifting from the notion of a distinct, full-fledged language to that of a prestigious speech register useful for specific expressive aims. At the same time, Sanskrit, as an idea, embodied cultural roles that encompassed both a rich complementarity to Tamil and a potential antinomy. Over centuries this set inspired continuous meditations on the Sanskrit-Tamil continuum, some of them even bolder than the grammar of the *LT.*

Take one example from sixteenth-century Tenkasi, in the far south, a site of intense cultural activity that we will study in Chapter 6. Circa 1560, King Ativīrarāma Pāṇṭiyaṉ composed an exquisite Tamil version of the great Sanskrit *kāvya* by Śrīharṣa, the *Naiṣadhīya-carita,* which tells the story of the love of Nala and Damayantī. When the beautiful Damayantī's father announced that she would ceremoniously choose her bridegroom from among all the princes who sought her hand, there was a wild rush of potential suitors from all over India, and also from the heaven of the gods, to her city, Vidarbha; and since each of the human candidates spoke a different language, there was a question as to how they could possibly communicate with one another:

*ciṟpa-nūl kaḻiyak kaṟṟor cittiritt' ĕṉa vāynta*
*pŏṟp' uṟu nĕṭiya veṟ kaṭ pūṅkŏṭi vatuvai veṭṭup/*
*paṟ pala teya ventar tŏkutaliṟ pāṭai tervāṉ*
*aṟpuṭaṉ ĕvarum teva pāṭaiyiṉ aṟaivar māto*[96]

They all wanted to marry this startling woman
with eyes long as spears. She was beautiful—as if
she'd been painted by the finest painters in the world.
Since these kings came from many different lands,
in order to understand one another, they all happily,
lovingly, spoke the language of the gods.

*Teva pāṭai,* the language of the gods, is, of course, Sanskrit—spoken lovingly, *aṟputaṉ,* by all the highly cultivated suitors. Sanskrit is their only shared medium of communication, and they have no difficulty at all, it seems, in shifting to it in the interests of mutual intelligibility. It is striking that Ativīrarāma joins this notion to that of a living person as beautiful as, or in effect more beautiful than, any masterpiece of painting. All kings want to marry this astonishing creature. They also speak a divine language, *pāṭai=bhāṣā,* perhaps more beautiful than others, but certainly functional in specific pragmatic contexts. In any case, Sanskrit here is very much a language in its own right. We can also note the complete absence of any sense that the language of the gods is foreign to the Tamil world.

Yet underneath this remarkable verse we can hear its Sanskrit prototype, *Naiṣadhīya-carita* of Śrīharṣa:

> *anyonya-bhāṣânavabodha-bhiteḥ saṃskṛtrimābhir vyavahāravatsu/*
> *digbhyaḥ sameteṣu nareṣu vāgbhiḥ sauvarga-vargo na janair acihni//* (10.34)

> You couldn't tell the gods apart from human beings,
> since the men who had come there from all over, afraid
> they wouldn't understand one another's language,
> spoke only in Sanskrit words.

Our Tamil poet has made an important change in the basic idea of the verse. Śrīharṣa stresses the fact that human beings and gods were indistinguishable at Damayantī's ritual of choice. As the commentator Nārāyaṇa says: *saṃskṛtasya deva-manuṣya-sādhāraṇatvād ete devāḥ ete manuṣyāḥ iti tatratyair na jnātāḥ iti bhāvaḥ,* "since Sanskrit was common to both gods and humans, none of the locals could say, 'These are gods' or 'these are human beings.'" Ativīrarāma has put this notion aside; he is interested in communicability. The wording of the critical phrase in the Sanskrit verse is telling: *saṃskṛtrimābhir . . . vāgbhiḥ* literally means not exactly "Sanskrit" as a language but rather "refined or polished words." So, while clearly the suitors were reduced to speaking to one another in Sanskrit, there is also a suggestion that "Sanskrit" is a potential property of all speech. This suggestion fits very well with one prevalent medieval south Indian understanding of what Sanskrit means. Tamil shares this same basic property of elevated or intensified speech.

The Tenkasi example is one of many—too many to be considered here. Tamil sources from post-Chola times right up to the modern era offer endless speculations on the nature of Tamil, on language in general, and on Sanskrit-in-Tamil. As we shall see, many of these passages have a Tantric cast to them, effectively divinizing Tamil in its sounds, in the graphic or visual representation of the latter, and in the musical and rhythmic patterns in which these sounds carried meaning.[97] The poets and scholars who produced such works were part of a wide trans-regional discourse, multilingual by definition, highly intertextual and dialogic, erudite, often contentious, and hyper-reflexive (particularly about language). Together they created what we might call a "Republic of Syllables" based on shared axioms of phonematic efficacy and on the grammars of sound and sense implicit in then current metalinguistic and metapoetic theories—the latter also embodied and reformulated in a new series of grammatical texts.

Today it is difficult even to evoke the full dynamism and intensity of this intellectual and artistic universe, conspicuously at work in Tamil, Telugu, Kannada, Malayalam, Sanskrit, and later in Marathi and Persian as well, just as it is difficult for us to reconstruct the protocols of reading that Tamil poets assumed to be active in the minds of their readers. I am going to concentrate here on a single eloquent example, the *Maturai Mīṉâṭciyammai Piḷḷaittamiḻ*, or "the Tamil poem about the childhood of the goddess Mīnâkshī in Madurai," by the great poet Kumarakurupara Cuvāmi, who was born in the late sixteenth century and may have died in 1688. Here is a major cultural figure emblematic of a type, or creative mode, very different from our projected image of the *LT* Maṇi-pravāḷam theorist. As such, he can help us bridge the transition from what could be called late-medieval to early-modern times.

Tradition tells us that this poet was unable to speak at all until his parents took him, when he was five years old, to the famous temple of Lord Murugan at Tiruccendur; moved to sing by the god, the boy uttered his first words, and indeed his first complete text, the *Kantar-kali-vĕṇpā* ("Songs in *vĕṇpā* meter to Skanda / Murugan"). From this point on, there was no stopping the flow of Tamil poetry. Although he initially fit the prototype of the high-medieval peripatetic poet, like Black Cloud, moving from patron to patron and from temple to temple, Kumarakuruparar was, in fact, mostly an establishment figure—and as such opposed to mildly antinomian mavericks among his near-contemporaries (such as Paṭṭiṉattār[98] and the Vīraśaiva poet Tuṟaimaṅkalam Civappirakācar). Thus Kumarakuruparar was both the pupil of the fourth head of the Tarumapuram mutt, Māc'ilāmaṇi Tecikar, and the putative founder of the prominent Kācimaṭam at Tiruppanantal in the eastern Kaveri delta—one of the three or four most prestigious institutions of higher learning in the Tamil country in the late-medieval and early-modern period.

He is said to have come to Tiruppanantal from Kasi/Varanasi on the banks of the Ganges, where he spent some years, learning fluent Urdu as well as Śaiva metaphysics. In popular woodcuts and lithographs one often still sees him depicted riding on the back of a lion, since the story goes that the Mughal emperor in Delhi, Aurangzeb, hearing of his fame, summoned him to his court and sent a lion to carry him there. The story has a suggestive truth at its core: this poet was a man of wide cultural horizons, at home in the northern traditions no less than in Tamil Śaivism. In addition to a vast number of poetic works, he wrote a learned treatise on metrics *(Citamparaccĕyyuṭ-kovai)* and *Nīti-nĕṟi-viḷakkam* on practical ethics. We might think of him as giving voice, in some ways, to a "modern" sensibility informing his relation to the deities he praised. At the same time, he is self-aware and reflexive, in particular about the role of Tamil and the modes in which Tamil is felt to exist and to work its magic. He perfectly exemplifies the Tamil poet-intellectual and scholar of the seventeenth century, a man rooted in the ritualized world of the delta-based mutts, a participant in the polyglossic pan–south Indian discourse of this period, and in tune with the aesthetic sensibilities that animated that learned environment.

I have to say something about the generic features of the composition that concerns us—a *Piḷḷaittamiḻ* or "Child Tamil," the oddest genre in the entire literary ecology of medieval Tamil and one of the 96 "Short Genres," *ciṟṟ'ilakkiyam.* The *Piḷḷaittamiḻ* corpus, well studied by Paula Richman (who has also addressed our particular text),[99] imagines the deity (or some august human personage) as a young child to whom the poet relates as a devotee but also, in a sense, as a parent, fondly nurturing and encouraging this godly baby, helping him or her to grow, to acquire language, to begin to walk, to play, and so on. Conventionally the *Piḷḷaittamiḻ* is divided into ten *paruvams* or "stages," each of which gets ten or more verses:

*kāppu*—invocations meant to protect the child (who is two months old)
*cĕṅkīrai*—literally "tender greens," the stage when the baby raises her head, presses her hands against the earth, and sways from side to side (five months)
*tāla*—lullaby (seven or eight months)
*cappāṇi*—clapping hands
*muttam*—asking the child for a kiss (eleven months)
*varukai*—first steps; calling the child to come (thirteen months)
*ampuli*—calling the moon to come to play with the child (fifteen months)
*ammāṉai*—playing with jacks
*nīrāṭal*—bathing
*ūcal*—swinging on a swing

There is some variation in this scheme; if the child is a boy, then the last three stages are replaced by *ciṟṟil* (the girls begging the boy not to destroy their sand castles), *ciṟu-paṟai* (beating a drum), and *ciṟu-ter* (playing with a toy chariot). As Richman notes, the word *paruvam* itself can refer either to the notion of maturation—a key theme in these works—or to a section or segment of a larger entity.[100] In short, the *Piḷḷaittamiḻ* both reveals the deity's ripening into full-fledged, self-aware personhood and enables that process of maturation to take place. By reciting the poem, we are, in a way, "nurturing or growing a goddess,"[101] and at the same time establishing and enacting conditions of radical intimacy with her. Once again I have to insist on the pragmatic aims of most premodern Tamil poetry.

As it happens, our particular *Piḷḷaittamiḻ*, on the goddess of Madurai, has a special fascination with this deity's connection to the Tamil language—no doubt because of the continuous link between Madurai, the supposed home of the third Sangam, and Tamil poetry and poetics. Not only is Kumarakuruparar interested in how Mīnâkshī learns to speak (Tamil)—a natural topic in works of this genre—and in how "normal" speech is related to presemantic, musical utterance; he also wants to explore the nature of this goddess as an embodiment of the Tamil language and as personally carrying through its primary, internal processes, including regrammaticalization, suggestion, and semantic condensation. These latter themes crop up regularly throughout the 102 verses of the text, eventually intensifying into a climax, as the literary tradition has noted. We will have to limit ourselves to four examples, beginning with one of the complex and quite typical invocation *(kāppu)* verses, formally addressed to Mīnâkshī's husband, Śiva / Sundareśvara at Madurai:

He bent the peak of the northern mountain into a warrior's bow.

He made a child's stumbling words float upstream in the
Vaikai River
in a contest with bald, malevolent Jains.[102]

He signed over to those who say the name "Hara"
all that the Goddess of Wealth
and the wishing trees of heaven can offer.

He has crowned himself with my humble words, as if they were
the ripe speech of those who know limpid Tamil. . . .

Not even Brahmā on his lotus could inscribe the rich Vedic
songs
in the book [*paṉuval*] he has written down.
Let us sing our praise to him while we fix our minds on
his feet
that dance the Bharata dance in the famous Hall of Silver.[103]
Let us praise him for *her* sake—
long hair flowing with fragrance,
a smile shooting moonlight,
eyes looking at our lord and at war with him,

breasts filling out and lovely that strain her fragile waist to
its limit.
She is worshiped by the goddess who is a flash of brilliance
on a white lotus rich in honey and by that other goddess on
a lotus
of a hundred petals,[104] since their beauty, which one might try
to capture
in a drawing yet never succeed in drawing, was shamed
by hers. She is the elixir from the sea with its dancing waves,

a parrot fluent in sweet, deathless sound,
a female elephant graceful in its movement as a goose

and the apple of her father's eye—I mean the Pandya king

who held the whole earth in his rocky arms and brought
 it comfort—
she, most luminous of all, who has the nature of Tamil
that is liquid honey.

We call her Marakata-valli, the Emerald Vine
from Madurai. (3)

What does this verse tell us about how Tamil, and indeed various other kinds of language, were understood in seventeenth-century south India? Almost at the outset we meet the child poet with his "stumbling words" *(matalaicŏl)* that were recorded on a palm leaf during the boy's contest with his Jain foes. Śiva is also given to writing: he has "signed over" *(kait tīṭṭiṉar)* vast wealth to those who can utter his name, Hara; and he himself wrote down, as a scribe, a whole book—probably the *Grammar of Stolen Love,* which we have met before; but possibly also Māṇikka-vācakar's *Tirukkovaiyār,* the sequence of lyrical and hermetic love poems that the god commissioned and recorded.[105] It is also possible that the reference is to the famous Sangam love poem, *kŏṅku ter . . .* (*Kuṟuntŏkai* 2) by Iṟaiyaṉār, "god," (thus the modern editor of our text, Pu. Ci. Punnaivanananata Mutaliyar).[106] In any case, the Tamil poem authored by god himself is a kind of Vedic song; as we by now expect, there is no conflict, not even a contrast, between the ancient Sanskrit canon and the Tamil one; these two are co-extensive. Writing, inscribing, fixing a text on palm leaf—all these are necessary and benevolent acts. But our poet's words, like those of Tiruñāṉacampantar, his prototype, are "humble" *(puṉ mŏḻi),* and only Śiva's forbearance can make them into "ripe speech" *(mutu mŏḻi)* acceptable to those who know "limpid Tamil" *(vaṭi tamiḻ).* Apparently, there are two kinds of language, ripe and unripe. Which is better? In any case, Tamil itself, or herself, is naturally limpid and, as we will see, can become more so.

Limpid Tamil speech, in the form of utterances of a good poet, seems to coexist with sheer music, unsemanticized and pervasive. Note the ease of transition from one domain to another. We are in a Tantric world where sound is always, by definition, effectual, and most so when it can be not merely heard but also seen. At the heart of that world we find the goddess herself, "a parrot fluent in sweet, deathless sound," who has "the nature of Tamil that is liquid honey." Mīnâkshī, a Madurai girl, speaks and also probably sings beautiful Tamil; more striking still is the fact that her nature *(iyal)* is identified with Tamil—that is, with something that is dense, luminous, golden-green (she is the Emerald Vine), sweet, musical, ripe, cool, refined, but also sometimes raw and unruly. One part of singing this verse is the latent goal of activating the goddess by speaking or singing to her in the hope that she will respond in kind.

Every time a Tamil speaker opens her mouth, it is the honeyed goddess who emerges into audible presence. So much for the opening. Our poet is eager to refine this initial characterization of Tamil. We follow him in verse 9, another invocation, this time to a different goddess, Kalaimakaḷ or Sarasvatī, the deity presiding over poetry, music, and art, who is asked to watch over baby Mīnâkshī:

> Generous, isn't she,
> this Pāṇḍya princess? She has a child's natural
> wish to give, so she's taught the parrot
> to murmur and lisp, a music sweet beyond words,
> and she's loaned the peacock her green splendor
> and the doe her gentle eyes
> and shown the royal gosling how to saunter
> and her young playmates how to be silly.
>
> Guard her, dear goddess!
> Sifting and sprinkling and savoring the liquid elixir
> that comes from God's book, the one that tells us
> about love in its five classic phases, the one that came
> from the sea of translucent, polished Tamil,
> you sit, a white goose, in your home
> that is the lotus with its golden pericarp,
> its thick fragrance, its long silver petals, wide open,
> where bees sing to enchant.
>
> We sit at your feet to beg you:
> Guard her, sweet goddess!

Sarasvatī knows Mīnâkshī,—knows, among other things, how she excels the standard objects of comparison (the parrot, the peacock, the doe, the gosling) in the very acts or features that the latter naturally embody. These opening statements all fit the classic poetic ornament *vyatireka,* where the subject of comparison outdoes the object. Mīnâkshī is the source of the parrot's "music sweet beyond words," of the "green splendor" of the peacock, and so on. Yet in this figurative field we find again the tension between two kinds of speech *(kiḷavi)*—a grammaticalized, rarefied Tamil connected to God's book about Tamil, and the pregrammatical music of ultimate sweetness that may well be Mīnâkshī's deeper form of expression. This time we know precisely which work is God's book: it is indeed the *Grammar of Stolen Love*; its opening *sūtra* on the "five classical phases" of love is quoted here verbatim. And it is at this point that we discover what the differential intensities of Tamil might mean. For Sarasvatī, goddess of poetry, is savoring—actually "devouring," according to the modern commentator's gloss—the liquid essence flowing from that ancient book, an elixir subject to processes of sifting and sprinkling so as to achieve translucent polish. Look at the relevant verbs: first we have *kŏḻi* (or *kŏḻitt'ĕṭu*), literally to separate the husk or bran from grains of rice, or to sift, to polish, to rinse (as, for example, sand is washed and cast by waves onto the shore); this gives us the idiomatic phrase *kŏḻi tamiḻ,* "refined or pure Tamil." Then there is *tĕḷḷit tĕḷikkum tamiḻkkaṭal,* the ocean of Tamil that is literally "cleared of sediment," or drained off, sprinkled, sifted, as one sifts flour *(māt tĕḷḷa)* or drains away lees, impurities, excess. *Tĕḷḷu tamiḻ* is thus "elegant Tamil"—language at its most refined but also at its most intelligible and perspicuous; *tĕḷḷat tĕḷiya* is "to understand clearly." (Two ancient roots, Burrow and Emeneau 1961: 2825 and 2827, appear to have a prehistoric link.). The liquid elixir is also *tĕḷ-amutu,* "perfectly clear."

Good Tamil is clarity itself, an intense and luminous, or translucent, form of being. It is clearer than clear. It is also delicious. Sarasvatī tastes, devours, or perhaps studies and learns by heart the essence of true speech that is both Tamil and the embodied Tamil goddess, composed of language: the two are one. Polishing and sifting are modes of reaching toward this inner existential core of the syllable or the word or, one might say, of touching, at least for a moment, the inner surface of sweetness, rather like the inner surface of in-ness.[107] That surface is a site of grammar in its most basic sense, including phonology, morphology, and the "stuff" of meaning, though in another sense grammar has been both reflectively reconceived and superseded by a deeper music that goes beyond words. If a poet or a listener does choose to stay with the words, for example by composing or reciting this text we are reading, then grammar offers a means of working on or through these words, cutting away their outer shells, and also, no doubt, enacting them as consequential sound bursts, for example by internalizing the combinations of sounds that serve any competent poet. All of this is inherent to Tamil as such and to the goddess as an expert in Tamil poetry; the Tamil poet thus offers a novel perspective on the interesting question of how god, or goddess, spends his or her time.

But there is more. The deeper reaches of language are connected here to the subtle, fateful, half-remembered moment when a child begins to speak and to think in sentences; the whole of the *Maturai Mīṉâṭciyammai Piḷḷaittamiḻ* deals with this process, which at least some of us may even remember. Let us, then, look at this goddess as she falls asleep, at the age of seven or eight months, to the sounds of a Tamil lullaby offered by the poet:

> Sleep now, little queen of Madurai, the Tamil place
> with its geese on their webbed feet, their crest brilliant gold,
>
> that are like the Golden Goddess Lakshmī given life by waves
> that pour thick moonlight mixed with golden pollen
> from green leaves of the gold-red lotus
> in pools rippling with sweet water mixed with milk
> that gushes from the udders of the red-eyed
> buffalo mother, recently delivered, her mouth
> wide open as she thinks with longing
> of her calf that hasn't yet learned to chew grass
> as she dozes in the shade of mango trees
> with their fiery buds
> while the southern wind blows, born together with Tamil
> in the land of the Pandya king.
>
> Sleep now, little goddess.
> Close your eyes, like flashing fish,
> pregnant with compassion. (23)

It's a long, complex sentence—musical, murmuring, baffling enough to put you to sleep—built up by a series of hierarchically nested clauses, though in Tamil these clauses are really sequential stacks of modifiers folded into one another, like a set of partially overlapping circles. It's worth remarking that the order of the latter is mostly the reverse of the English, given the left-branching nature of Tamil. The poem thus begins in Tamil with the Pandya king and proceeds via the southern wind, the buffalo and calf, the pools where a mother's milk mingles with moonlight, and the goddess Lakshmī, eventually culminating in the geese to whom this goddess, the little queen of Madurai, is implicitly compared. Madurai, remember, is "the Tamil place." We might ask ourselves what is the most deeply embedded point of reference, for it is there that we will touch on the core reality within this poem. And the answer in this case is quite clear: the deepest point we can reach, where the series finally subsides, is that sleepy little queen, her cradle presumably rocked by the same southern wind that was born together with Tamil and that caresses the buffalo mother as she, too, dozes in the shade of the mango trees.

But look at the tonality of the images. We have a typical south Indian pairing of red and white: the fiery mango buds enhance the brilliant gold of the goddess Lakshmī, the pollen, the lotus, the crest of the geese (red and gold are variants of the same color in Tamil); and there is the moonlight pouring from the waves of the Ocean of Milk from which Lakshmī emerged and mingling with the buffalo mother's milk—a creamy flood of white. But the poem is a lullaby: night is falling, so a deepening darkness forms the backdrop to this play of red and white. Tamil poets love the theme of mixing and mingling,[108] here intimately linked to seeing and reflecting: milk and moonlight are originally distinct, perhaps reflections of one another; as the poem proceeds, they become indistinguishable. The milk and water of the pond are also inextricably mixed and then absorb the moonlight, itself no longer separate in any way from this liquid mixture—like Tamil and Sanskrit, in theory distinct yet in practice so thoroughly fused as to constitute a new third-order entity, the true subject of this poem.[109] On one level, the moonlight allows us to see milk flowing through water;

on another, the moonlight is itself a part of what the eye perceives, another moment in the continuous mutual reflections that produce the thick texture of reality. Mīnâkshī's eyes are "like flashing fish / pregnant with compassion"—eyes that give the goddess her name, "Fish-Eyes," and that are themselves pools of water-milk-moonlight. This goddess is in the world as the world is mixed into her, and both are afloat in the creamy moonlight that is Tamil.

Kumarakuruparar knew what he was doing, and he was also making a statement that we should take seriously. In effect, he tells us, in so many words, that (1) god(dess) *is* Tamil; (2) Tamil, in its ripe, polished, sifted essence, is a perfected and intensified form or register of language at its most creative and pragmatically charged (in this sense Tamil is like Sanskrit, or maybe Sanskrit is a kind of Tamil); and (3) poetic speech is ultimately a third language, like the amalgam of milk-water-moonlight, a dense linguistic medium that can no longer be defined in terms of its original components such as "Tamil" and "Sanskrit" in the diachronic, rather limited sense of these terms. Something new has arisen from the middle space of mixing.

Take this understanding of language as emblematic of the mature culture of the seventeenth century in the Tamil world, particularly in its primary institutionalized settings—temples, mutts, courts—with their inherent polyglossia, including even Persian, Urdu, and Hindustani, which Kumarakuruparar presumably learned in Varanasi. As I have said, the historical frame within which this vision of language crystallized is a Tantric one; the goddess is made up of visible sounds, or rather, she is sound itself in both its prearticulate, musical aspect and its grammaticalized, fully elaborated aspect. A certain tension remains between these two different vectors.

We cannot leave the *Maturai Mīṉâṭciyammai Piḷḷaittamiḻ* without looking briefly at verse 61, for the literary tradition marks this verse as the true climax of the poem as a whole. The verse is the penultimate one in the decade devoted to the baby Mīnâkshī's first steps *(varukaipparuvam)*:

> Come now, daughter of King Malayadhvaja,
> fruit of the ancient poems of god woven together like a garland,
> sweet flowing taste of Tamil that is fragrant, ripe with meaning,

you who are a lamp lit in the temple that is the mind of your
  lovers,
you who uproot their self-obsession, come
    like a young elephant-girl playing on the peaks of the
      highest mountains,
    like a picture painted and brought to life in the mind of
      that One Lord
    who lives beyond this world with its land washed by the sea,
you who, lithe as a young vine, are graced by a forest of dense
  dark hair
where bees sip honey,

come to us,
come,
come now.

The story is that when the poet sang this verse for the first time, in public recitation in the presence of the king of Madurai, Tirumalai Nāyakkar, and then expounded the meaning of its opening phrases, the goddess herself appeared in the form of the young daughter of the temple priest; she tore a pearl necklace off the neck of the king and placed it on the poet's neck before she disappeared. Very typically, the verse selected for this epiphany appears about two-thirds of the way through the text as a whole, at a point where the prime listener, Mīnâkshī, can no longer contain the overpowering emotion generated by the words and must stir herself to act. Moreover, this climax is intrinsically related to the defining role of this goddess as the inner liveliness of Tamil poetry, its sweetness, its particular taste or range of tastes, its fragrance, and its pragmatics—since the verse, unfolding on the edge of silence, manages to put her into movement, to make her walk or stumble toward us in visible form. She is the fruit of the ancient poems, divine by nature, that have been woven together as a garland, a continuous tradition *(tŏṭai)* of Tamil poetry with its inherited sweet themes and topics *(tuṟait tīn tamiḻ)*. In another sense, she is herself that unbroken string.

The *Maturai Mīṉâṭciyammai Pillaittamil* offers us one incisive way of modeling the relations between Sanskrit and Tamil at the height of the late-medieval synthesis that produced many truly creative poets—Kumarakuruparar, Tuṟaimaṅkalam Civappirakācar, Nirampavaḻakiya Tecikar, Antakakkavi, and others. In the works of all these poets, we find a far-reaching blending of the two literary languages, often accompanied by passages reflecting on this very theme. The poetic fusion of two ancient linguistic traditions is predicated on the initial distinctiveness of each of them but always entails a new stage in which this distinctiveness is superseded in the interests of forging a new, highly charged idiom. We call this new idiom "Tamil," and Tamil it is, largely by virtue of the linguistic synthesis we have been exploring. As we will see, in the seventeenth- and eighteenth-century corpus of Tamil poems, this kind of reflection is deepened, and other languages and registers are added to the volatile concoction I have described.

We began with Black Cloud, the first conspicuous exemplar of the new poetics, rich in pragmatic results and pyrotechnical feats. We observed a continuum of linguistic and aesthetic experiments in which poet-magicians rivaled their erudite and courtly counterparts, such as Pukaḻenti, in sophistication, popularity, and power. Both groups had assimilated fully the poetic grammar going back to Daṇḍin, either in its original, Pallava-period Sanskrit version or in its Chola-period Tamil reworking. Concomitant with this reorganization of the linguistic and cultural ecology of the Tamil south are the emergence of classicizing tendencies, on the one hand, and of attempts to thematize and/or formulate a possible grammar of the mixed literary languages that had crystallized both in Tamil Vaishṇava contexts and in the special cultural universe of Kerala. A boldly formalized grammar such as the *Līlā-tilakam* recognized the diglossic, or, better, polyglossic character of Tamil while still adhering to a notion of a rule-bound register of aesthetic expression.

Clearly, the period from the thirteenth to early sixteenth century was a time of continuous creative experimentation. Once we venture past the somewhat arbitrary boundary of ca. 1500, we find works that, building on the foundations put in place by the scholars and poets before them, elaborate an understanding of Tamil as, at base, a divine being, variously embodied in goddesses such as Mīnâkshī and her male counterpart and consort, Cŏkkanātar/Sundareśvara-Śiva[110]—both very naturally situated in Madurai, the home of the Sangam. As with any south Indian divinity, Tamil-as-god/goddess invites far-reaching meditations on the composition, systemic dynamics, and existential intensities of such a deity, a restless being striving to speak. Such meditations, prevalent in a wide range of literary works, tend to envision Tamil not as a first-order, primordial entity but as a third-order, internally complex, magnified, mixed being, at once local and translocal, or rather, universal and cosmopolitan *by virtue of* being entirely at home in the local reality of Tamil speech.

SIX

# A Tamil Modernity

## *Caraṇam* 3

### The Tenkasi Breakthrough

As we approach modern times in the Tamil world, a certain stridency enters both public and scholarly debates. We can easily see where it comes from, as we see its continuing effects in the social and political spheres of today's Tamil Nadu; we can also define somewhat unexpected continuities from the courtly and popular cultures of the seventeenth and eighteenth centuries. It is not so easy to escape this acrimonious, impassioned tone, present at every step one takes. One way to slip into the discordant modern world is to ask ourselves when it began to take shape—or more generally, what a word like "modern" might mean in Tamil. In fact, we moved in this direction in the final section of Chapter 5: I think a poet such as Kumarakuruparar is already rather modern, in ways we can specify, appearances to the contrary notwithstanding. Without lingering over these features now—it is surely preferable to let the reader form her own impressions inductively from the materials we'll be studying—I will simply list a few themes and domains that seem to me to be critical to any synthesis of the modern, or the early modern, in the far south. I think of notions of self and the integrity, also the dis-integration, of self; of dissonant and overlapping temporalities; of irony, broadly defined, and self-parody, or a reflexive reframing of experience that foregrounds cognitive disharmonies and dissent; of shifting models of the mind and of the person; of redefinitions or differential, nuanced theories of what is real; of the relation of human and cultural worlds to the rule-bound natural domain that envelops them and of which they are part; of a reconceived politics and innovative, restructured polities; of cash-based economics and the reconfigured social order; of radical experiments in the erudite sciences, including mathematics, physics, logic, poetics, and linguistics—and so on. It is, of course, often the case that major shifts in all the above areas and topics mask themselves in highly traditional modes of speaking and writing; it is also the case that we can isolate new expressive forms, in syntax, lexis, genre, and style, so that the very sentences that we read take on a freshness, a modern tone, instantly apparent and familiar to us. Usually, such continuity and novelty go hand in hand.

Modernity is always a relative concept, privileging the more recent over the more distant past and thereby habitually distorting the latter. It never happens in a single shot. It emerges in some organic way, surely conditioned or triggered by social and structural change, usually gradual; it is necessarily continuous with its own prehistory; and it is never a single, homogeneous set of features. All sorts of amalgams and confusions are the norm. In the case of south India, in particular, we have to contend with a relatively shallow notion of reformist modernity that arrives as a result of the colonial regime.[1] Much of the scholarly literature on modern south India deals almost entirely with this latter, impoverished, set of themes. I will try, in this chapter, to go a little deeper, inspired by creative figures such as Giambattista Vico, in early-eighteenth-century Naples, and his astonishing and no less creative predecessors and contemporaries in sites such as Tenkasi, Penukonda, and Tanjavur.

Let's start with Tenkasi, in the far south of today's Tamil Nadu, just east of the Western Ghats dividing the Tamil country from Kerala. By the middle of the sixteenth century, something very new was under way in Tenkasi. A line of rulers claiming to be descendants of the medieval Pāṇḍya kings consolidated a small-scale state in this far southern corner of the Tamil country in the course of the fourteenth and fifteenth centuries.[2] By the decade of the 1440s this Pāṇḍya state had attained a solid economic base, at least partly sustained by the lucrative trade passing over the Ghats, that enabled the rulers, among other projects, to build the great Viśvanātha-Śiva temple still standing in the city, with its monolithic portrait-sculptures that are among the artistic masterpieces of Nāyaka-period south India. The boom in temple construction or reconstruction and the related investment in painting and sculpture—for example, the magnificent paintings inside the gopuram at Tiruppudaimarudur—have been studied by Leslie Orr and Anna Seastrand.[3] In Tamil literature the rule of Ativīrarāma Pāṇṭiyaṉ, beginning ca. 1564, witnessed a burst of activity unparalleled elsewhere in Tamil Nadu; the king was himself a powerful poet, the author of the complex work known as *Naiṭatam,* which we have already quoted.[4] Once considered the basis of an education in Tamil, this work is, sadly, little read today, as are Ativīrarāmaṉ's other monumental narrative poems, based on purāṇic themes, such as the Tamil *Kāśi-khaṇḍa* and the *Kūrma-* and *Liṅga-purāṇas.*

It is surely significant that two of these works—the great literary feat of the *Naiṭatam* and the *Kāśi-khaṇḍa*—were also reconceived in Telugu by the fifteenth-century innovator-poet Śrīnātha, a revolutionary figure in the Andhra tradition. It is certain that the Tenkasi literary circle of the sixteenth century was well aware of developments in Telugu, on the one hand, and in Malayalam, a close neighbor, on the other; this supralocal awareness is entirely typical of the Republic of Syllables of which I have spoken. Among the major figures at Tenkasi was Ativīrarāmaṉ's brother, Varatuṅkarāmaṉ, whose Tamil *Brahmottara-khaṇḍa* was once a highly popular and widely diffused work (recording the local tradition of Gokarna on the western coast).[5] An imaginative metrical retelling of the ancient story of Purūravas and Urvaśī, the *Purūrava-caritai,* was apparently composed in Tenkasi by a contemporary of Varatuṅkaṉ, Ayyam Pĕrumāḷ Civanta Kavirācar.[6]

It is always difficult—usually impossible—to assert causal connections leading from the social-political and / or economic domains to creative, artistic production. Great art has a habit of turning up of its own accord, however powerfully it may reflect the material conditions that were there at its birth. Elsewhere I have suggested that the Tenkasi Tamil works of genius give voice to a newly emergent model of the mind, one in which the faculty of imagination had hypertrophied to the point where it was, in many ways, the defining feature of the human.[7] We see varying embodiments of this new model and of the sensibility that informed it from major cultural sites all over sixteenth-century south India. *Naiṭatam* offers a particularly trenchant set of examples.

It is hard to overstate the freshness of vision, and the presence of a refashioned poetics, that one gets from reading this work, which ostensibly follows its Sanskrit prototype rather closely even as it repeatedly, indeed systematically, exceeds this model. Look at the following two verses:

> He, Nala, the warrior king, wants
> to paint your portrait. He's collected many
> precious stones and polished them
> for this collage (each for one
> of your perfect features).[8] It's not so easy.
> He grumbles: "This damned canvas is not wide enough
> to paint her breasts," or "The tip of my paintbrush
> is nowhere near fine enough to paint
> her waist." He's frustrated: deep
> psychic despair. All he can do is stare,
> unblinking, yearning.[9]

The goose, sent by Nala as a love messenger to Damayantī (whom Nala has never seen), is reporting to Damayantī and trying to convince her that Nala is truly in love with her. This verse has its prototype in the Sanskrit *Naiṣadhīya* 3.103–105, where Nala is also desperately trying to paint Damayantī's portrait; but Ativīrarāma has taken an utterly conventional *topos* in a new direction and, what is even more striking, articulated his thought in a complex, somewhat jagged syntax that can only be called "modern." The goose is improvising, at the same time toying with his listener, probably also trying to make her smile (even as the poet is trying to make *us* laugh with her). So the verse has an unobtrusive but crucial undertone of self-conscious comment by the narrator; I've tried to capture this in English. Nala's despair, says the goose, is active deep inside his psyche, *uḷḷam*—that is, his inner self, generally, but, in this period, more specifically the mind, seen as an integral, personal unit capable of all kinds of hallucinatory excess.[10] It is the *uḷḷam* that has generated the imagined image of the beloved that Nala stares at without blinking in a strange, yet strangely familiar, form of introspection.

All in all, it's a modern, or early-modern, verse structured with the standard building blocks of earlier *kāvya*. The waist of the beloved, as everyone knows, is so tiny that it might not even be there—so, naturally, no brush-tip can be fine enough to paint it. The opposite problem relates to the canvas and the enormous breasts. The frustration Nala supposedly feels is perhaps not so different from ours as we encounter yet another variation on well-known tropes. But just here lies the point. We are close to the principle associated with the name of Pierre Menard, "author of the Quixote," as presented by Jorge Luis Borges. In the twentieth century, the fictional Pierre Menard manages, with vast effort, on the basis of his own experience, to produce paragraphs that coincide precisely with paragraphs by Cervantes; but their meaning has been changed irrevocably. "The text of Cervantes and that of Menard are verbally identical, but the second is almost infinitely richer."[11] This principle operates regularly in south Indian literature and is in no way limited to modern works; but in a sophisticated text such as the *Naiṭatam,* it enhances an already modernist tone, much as in Borges's example. A thought that could, in theory, have occurred to Pukaḻenti in the thirteenth century, in the course of the latter's playful rethinking of Daṇḍin's classical figures,[12] comes to the surface in late sixteenth-century Tenkasi with an added tinge of gentle, pointed irony and a slight but unmistakable inner distance. It is as if the poet were saying to us: "Listen to this learned yet rather silly goose. We've seen this figure a thousand times, and here it comes again. It's no doubt true—beautiful women have, by definition, full breasts and an infinitesimal waist. Then again. . . ." A playful skepticism is integral to the "infinite richness" such a verse offers connoisseurs of Tamil poetry. Even without Borges, we know we are in a bold new era.

The *Naiṭatam* happens to be particularly thick with illustrations of this thesis, although the other great works from Tenkasi are clearly part of the same enterprise. Once again I want to stress the porous nature of this sixteenth-century world and the active intertextual presence of Telugu and Malayalam works in the Tamil masterpieces from this extended moment. It would be absurd to limit our discussion of novelty and systemic change to what happened in Tamil. Thus, to mention only two more features: first, we find in the *Naiṭatam* the same kind of focused, protoscientific observation of the natural world—itself reconceived as an autonomous domain governed by natural laws amenable to empirical observation—that we see in the Telugu and Kannada *prabandhams* from the early sixteenth or late fifteenth century. Here is one simple example:

> The male cuckoo, dusted white with cool,
> fragrant pollen from silky flowers weighing down
> the boughs in spring, is full
> of passion. She—his new wife—sees him
> approaching; or rather, she smells
> something a little new. She's dark,
> with red eyes and a voice sweeter
> than the lute, and she's happy
> to tease him. She hides herself
> among the tender leaves of the growing
> plantain with its thick virginal trunk.[13]

A moment of first blossoming—of flowers, trees, love—is held in focus; it is also humanized, since the cuckoo couple is in the state of being *kaṭi maṇam,* "newlyweds," but by *ślesha* paronomasia, these words also mean "sharp fragrance"; and indeed, the special fragrance and emotional novelty are fully fused. The young plantain, closely described, brings the verse to its climax and close. Meticulous observation (by the poet) underpins the necessary imaginative component of seeing. To begin to grasp the full significance of such descriptions, one needs to examine them in the context of the newly burgeoning literature of naturalistic and technological-scientific treatises that we find in all the languages of the south in this period.[14] Such works in the south Indian vernaculars created the basis of well-known compendiums produced by colonial-period authors of entire scientific domains, notably botany, zoology, mineralogy and geology.[15] Conceptually, such domains now form part of a much wider notion of nature itself: indeed, I would argue that Nature, in the sense I have outlined, is the true heroine of Bhaṭṭumūrti's Telugu masterpiece, possibly the acme of classical Telugu literary culture, the *Vasu-caritramu* (mid-sixteenth century). Interestingly, within a few years of its "publication" Bhaṭṭumūrti's book was adapted into elegant Tamil poetry by a poet from the northern Tamil country, Tŏṇṭaimāṉtuṟai Ampalatt'āṭum Ayyaṉ—testimony both to the regionwide awareness of developments within neighboring languages and literatures and to the salience of this theme of nature as a rule-bound, creative domain inviting observation.[16] A Sanskrit adaption also exists, the *Vasu-caritra-campū* of Kālahasti Kavi.

Second, the Tenkasi poets produced, along with a lyrical masterpiece such as *Naiṭatam,* major works of what we could call poetry-as-prose. We notice a gradual shift to an emergent style of writing (with an emphasis on actually writing things down) in experimental prose even before prose itself had been fully defined in terms of the modern genres. One sees this style, individually inflected, in works such as Ativīrarāmaṉ's *Kāci-kaṇṭam,* where narrative urgency often sweeps the reader along in straightforward protoprose; the new style is also conducive, as in the early-modern novels, to passages of psychological realism (for example in the nuanced depiction of the rebellious king of Benares, Divodāsa). Poetry-as-prose of this sort also crystallizes in Telugu in the sixteenth century, notably in the works of Piṅgaḷi Sūranna such as *Kaḷāpūrṇodayamu* ("The Sound of the Kiss") and *Prabhāvati-pradyumnamu* ("The Demon's Daughter"). In Tamil, believe it or not, one could draw a line leading from late-sixteenth-century Tenkasi poetic narratives to twentieth-century prose artists such as Putumaippittan, with a big but necessary detour around late-nineteenth-century novelists such as Vedanayakam Pillai and Rajam Iyer.[17]

## Prose, History, Realism

In a polyglossic reality such as Tamil speakers have probably always inhabited—including systemic diglossia or triglossia[18] and a continuum of distinct spoken dialects, not to mention the presence of sister languages such as Telugu and Kannada and of Sanskrit—prose is at once a problem and an achievement. What do we even mean by this common term? Premodern literature is overwhelmingly couched in metrical verse, though rhythmic prose passages, *vacaṉam* or *urai-naṭai,* do appear in the *Cilappatikāram* and in some later works. As we have seen, Tamil inscriptions, from Pallava-Pandya times onward, are largely in prose; indeed, they are our richest sources of eloquent early prose in both pragmatic and expressive styles.[19] We also sampled the precise and lyrical prose style of the commentary on the *Grammar of Stolen Love;*[20]

and it has become something of a truism, or a scholarly convention, to trace the origins of modern Tamil prose to the great medieval commentators, such as Naccinārkk'iniyar, Aṭiyārkkunallār, Cenāvaraiyar, and Iḷampūraṇār, in a general way.[21] Genealogies, however, are usually deceptive.

Tamil speakers, of course, have always spoken prose, perhaps, like Molière's M. Jourdain, without knowing it. We can be sure that colloquial speech, from the beginning, was, like all spoken language, syntactically complex, rich in figuration and transferred (metaphoric) meanings, and naturally rhythmic, even semimetrical. Hints of this kind of speech have survived in medieval inscriptions—also in late-medieval and early-modern inscriptions such as the long captions to the Mucukunda paintings in the Tiruvarur temple, from the late seventeenth century.[22] Modern *literary* prose, however, is of a different order entirely, as Kamil Zvelebil noted long ago;[23] nothing can quite prepare us for the expressive power and stylistic range of nineteenth-century Tamil prose works, which "bespeak a change of consciousness, of conscience," as Sascha Ebeling has justly stated.[24] It is that transformation that needs to be defined and, perhaps, explained.

Its roots lie in the Tenkasi Renaissance and other protomodern sites. Prose, of different sorts, is one, but only one, major indication of the change. We can't understand this development without reference to the newly crystallized genre of historiography—that is, the appearance of novel notions of temporality—and to no-less-novel forms of humanistic realism in relation to the natural world. I think, in contrast to Zvelebil's view, that contact with external, non-Indian cultural practices had little to do with this set of features, including the growing dominance of prose within the cultural ecology of the far south. Incipient modernism of the type we are exploring seems to be primarily an indigenous and organic development occurring more or less simultaneously in all the languages and cultures of the far south.

Who were the carriers of this new "prosaic" reality? One major group, active mostly though not solely in an early proto-urban environment and reflecting the values and worldview of an educated and literate elite, were the record keepers and local historians whom we refer to as *karṇams* (*ūrkkaṇakkar* in earlier inscriptions). In Tamil, as in the other southern languages, *karṇams* wrote history in a style, or set of styles, of their own creation.[25] In all the major languages, historiographical discourse stands in marked contrast to the so-called pandits' prose, archaic and stiff, that acquired particular prestige and influence by the middle of the nineteenth century under the colonial regime.[26]

For a good example of what I am calling "*karṇam* prose," the reader is referred to translations of the *Koyil-ŏḻuku*, or *Temple Register,* which tells the history—political, bureaucratic, ritual-liturgical, economic—of the great Srirangam temple. No one knows when the accountants and other temple servants in Srirangam began to compile this written record, which has a lot to say about quite early Chola and post-Chola times. It is clear that the work had many authors and that it grew to its present, rather unwieldy, even chaotic state, over centuries, possibly settling into some relative fixed form in the late eighteenth or early nineteenth century.[27] Despite the range of expressive styles, certain features remain stable: a rich, multilingual vocabulary, with occasional chunks wholly in Sanskrit (embedded verses, for example) and lexical borrowings from all registers of speech and from sometimes distant languages, including Persian and Urdu; a tendency toward strung-out, hypotactic sentences that seem, with their convoluted rhythms, to mimic the uneven flow of time itself; within such syntactic experiments, discordant temporalities—a preexisting future nesting inside the past, or sudden transitions into a timeless and eternal present—as the very stuff and color of a precise historical record. We have argued elsewhere that it is just this temporal discord that makes modern historiography possible, not only in South Asia.[28] Several typical features of the *karṇam* style, in particular the syntactical looping and embedding, carry over into the prose of the nineteenth-century Tamil novelists;[29] the contrapuntal temporal rhythms have survived in the eloquent Tamil prose of authors of our own generation (very conspicuously in Na. Muthuswamy and Imayam).

Other such continuities exist: scholars interested in early Tamil prose are fond of referring to the first surviving full-fledged diary in Tamil, that of the *karṇam*-like entrepreneur, colonial factotum, and local politician Ananda Ranga Pillai, in mid-eighteenth-century Pondicherry. This long and often rather boring text was written in a mixture of colloquial and formal, semiliterary Tamil.[30] It is, of course, in prose. Occasionally, this record of daily events transcends itself and reaches toward descriptions graced by color and telling observation. The diary is not, however, an example of modern subjective introspection, as we might perhaps have expected from someone living in the same century, and at times in the same language, as Jean-Jacques Rousseau. For a little more lively feeling finding its voice in the new prose style, we would do better to turn to the cache of Tamil letters from Sri Lanka recently published by Herman Tieken.[31]

These letters, sent by members of the well-known Ondaatje family of Christian Chettiyar merchants to Nicolaas Ondaatje, who was exiled from Sri Lanka to the Cape of Good Hope in 1727, are couched in a ravishing blend of archaic formal and intimate semi-colloquial speech levels, with an overlay of Christian missionary style; they are peppered with foreign words—Dutch, Portuguese, even Chinese—and, inevitably, second- or third-hand Sanskrit, like the English and other foreign loan words we hear in modern colloquial Tamil. A powerful interlinguistic permeability is one feature of a language dramatically expanding its expressive range and depth, though the true explosion into fully modern prose comes later. Still, the new, unassuming prose style that we see in the Ondaatje letters and, to some extent, in Anandraranga's diary is steadily striving, unawares, toward a translocal register of increasing semantic density and scope. Tamil of this sort has no real precedent in the literature of past centuries. Empirical observation and colorful description are natural to it, as are the mixed temporal nodes I have noted and—most salient of all—a pervasive realism, evident in all the south Indian literatures of this time. I need to say a little more about this theme.

## Hyperglossic Speech and Tamil Islam

"Realism" is one of those words that tend to break down upon close inspection, so I had best try to explain what I mean by it. In the case of natural science, including technical treatises as well as the detailed naturalistic description we now find in abundance in literary works, realism in early-modern Tamil entails precision, inductive categorization, and a certain ontic solidity of the observed object. It does *not* preclude a strong notion of imaginative perception; in fact, as I have argued elsewhere, we find throughout south India persistent claims that all perceptual acts contain, indeed emerge out of, an imaginative faculty inherent to the human mind. What is perceived as real is thus accessible to us not in spite of, but rather as a result of, our active imaginative capacity.[32] Moreover, in a comparative and theoretical vein, realism as a conscious literary mode is no less "fictive" than, say, the novel, various dramatic genres, or the *Märchen,* as one can easily see in the genre ecologies of both ancient and modern literary cultures.[33]

We can also speak of realism in relation to the social universe, that is, to diverse forms of life that include communities hitherto largely ignored by Tamil poets and now suddenly brought to the thematic center of the dominant genre ecology. Many of the "Short Genres" focus attention on the social and cultural margins of the far south. For example, *nŏṇṭi-nāṭakam,* the once-popular "Dramas about a Cripple," are picaresque parodic works whose heroes are thieves, usually horse thieves.[34] *Paḷḷu* "Peasant-poems" offer vivid pictures of agricultural life, incidentally recording its regional dialects. *Tūtu* messenger poems are frequently hyper-realistic in their descriptions of Tamil geography and landscape. And so on. Although some of my colleagues may protest, it is clear to me that these now forgotten texts lead directly, both as essays in hard-core social realism and as comic or comi-tragic studies of marginal types and low-caste heroes, to the self-conscious realism of twentieth-century short-story writers in Madras and Madurai.

What about the linguistic concomitants of this widening cultural and social horizon? Does realism of the sort we are seeing imply a new kind of language, and possibly the explicit thematization of that language? Definitely yes. Acute polyglossia now coincides with hyperglossia, the intensification of language through what might be called complexity effects, the elevation of language to divine or semidivine status and, in our period, an enhanced autonomy of community-based literary speech. All these features invite reflexive attention and precise formulation by the intellectual elite. As for acute polyglossia, which may, in fact, have been the linguistic norm in the south for most of the second millennium A.D., the early-modern Republic of Syllables knows few linguistic borders. By the sixteenth–seventeenth centuries, this multilingual set of interlocking cultural contexts has achieved a dynamism that reflects an astonishing rapidity in the diffusion of new texts—many of them from the north, especially from the rich erudite world of Mughal Benares—and a strong impulse to respond rapidly to these novel works in whatever language is most fitting: Tamil, Sanskrit, Telugu, Maṇi-pravāḷam / Malayalam, Kannada, all of the above.[35]

This osmotic linguistic republic is explicitly described in seventeenth-century and eighteenth-century Tamil works, usually produced by scholar-poets combining vast erudition in many languages with literary ambition. A good example is the remarkable *Cīkāḷatti-purāṇam* ("Story of Srikalahasti") collectively composed by three brothers, Karuṇaippirakāca cuvāmikaḷ, Civappirakāca cuvāmikaḷ, and Velaiya cuvāmikaḷ (mid-seventeenth century). This book opens with an invocation to the Tamil Divinity, *tamiḻttĕyvam:*

> First the god with the crescent moon in his long hair,
> who spoke the root-words of the Veda,
> made a grammar that established his name
> for the Tamil divinity that has conquered all languages
> in the world bounded by the roaring sea
> and that compares (and contrasts with) Sanskrit [*āriyam*].
> Let us be aware of this divine being and praise it
> in our mind.[36]

We know this grammarian-god, Śiva, the author of the *Grammar of Stolen Love.* Interestingly, we are told that he composed and recorded this grammar not only for the sake of the Pāṇḍya king but also to "establish his name."[37] As for the Tamil language itself, not only does it have a divine nature, as we have seen in the previous chapter, and not only is it linked intimately with the great god as grammarian, but it has also triumphed over all other languages. The most striking element in this verse, however, is the attempt to formulate, once again, the relations of Tamil and Sanskrit. The relevant phrase—*āriyattoṭ' uṟaḻ taru tamiḻttĕyvattai*—has a subtle complexity suited to this era. The verb *uṟaḻ* means, among other things, "to be comparable to," "to resemble," also "to contrast with," even "to be hostile to," "to rival."[38] This double-edged semantic thrust is certainly intentional. Tamil is simultaneously a rival, possibly even an enemy, of Sanskrit and a necessary complement to the latter, comparable to it: thus Tamil "compares (and contrasts) with Sanskrit" in my translation. The two languages are distinct entities, wedded, not without tension and conflict, within a single package that, as such, overpowers all other tongues.

Once we get beyond the anachronistic modern notion of an exclusive Tamil-ness, a vast horizon opens up. Sanskrit is only one, clearly prominent element in this expansive landscape. By the late seventeenth century, two new languages have entered into Tamil-ness from the outside—Persian and Arabic. They are assimilated, both lexically and, more important, culturally and conceptually, at a time when polyglossic hyperglossia articulates anew what Tamil means. Hyperglossia and polyglossia occupy the same cultural space. Thus one particularly prevalent and privileged mode in the late-medieval or early-modern Tamil country is that of sustained paronomasia, *śleṣha* (*cileṭai* in Tamil), almost always operating with the lexical and grammatical resources of more than one language.[39]

Some poets specialized in this kind of poetry. Take, for example, Kaṭikaimuttup Pulavar, a poet from the dry lands of Ettayapuram in the far southeast (roughly 1665–1740).[40] This gifted artist seems to have been incapable of saying anything that was not paronomastic and / or bilingual, assuming that we can still disentangle Tamil and Sanskrit readings of a single phonetic sequence. For example, on the first anniversary of his wife's death, the poet bought some items needed to perform the rituals; he was carrying them home on his head when he encountered a friend, who asked him what they were for. The poet answered: *talaivitivacam,* that is: "the death date of my beloved" (Tam. *talaivi,* "wife," "heroine" + Skt. *divasam,* "day"); but also, segmenting differently, "the burden of fate" (*talai-viti* < Tam. *talai,* "head" and Skt. *vidhi,* the fate that Brahma writes on one's forehead at birth, + Skt. *vaśa,* "power," "compulsion"). Notice that however one segments the sequence, a Tamil-Sanskrit compound will turn up—so, in effect, we have a double bifurcation, Tamil and Sanskrit welded together in both decodings. They say the poet's friend smiled when he heard this reply—bilingual punning of this order requires the presence of an attentive and educated listener.[41] Kaṭikaimuttuppulavar was also capable of what might be called single-order punning (the analytical distinction is mine, not his). Thus when he lay on his deathbed, with his children weeping beside him, afraid of the future, he said to them: "Why are you mourning for this one father *(appaṉ),* when you have Ĕṭṭappaṉ—literally "eight fathers"—to look after you?" Veṅkaṭecura Ĕṭṭappaṉ, the zamindar of Ettayapuram, was the poet's patron and guardian. It is of some interest that both these stories of paronomastic improvisation take place on the border of life and death, as is only fitting for exercises exploring the deeper reaches of human speech.

We need to explore this point, typical of our period, a little further. The overlapping of hyperglossia and polyglossia has consequences for the entire genre ecology of Tamil and for the social and political universe that Tamil shapes and inhabits. Kaṭikaimuttup Pulavar's most brilliant work is the "Play of the Ocean," *Camuttira-vilācam,* consisting of one hundred bitextual, and often bilingual, verses that carry the lament of a young woman who has caught sight of this same patron, Veṅkaṭecura Ĕṭṭappaṉ or Veṅkaṭecurĕṭṭaṉ, in procession and fallen hopelessly in love with him (unbeknownst to him). She can't eat or drink or sleep; she sees her beloved everywhere; she cannot bear to be so distant from him. In this sleep-starved, hallucinatory state, she addresses the ocean, which in many ways reminds her of her deeply dignified beloved and of her surging desire for him, and also, in some ways, of her own inner tides and riptides. For example:

White the jasmine garlands on the shoulders
of Veṅkaṭecurĕṭṭaṉ, white as the smile
of the Warrior Goddess sitting there,
white as a regal goose,
white as the laughter those shoulders laugh
when they see his enemies turn their backs.
Ocean surging and swelling
like the wealth *he* gives to help Tamil:
worst of all is this killing blackness,
oh deep dark ocean washing over me
like the swishing arrows of Love, even my belt
you have swept away and by now I'm entirely

mad, so mad my mother
won't look at me, those huge waves
of yours make me crazy with pain
but do nothing to stop
tongues wagging like mad
in the village. (29)

It's a mad world and a kind of crazy Tamil; every line in the second half of the poem cracks open to reveal two homophonous but semantically separate phrases—the horizontal paronomasia called "twinning," *yamaka* in Sanskrit, *maṭakku* in Tamil (a general term encompassing several distinct subtypes).[42] Thus:

***vaḷamaik kaṭaley*** *ĕṉai nĕruṅku/*
[oh deep dark ocean washing over me]
***vaḷa' maikk' aṭale*** *piratāṉam*
[worst of all is this killing blackness]

and so on; note the very conspicuous Sanskrit loan word *piratānam* (*pradhānam*, "the main thing," "worst of all"). Unlike the thick intermingling of milk and moonlight, Tamil and Sanskrit, in the *Maturai Mīṉâṭciyammaip piḷḷaittamiḻ*, here a surreal, joyful white mixes with tormenting black, as if the combination of the two linguistic registers and the compulsive bivalent phonetic repetition were more than enough to drive any speaker or listener mad. Verses like this one, overdetermined both phono-aesthetically and semantically, defy translation; their charm derives largely from the deliberate distortion of everyday speech. It is nonetheless apparent even in translation that the patron-hero's love for Tamil and active support of Tamil letters is one major expressive vector at work in the poem, no doubt meant, inter alia, to augment this support in entirely pragmatic ways.

Such is hyperglossia in poetic practice. It goes on and on until finally, somewhere in the heroine's mind, she finds a messenger whom she can send to the king:

Ocean! I saw someone
just like you. I was happy. Her words
were sweet as solid sugar, and all true.
I *really* saw her. She asked me,

"Why is your body so pale? Who
is the one you love?" I said: "I have no one
to give my message." "True," said she,
nodding her head. She promised, and off she went
to the court of the king, Veṅkaṭecurĕṭṭaṉ,
who is God, who takes care of this world.
She told him about me. "Among the young courtesans
who saw your procession, there was one,
a Lotus Girl. You have to send her
a garland *now.*" And the king took this
to heart. (85)

A messenger poem like this is called *tūtu* in Tamil, from Sanskrit *dūta,* "messenger" (the reference is to the prototypical courier poem in Sanskrit, Kālidāsa's *Megha-dūta* or "Cloud-Messenger"). *Tūtu* is a major genre in medieval Tamil, with its own logic of composition and unique features, including the requirement that the messenger, whoever it may be, bring back a concrete sign, usually a garland, from the beloved to the sender of the message.[43] We see this feature in our text as well; the dream messenger explains to Ĕṭṭappaṉ how much he is loved, and he, acknowledging his own incipient feeling for the girl, sends her a ring and pearls. The messenger delivers them, to the girl's intense delight and relief; now at last she can sleep—and dream, apparently a dream within a dream, in which her lover actually appears and makes love to her. "Actually" is the right word for the level of reality inside the dream.

This level of reality is capable of being expressed only through the intensified amalgam of a multilayered Tamil and a thickly Tamilized Sanskrit. No simple, unidirectional stratum of denotation could possibly be adequate to the experience of the young woman in love. Her inner life, she tells us, is fractured, denaturalized, disintegrating, and the syntax of her statements is similarly fragmented, also continuously paronomastic, as if she were trying to reassemble the scattered bits of language and awareness through rhyme and phonetic repetition.

This language, which we continue to call "Tamil," has enriched itself so thoroughly with new resources that it bears little resemblance to the language of, say, Kamban or Cekkiḻār. The bitextual-bilingual world of Kaṭikaimuttup Pulavar and his contemporaries has gained in depth and in dynamism (there are verses where the paronomastic utterances split into three or even four phonetically identical levels); moreover, colloquial speech has infiltrated the rarefied registers of Sanskrit-as-Tamil along with quotations from earlier Tamil classics, so that the experience of reading a poem becomes something quite new, a, dizzying pleasure. At the same time, we find direct, immediately intelligible statements (as in the verse I have just quoted) combined with dense, arcane phrases that require rereading and decoding. Strange to say, this series of intersecting speech levels is in some ways remarkably close to spoken Tamil as we know it today. Yet the tag "bilingual" cannot do justice to the literary dialect we are observing, which is at least trilingual (with colloquial Tamil as the third, after Tamil and Sanskrit) or quadrilingual (if the Tamil-Sanskrit hybrid compounds constitute a mild and novel kind of Maṇi-pravāḷam). In fact, tri- and quadrilingual registers have become standard in the best Tamil poetry of this time.[44]

Now let us take the next step, located in the generation of Muttuppulavar's students, among whom was the great Muslim Tamil poet Umaṟuppulavar. Here we find something new. Umaṟuppulavar, like his teacher, exemplifies the mixed cultural worlds of the southern Tamil country (Ettayapuram). He was patronized by a famous Muslim merchant-politician and culture hero of the Maraikkāyar community, Cītakkāti (Shaikh 'Abd al-Qādir, also known as Pĕriya Tambi Maraikkāyar, d. 1715), from the Muslim coastal center at Kilakkarai, near Ramnad.[45] This Cītakkāti, whom we also know from non-Muslim poets such as Paṭikkācuppulavar and Namaccivāyappulavar, is said to have sent the young Umaṟuppulavar to study the Arabic sources on the Prophet's life (Ar. *sīra*) with the prominent Qādiri Sufi teacher Shaykh Sadaqattullah (1632–1703)—but the latter refused to teach Umaṟu since he came to him wearing Hindu garb, with gold rings on his fingers, as befits a gifted Tamil poet. God himself had to intervene by sending a dream to both teacher and student to arrange for the necessary tuition.[46] The result was the best-known literary work of Muslim Tamil, the *Cīṟāppurāṇam*, probably the finest large-scale narrative poem in Tamil in the seventeenth century; this vast work, largely modeled on Kamban, tells the story of Muḥammad in a Hijaz that has been reimagined as the verdant Tamil land, complete with the classic *tiṇai* landscapes (see

*Cīṟāppurāṇam, Nāṭṭuppaṭalam* 13–14). Like all the texts produced by Tamil Islam, the *Cīṟāppurāṇam* is packed with Arabic loan words (some transmitted via Persian) and, while conforming to the hyperglossic literary dialect of the late seventeenth century, also exemplifies a newly emerged language: Muslim Tamil, the idiom of a vast literature produced over the past three to four hundred years and only recently benefiting from sustained scholarly interest.[47]

This literature has come down to us in two main written forms: one large group comprising nearly all of Tamil Muslim *belles lettres* is recorded in Tamil script, while another considerable segment, primarily though not exclusively religious in aim and orientation (prayers, jurisprudence, praises of the Prophet, and so on), is in Arwi *(lisān al-arwi),* an adapted version of Arabic script, studied systematically by Tschacher.[48] Both streams of this corpus reveal highly intertextual modes of quadrilingual Tamil—a thorough mix of normative grammaticalized Tamil, Sanskrit, Arabic, and a dash of Persian, to which we can add a flavoring of colloquial Tamil. The image of Umaṟuppulavar dressed as a Hindu yet studying Arabic and writing a Tamil *sīra* perfectly encapsulates this organic, interwoven polyglossic culture, which, as Ronit Ricci has shown, reflects the creative overlapping of both Sanskrit and Arabic cosmopolitan, trans-regional idioms, always locally inflected and transformed.[49] More precisely, we might say that both cosmopolitan Sanskrit and Arabic were in fact created and continuously reconfigured by vernacular literary and political cultures, as Ricci argues and as we have seen in our discussions of second-millennium Tamil. Incidentally, the same theme of a Tamil Muslim poet trained by a non-Muslim literatus (in this case, one Tiruvaṭikkavirāyar) recurs in the life story of the eighteenth-century Tamil Muslim virtuoso Kācimpulavar of Kayalpaṭṭaṇam, whose *Tiruppukaḻ* is a conscious attempt to outdo the classic Śaiva collection of the same name by Aruṇakirinātar (fifteenth century).[50] Both Umaṟuppulavar and Kācimpulavar fit the standard type of the Tamil poet-sorcerer; Umaṟu, it is said, was capable of defeating a north Indian rival by making his metal stylus improvise and recite a Tamil verse (note the necessary role of graphic literacy in this context).

With astonishing ease, the pan–south Indian Republic of Syllables expanded to make room for the seventeenth- and eighteenth-century

Muslim Tamil literati who, though clearly seen as distinct in their cultural formation, were integral parts of a wider literary world. One might even go so far as to characterize that world as "secular," in the sense that communal identities, hypertrophied today under the pressure of modern nationalism, were configured differently, and less antagonistically, three hundred years ago. The syllables worked their magic and generated aesthetic delight without reference to the religious proclivities and ritual performances of the poets who uttered them. Indeed, in the case of Tamil Islam and its cultural products, we would do well to envision a still wider complex stretching from southern Arabia to the Malay world and the deep reaches of Javanese civilization, with Sri Lanka firmly inside this fertile, criss-crossing cultural cosmos.[51] Tamil-speaking Muslim merchants were active in the gradual Islamization of the Malay-Javanese sphere from the fifteenth century on, and Malay Muslim culture bearers also influenced the formation of Tamil Islam, as Tschacher has shown. The effervescence of the Southeast Asian Tamil diaspora over the past half-millennium should not be underestimated; its ritual, linguistic, and textual products can still be seen today in Tamil-speaking communities in Singapore, Malaysia, and Sri Lanka (where, interestingly, the large population of Tamil-speaking "Moors" have resisted attempts to subsume them under a generalized, and newly nationalistic, Tamil identity).[52]

From the sixteenth century onward, and probably even earlier, the Tamil coast was dotted with major cultural sites where Islam and Tamil Śaivism flourished side by side: thus we have Nagapattinam / Nagur[53] and Adirampatnam in the central Tamil delta and Kilakkarai and Kayalpattanam, among other small towns, on the Fishery Coast in the far south. In all these settlements, mosques, madrasas, and other vibrant institutional milieux generated works of classical Islamic learning in Arabic and Tamil,[54] as well as Tamil Sufi works, folk epics, eclectic devotional and mystical (sometimes antinomian, utterly nonsectarian) texts such as the songs of Mastāṉ Cākipu (nineteenth century), a huge corpus of prayers *(munājāt)* and celebrations of the Prophet, and complex courtly poetry of the kind I have mentioned. The latter set of genres were closely linked to political figures such as Setupati Vijaya Raghunātha II of Ramnad (d. 1710), patron of Cītakkāti and Umaṟuppulavar, and to the changing fortunes of the Nāyaka states of Madurai and Ramnad in the period of early colonial (especially Dutch) settlement on the coast.[55]

This Tamil diaspora is not, of course, only Islamic; Sri Lankan Tamil "Hindus," if that is the right word, went through a centuries-long cultural trajectory that culminated in a unique, still largely unstudied Sri Lankan Tamil literary corpus, a body of major works not divorced from contemporaneous sites in southern India but distinct from the latter both in language and in themes. To mention but two particularly eloquent examples: the early-eighteenth-century Jaffna poet Varatarāca kavirācar, or Varata Paṇṭitar, composed one surpassing masterpiece, the *Civarāttiri purāṇam* or "Story of Śiva's Night," along with the *Ekātaci purāṇam* ("Eleventh Day Vow") and a *tūtu* messenger poem that may be linked to the vogue in this genre in medieval Sinhala; this gifted and erudite author, at home in Tamil, Sanskrit, and the traditional sciences of medicine and astrology, became in some sense emblematic of early-modern Tamil Sri Lankan literary production, as was Umaṟuppulavar for Tamil Islam. Varatarācar's contemporary, Yāḻppāṇam Nallūr Ciṉṉattampip pulavar (1716–1780), mixed the *antâti* genre—the final syllables of one verse becoming the first syllables of the next—with the virtuoso poetic devices of *maṭakku* ("twinning" or "folding," Skt. *yamaka*) and *tiripu* ("replacing" only the initial syllable of a polysyllabic sequence in each line of a four-line verse, with a consequent change in meaning). The lyrical and musical effect of these cumulating intralinguistic maneuvers is staggering. Ciṉṉattampi's *Kalvaḷaiyantâti,* on Lord Kaṟpaka Vināyakar at the temple site of Kalvaḷai near Jaffna,[56] was taught in Tamil schools in south India well into the twentieth century as an introduction to the intricacies of Tamil poetry at its best.

To take the Sri Lankan case a step further: among prominent sites of the early-modern Tamil diaspora one has to mention the Nāyaka court at Kandy in the central hills. This Nāyaka dynasty (1739–1815) was linked by marriage, strong kinship ties, and military-political expediency to both the Tanjavur and Madurai Nāyaka courts; the Kandy kings were Tamil speakers from birth, though Sinhala also no doubt qualified as their mother tongue. Modern historians have debated whether or not an anti-Tamil backlash took place among the Kandyan Sinhala elite around 1760, the Tamil king having been seen, at least as reported in some Sinhala documents from this period, as "heretical" (originally non-Buddhist) and thus possibly "alien."[57] This reading seems, on the whole, not to do justice to the complex cultural economies and political dynamics of the time. Anti-Tamil sentiment, however, was not unknown in Sinhala works from the eighteenth and early nineteenth centuries. In any case, the Tamil speaking Nāyakas of Kandy presided over a cultural "renaissance" in Sinhala Buddhism at a time when Tamil literati were also intensely active in other parts of the island. Let us then add to the Republic of Syllables in its widest geographic extent, rooted in Tamil as one of its primary cultural vehicles, both the active Islamic component, embodied in an entire library of powerful works, and a more localized Buddhist variant tenuously linked to the very old and extraordinarily creative Tamil presence on the island. For lack of space, we will sadly have to leave Christian Tamil from this period, created first by missionary scholars and then deepened and elaborated by Tamil Christian poets, for another scholarly occasion and the forthcoming work by Margherita Trento.

## Tantric Tamil

For a particularly rich expression of what Tamil—as a concept, as a body of literature, as a grammar, and as a privileged expressive medium within the wider linguistic ecology—meant for literati in the far south on the cusp of the modern era, we are fortunate to have a highly unusual, indeed uniquely imagined, text: the *Maturai cŏkkanātar tamiḻ viṭu tūtu (TVT),* or "Tamil Sent as a Messenger to the Lord of Madurai." We don't know who composed this work in 268 head-rhyming couplets; it was recovered from a single manuscript by the great savant U. Ve. Caminat'aiyar, the founder of modern Tamil studies, in 1900 and edited and published by him in a lucidly annotated edition. We can only guess at its date—perhaps the seventeenth or early eighteenth century, the heyday of compositions in the genre of *tūtu* or messenger poems, to which it belongs.[58] Most Tamil *tūtus* offer lengthy descriptions, in ornate and allusive language, of the beloved; inevitably, the messenger is also pointedly characterized, and his (its) suitability for the mission explained. In the present case, the unlikely messenger of love is none other than the Tamil language itself, sent on a mission to the god of Madurai, Cŏkkanātar. Most of the poem is devoted to depicting this strange, and strangely suggestive, messenger in all its features and in the light of its centuries-long literary, cultural, and pragmatic achievements. In English it is hard not to speak of Tamil as an "it"; but the text boldly portrays Tamil as a subjective being or, more precisely, a king. In the course of doing so, the anonymous poet produces a compendium of Tamil literature and grammar—in effect, an idiosyncratic canon of Tamil as present in the minds of educated Tamil speakers of his period.

There is an excellent study of the *TVT* by Sumathi Ramaswamy, probably the first scholar to take this work seriously as embodying an entire linguistic cosmology typical of its time and distinct from earlier, and later, ways of "thinking Tamil."[59] Yet it remains somewhat difficult to read the *TVT* without slipping at moments into the retrospective frame of twentieth-century nationalist interpretations, with their attendant dichotomies. To see the full force of this strange work, we have to think ourselves back into the mind of the seventeenth century and to see what links the *TVT* with its roughly contemporaneous works, including the famous *purāṇa* text from Madurai, the *Tiruviḷaiyāṭaṟpurāṇam* (Śiva's "games") of Parañcoti muṉivar, another book pregnant with a particular set of understandings about Tamil and full of love for and pride in the language.

One has to keep in mind as well that the choice of Tamil as the messenger of desire implies, at the very least, that the communication will be persuasive and powerful: will the god, a Tamil god, be able to refuse a request conveyed in eloquent Tamil? The medium establishes a necessary intimacy and thus, on one level, strongly affects the god, impinging on his self-awareness. Although other linguistic forms, including Vedic Sanskrit, have roles to play in this drama, there is a recurrent sense that Tamil, in its inherent sweetness, is, in a way, equivalent to speech itself. On the other hand, within the Tamil cosmos over which Tamil rules as a king, Sanskrit is fully at home, a necessary and, indeed, protective presence. I see no sign whatsoever that "for the author of the

*Tamiḻ viṭu tūtu,* Tamil was the master of that master language of the Hindu-Indic world, Sanskrit"[60] or that the *TVT* deliberately challenges a deepening hegemony of Sanskrit language and culture in the early-modern south.

Like all messengers in the *tūtu* genre, I have to hurry on to my goal.[61] Let me just say, for the record, that the *TVT* offers a refreshing perspective on who "Tamil" really is. Thus in addition to being a language, a king, and a (male) god, as Ramaswamy has clearly shown, Tamil is now, first and foremost, a full-fledged person, with all that a concept like "person" means in the seventeenth or eighteenth century in south India: a sense of singularity and wholeness, a nascent subjectivity expressed in moods, an interactive in-ness that positions itself vis-à-vis a realistic natural world, an active memory, an idiosyncratic manifestation of character, and so on. In this period, such a person, who either constitutes a language or, conversely, is made up of language and sound, is also polyglot. So we have Tamil as a singular but multifaceted linguistic entity with its own tradition of grammar, poetry, and music; and we have Tamil as a pragmatic medium of speech, also a continuum of dialects, riddled with other kinds of language, indeed inhabiting some space within them even as they pour into Tamil. The first vector exists by virtue of the second and cannot easily be distinguished from the latter. Tamil-as-person is also intensely personal: this is the language of intimate experience, clarified, sifted, and resonant, that is carried by the *uyir.* And it is also something more.

The *TVT* points us in the direction of a fully Tantricized understanding of the Tamil language as a divine force or being that is both effective in pragmatic ways, working on the world in accordance with the will of a trained and gifted poet, and present in this world in both aural and visual forms. We need to take a short step back to observe this notion in its earlier forms before we trace its evolution in the domains of early-modern music and dance. I will be arguing that the road to modernism in Tamil—not the superficial reformist modernity derived from the colonial experience but an organic and mostly autonomous development from within south Indian culture—leads through the rich and diverse spectrum of Tantric praxis and teaching, especially as embodied in lines of transmission outside the major institutional network of the Śaiva mutts, yet tied to the patronage of the royal courts (first and foremost, the Maratha court of Tanjavur). In order to present the main elements of this thesis, I will begin with a few words about Tantra in general and its presence in the far south.

The topic is of crucial importance to any discussion of Tamil, and ideas about Tamil, in the early-modern period. A central defining feature of this protean term, "Tantra," is a pragmatic metaphysics of sound and syllables as the medium of creation of the cosmos and, if these sounds are used effectively, of potential modes of liberation from or within that cosmos. The Tantric world is made up of vibrating sounds, many of them inaudible to our ears, but eventually devolving into the vowels and consonants of everyday speech and thought.[62] The notion of cosmogonic vibration, *spanda,* includes an oscillation between two intradivine modes, an innate illumination *(prakāśa)* and a recursive-reflexive movement of contemplation *(pratyavamarśa)* leading to self-recognition *(pratyabhijñā)* that, together, generate wonder, *camatkāra.* In the Tantric systems that were most firmly established in the south, including the Śrīvidyā,[63] such wonder, both on the human and the divine levels of awareness, is firmly focused on the goddess Tripura-sundarī, "Most Beautiful in All Three Worlds."

From early on—middle-Chola times at the latest—we find traces of the Śrīvidyā in the great Tamil temples of Śiva and his local consort, most conspicuously at Cidambaram and Tiruvarur. Eventually, all the major Śiva temples in the Tamil country were radically "Tantricized," in both their ritual-liturgical order and their conceptual organization; this process took centuries to come to fruition, leaving behind ample historical markers of its several stages in each large temple site.[64] The post-Chola centuries witnessed complex interactions between these Tantric temples and the mainstream, normative, and orthodox Tamil Śaiva Siddhânta system, strongly affiliated with the northern Tantra in its so-called dualistic variants but with its own Tamil canon and institutional basis in the mutts, primarily those situated in the eastern Kaveri delta—at Tiruvavaduturai, Dharmapuram, and Tiruppanantal. In the seventeenth and eighteenth centuries, these two sociopolitical currents, Tantra-in-temples and mainstream Śaivism taught in the mutts, were further enriched and galvanized by the autonomous, active lines of Tantric teaching outside the standard frameworks mentioned above.

It is the latter forms of what I will call "Deltaic Tantra" that are of most interest to us here. Two things have to be borne in mind from the start. First, there is the broad division into two competing streams: the moderate and orthoprax Samayâcāra, which generated repeated attempts at synthesis with the Śaiva mainstream and in effect came to constitute the modern Tamil Smārta-Brahmin consciousness,[65] and a more radical, sometimes antinomian set of Kaula traditions, widely distributed in the south as a whole (including Andhra) and in the Tamil heartland in particular.[66] Both these streams were, in distinct senses, Advaitic—that is, committed to a notion of nondualistic reality that was also theistic and oriented to the worship of the all-embracing goddess.[67] The Samaya theoreticians have an explicit preference for internalized worship, through visualization, of this goddess rather than externalized material forms of *puja*.[68] I will return to this point. In general, the Tantric Tamil Advaita of the Kaveri delta has not yet been adequately studied and defined, though remarkable eighteenth-century sources exist in plenty, in both Tamil and Sanskrit.

Second, all the southern Tantric systems, inside and outside the mutts and temples, developed yet another new grammar of sounds, mantric syllables, and power-packed words and sentences—a kind of cosmo-phonetics together with coded, rule-bound morphology and syntax.[69] Much of this grammar crystallized only in ritual practice and has to be reconstructed inductively on the basis of usage as recorded in the major southern Tantric texts and in their single most eloquent surviving witness, the verbal and nonverbal texts of classical Carnatic music. Such grammar-based pragmatics should properly be seen in juxtaposition with the fierce internecine wars of the learned traditional Tamil grammarians, mainly working in the great mutts, during the seventeenth and eighteenth centuries.[70] At this point I cannot go into the details of this dramatic story of reconfigured relations between Tamil and Sanskrit, though it, too, belongs to the wider narrative of an emerging modernism, as I hope to show in a future study.

As I have already stated more than once, Tamilized Tantra or Tantric Tamil brings into play a new and critical role for written words. The

Tantric grammar of syllables, although still rooted in the primacy of audible or almost audible sound in carrying out the work of personal transformation into a divine (female) being and of reordering the objective world generated by that being, requires that sound also be made visible, in various ways. In this, the new grammar of praxis extends the poeticians' theory of what is called *citra-kāvya* or "fancy poetry," lucidly articulated by Daṇḍin in his *Mirror of Poetry* and formalized in Tamil in the Chola-period *Taṇṭiyalaṅkāram,* modeled after Daṇḍin's Sanskrit textbook. Here we find picture poems in which careful arrangement of syllables produce visual patterns such as the zigzagging "cow's piss" *(go-mūtrikā),* verbal constructions of swords or carts, or the ingenious magic square *(sarvatobhadra)* allowing for simultaneous readings forward and backward as well as vertically and horizontally.[71] Delinearization of a metrical musical utterance is one evident principle of this set of poetic genres, one that applies to Tantric grammatical practice as well. Visual sound might be said to be the first step toward the meditative mode of "auralization"—that is, putting together a goddess through a mental process of listening for her—the sonic equivalent of the more familiar act of visualization, as we shall see.

Take a concrete example. In the early sixteenth century, at the very moment of incipient modernist transformation, a Brahmin poet, Kavirāca Paṇṭitaṉ Vīraiyaṉ, as he calls himself,[72] produced a remarkable Tamil version of the much-loved south Indian Sanskrit poem *Saundarya-laharī* or "The Wave of Beauty."[73] The Sanskrit original, still recited daily by many thousands of devotees in the Tamil country, offers a fine-grained depiction of the goddess named Most Beautiful in All Three Worlds, a guide to her *yantra*-diagram or *maṇḍala* (which we can see today in many Tamil temples), and a do-it-yourself kit to using it in the interest of self-transformation. Traditionally, the Sanskrit prototype is divided into two segments—verses 1–41, the so-called *Ānanda-laharī* or "Wave of Joy," on the practicalities and teleological effects of the *yantra* and *mantra* of the goddess (including a map of her, and our, psychophysiological subtle body with its invisible *cakra* energy centers), and verses 42–100, the "Wave of Beauty" proper, which slowly builds up the ravishing image of this deity. Kavi-rāca Paṇṭitaṉ follows this same division.

But how did this bifurcation of what is clearly a unified text come about? Here is where writing comes in. The text is ascribed (wrongly) to the philosopher Śaṅkarâcārya who, so it is said, was visiting Lord Śiva at his home on Mount Kailāsa; there he noticed the book of the *mantra-śāstra,* which the goddess had left lying on Śiva's throne. Śaṅkara at once picked it up and rushed toward the exit; but he was intercepted by the god's doorkeeper, Nandikeśvara, who tried to tear the book out of the sage's hands. Śaṅkara managed to hold on to the fragment that contains verses 1 to 41, which he brought down to earth; he later added fifty-nine new stanzas of his own, describing the goddess.[74] We have several variations on this theme, with its central notion of an existing written text. Verse 75 of the text refers to a *draviḍa-śiśu* or "Tamil boy," undoubtedly the *Tevāram* poet Tiruñāṉacampantar, who, later commentators say, both composed the entire work and inscribed it on Mount Kailāsa.[75] Śaṅkara saw the verses there and started to memorize them even as the goddess moved the author to erase them; fortunately, he managed to retain the first 41 stanzas.[76] The very existence of a written text is somehow not to the liking of its subject; the philosopher thus has to transfer the graphic form of these verses from the rocky mountain face to his invisible neurons, with only partial success. The text disappears before our eyes (or the eyes of its putative copyist-author). By this period, writing it down on palm leaf is one key to preservation.

But the Tamil poet tells the story in a more elaborate and rather moving manner well suited to the early sixteenth century in the south. Sarasvatī, goddess of wisdom, composed a book that strained and filtered the four books of the Veda, in praise of the goddess Yāmalā (Tam. Yāmaḷai). She recited the work, which she thought was her own, to Śiva, who laughed and, calling her near, showed her that it was already inscribed on the mountain (Kailāsa). "It is this poem, this great treasure *(cema-niti),* that I," says Kavirācaṉ, "have made into my poor Tamil verses *(puṉ-kavi).*" The treasure, we might note, is one to be safeguarded and carefully preserved, *cemam*—but this word also indicates the tying of long wooden boards on the top and bottom of a palm-leaf manuscript to protect it. So again, the association with writing is very pronounced; the text the goddess was sure that she had produced from her own mind is already present in durable graphic form on the slope of Śiva's mountain. Sarasvatī, like Pierre Menard, has thus mysteriously composed a preexisting work. As if this were not enough, an ascetic, Pushpadanta, copied and firmly reinscribed the text on another northern mountain, apparently Meru, where the Advaitin Gauḍapāda saw it and imprinted it on his heart *(uḷam patittu)*—another way of recording it—and then taught it in toto to his student Śaṅkara; the latter poured it out into the world where living beings, *uyir,* were languishing, in order to revive them as the rain cloud gives life to the crops.[77] Significantly, this final stage requires a reversion to oral recitation, the only true guarantee of massive diffusion.

Why this new obsession with writing things down? On the simplest level, it may reflect more technical competence, greater production and wider circulation of texts recorded by the standard south Indian technology of writing on palm leaves.[78] Fifteenth- and sixteenth-century poems often describe this business of preparing the leaf, covering it with oil, making the incisions with the stylus, and smearing the black inky mixture into the grooves.[79] Private libraries exist: the sixteenth-century Telugu *Pāṇḍuraṅga-māhātmyamu* of Tĕnāli Rāmakrishṇa describes the three main dangers to such a collection—fire, loose bindings around the manuscripts, and borrowers who fail to return the books they've taken on loan.[80] Beyond these materialist explanations, however, there lies a conceptual revolution. Consequential sound exists and acts both in the ear and the eye; the two senses are synaesthetically fused in a mantric hypersemanticism that transcends by far the limited natural semantics of everyday language. In this heavily overdetermined phonetics, there is meaning to the entire process of generating sound from deep in the body—the empty space in the heart, for example—and articulating it externally via the organs of speech (as one sees already in the first book of the *Tantrâloka,* the magnum opus of the Kashmiri Tantric theoretician and systematizer, Abhinavagupta). Externalized sound also exists in graphic form.

Each component of every utterance has carefully defined metaphysical properties rooted in the primordial vibration described above, with varying intensities of combined luminosity and reflexivity and, in all cases, an inner struggle between the urge to speak, *vivakshā,* and a profound resistance to audible utterance. All of this is well known. Added to it, however, is a similar specification of occult metaphysical implication in the sheer tangible and visible form of the Tamil letters, a form that, on principle, can never be accidental or contingent. Written syllables embody and reveal divine energies, qualities, and evolutionary directions, all entirely isomorphic with the fluid lines, curves, and loops of the Tamil script; the hand that inscribes these signs, like the tongue that utters the corresponding phonemes, in effect builds up a god or goddess at every sequential moment. There are also ways of reading this theographic set of principles back into the ancient *sūtras* of *Tŏlkāppiyam*, among other grammatical texts, as one can see from a somewhat far-flung modern restatement of Tantric theories of the written character by P. V. Manickam Naicker.[81]

Thus when Kavirāca Paṇṭitaṉ records for his readers—for that is who they are, not listeners—the root mantra of Most Beautiful, precisely following the Sanskrit parent text, he apparently uses the word for syllable, *ĕḻuttu*, to mean both audible and written variants of the godly entities that, in coded form and in specific patterns and sequence, can be used literally to compose (unfold, unwind, make present) a goddess. If the sequence is reversed, the same syllables can decompose, fold, rewind, and dissolve her.[82] That the Tamil poet has managed to produce Tamil equivalents of the Sanskrit code words in elegant metrical verse is itself a staggering achievement. And like the Sanskrit original, the Tamil mantric idiom, incorporating a hypersemantics moving into trans-semantics, is fully grammaticalized, with rules and metarules that can be inferred from usage. Thus the verses in question allow us to state, as I have shown elsewhere, that "a word indicates not itself, not its audible sound-sequence, not its usual meaning, not any of its synonyms, but a certain phonic pattern."[83] Traditional grammar, whether Pāṇinian or Tamil, has been Tantricized in the interest of pragmatic performance. There are more ways than one to see a newly fashioned goddess. Aural vision is perhaps the most effective of all. Note how close we are, at this point, to études in musical theurgy.

The latent grammar of a popular text like the Tamil *Saundaryalaharī* may seem a little exotic, but there is no way we can bracket it out or relegate it to the cultural margins. If anything, it came continuously closer to the political and social mainstream of seventeenth- and eighteenth-century Tamil Nadu and served to complement the erudite grammars of scholars and poets based in the Śaiva mutts. Kavirācar's work thus easily sparked a Tamil commentary by one of the major establishment poets of the mid-sixteenth century, the mutt-based Ĕllappa Nayiṉār (here is another unstudied work worth exploring). Tantric lineages of teaching and prominent Śaiva Siddhântin literati came together in the mutt-dominated temples and, more dramatically, in the royal courts. Let us take a moment to characterize these courts as fertile arenas for cultural production.

Recent studies by Davesh Soneji and Indira Peterson have revealed the striking originality—also the naturally multilingual reality—of expressive genres at the royal courts of seventeenth and eighteenth Tamil Nadu. We see this remarkable effervescence at all three of the major Nāyaka courts in the far south—Tanjavur, Madurai, and Senji—with powerful continuities stretching into the post-Nāyaka colonial period (much the same could be said of contemporaneous states in coastal Andhra, Ikkeri, and Sri Lanka). In the Kaveri heartland, dynastic history stands in somewhat oblique relation to the continually intensifying cultural visions, although the Maratha conquest of Tanjavur in the mid-1670s did bring into play very rich and active literary and musical traditions from the western Deccan.[84] We can now clearly see how Nāyaka and Maratha Tanjavur, in particular, shaped the artistic and intellectual universe of modern twentieth-century Tamil Nadu. It makes no sense to focus on Tamil production alone in a period of such intimately interactive linguistic and cultural realities: to take but two examples among many, we have the outrageous court comedy by Purushottama Dīkshituḍu, "Love in the Soup Kitchen" *(Anna-dāna-mahānāṭakamu),* from seventeenth-century Tanjāvur, a work nominally in Telugu but filled with colloquial Tamil (recorded in Telugu script).[85] Under the aegis of the great connoisseur-king Shahaji (1684–1712), we have the "Play of Five Languages" *(Pañca-bhāshā-vilāsa),* in which Tamil, Telugu, Marathi, Braj-Bhasha, and Sanskrit, the first four embodied as love-stricken princesses, compete, each in her own language, for Krishna's love.[86] By now, the very notion of a hegemonic Sanskrit, if it ever really existed, has given way to a democratic multilingualism:

as Peterson notes with respect to this remarkable work, "While Sanskrit is not entirely rejected as a visible language on the aesthetic plane, its cosmopolitan status and claims to mediator status are challenged, yielding to a dialogic cosmopolitanism of the vernaculars."[87]

We should take note of the continuous experimentation with genre in the courtly culture of this time. A large corpus of Telugu *yaksha-gāna*, "dance dramas," evolved; this newly dominant genre "permanently blurs the boundaries between literature and performance at the court."[88] Among the *yaksha-gāna* texts the subgenre of "gypsy dramas" (Tamil-Telugu *kuṟavañci*) has a special place; some, like the *Tiyakecar-kuṟavañci,* focused on the god Tyāgarāja in Tiruvarur, became integrated into the staple temple liturgical-ritual cycles.[89] Here we find, along with the relatively familiar love-struck devotees, a pair of gypsy bird-catchers, whose straightforward sensual love serves as a pointed contrast to the romantic hallucinations of the "high" courtly hero and heroine. In Tamil, the most famous and still current representative of the genre is Tirukkūṭarācappa kavirāyar's *Tirukkuṟṟālakkuṟavañci* from the early eighteenth century, centered on the lord of the famous Tirukkurralam temple near Tenkasi. A somewhat tenuous but, I think, credible line of transmission, with defined carriers, links these Tamil-Telugu "gypsy dramas" to late-eighteenth-century Vienna and to Mozart's *Magic Flute.*

The courtly literature-in-performance leads directly to the vast corpus of courtesan dance and musical texts—*padams, jāvaḷis,* and other genres.[90] Telugu- and Tamil-speaking courtesans, active both in royal venues and in the great temples, preserved, performed, and extended this astonishing corpus throughout the early-modern and colonial periods, down to the demise of the latter (1947) when the very institution of temple dancers, *devadāsīs,* was proscribed by the British as one of their last, and particularly destructive, acts in India. Courtesan culture and temple musical traditions, along with popular musical dramas such as Aruṇācalakkavirāyar's *Irāma-nāṭakam* (eighteenth century) and the Marathi devotional songs mentioned above, fed into the great classical synthesis of Carnatic music in the late eighteenth century. The three great composers in this tradition, Syama Sastri, Muttusvami Dikshitar, and Tyagaraja—contemporaries of Haydn, Mozart, and Beethoven—shaped the Carnatic repertoire as we know it today. Among them, both Syama Sastri and Muttusvami Dikshitar show us the formative influence of Kaveri delta Tantric schools (in the Samaya mode). Dikshitar had a Tantric master, Cidambaranātha, who initiated the budding composer into the Śrīvidyā and the worship of Tripurasundarī; but even earlier antecedents of Dikshitar's theurgic vision include the eighteenth-century Advaita composer and commentator Upanishad Brahmam, as the family tradition tells us.[91]

In the Dikshitar corpus, as I have argued elsewhere,[92] the composer activates in his sensitive and cultivated listeners modes of internal "auralization," that is, the patterned imagining of the goddess into presence through musical and verbal signals, working in tandem. Note the Samaya preference for internal worship, *antar-yāga,* now taken to a new level and ruled by a musical grammar in which the older Tantric phonematic progression from presemantic quivers and buzzes to discursive speech is combined with purely musical signals and iconic expressivity. This kind of inner ritual, transpiring in the mind of the trained listener, presupposes the classical Carnatic system of *rāgas* first formalized at the Nāyaka court in sixteenth-century Tanjavur. Seen together with parallel developments in poetic practice, this mode of "auralization" superimposes a novel Tantric grammar of sound and meaning onto the system of efficacious, pragmatic sound combinations already in place in second-millennium Tamil. The crucial point, however, lies in the personal, individualistic, and entirely modern character of this revolution in form and taste: all three of the great eighteenth-century composers produce melodic lines that are like personal signatures, and both Muttusvami Dikshitar and Syama Sastri molded dense Tantric content into this individualistic new style. Dikshitar, above all, then proceeded to detach musical composition from its earlier ritual moorings, especially in the major Tamil temples, and to make it the property of a newly secular middle-class audience. We would do well to go beyond the conventional image of Dikshitar as a pious devotee and begin to think of him as the radical experimentalist-shaman that he was.

A final remark in this same context: to understand the emergent artistic world of the eighteenth century, we need to see it in relation to the erudite traditions flourishing, in part, under royal patronage and recorded in Sanskrit, Tamil, Telugu, and Marathi. Musicology is one such tradition, particularly conspicuous in the Kaveri delta;[93] but no less conspicuous are the major works of synthesis from this period in law, grammar, the natural and empirical sciences, and the various philosophical schools—especially Tantra-infused Advaita. If we look carefully at the major erudite works, it is often easy to see why a given author chooses to write in Sanskrit, for example, or in one of the other current literary languages. There are intellectual domains, such as Mīmāṃsā hermeneutics, so profoundly saturated with Sanskrit terminology and conceptual *Fragestellungen* that it would have made no sense to enter the debates with a new work in any language but Sanskrit.

We can formulate a principle of linguistic selectivity that applies both to scholars and to poets (in any case, these two cultural roles had merged to a large extent by early-modern times). The primary criterion of choice is the language-specific expressive resources available for any given work. There are earlier, seventeenth-century examples that already establish the paradigm. Thus, as Elaine Fisher has cogently shown, the great poet Nīlakaṇṭha Dīkshitar in Madurai—"a sort of pre-modern public intellectual, remembered primarily for his interventions in the local and regional circulation of Sanskrit discourse"[94]—decides, for his own no doubt overdetermined reasons, to compose a Sanskrit version of the famous series of "games" played by Śiva-Sundareśvara, the *Śiva-līlârṇava* or "Ocean of Śiva's Amusements." Why Sanskrit? It is possible to see the choice as part of a wider contestation between Sanskrit and vernacular Tamil—a "de-regionalization of local culture" entailing an "intriguing inversion of the vernacular by the still-vibrant values and presuppositions of a Sanskritic world-view."[95] The truly competent Sangam poets thus turn into *śāstric* pundits at home in the translocal traditions of poetics, logic, and Mīmāṃsā. But is this necessarily a passionate contest between cosmopolitan and vernacular ways of thinking and feeling? A Sanskrit-speaking Sangam has its own surprising charm, not devoid of a certain teasing irony, not to mention the powerful intertextual resonances that Sanskrit can offer both poet and reader. Each case needs to be seen on its own terms and in relation to an always large repository of intertexts. In short, for these early-modern centuries we would do well to follow Fisher's practical suggestion that we "bracket the Sanskrit-vernacular binary in favor of a model that situates multilingual production in its diverse social and institutional settings."[96]

Faced with the thickness and richness of cultural production we have been examining, a word like "modernism" itself begins to pale. In institutional terms, the period between ca. 1500 and 1800 saw the creation of the Nāyaka-style states, built by self-made adventurers and entrepreneurs working in a monetarized cash economy and animated by an ideology of hardy individualism and innovation. During the same period, the great mutts, especially in the Kaveri delta, came to dominate both temple economies and literary and erudite culture. The poet-pandits active in the mutts, many of them non-Brahmin, most of them thoroughly at home in Tamil, Sanskrit, Telugu, and other languages present in the south, composed an immense, intricately fashioned literature, very closely linked to the domains of music and visual arts as well as to the continuous, often polemical attempts to reformulate Tamil grammar.

Comprehensive, integrative grammars such as Vaittiyanāta Tecikar's *Ilakkaṇa viḷakkam* (seventeenth century) and the slightly later *Ilakkaṇak-kŏttu* of Cuvāmināta Tecikar developed a new linguistics, in which Tamil and Sanskrit grammatical science, embodied in a wide selection of classical source texts, were deliberately intertwined, in different degrees—partly under the impact of the radical reformulation of Sanskrit grammar by Bhaṭṭoji Dīkshita and his students in the sixteenth century. The most far-reaching attempt to combine Sanskrit and Tamil in a single system was Cuppiramaṇiya Dīkshitar's *Pirayoka-vivekam* (mid- to late seventeenth century), which provides an idiosyncratic theoretical basis for the polyglossic literary ecology of this time. More generally, the Republic of Syllables embraced all the major regions of southern south Asia and assumed knowledge of all the relevant languages and their literary traditions. Innovation in sensibility, taste, and theme is a hallmark of the period, beginning perhaps, as so often happens, on the periphery, in sites such as Tenkasi and the vibrant Muslim centers on the eastern coast.

This world of sparkling, multilingual intellection broke new ground, orienting itself in the direction of extreme realism, naturalistic and empirical observation and bold attempts at classification of species, highly personal expressive forms, a new sensibility highlighting the female voice, and complex parodic genres flourishing, above all, in the Nāyaka and Maratha courts. In both Tanjavur and Madurai, the royal courts sought the services of Tantric masters; Tantric principles and concepts, primarily in the moderate Samaya schools, came to color Tamil literary practices generally, including the drive to create texts that were both audible and visible in graphic form, not only in the classical *abhinaya* mode of writing in empty space. Poetry was now, if anything, even more effective in working on the world: the grammatical pragmatics of the post-Chola centuries were integrated into musical grammars of "auralization" and shamanic magic aimed at generating divinity and concomitant forms of understanding in the listener's mind. Tamil itself, one powerful and prestigious medium for such effects alongside its sister languages, was now a full-fledged deity, sometimes capricious, situated in the core of the speaker's inner self.

SEVEN

# Beyond the Merely Modern

*Rāgamālikā*

## New Ambrosia in Old Vessels

The history of Tamil over the past two centuries or so can be (and indeed has been) told in various ways, among which three master narratives can easily be delineated. There is a tale of severe disjunction, a massive break in the cultural and literary tradition linked largely to the insidious and demoralizing impact of a newly dominant colonial culture; the "colonial modernity" that I have mentioned, with its reformist ideologies and its novel genres, is a central part of this narrative. Then there is an epic story of recovery and reconstitution driven by the gradual reappearance and publication of the ancient Tamil classics and the forging of a new canon centered on them. And we have a tale of a Tamil or Dravidian "renaissance," in some ways akin to the so-called Bengali Renaissance, and of a social and political revolution that generated a fresh cultural and literary sensibility, sometimes militant and strident, sometimes creative and original in ways quite new to the Tamil tradition. All three of these master narratives, each in its own way, is both true and false (this ambiguous but overriding truth value may itself be a diagnostic feature of modernity). We should, perhaps, think in terms of yet another, colonial period, grammar, not yet formalized, that has restructured the entire domain of Tamil as a language and as a major culture.

Certainly, there has been a break: the old protocols of reading have been eroded, and by now much, perhaps most, of the rich literary and erudite production of the last millennium or so has gone out of currency. Traditional scholars such as the late T. V. Gopal Aiyar, masters of the entire range of Tamil sources and of the various competing grammars that evolved over many centuries, have almost disappeared. Jennifer Clare writes cogently of the "erasure of [knowledge of] the Tamil intellectual tradition" in our generation and of the concomitant "tyranny born of linguistic nationalism,"[1] which has strikingly narrowed the field of vision and done away with the polyglossic plurality of interwoven forms of discourse so characteristic of premodern Tamil. We can trace the stages through which this process of erosion gathered momentum in tandem with an emergent radical revolution in taste. One prominent modern Tamil writer is said, incredibly, to have complained that there is nothing to read in Tamil. (Clearly, he was thinking about the silent, private reading of printed books, mainly in prose, preferably something akin to Joyce or Musil.) Yet in my view, strong though perhaps shadowy and largely unconscious elements of continuity with the premodern tradition can still easily be discerned, even in modern texts that seek to reject that tradition outright. I will point to some of these in the final sections of this chapter. As we all know, it is not so easy to escape the constraints of the past; often, attempts to attack and destroy these constraints end up by unwittingly reconstituting them.

Thus the story of very modern Tamil is a complex one; large parts of it have been told in detail by scholars more competent than I, to whose works the reader is referred.[2] I will concentrate here on what could be called the underground history of nineteenth- and twentieth-century Tamil without repeating at length what can easily be found elsewhere. I will begin with some remarks on literary masterpieces of the nineteenth century and the revolution that took place largely within traditional genres and generic conventions; from there we move to the exciting moment of recovery and the emblematic figure of U. Ve. Caminat'aiyar; and, in conclusion, we will trace the cultural and intellectual roots of modern Tamil linguistic nationalism, with a short glance toward the unknown future.

The year 1800 is no more than a scratch in the sand of time; the vibrant courtly and popular cultures of Maratha-period Tanjavur and its contemporaneous polities in Pondicherry, the far south, and the still-young urban center of Madras continued to shape artistic and scholarly production in Tamil and its sister languages. Stuart Blackburn has traced the dramatic impact of the new print culture and the huge expansion in both the volume, and the readership, of Tamil literary and other discursive works, including the whole new world of Tamil journalism, which gradually produced a language of its own.[3] He also writes of new literary practices such as translation into Tamil from Western languages, especially English (note the bilingual Tamil-English 1793 edition of *The Pilgrim's Progress,* an important experiment in the emerging prose styles), and of a series of new grammars, some in Western style, written by missionaries, as well as the first alphabetically arranged dictionaries. For example, we have Proença's pioneering Tamil-Portuguese dictionary in 1679;[4] Fabricius's 1779 Tamil-English dictionary, still useful today; Ziegenbalg's grammar from 1715, published in Halle; and the great polymath Beschi's multilingual or interlingual Tamil dictionaries, from the 1740s, and his two Latin grammars of Tamil, 1728–1730, the former, translated into Tamil as *Tŏṉṉūl viḷakkam,* "probably the most widely used and influential printed book in Tamil before 1850").[5] Eventually, in the second half of the nineteenth century, innovative practices would include the adaptation to Tamil of imported genres, first among them the novel—although one could argue that novelesque modes were already current in both Tamil and Telugu from as early as the sixteenth century.[6]

Sascha Ebeling has shown in detail how the institutional settings of Tamil cultural creativity, in both the learned and prevalent literary modes, went through a major upheaval in the early-to-mid-nineteenth century:

> Already from the 1820s onward, the pulavars [poet-scholars] felt the wind of change in their face. On the one hand, the major traditional patrons, zamindars and monasteries, both gradually lost more and more of their economic power and thus their ability to sponsor Tamil literary activities and scholarship. On the other hand, an expanding colonial state machinery offered secure jobs for language teachers and invested in campaigns to foster and reform Tamil language and literature.[7]

Some of these scholars, such as Kottaiyur Civakkoḻuntu Tecikar, gravitated to the College of Fort St. George in Madras, where they had an impact on English scholars and administrators-to-be. The radical transformation in the self-perception and in the nature of the creative work of such men also coincided with the incipient shift to a print-based culture of diffusion; no longer poets in their own rights, they sometimes became publishers or editors of manuscripts awaiting printing. With this change came a no less far-reaching reshaping of sensibility in line with the evolving, or devolving, taste of the new social elites ("colonial administrators, lawyers, advocates, traders, or bankers"[8]—all urban and in some sense middle class, with knowledge of English).

But what can we say of nineteenth-century Tamil works that ostensibly held to the medieval generic forms and conventions? There are hundreds of such works, among them undoubted masterpieces that, in my view, are far more radical and engaging than the early Western-influenced novels. The modernizing impulses present in the hyper-realistic and naturalistic modes of the seventeenth and eighteenth centuries, often couched in parodic tones, developed further in the nineteenth century, partly in response to the deepening colonial culture but also as an organic extension of the still-dominant literary tradition. Parody turns into sustained and subtle irony inherent in the choice of genre per se. We have many examples of this trend, some cogently analyzed by Ebeling. In general, the hallmark of this period was daring experimentation both within the traditional forms and beyond them. Probably the most impressive works in the former category are those of the polymath genius, a "poet's poet," Tiricirapuram Minatcicuntaram Pillai (1815–1876).[9] Here is a poet who looks and sounds like the last of the great premodern stylists, a man working within the literary and linguistic grammars he inherited, in a line of artistic transmission going back to Kumarakuruparar, Tuṟaimaṅkalam Civappirakācar, and Kaṭikaimuttup Pulavar. He is at least as modern in content and concept as these venerable figures, though in some important senses he also transcends them. Let me show you, with one slight example, what I mean.

We are fortunate to have a detailed biography of Minatcicuntaram by his main student, U. Ve. Caminat'aiyar, who traces his master's life in the mutts and temples and small market towns of the Kaveri delta such as Mayavaram and Kumbhakonam.[10] Already at a young age, this virtuoso poet was capable of producing immensely complicated *citrakavi* verses keyed to underlying graphic templates and rich in paronomasia and other difficult figures of sound and sense. He was also able to create huge numbers of verses entirely in his head and to dictate them to scribes writing on palm leaf at a pace no human hand could keep up with (one of his student scribes was disabled for some days after one particularly intense session). He specialized in long, well-integrated texts in traditional genres, including, above all, the *talapurāṇam* or "Story of a Shrine." These latter works reveal the vast range of his talent as well as a powerful coherence of content, narrative, and lyricism that serves as his hallmark. *All* of these large-scale texts remain to be studied—and the results of such studies will be more than surprising. But he also composed shorter works in many traditional genres, such as *kovai, tūtu, piḷḷaittamiḻ,* and *ulā,* all of which we have seen in action in earlier chapters; and it is in precisely these seemingly conventionalized, fully grammaticalized forms that we can hear that unsettling, even subversive, always playful new tone. Take the following invocation verse from the *Akilāṇṭa Nāyaki Piḷḷaittamiḻ,* "When the Goddess of All Worlds was a Baby,"[11] composed when Minatcicuntaram was still a young man just beginning to make a name for himself in the world of Tamil letters:

*cīr ulavu vaṉacamakaḷ puraiyu' maṭavār ikal tīrntom ĕṉak kaḷippac*
*cĕṟiy uṭuk kaṇam uruvil putte' ṭikaippav itu tīṅk' avaḷam ĕṉṟ' utaṭi toy*
*kār ulavu' māka naṭuvaṭ pŏliyum āmpal aṅ kātaṉ mati mīp paṉaiyĕḻil*
*kāṭṭuṅ kai nīṭṭum ŏru koṭṭiru patat tiri kaṭāk kuñcarattai niṉaivām*

Young women radiant as the Lotus Goddess no longer have to fight
for recognition. They're happy, but the stars are worried,
and so is the Love God. "Something very very bad
has happened!" All this because that elephant—
to whom we humbly pray—

has stretched out his trunk, long and tapering
as a high palmyra tree, into a sky thick with clouds
to swallow the moon, luscious, beloved
as a white lily.[12]

All right, I confess: the Tamil says simply that the radiant women no longer have to fight; I've made them into suffragettes in the hope that something of the modernist, tongue-in-cheek tone might come through. Readers who know Tamil will instantly note the staggered, recursive syntax and complex metrical patterns that are also signs of the changing times. The evident ellipsis—that is, the unspecified content that makes sense of all the initial statements—is, however, entirely traditional; a skilled reader will know that all beautiful women are embroiled in conflict with the moon, the standard object of comparison to which their incomparable faces are compared, and also a source of tormenting white heat when these women are in love. Their rival has been neatly removed, and they can relax. The stars or constellations, on the other hand, are worried because the moon is their husband, and he has disappeared; and the Love God, Manmatha, has lost his lunar parasol. All this has happened because the baby elephant-headed Gaṇapati has mistakenly identified the moon as a succulent ball of white rice and stretched out his trunk to seize it (thus the underlying figure is *bhrāntimat,* Tam. *mayakkav-aṇi,* "mis-perception," with additional superimposed figures such as *utprekshā,* Tam. *taṟkuṟipp'eṟṟav aṇi*).

The same event thus produces polarized and differential effects on various interested parties. The thought itself is a good nineteenth-century idea, with older precedents in the literature of poetics; the figuration that embodies it is at once highly traditional and strangely fresh and amusing; the disjunctions built into the syntax are not far removed from complex prose sentences. This is an early, but entirely mature, indeed perfect attempt to say something that was never said before in Tamil, though it gathers together fragments familiar to any trained reader. As in much of this poet's oeuvre, much depends on the sensibility of such a reader, who might well hear the verse as a wholly traditional one, but who might also catch its playful tone and feel a slight, but crucial, ironic twinge. That twinge tells you that we are standing on shifting ground. One could also say that by jumbling together conventional images and undercutting their naïve, first-order meanings (in jagged syntax) this modern poet has generated the second-order, reflexive distance and dissonance that are stable hallmarks of a modern sensibility, by no means only in Tamil.

This is a relatively simple, though eloquent, example; I wouldn't want to overload it with latent meanings. But what happens when an entire composition in a traditional genre such as *tūtu* or *ulā* presents us with a vision that cannot but appear outlandish in colonial Tamil Nadu? I can't demonstrate these experiments in subtle, mind-boggling irony, for want of a better term, as this final chapter races to conclusion. Ebeling has nicely stated the principle: "If the combination of erotic excess and excessive praise of the king was linked to a specific society at a given historical moment, how are we to make sense of such poetry once the social environment changes?"[13] By the middle of the nineteenth century; the Tamil world has changed almost beyond recognition. English savants and missionary educators like the Rev. Peter Percival—professor of vernacular literature at Presidency College, Madras—spend, or rather waste, their energies blasting Tamil poetry as puerile, decadent, and obscene.[14] Such men (they were of course men) clearly had no access whatsoever to the sensibility active in the texts then still being produced, although some of them knew Tamil well. Subtlety, playfulness, and the telltale reflexive gesture were beyond their comprehension. In short, they were unable to read real Tamil, and their blindness and deafness infected generations of modern Tamil speakers as well. But in colonial Mayavaram, deep irony, or self-parody, was the name of the game.

My claim is that Minatcicuntaram Pillai, an enormously prolific poet working within the traditional genres and supported mostly through traditional modes of patronage, is a modernist *manqué,* in many ways more daring than those nineteenth-century Tamil authors experimenting with Victorian-style "novels" and other new forms. Interestingly, he still inhabits a world where literary works are recorded on palm leaf (the author dictating to his scribes); only later do they sometimes make their way into print. The new print culture, with its elite readership that had no access to manuscripts,[15] was by no means an unmixed blessing. As Velcheru Narayana Rao has cogently argued, print also "silenced" the deeper resonances that informed all classical and premodern, indeed also protomodern, south Indian texts.[16] The printed book gives us the "recorded text," a mechanically reproduced graphic image of the work as a whole as the author thought it into existence. This same printed book obscures what Narayana Rao has called the "received text," that is, the work as circulated and performed orally as a collectively generated selection of segments / verses with their unrecordable modes of musical recitation, their eloquent pauses and caesuras, their particular emphases and intonations possible only in audible performance, and their implicit commentaries. In effect, we are left with less than half of what made up any premodern text. The loss is immense by any standard.[17]

In the Tamil case, the damage was compounded by the fact that the very early texts—the classical *akam* and *puṟam* anthologies—had largely gone out of circulation by the middle of the nineteenth century and were in need of "recovery," as we will see in the next section. Our knowledge of how these poems were sung is limited and conjectural. Traces of the performance tradition for medieval and premodern works have survived, and we are fortunate to have the live *Otuvār* performance of *Tevāram* and the Araiyar renditions, complete with crucial *abhinaya* gestures, of parts of the Śrīvaishṇava corpus.[18] But in general, mechanical reproduction, à la Walter Benjamin, has wrought havoc with Tamil sensibilities and, together with other factors already mentioned, contributed to the disjunction, even crisis, that set in during the second half of the nineteenth century and has continued till today. In this period, luminous writers such as Minatcicuntaram Pillai and the one slightly later author I am about to discuss effectively changed the terms and dominant practices of Tamil literary composition, opening a new imaginative horizon. It is, however, sometimes hard to see their greatness from our vantage point after the break, after whole chunks of the tradition have become remote.

In passing we should note that this very situation of incipient disjunction was powerfully highlighted, and sometimes explicitly thematized, in Telugu and Kannada, and to some extent also in Tamil, by the so-called *avadhānam* poets of the late nineteenth and early twentieth centuries. These were oral poets specializing in improvisation under demanding circumstances, on the cusp of the emergent print culture. Such poets (in Andhra they tended to come in pairs such as the famous Tirupati Venkaṭa Kavulu) improvise lines of verse in response to demands coming from an audience of eight, or sixteen, or a hundred, or, in theory, even a thousand *pricchakas:* "Produce a verse in which Rāvaṇa defeats Rāma," or a verse about some local political situation, or a *ślesha* verse comparing a mirror to a king,[19] or a tantalizing riddle, or a poem about the weather, and so on. The *avadhāni* makes the rounds of the audience four times, each time adding a new line to the verse that was started on the first round. Usually there is also someone to distract him by asking ridiculous questions or poking fun at his verses; and the poet may also be playing chess at the same time, or counting the number of rings of a bell in the background. By the end of the fourth round, there will be eight or sixteen or a hundred complete, polished, four-line verses on the various topics the *pricchakas* have requested.[20] This art, requiring prodigious feats of memory as well as poetic genius, has not disappeared; in our generation, in Tamil, there is the well-known *avadhāṉi* Kanaka Subburattinam,[21] and I myself have witnessed remarkable *avadhānam* performances in Telugu. Many of the great *avadhānam* works were recorded and printed, close to the time of their improvisation, in newspapers or pamphlets, as if the literary culture itself wanted to preserve a record of this dying oral art. Anxiety at imminent loss is another diagnostic feature of south Indian modernity.

Ebeling has given us a penetrating analysis of the first, or almost-first, Tamil novels, ostensibly in the European mode, and in prose, beginning with the brilliant *Life and Adventures in Tamil of Pradapa Mudalliar* (1879) by Mayuram Vedanayakam Pillai, a friend of Minatcicuntaram Pillai, and the *Suguna Sunthari, An Interesting Tamil Novel* by this same author (1887), followed in the early 1890s by B. R. Rajam Aiyar's *The Fatal Rumor or the History of Kamalambal.*[22] I pause only to note that, as Ebeling has said, the Tamil prose style evident here (particularly in Vedanayakam's work) is characterized by "hypotaxis and sanskritization"[23] and thus, in my view, is entirely continuous with earlier Tamil prose of the popular urban narrative, *kathā,* genres. More precisely, Vedanayakam Pillai exemplifies the long-standing amalgam of what is called *nīti* (pragmatic ethics) and juicy but often long-winded *kathā*, to which we can add, as a somewhat secondary overlay, the reformist agenda of the high colonial period. The continuities with earlier, indigenous Tamil sources are, to my mind, far more impressive than the somewhat shallow reformist program. To do at least a little more justice to this rich topic, I should mention that earlier candidates for the "first" Tamil novel have been suggested (quite apart from the novelesque features of the Tenkasi works of the sixteenth century); among them is an Arwi or Tamil-Muslim version of the well-known surrealist novella from the *Arabian Nights*, the "City of Brass," by Sayyid Muhammad or Imām al-'Arūs (ca. 1858).[24] This would not be the first time the "City of Brass" was recycled for quasi-modern use.

We cannot leave nineteenth-century Tamil literature without looking at the most impressive example we have of the sea change in taste and technique that became evident by the end of that century.[25] In 1891, P. Sundaram Pillai, born in Aleppy, in Kerala, later professor of philosophy at Maharaja College in Trivandrum and without doubt one of the major Tamil intellectuals in the second half of the century, published a play, never intended for performance. This play, often said to be the first in modern Tamil, is called *Maṉoṉmaṇīyam*, "Madness of the Mind," after the name of its heroine, Maṉoṉmaṇi.[26] It is a magnificent work, exactly contemporaneous with, though formally very different from, Gurujada Appa Rao's modernist masterpiece in Telugu, *Kanyā-śulkam*, "Girls for Sale."[27] A closer look reveals tantalizing affinities between these two plays. I hope to write a full study of Sundaram Pillai's text; for now, let me mention only a few major points.

The play is based—so the author tells us, possibly a little disingenuously—on a narrative poem by Sir Edward Bulwer-Lytton: "The Secret Way," published in 1866 in his *Lost Tales of Miletus*. Lytton himself found the story in Athenaeus (*Deipnosophists* 13.35, late second century A.D.), who says that it is "often told by the barbarians who live in Asia." It's unlikely that by this Athenaeus meant India, although the dénouement of the tale is an Indian-style *svayaṃvara* where the heroine and bride-to-be chooses her bridegroom from among an assembly of suitors. It would be nice to think that an Indian narrative thus came home, as it were, after a long detour through the Rome of Marcus Aurelius and the rather tedious retelling, unreadable today, by a once-popular Victorian author. Bulwer-Lytton added to his laconic source the crucial motif of a hidden passageway or tunnel (which becomes *caruṅkai* in Tamil). Sundaram Pillai has expanded Bulwer-Lytton's expansion and thoroughly Tamilized (or perhaps Malayalamized) the story. The somewhat bizarre and confusing plot, with many twists and turns, shows us the Pandya king Jīvakaṉ (=Tamil *uyir,* "the breath of life," "the inner being") and his crooked, manipulative minister, Kuṭilaṉ, who wants the throne for himself or for his dissolute son, Palatevaṉ. There is also a wise and humane guru, Cuntaramuṉivar, the voice of reason, modeled after a venerated historical figure, Cuntara Cuvamikaḷ (1831–1878).[28]

The king has a daughter, the beautiful Maṉoṉmaṇi, and this daughter has had a dream in which she sees, and falls in love with, the Travancore king Puruṭottamaṉ—who has himself had a commensurate and complementary dream about Maṉoṉmaṇi, his ideal beloved. The corrupt and self-seeking Kuṭilaṉ manages to spark a war between the Pandya kingdom and Travancore; he uses the secret tunnel beginning inside the palace to defect to Puruṭottamaṉ, but the latter has no patience with treachery, even politically useful treachery, and thus puts Kuṭilaṉ in chains. Puruṭottamaṉ does, however, make his way through the tunnel into Jīvakaṉ's palace, arriving there just in time to save the princess from a miserable marriage to Palatevaṉ; Maṉoṉmaṇi, astonished to see her dream lover standing beside her, garlands him as her husband-to-be, and peace is restored to the southern tip of India, the "Dravidian land" (*tiraviṭa naṟ ṟirunāṭu,* as Sundaram Pillai calls it in his famous invocatory verse). This poet is an early predecessor of what would soon become the Dravidian Movement, discussed below.

The actual setting of the entire play is in Tirunelveli, in the far south, but not so far from Kerala; very close, too, to Tenkaci, the first great center of Tamil modernism, as we have seen. I think this suggestive geography is intrinsic to the kind of statement Sundaram Pillai is making; we can trace a definite link to the sixteenth-century Tenkaci poets and also to parallel developments in southern Kerala, the author's first and most significant home. But there is also a second, unspecified but certain, source for his story. *Maṉoṉmaṇīyam* is, as Sundaram Pillai tells us in his introduction, an allegorical play—or at least capable of being read as such[29]—in which the inner living person, *jīva* (=Jīvakaṉ), is endangered by the crooked power of illusion *(māyā-śakti)*, and Maṉoṉmaṇi is the pure element *(śuddha-tattva)* that triggers release from worldly suffering; this happy conclusion requires a wedding with the divine faculty of compassionate blessing *(anugraha-śakti)* embodied by Puruṭottamaṉ—that is, God. Moreover, the mysterious tunnel running through, or under, the whole plot is the necessary means to achieving the direct experience of reality, *pratyakṣânubhūti;* and King Jīvakaṉ's birthplace and original capital is the Site of Freedom, Muttipuram—that is, Madurai, not coincidentally the first home of Tamil letters. This allegory is firmly located in a concrete, familiar landscape. The allegorical reading is reinforced by cryptic verses that conclude many of the scenes. But, as others have noted, it has a model, which Sundaram Pillai must have known in one form or another, in Ratnakheṭa Śrīnivāsa Dīkshita's great sixteenth-century Sanskrit play, the *Bhāvanā-puruṣottama* or "The Wedding of Imagination and God."[30] Again we find ourselves thrown back to the extended breakthrough moment of the sixteenth century, resonating now in a late-nineteenth-century masterpiece of modern Tamil.

And modern Tamil is, indeed, the idiom of this work, composed in the formal literary style but alive with immediately audible colloquial tones and the highly distinctive personal voices of each of the characters. Moreover, as Sundaram Pillai himself tells us, the dominant meter—*akaval-pā*—is "equivalent to prose" (*vācaka naṭaikku camam*), Introduction, p. 21); thus, like the Tenkasi purāṇic texts I have mentioned, the play belongs, syntactically and lexically, to the recent history of Tamil prose, another clear indication of its modernity. Complex enjambment—thus again the author—is a natural syntactic feature of such poetry-as-prose. Sundaram Pillai knew very well what he was doing. Many readers of the play have correctly noted, and loved, its brilliant lyricism and rhythmic virtuosity; the lines tend to stick in your mind even after a first reading. Perhaps most famous of all is the long invocation to the Tamil language, the divinity who is Tamil *(tamiḻttĕyvam)*, with which the play begins.

Here we see clearly the changing configuration of Tamil, now a woman or goddess, *aṇaṅku,* delicate and pervasive as the fragrance of the sandal-paste dot, *tilakam,* (that is, the Dravida land), on the forehead (the South, *tĕkkaṇam*=Madras Presidency) of the face (Bharatakhaṇḍa or India,) of the Goddess Earth (verse 1). Never mind the details of this complex metaphor; the point is the existential hierarchy that situates fragrant, ethereal Tamil at the very acme of the inhabited world.[31] In the next verse we learn that Tamil is the source of all other south Indian languages (by 1891, thanks to Bishop Caldwell, everyone knows that they constitute a linguistic family, Dravidian): Kannada, "delightful" Teluṅgu, "beautiful" Malayalam, and Tulu. In his prose preface to the play—itself a foundational text for late-nineteenth-century Tamil-modernism—Sundaram Pillai says that he wrote this work in order to restore to the Tamil people a natural pride in their language, since many of them do not know if Tamil is on the same level as, or perhaps even inferior to, languages such as Telugu, "which arose only yesterday" (*neṟṟ' utitta tĕluṅku mutaliya pāshaikaḷ,* p. 9). This claim to primordial antiquity is a staple theme in the crystallizing proto-nationalist view of Tamil, a view strengthened by the recovery of the ancient Sangam poems in these final decades of the century, as Sundaram Pillai himself tells us in his preface (p. 10).

Let us stay a moment longer with the invocatory verses. Tamil is both the oldest of languages and yet eternally young *(cīr iḷamait tiṟam),* like the First Substance, *param pŏruḷ,* that preceded even the creation of the universe and that survives the periodic reabsorption of the latter by that Substance. So Tamil is not "only" a great goddess; it, or she, is the metaphysical principle of unity itself, the substratum of all existence and the embodiment of time as both changeless—an undying present—and as devolving into the human experiences of aging and death. Moreover, good spoken language *(ulaka-vaḻakku)* tends inevitably to become corrupt *(aḻint' ŏḻintu citai);* but Tamil, like Sanskrit *(āriyam),* is immune to such processes.[32] However, this affinity with Sanskrit needs to be formulated more precisely: Sanskrit, the northern tongue *(vaṭa mŏḻi),* and Tamil, the southern tongue *(tĕṉ mŏḻi),* are the two eyes of the goddess of knowledge, Kalaimakaḷ. But which of these two eyes is the right eye and which is the left? The goddess faces east; so Tamil, to the south, must be her right eye (verse 9). Anyone who says that Sanskrit is the right eye is ignorant of the east (*kuṇa ticaiy aṟiyār,* verse 8), or rather, the (no longer soporific) East. A novel opposition between the colonial West and the "real" or authentic East is conscripted, possibly for the first time in Tamil, to an effort to establish the clear superiority of Tamil over Sanskrit, though the two languages remain symbiotic and interdependent.

As if this were not enough, this series of beautiful short verses mentions several emblematic Tamil moments: Nakkīraṉār's stubborn insistence that there was a mistake in the famous verse *kŏṅku ter vāḻkkai* (*Kuṟuntŏkai* 2), which left Śiva speechless and forced him to open his third eye to burn the pedantic scholar-poet—a sign of how rare and rich is *your* (Tamil's) grammar (v. 2);[33] the floating of the palm leaf with a *Tevāram* verse inscribed on it by Tiruñāṉacampantar against the current of the Vaikai River, in his contest with the Jains in Madurai—proof that Tamil itself flows *against* the current of time (*kāla-nati,* v. 4);[34] Śiva's recording the text of the *Tiruvācakam* as dictated by Māṇikkavācakar in Cidambaram, so that the god himself would not be all alone at the time the cosmos is destroyed (he will have the good company of the Tamil poem, v. 5); the remarkable fact that the Sangam Plank could expand infinitely to make room for any real Tamil poet (v. 6). Moreover, those who know the *Tirukkuṟaḷ* have no need to study the Sanskrit works of *nīti,* such as Manu's (v. 11);[35] and anyone who goes deeply into the *Ten Songs*—the Sangam anthology only recently recovered that became a particular interest of Sundaram Pillai's—has no need for other books that lack a grammar rich in topics of great substance (*pŏruḷ,* probably a reference to the ancient *akam* grammar of love, v. 10). There are those who recite the Veda with eyes shut, using the mnemonic techniques of reciting forward and backward and so on (*kaṉam* and *caṭai*); those who appreciate the greatness of the *Tiruvācakam,* which melts the heart and does away with all impurities *(malam),* have no need for such things (v. 12).

In short, before Sanskrit and the Vedas appeared in the world, the whole universe belonged to Tamil, the most ancient and eternal tongue (v. 3). "There are those today who are renewing Tamil's primeval greatness and those who are making new poetry of all four kinds (*ācu,* improvised; *maturam*, sweet; *cittiram*, fancy / figurative; *vittāram*, extended, narrative); putting these aside, I, Sundaram Pillai, the lowest of all your servants, living in the fierce Malayalam world, but still a son of Tamil, have done my best in offering you this play. Please accept it, though it is made only of silver, as a toe-ring, a token of my love."[36]

Sundaram Pillai was a scholar of profound erudition in Tamil and in English literature, a man of unconventional interests and taste; also a critical historian at a time when the historical reconstruction of medieval Tamil was still at a very early stage. We can see in his great play, and in the introduction he prefixed to it, still inchoate themes of an emergent linguistic nationalism with its attendant mythology. Tamil was there—everywhere—first; Sanskrit, still a kind of sister language, came second, apparently from the north; but Tamil has been corrupted and desperately needs to be revived, especially by scholars such as Damodaram Pillai and Caminat'aiyar, publishers of lost texts, and by young authors who will write ravishing new works. Not by chance, Sundaram Pillai cites at the very opening of his preface the verse from *Cīkāḷattippurāṇam* that we studied in Chapter 6 (in the section "Hyperglossic Speech and Tamil Islam")—the verse that formulates in sophisticated and somewhat ambiguous terms the systemic relations between Tamil and Sanskrit in the early-modern south. What is more, the *Maṉoṉmaṇīyam* alludes continuously to the entire past tradition of Tamil, citing works from the *Puṟanāṉūṟu* (not yet in print in 1891), the Śaiva poets, *Kamparāmāyaṇam* and onward through the poems of the seventeenth- or eighteenth-century mystic Tāyumāṉavar, and the very late metrical *nīti* collections on the pragmatics of a good life. This play is thus, in its own way, a statement of the current literary canon and strong evidence of a mostly unbroken tradition at the very moment when this tradition was just beginning to expand with dizzying velocity backward, toward Sangam times.

## Recovery and the Gap

There is no doubt that something dramatic happened in the world of Tamil life and letters in the last third of the nineteenth century. Suppose the literature of fifth-century B.C. Athens had been forgotten for centuries and then suddenly came to light in early-modern Athens. Imagine the excitement, the passionate responses, the suddenly explosive horizon, the attempts to reconceive and reappropriate Greece in its ancient glory. Imagine, too, the inevitable and sudden downgrading of most of Greek literary production from, say, late-Antique or Byzantine times on, up to the arrival of a devoutly wished-for modern Renaissance that stood in active relation to the newly recovered masterworks. Here is a paradigm—not, incidentally, entirely remote from certain currents in modern Greek intellectual history in the period when a learned style, Katharevousa, was beginning to retreat before the "vernacular" Dimotiki—that might work for the Tamil case. Indeed, in a sense this kind of model was invented or appropriated by Tamil literati in response to the return to currency of Sangam-period works. Like any overly abstract and simplified paradigm, this one, too, tends to obscure almost as much as it reveals.

But I should probably begin with the standard narrative, by now endlessly retold in works on modern Tamil. It is October 21, 1880, a mythic moment in two senses of the word—first in the sense that this moment creates and constitutes what it purports to describe, and second in the semantic urgency and excess that it embodies and in the inevitable loss of detail and perspective that follows upon this excess. It in no way diminishes the greatness of U. Ve. Caminat'aiyar, the hero of our story (and the revered founder of my own line of teaching), if we note, in advance, that he was not alone in the enterprise of recovery and that the very notion of "rediscovery" may be a hyperbole that serves the myth. Still, something happened in Kumbakonam on that day, something that changed the way Tamil thinks about itself or herself.

There is a man, a *munsif* or judge at the local civil court, a connoisseur of Tamil, named Celam Ramacuvami Mudaliyar. Caminat'aiyar, newly appointed Tamil pandit in Government College in the city, goes to visit Ramacuvami. Caminat'aiyar was, as we know, a student of Minatcicuntaram Pillai, the outstanding poet of nineteenth-century Tamil Nadu; there could be no better intellectual pedigree. Minatcicuntaram Pillai died in 1876. Caminat'aiyar has internalized the huge corpus of classical and medieval texts that his teacher taught him, in the old, largely oral, style. But he has never read more than a few verses, preserved in the medieval commentaries, from Sangam times. He of course knows about *akam* and *puṟam* and their respective grammars but not about the whole literary world structured around these terms. All this is about to change.

Ramacuvami Mudaliyar asks the young master who his teacher was and what Tamil books he has studied. Caminat'aiyar proudly says he was a student of Minatcicuntaram Pillai; he then launches into a long list of the books he knows (probably by heart), including some twenty *antātis,* twenty *kalampakams,* fifteen *kovais,* thirty *piḷḷaittamiḻs,* twenty *ulās,* some *tūtus*—all of them included in the Short Genres that were so popular in early-modern Tamil Nadu. The *munsif* is obviously not impressed, and the young scholar, too sure of himself, is already beginning to feel peeved. Ramacuvami Mudaliyar suddenly says, "What's the use of all these books?" Caminat'aiyar presses on, this time citing the many *purāṇas* he has studied, including Parañcoti's *Tiruviḷaiyāṭal-purāṇam* and Cekkiḻār's *Pĕriya purāṇam.* There is no response from his host. Now come the names of *Naiṭatam* (no small work to have taken in fully), the *Pirapu-liṅka-līlai,* then classic texts of Tamil Śaivism, followed by various medieval grammatical and metrical treatises. No comment. "Ah," thinks Cāminat'aiyar, "I've forgotten the most important book of all, *Kamparāmāyaṇam.*" He mentions that he's read it in its entirety two or three times. "Fine," says Ramacuvami, "is that all?"

The young scholar is bewildered and more than a little suspicious. The judge now shows what he's thinking. "It's very good that you've read all these rather late books, but haven't you read any old books?" Says Caminat'aiyar: "I've mentioned the names of plenty of old books." "But what about the books that were the original source of all those you've mentioned?" "What books do you have in mind?" Ramacuvami Mudaliyar: "Have you read the *Cīvaka cintāmaṇi?* The *Maṇimekalai?* The *Cilappatikāram?*"

The answer, of course, is no. He hasn't read them, or even seen them, and his teacher also, he tells us, had never read them. Here it's of some importance to mention that these names, at least, are known. The first section of the *Cīvaka cintāmaṇi* had even been printed by H. Bower and Muttaiya Pillai in 1868 and was part of the curriculum prescribed for students of Tamil in government colleges; Minatcicuntaram Pillai had also contemplated editing the work and had even made a manuscript copy of it that was preserved in the Tiruvavatuturai Mutt. One canto of the *Cilappatikāram* was, in theory, meant to be part of the college syllabus, though available copies of it were hopelessly corrupt. But it is one thing to have heard the names, another to try to read the texts. A feeling of humility is beginning to percolate upward in Caminat'aiyar's mind. On his next visit, Ramacuvami Mudaliyar gives him a paper copy of the *Cintāmaṇi,* and Caminat'aiyar begins to delve into Chola period Jaina Tamil—the first step in a long journey backward in time.[37]

Another decisive event is Caminat'aiyar's discovery of a bundle of palm-leaf manuscripts in the library of the Tiruvavatuturai mutt on a Sunday during vacation time in 1883.[38] The bundle, with a note written by one Kumaracamit Tampiran saying "Looks like Sangam works," contained the text of six of the eight Sangam anthologies (minus *Paripāṭal* and *Kalittŏkai*). Caminat'aiyar would spend much of the rest of his life scouring the Tamil country for more manuscripts and editing the Sangam corpus. Thanks to the meticulous work by Eva Wilden, we now know a lot more about the manuscripts he found, the current location of those that have survived, and critical features of their textuality; she has also carefully described the transition from such manuscripts to the early printed editions.[39] Caminat'aiyar certainly earned the compliment Sundaram Pillai paid him in 1891: he brought to light the ancient, largely forgotten masterworks of Tamil, thus renewing the tradition and setting it on a new course. His was a lifetime of immense achievement. He was, however, as he himself acknowledged more than once, part of a wider current flowing through the worlds of Tamil erudition in the nineteenth century.

The movement from manuscripts, whether palm leaf or paper, to printed books—including the publication of both Sangam-period and rather rare medieval works—began already in the first half of the nineteenth century and accelerated in the second half: Malavai Mahalinga Aiyar published the first book of the *Tŏlkāppiyam,* on phonology, together with Naccinārkk'iṉiyar's commentary, in 1847–1848 in Madras; Ceṉāvaraiyar's commentary on the second book was published by the famous Jaffna-born publicist-scholar Y. N. Arumuka Navalar, together with Komalapuram Iracakopalap Pillai in 1868 (reprinted in 1886); this same Arumuka Navalar founded his own printing press and was responsible for very early editions of many works, including the *Ilakkaṇakkŏttu* of Cuvaminãta Tecikar, the *Cūṭāmaṇi nikaṇṭu* lexicon of Maṇṭalapuruṭar, the Tantric poem *Saundarya-laharī,* the *Pĕriya Purāṇam,* and so on. If we focus on Sangam-period classics, we can mention the great scholar-poet Tirumayilai Canmukam Pillai's *editio princeps* of *Maṇimekalai* (1891, 1894), several years before Caminat'aiyar's definitive edition. A complete list of early print editions would be rather long.[40]

Caminat'aiyar's main counterpart, ally, and sometime rival was Ci. Vai. Damodaram Pillai (1832–1901), another Jaffna Velala like Arumuka Navalar, a successful lawyer and judge on the Pudukottai High Court, but above all a critical scholar obsessed with ferreting out and publishing Tamil manuscripts. He played a part in the publication of *Ceṉāvaraiyam,* mentioned above. He also edited and published, among other works, the *Grammar of Stolen Love,* with Nakkīraṉār's commentary (1883); the *Ilakkaṇa viḷakkam* of Vaittiyanāta Tecikar (1889); the Buddhist grammar, *Vīracoḻiyam* of Puttamittiraṉ (1881); Kacciyappa muṉivar's *Taṇikaippurāṇam* (see below); and his chef d'oeuvre, the Sangam anthology *Kalittŏkai* with Nacciṉārkk'iṉiyar's commentary (1887). Caminat'aiyar records a tense and awkward moment during his work on the *Cīvaka cintāmaṇi,* his first major challenge in editing, prompted by Ramacuvāmi Mudaliyar, as we have seen. Damodaram Pillai, the far more senior scholar with a splendid record of editing Tamil texts, also wanted to publish the *Cīvaka cintāmaṇi;* he came to Caminat'aiyar in Kumbakonam and exerted tremendous pressure on the latter to hand over the task and the draft of the edited text. Caminat'aiyar, in an agony of indecision, in fact gave Damodaram Pillai the thickly annotated draft. Only after consulting with his father, who immediately told his son that it was *his* responsibility to complete this work, and who instructed him to pray to Lord Sundareśvara in Madurai for help (in publishing this Jain text!), did Caminat'aiyar summon up the courage to say a definitive no to Damodaram Pillai and to retrieve his draft.[41] We can, I think, refrain from asking ourselves about the relative proportions of personal ambition and selfless devotion in the business of recovering and printing ancient texts.

Occasionally, when I teach Sangam poems in translation, students say to me: "It's impossible that these ultramodern texts could have been composed two millennia ago; Caminat'aiyar, or A. K. Ramanujan, or maybe you, must have written them yourselves." Ramanujan is on record saying that he sometimes heard similar statements. There must have been such remarks as far back as the 1890s, when the first editions started to come out. Some scholars, perhaps even ordinary readers, found it hard to come to terms with the sheer beauty of these texts, even as they were amazed, even hypnotized, by them. Hence the importance of the public statement by Damodaram Pillai, meant to demonstrate the integrity of both editors: "Caminat'aiyar is my witness, as I am witness to him."[42]

There is another, somewhat hidden, even paradoxical aspect of the story I have been telling. As Venkatachalapathy has rightly said,

> print was constitutive of this process of discovering and constructing the [new] canon. . . . The underlying premise seems to be that of print as a panacea: somehow the printing of these texts in itself would render them immortal, defeating Time.[43]

This idea is explicitly and repeatedly stated by the great editors.[44] We can easily understand them. They knew what it meant to find a rare copy of an ancient book in a manuscript ravaged by dust, white ants, broken leaves, and general neglect. Publishing a good edition was, in their minds, a salvage operation of great urgency. But the printed text also had talismanic properties holding out a promise of immortality. Contrary to popular views, such a promise is vastly overrated. Printed editions cannot in themselves defeat Time or Death, especially in the absence of a continuous tradition of reading and reciting.

Publication of lost classics was a colonial-period value, not unrelated to the Western and colonial romance of the antique; "old" was synonymous with good. Tamil intellectuals at the turn of the twentieth century internalized this value with truly astonishing thoroughness. In the case of the Sangam poems, the equation happens mostly to hold true; however, it exacted a cost. What was found, so to speak, displaced what was newly lost—large chunks of the last centuries of Tamil literary production. It is a commonplace to assert that there is a caesura between the most ancient strata of Tamil and the collective awareness of late-medieval or early-modern Tamil literati. Such a gap did exist, as Wilden has shown. But the deeper gap—more like an impassable chasm—opened up only *after* the rediscovery and publication of the Sangam works. It is still in place today. Sometimes I think it is time to reverse the trend that overtook Tamil, beginning on October 21, 1880, and to recover or rediscover, without letting go of the Sangam classics, the forgotten *tūtus, kovais,* and *antâtis* that the young Caminat'aiyar had studied. Seen from a wider angle, the whole story of loss and recovery is perched precisely on the sensitive point of transition to ultramodern Tamil and, indeed, embodies, articulates, and illuminates that moment, with the tensions and incipient distortion inherent to it.

We can still ask: were the Sangam texts ever actually lost? The answer to this question is ambiguous: yes and no. We might also ask what exactly it means to be lost. Wilden has shown definitively that many of the Sangam texts, including the *Ten Songs,* were still known, cited, and copied in the seventeenth century.[45] We can push this firm dating forward by another half century or so, perhaps more. A very well known passage by Cuvāmināta Tecikar in his *Ilakkaṇakkŏttu,* roughly at the turn of the eighteenth century, contrasts works such as the *Tevāram,* the *Tiruvācakam,* and other Śaiva canonical texts—but also the *Grammar of Stolen Love*—with medieval grammars such as *Naṉṉūl, Ciṉṉūl,* the [*Nampi*] *Akappŏruḷ,* the [*Yāpp'aruṅkala*] *Kārikai* and *Taṇṭiyalaṅkāram* and the literary collections of the *Ten Songs,* the *Eight Anthologies,* and the *Eighteen Minor Works,* among other texts. The first group is worthy of praise; studying the second is a waste of time, like fish who live in the ocean of milk but never taste the milk. Aligned with the first set is the *Tirukkovaiyār* of Māṇikkavācakar, which some people, so the author tells us, unthinkingly link to the *Cintāmaṇi,* the *Cilappatikāram,* the *Maṇimekalai,* the Sangam poems, and the *Great Tale of Kŏṅkuveḷ.*[46] Look at the range of texts this grammarian seems to know! He cites passages from many of them in his own work. That he prefers Śaiva classics (including, as it happens, the *Grammar of Stolen Love,* since Śiva himself wrote it) should not surprise us; nor should we rush to conclude, as Zvelebil did,[47] that he would happily have proscribed the non-Śaiva (including Buddhist and Jain) texts he mentions. Some texts are more effective than others if what you want is final freedom.

Even in the middle of the eighteenth century the outstanding poet-scholar Civañāṉa muṉivar (d. 1785), commentator, grammarian, logician, and fierce polemicist, was credited with a hostile attitude toward heterodox (non-Śaiva) Tamil classics—but he, too, knew they existed and may have even read them.[48] I don't think he was alone in this. His famous pupil Kacciyappa muṉivar (d. ca. 1790), a prolific and gifted poet, inserted some five hundred verses of an independent *kovai,* supposedly composed by the god Murukaṉ himself and sung silently in his mind, into his purāṇa on the Tiruttani shrine (*Taṇikaippurāṇam, kaḷavuppaṭalam*). Like all *kovais,*[49] this one, still entirely unstudied, offers its listeners a revised *akam* scenario with a superimposed metaphysical agenda. These verses are not Sangam-style poems, but they are profoundly informed by the ancient grammars of in-ness, including the *Grammar of Stolen Love.* The content of these older texts on *akam* poetics (especially the *Nampi Akappŏruḷ*) was thus still current, perhaps through second-hand mediations, in this period, just as it was (through first-hand knowledge) two centuries earlier—as we see clearly in the works of the unusually creative poet Kurukaip Pĕrumāḷ Kavirāyar of Alvartirunagari.[50] These same rules and conventions turn up even in nineteenth-century grammars such as the *Muttuvīriyam* of Uraiyur Muttuvira Vattiyar, the teacher of Minatcicuntaram Pillai.[51]

And what about manuscript copies of the ancient works? One, probably anomalous, was a paper copy of *Kuṟuntŏkai* made for the great scholar A. C. Burnell in 1874 (received by Burnell in 1878; now in the British Library).[52] Most of the manuscripts collected by U. Ve. Caminat'aiyar and his contemporaries cannot be closely dated, but it is by no means unlikely that some of them were relatively recent, no earlier than the eighteenth century. Moreover, manuscripts are only one, albeit from our point of view privileged, track of transmission. Were none of the Sangam poems—say *kŏṅku ter vāḻkkai,* that is, *Kuṟuntŏkai* 2, so often cited throughout the medieval period—learned by heart and sung orally?[53] At the very most, we can speculate on a hiatus of little more than a century between the time when large parts of the ancient corpus were still current and the moment when they had to be "rediscovered."

We should also distinguish among three linked but distinct kinds of knowledge: that of the literary texts themselves, in quotable form; that of the richly elaborated narratives about these texts, such as we find in the Madurai materials about the Sangam and the role of Lord Śiva in establishing and regulating it;[54] and of the poetic grammars of *akam* and *puṟam* that served the ancient corpus, in whatever new forms these grammars adopted. The last category is well represented in grammatical works from the sixteenth and seventeenth centuries and beyond.[55] Indeed, it is still alive, though reconfigured, today, as we shall see. The first two categories are less amenable to dating, but I think that Wilden's conclusion that "by the early 19th century, the bulk of early Tamil literature . . . had faded away from common consciousness"[56] may be overstated. Whose consciousness are we talking about? How common was it? A recent study by V. Rajesh goes to the other extreme of claiming that the so-called recovery has been "overemphasized."[57] We find ourselves on the shadowy and usually elusive surface of what might count as certain knowledge. We cannot know for sure what Kacciyappa muṉivar did or did not know less than a hundred years before Caminat'aiyar began his life's work, though we could definitely make a good guess.

What can be said with confidence is that, by a spooky synchronicity, the publication of the Sangam classics and the historical visions this process inspired were very rapidly recruited "to fashion a new identity for Tamils"[58] at the very moment that the first tentative shoots of Tamil nationalism, with language at the heart of its program, began to burst out. As Sheldon Pollock has shown, "linguism," or language-based ethnicity, was never dominant in premodern India—though we have seen at least one example of *tamiḻar,* the "Tamils," serving as a collective sociocultural category in the medieval south.[59] By the early twentieth century, identity-driven linguism was a major force in the Tamil country; it has remained so to this day. Venkatachalapathy rightly states that the reentry into circulation of the Sangam classics generated a new literary canon, which he identifies as a product of secularization—since the regnant canon of premodern times was largely organized around a hierarchy of religious texts, as we saw in the citation from Cuvāminātа Tecikar.[60] But the term is somewhat misleading: a very large percentage of seventeenth- and eighteenth-century literary texts in the Short Genres were entirely secular, addressed to local human patrons and small-scale kings. One might even argue that a nonsectarian, noncommunal, secular aesthetic culture was the literary mainstream throughout the Deccan and the royal courts of the far south from the fifteenth century on, as is clear from Telugu and Kannada sources and from the courtly production in Nāyaka and Maratha Tanjavur. It is not so much that Tamil literature was secularized at the turn of the twentieth century as that it was radically nationalized and appropriated by a rising, largely non-Brahmin elite. We could also say that one older and outmoded mythology was replaced with a newer one.

## Dravidian Dreams

The beginnings are evident in Sundaram Pillai's proleptic play, the *Maṉoṉmaṇīyam,* though there were still earlier adumbrations of beginnings. Apart from the play, Sundaram Pillai offers a tentative version of embryonic Dravidianism set forth mainly in historical writings such as his book *Milestones in the History of Tamil Literature* (1897, the year of his death) and an important essay, "The Basic Element in Hindu Civilization."[61] That basic element is south Indian, and more specifically, Tamil, now set off in opposition to "Aryan philosophy" and "Aryan civilization" couched in Sanskrit. Moreover, "Tamil" slides into "Dravidian," no longer a linguistic term as used by Bishop Caldwell in his *Comparative Grammar* (1856)[62] but now an adjective qualifying words like "civilization," "culture," and "thought." The adjective soon begins to conjure up an idealized image of origins: not only were the "Dravidians" in place in southern India from the beginning of time; not only were they subject to invasion and subjugation by the Sanskrit-speaking Aryans, as the Agastya story suddenly seems to show us; but the "manly and virile Dravidian" (Rāvaṇa) was obviously and infinitely superior to the "flaccid and effete Aryan" (Rāma),[63] as Sundaram Pillai's friend, T. Ponemballem Pillai, suggested in an early essay on "The Morality of the Ramayana."[64] Before long this primordial Dravidian person was also being lauded as egalitarian, casteless, exemplary in moral terms, a democrat *avant la lettre.*

It isn't hard to guess who was cast as the antidemocratic oppressor in this emergent historical scenario. Colonial Madras carved out significant, highly visible domains of Tamil Brahmin privilege, particularly in the civil service, the courts, education, and prestige professions.[65] High rates of Brahmin literacy, following a centuries-long tradition of commitment to learning, explain something of this phenomenon; but anti-Brahmin feeling had older roots as well, as we know from significant voices in the medieval period (see below). Lavish royal land grants to Vedic Brahmins go back to Pallava times, as we have noted, and remained a feature of the medieval sociopolitical and agrarian order; recall Stein's theory of the "entrenched secular power of Brahmins" in the Tamil country.[66] Whatever we may think today about this description, especially given the shifting power relations in post-Chola and Vijayanagara-Nāyaka times, it is clear that surviving symbiotic aspects of Brahmin and non-Brahmin (especially Velala) social roles broke down dramatically toward the end of the nineteenth century under the colonial regime. A powerful current of resentment swept through non-Brahmin Tamil communities and has still hardly abated. At the very heart of this movement, which eventually, decades later, captured the political center (1967), lies a novel notion of Tamil language, now fully ethnicized and perceived as the primary marker of collective identity. At a stroke, Tamil Brahmins—living in Tamil, shaped by Tamil culture, entirely at home in the various interwoven and overlapping Tamil worlds—were perceived as foreign interlopers, the bearers of an alien, Sanskritic culture at odds with an imagined, autochthonous, purely Dravidian civilization.

Scholars have traced the evolution of this movement through several stages in both the ideological and sociopolitical realms. As Irschick writes, "the formulation of the concept of Dravidian civilization quickly became involved not only with a full-scale attack on the Brahman's cultural position but also with political issues."[67] Early portraits of a primeval Dravidian south India by historians such as V. Kanakasabhai Pillai[68] and Śaiva or neo-Śaiva authors such as J. M. Nalluswami Pillai (1864–1920)[69] crystallized into a default narrative current throughout early-twentieth-century Tamil Nadu. It is important to see clearly the neo-Śaiva component in this process: the Śaiva Siddhânta philosophical and ritual synthesis of the thirteenth century onward was recruited, and powerfully distorted, as evidence of a non-Brahmin, original Dravidian religion that could be pitted against the Aryan-Brahmin systems with their alleged Sanskritic bias.[70] By the second decade of the twentieth century, rampant mythologizing generated a purist movement aimed at "cleansing" Tamil of its Sanskrit elements: the colorful, emblematic figure spearheading this Pure Tamil movement, *taṉittamiḻ iyakkam*, was Maraimalai Adigal (born as Vedachalam Pillai, 1876–1950).[71] Focused primary on lexical substitution—nouns derived from Tamil roots replacing prevalent Sanskrit words both in colloquial and in written Tamil—but eventually progressing to sustained efforts to generate neologisms needed for modern domains of science, technology, and government bureaucracy, the movement was ultimately no more successful than were the Young Turks who sought to discard the Arabic and Persian legacy in modern Turkish.[72] Tamil today, like the Tamil of yesterday, indeed like nearly all major living languages, remains saturated with borrowed vocabulary. What is more, the very intensity of anti-Sanskrit feeling that we see in the Pure Tamil fanatics is itself a sure sign of the deep interdependence of the two languages (if, indeed, we can even isolate them from one another in some artificial manner).

Tamil anti-Brahminism turned out to be a heterogeneous, dynamic, and politically effective force. It entered into the public sphere in Madras in 1916 with the founding of the Justice Party, among whose leaders were Dr. T. M. Nair and P. Tyagaraja Chetti, the latter coming from a Telugu merchant community (interestingly, Telugu Komatis and Chettis were among the first politically oriented "Dravidianists" in Madras).[73] The new party immediately found itself locked in debate with the India nationalists and their domineering spokeswoman, Annie Besant, who disliked the narrow focus of anti-Brahmin politics. This tension endured for decades and came to a head when Gandhi came to Madras in 1921 and again in 1927.[74] Meanwhile, a novel voice had a deep impact on the non-Brahmin movement, beginning roughly in 1927 and continuing until 1944 in its initial form, "when the Dravidian movement was at its radical best," in the telling phrase of A. R. Venkatachalapathy.[75] This was the Self-Respect Movement, *cuyamariyātai iyakkam*, of a maverick genius, E. V. Ramasami Naicker, popularly known as "the Great

One," Pĕriyār. It is of some significance that this fearless iconoclast came from Erode, in the west of the Tamil country or, better, in the southern reaches of the early-modern Deccani culture, and from a Kannada Balija Naidu community. In stark contrast with both the neo-Śaiva ideologues and the classicizing mythologists, Ramasami Naicker was a professed atheist, utterly unromantic about the glories of the early Dravidians, and even skeptical about, or indeed indifferent to, the mystique of the Tamil language: "I do not have any devotion for Tamil, either as mother tongue or as the language of the nation. I am not attached to it because it is a classical language, or because it is an ancient language, or because it was the language spoken by Shiva, or the language bestowed upon us by Agastya. . . . Such an attachment and devotion is foolish. I only have attachment to those things that have qualities that have utility."[76]

The pragmatic, skeptical, and fervently rationalist ethos of the man comes through clearly. Emancipating the Tamilians from social inequality and Brahmin domination, as he saw it, was his goal; if English were to prove more effective politically, then Periyar was for it. At a conference in 1948 over which he presided, he wrote a note to himself: "Down with Tamil!"[77] Throughout his long career he consistently opposed what he called "language madness" (*mŏḻi paittiyam,* incidentally a typical Tamil-Sanskrit hybrid). He was also an early advocate of reforming the Tamil script. Even more striking is the fact that, unlike his successors in politics, he preferred a juicy spoken Tamil to the elevated hyperglossic "Platform Tamil."

Welding such views together with those of the Dravidian nationalists was, clearly, no simple matter; there were many sharp twists and turns on the road to founding the Draviḍa Kaḻakam (DK) or "Dravidian Association" in 1944[78]—the party out of which the Draviḍa Muṉṉeṟṟak Kaḻakam (DMK), "Association for Dravidian Progress," emerged in 1949 under the leadership of C. N. Annadurai. (There was a further split in 1972.) Extreme divergence among the several discrete components of the Dravidian movement in fundamental orientations toward life, language, and politics was partly submerged under a common revulsion against the attempt, led by the Brahmin (Aiyangar) premier of the Madras Presidency and National Congress politician

Rajagopalachari, to make instruction in Hindi mandatory in schools (1937). Hindi now occupied the slot previously allocated to Sanskrit as a malevolent northern (Brahminical) import to the deep south. The first highly visible self-immolations by individual Tamils terminally devoted to their language took place during this period, with another round in the mid-1960s. Even the pragmatic Periyar joined in the anti-Hindi agitation in the 1930s and thus achieved temporary elevation to the pantheon of pro-Tamil saints.

Bernard Bate is undoubtedly right to characterize Periyar's DK as a "classically modernist movement in the sense of distinguishing itself from what it considered a moribund 'tradition' (that is, Brahminism) and proposing a new, enlightenment-based philosophy of self-respect *(suyamariyathai)* and rationalism *(pakutharivu)* that would wipe away the irrationalities of caste and gender oppression."[79] No less modern was the marriage of linguism with long-standing social and economic resentment. Extreme Tamil linguism even came to deny the separate existence of the other south Indian Dravidian languages: at times "Dravidian" came explicitly to mean only "Tamil," rather like the usage of the late-medieval Kerala *Līlā-tilakam*.[80] Tamil language madness could be directed against Telugu, Kannada, and Malayalam as well as the primary target, Sanskrit (or Hindi). On the other hand, Tamil-based Dravidianism eventually spread far beyond the borders of Tamil Nadu and, in local mutations, reached the other south Indian states by the last quarter of the twentieth century. There is much more to be said about regional inflections of this process of diffusion.

So far in this section I have stuck to what we might think of as the standard narrative. Unfortunately, I don't think it really explains the dynamics and astonishing power of Dravidian anti-Brahmin nationalism in twentieth-century Tamil Nadu. We need a wider or thicker description. Resentment, undoubtedly one of the driving forces of human history, coupled with the literally fantastic consequences of the recovery of Sangam-period Tamil, created and shaped a potent matrix for political action—but not without drawing on much deeper roots than the colonial-period phenomena apparent on the surface. To spell out the precise lines of filiation would require another book, but I think a skeletal shadow image can be projected onto the partially illumined historical screen. I will limit myself to four main thematic-historical clusters clearly present in the intellectual and social world of the nineteenth century.

*1. Siddha antinomianism.* Egalitarian, iconoclastic, skeptical, and strongly rationalistic tendencies were not so new in the Tamil south. From roughly the fifteenth century on, we have texts, some of them orally transmitted, by antinomian mystics known collectively as Siddhas or Tamil Cittar (we briefly discussed one of them, Paṭṭiṉattār, in Chapter 3).[81] It's not a good idea to lump these twilight figures together, especially since their voices tend to be highly idiosyncratic; but broadly we can see common traits such as hatred for caste hierarchies and orthodox rituals, a Yoga-oriented universalistic ethic, anti-Brahmin sentiments and a generalized social critique, and intimate links to a separate system of medicine, pharmacology, and a Tantric metaphysics of body, self, and language. To this day, Siddha medicine is one of the major surviving indigenous schools of south Indian medical learning and practice.[82] Siddha poetry proliferated, in an accelerating trajectory, throughout the early-modern period. One of the major Siddhas, Civa-vākkiyar, was often quoted by Periyar, among other Dravidianists;[83] indeed, it would be fair to say that Siddha sources were regularly recycled by this branch of the movement, and that such citations fit well into the nonconformist secular Erode-Deccani context that formed Periyar himself. There is every reason to believe that we are seeing traces of a continuous tradition surfacing in and informing the modern political arena. Ramalinga Svami (1823–1872), the greatest of the nineteenth-century Tamil mystics and a protomodernist, is usually said to be the last (so far) of these Siddhas. I'll come back to him in a moment.

*2. Heterodox Tantra from the Kaviri delta.* Possibly the single most influential factor in the reconfiguration of Tamil intellectual life in the second half of the nineteenth century, especially in its nationalist-linguistic aspect, was the ongoing transmission of Tantric themes and content, in both the Samaya and Kaula streams, from the lines of teaching prevalent in the Kaveri delta and elsewhere (notably Madurai) in the sixteenth to eighteenth centuries. If we ask ourselves where the obsession with Tamil language came from, *before* the translation of this obsession into an exclusivist identity-related track, we cannot ignore the vector leading back to language-specific mantric practices that we noted in Chapter 4. God, as you may recall from our earlier discussions, prefers to speak in Tamil. Tamil syllables, both in their aural and their graphic forms, are the stuff of reality; pragmatic Tantric grammars regulate their use.

Even beyond these grammars, Tantric transformative metaphysics slowly found their way into the orthodox mainstream, including the prestigious world of classical music. Indeed, what is today referred to as the movement of Tamil music *(tamiḻ icai),* a major historical development, largely nationalist in tone, in twentieth-century Madras, goes back to the great seventeenth- and eighteenth-century composers working in Tamil—often also in Telugu and Sanskrit—such as Tiruvārūr Pāpanāśa Mutaliyār, Muttut Tāṇṭavar, and Upanishad Brahmam.[84] The classical texts of early *tamiḻ icai* were part of the Tantricized world of the delta, as were the musical poems of Tāyumāṉavar from this same period. To no small extent, Tamil modernism sprang from these heterodox materials, which were current at the royal court of Tanjavur, thus imbued with political resonance, but also familiar to the emerging urban elite audiences for classical music in early colonial times.

We know something about the links in transmission. Ramalinga Svami was certainly a major figure in this respect, offering an "esoterical phonological analysis" to drive home his commitment to the Tamil language as the high road to ultimate (Śaiva) experience[85]—just as one would expect. But he was not alone in the field. Among the early Tamil nationalists endowed with a special passion for the language and its classical poetry is the provocative and prolific ascetic known as Dandapani Swamigal (Caṅkaraliṅkam Murukatācar, ca. 1840–1899), the author of a compendium in verse of the legendary vitae of Tamil poets, the *Pulavar-purāṇam.*[86] Tantric teaching did not dry up in colonial Madras; rather, it transmuted itself into modern language-based theories and praxis. Modern Tamil identity-politics have unacknowledged Tantric roots.

*3. The Jaffna-Sri Lanka connection.* Tamil neo-Śaivism, to use Sumathi Ramaswamy's term, grew out of the mutt-based system of ritual, temple economics and administration, and education when this system came under the magnetic force of colonial concepts and colonial authority. Historically, the mutts themselves were largely non-Brahmin (Velala) operations that, as Elaine Fisher has noted, cultivated Velala pride and a Tamil Śaiva identity;[87] they adapted well to the new administrative and economic reality and served as institutional moorings for the new articulation of non-Brahmin (then anti-Brahmin) politics. Yet as far as I can see, nothing in the long history of Tamil Śaivism and its institutional nodes was conducive to the formation of a romantic myth of pure Tamil origins. We will have to look elsewhere for factors triggering the modernist neo-Śaiva worldview, focused on Tamilness as the primary ingredient of an autochthonous Velala-Dravidian religion and engaged in intense reformist polemics with Christian challenges, at once institutional and theological. Missionary sources are an obvious place to start.

In particular, we should notice the outstanding figures who moved to Madras from Jaffna in the middle of the nineteenth century. Foremost among them were Ka. Arumuka Navalar and Ci. Vai. Damodaram Pillai, both mentioned above, though there were more. Both these men grew to manhood within the orbit of Christian missionary institutions in Jaffna and elsewhere on the island; both were intellectually formed by eminent missionary educators and by traditional Tamil pundits working under their aegis. Underlying this Western-style professional training was a deeper, more pervasive level of Sri Lankan Tamil literary culture, with its own particular thematic emphases and a distinctive social context. I have already remarked on the scintillating, modernizing character of Sri Lankan Tamil culture in the early-modern period—fertile ground, perhaps, for early manifestations of a proselytizing, reformist, neo-Śaiva, language-based nationalism, exported from Jaffna to the mainland in the mid-nineteenth century.

*4. The colonial bureaucracy, Fort St. George, romantic folklorists, and other exogenous factors.* None of the above, separately or together, would have sufficed to produce a European-style nationalist movement in Madras. Nationalism, linguism, separatism—the next stage after Dravidianism defined itself in opposition to an Aryan north—were shaped by conceptual input from the colonial system with its imported reformist agenda. It is amazing, also strangely ironic, to see how English administrators, missionaries, educators, and scholars promoted a romanticized narrative of a Dravidian, non-Brahmin, non-Sanskrit past akin to the new nationalist mythologies of nineteenth-century Europe, notably in the Hapsburg state, Russia, Finland, and Scotland. Blackburn has shown how European folklorists such as Charles Gover and E. J. Robinson, working in Madras, imagined a Dravidian folk that had long ago produced folksongs in "pure Tamil" antedating Sanskrit, indeed as ancient as Old Testament times, and also vibrating with a somewhat surprising "Protestant" ethos.[88] A crude anti-Brahminism accompanied this vision; Gover wrote in 1871, "The Brahmins have corrupted what they could not destroy."[89] (We might note in passing that Gover's book gives pride of place to the Tamil Siddhas.) Linguists such as Caldwell and missionary students of "Dravidian folk religion" such as Henry Whitehead and Wilber Theodore Elmore eagerly contributed to this crystallizing colonial story of origins, which had become the received wisdom in the Madras Presidency even *before* the days of Sundaram Pillai and Nalluswami Pillai.

By the 1880s, the governor of Madras, Mountstuart Elphinstone Grant-Duff, in an address at the University of Madras, could thus assure a (mostly Brahmin) audience: "You have less to do with Sanskrit than we English have."[90] He thought he was ruling over a "pure Dravidian race" that had been corrupted by invaders from the north (not as far north as London).[91] Colonial scholarship, at first centered in the College of Fort St. George in Old Madras, generated early grammars of Tamil and other south Indian languages along with theories of linguistic and literary history at times continuous with, at times dissociated from, the living traditions of these same languages.[92] Indeed, it is not clear that European scholars and young civil servants working in the college, with some notable exceptions, had internalized anything of the sensibility that informs classical Tamil and Telugu texts, despite the presence there of the proficient south Indian poet-scholars who taught them.[93] Linguism, like modern nationalism generally, tends to flatten out the object it purports to celebrate.

After all this, and more than a century of Tamil nationalist politics, one might well wonder if the ideological disjunction between the "northern language" and the "southern language" has penetrated as deeply as it might seem. Dravidian separatism—the dream of an independent Tamil state, Dravida Nadu, in south India—was once the ostensible program of the DK and, to some extent, of its successor parties; it has died away, so much so that the Tamil separatist movement is cited by political scientists as a good example of the co-option of such collectives by the wider nation-state. In some, often subterranean ways the old symbiosis of Brahmin and non-Brahmin in the far south is still alive. If not in Chennai then in Delhi: for the past several decades, Tamil Brahmins, "Tam Brahms," have, some would say, run the Indian state.[94] Anti-Brahminism remains a potent political force in the far south, while Sanskrit—even the *idea* of Sanskrit, not to mention the now somewhat exotic notion of learning the language—has become attenuated as a cultural force, although not across the board (Sanskrit is alive and well in the critical sphere of ritual, both in temples and in homes, and also in classical Carnatic music, flourishing today as never before). But it is important to remember that all along there were voices that positioned themselves somewhere between the apparent antinomies—not least among them that of Subrahmania Bharati (1882–1921), a Smarta Brahmin, probably the finest talent among all modern Tamil poets, a nationalist, iconoclast, and passionate partisan of Tamil who seems never to have thought of Sanskrit as an alien presence. With some grinding of teeth, Dravidianists, too, were mostly ready to acknowledge him as the "national poet" of the Tamils.

## Tillāṉā (Meditative Finale)

We know when the Republic of Syllables came to an end. In 1956 the borders of the states making up the Republic of India were redrawn to coincide, as much as possible, with language distribution. Tamil Nadu is thus the state where Tamil is spoken; Andhra Pradesh, before it was split into two states in 2014 (Andhra Pradesh and Telangana), was home to Telugu speech; and so on. As noted in Chapter 1, there are spillover zones with large numbers of bilinguals and multilinguals; in general, however, remapping the subcontinent to produce linguistically homogeneous states has had the effect of reducing what was once a normative polyglossia to lonely and impoverished monolingualism, tempered to some extent by the strong role of English and Hindi, both present in schools and the modern media as the new "northern tongues." Along with this structural trend we have widespread parochialism and ignorance as the points of departure in cultural domains. Nannayya, the first Telugu poet, apparently knew about Sangam poetry, but today's speakers of Telugu have, for the most part, never heard of it. By the same token, educated Tamil speakers may know the name of Krishṇadevarāya, the synoptic Telugu poet-king of the early sixteenth century; but how many of them could read his great book, the *Āmukta-mālyada*, in Telugu? For that matter, how many would want to? (The same two questions could also be directed to native Telugu speakers.) The days when a court poet in Tanjavur could compose a play in five languages and expect his audience of connoisseurs to engage with it are, sadly, long gone.

Yet there was something like a Tamil Renaissance after all, not in nineteenth-century Madras but in the mid-twentieth century; indeed, it is still going on, even accelerating. There have been revolutionary developments, in more than one sense of the word, in Tamil poetry: first the "new poetry" *(putu kavitai)* of Na. Pichamoorthy, and a little later the breakthrough poems of Ci. Mani (*Narakam*, "Hell," 1962), Ñānakkūttaṉ, and the Vanampadi poets of the 1970s (notably Agniputhiran). At the same time, dozens of great prose writers collectively reinvented and extended the expressive potential of Tamil prose. To mention only a few exemplary names is to do injustice to many others. Nonetheless: Putumaippittan; Kalki; Mauni; Ashokamitran; Ki. Rajanarayanan; T. Janakiraman; Ka. Na. Subrahmanyam; Sundara Ramaswamy; Dilip Kumar; Poomani; G. Nagarajan; Na. Muthuswamy; Imayam (the last three particularly noteworthy for their experiments with writing in colloquial dialect). As in other regions of south India, Marxist ideologies, orthodox and heterodox, shaped the work of Tamil writers from mid-century on. Two Sri Lankan Tamil writers from the

Sri Lanka Progressive Writers' Association, S. Ganeshalingam and Dominic Jeeva (among many others), showed again the particular effervescent effect on Tamil Nadu of artist-intellectuals from the island next door. I had best stop stringing out such invidious lists.

What has happened in recent decades with Tamil diglossia? What do Tamil literati think about it? Where is it going? Is Facebook Tamil diglossic? Do we now have something like a standardized dialect? Thoughtful answers to questions such as these are offered by E. Annamalai. He records some movement toward standardization in speech; written Tamil and the so-called Platform Tamil are in any case relatively homogeneous, conforming in at least some major parameters to grammatical norms of *cĕntamiḻ* going back to medieval times—although it would be a mistake to think of modern formal Tamil as isomorphic with the earlier literary dialect. But even assuming the still precarious emergence of a standard spoken dialect, Annamalai rightly concludes: "The standard dialect of Tamil contains a range of acceptable features, which are larger than the variations found in the standard dialect of most languages."[95] There is no doubt that modern media of communications, including television and film, have contributed to partial standardization both in formal and in colloquial styles. There are centripetal tendencies within modern Tamil. On the other hand, centrifugal forces conducive to the survival and legitimation of social and regional dialectical speech are also very active.

One might have thought that under the pressures of modernity the deep structural diglossia of Tamil would have generated a powerful middle-level register, a Standard Modern Tamil that would have assimilated elements of colloquial speech to a new formal style used both in writing and in speeches, lectures, and other public contexts. Something like this is supposed to have happened in Tamil's northern neighbor, Telugu; the archaic, rather stiff learned style (*grānthika* Telugu), reminiscent of Greek *katharevousa,* was superseded in the twentieth century, not without fierce struggle, by a morphologically and syntactically distinct *vyavahārika* or "usage-based" dialect, now in common use in formal genres.[96] This modern, relatively standardized register is indeed closer to colloquial Telugu than the old *grānthika* style was. Thus a kind of Standard Modern Telugu (SMT) has taken root—though anyone from outside who learns Telugu discovers very rapidly that this SMT is something of an illusion. In fact, Telugu diglossia is still very much the norm, and there is a staggering range of prevalent dialectical speech, utterly nonstandardized, and phonologically, morphologically, and lexically distinct from the theoretically mediating *vyavahārika* forms. This diglossic or polyglossic reality has, if anything, deepened with the creation of the Telangana state and the rising cultural role of the Telangana dialect, now also present in various registers of literary Telugu from this region.

In Tamil, too, modernity has, somewhat surprisingly, not only perpetuated but even intensified the diglossia, without giving birth to a widely accepted *vyavahārika* or usage-based formal dialect. The gap between colloquial-dialectical speech and formal Tamil has hardly shrunk. What we do have is *meṭaittamiḻ*, the Platform Tamil of political speeches and other public occasions. Something very remarkable happened in this arena. Political oratory in the early decades of the twentieth century—for example, by E. V. Ramaswamy Naicker / Periyar but also by Congress politicians such as Rajagopalachari—was largely based on colloquial speech *(kŏccaittamiḻ)*, a conscious mark of democratic and egalitarian claims by the speaker. By the middle of the twentieth century, Dravidianist orators such as C. N. Annadurai and Mu. Karunanidhi adopted in the public space a version of *cĕntamiḻ* or "high," "pure," grammaticalized Tamil, as Bernard Bate has shown.[97] "This transformation, this oratorical revolution, coincided with the establishment of mass suffrage, the emergence of a mass electorate, and the full-scale politicization of the Dravidianist historical and cultural paradigm."[98]

Two primary aspects of this shift deserve mention. On the one hand, we see the astonishing depth of Tamil diglossia as a cultural choice continuous with premodern Tamil linguistic practice. Politically effective mass Tamil is formal "high" Tamil derived from the written registers. In this, Tamil is very similar to modern Arabic, famous for its glaring diglossia and for its recourse to standard elevated speech *(fuṣḥa)* for most translocal, nondomestic usage. On the other hand, modern Tamil literature has shown an increasing preference for the colloquial. As Bate says, "Strikingly, at the very moment when Tamil purist politicians began to speak on the model of the written word, the vanguard of the Tamil literary movement, especially those writers associated with the publication *Manikkodi*, began to write on the model of the spoken word."[99]

There are several ways to theorize this apparent paradox. *Cĕntamiḻ* is a cultural construct of such immense resonance and historical weight that, despite the fact that it actually embraces a considerable range of usage and style and has evolved significantly over many centuries, there is no acceptable option of seriously compromising it, let alone jettisoning it, as a privileged medium of communication in most formal domains. *Cĕntamiḻ* also offers expressive possibilities more or less unique to its internal logic; indeed, these possibilities have expanded tremendously over the past century or more. But so has the context-specific cultural expressivity of dialectical speech, especially in defined arenas such as modern literary usage and the modern stage; it is also the case that some things can best be said, or indeed only be said, in dialect.

In a way, hypermodern Tamil is close to a model of incipient vernacularization not so different from what Sheldon Pollock has described for Sanskrit at the turn of the second millennium: without sacrificing the overwhelmingly prestigious role of the translocal high idiom, but through a long process of internalizing and replicating many of the formal features and much of the content of that idiom, the vernacular conquers ever larger areas that were previously the preserve of the cosmopolitan language (Sanskrit ca. 1000 A.D.; *cĕntamiḻ* a thousand years later). No one can predict at this point whether Tamil will eventually vernacularize itself in this mode in an expanding range of normative, relatively autonomous domains.[100] It is possible, however, that modern communications create better conditions for centrifugal vernacularization—the full autonomization and cultural privileging of colloquial dialects—than existed in medieval times.

Whatever happens over time, the future of Tamil is more than bright; I see no danger whatsoever of serious attrition or erosion, despite the complaints one regularly hears among connoisseurs of Tamil in Chennai and farther south. The fact that a globalizing English (as distinct from the earlier colonial English) has made its way into Tamil—first lexically, but also to some extent in syntax[101]—has conceptual consequences within the language but is, in principle, hardly different from massive linguistic borrowings in the past. Purists are invited, if they really want to, to lament this infusion of fresh linguistic material. No statistical percentage of English usage in Tamil, however high, is going to wash this language away. Creativity in Tamil, both in the expressive genres and, even more important, in playful, personal, everyday speech and thought, is as intense today as it was before, whatever "before" might mean. This statement applies not only to south Indian Tamil in its diverse continuum of levels and forms but also, emphatically, to Sri Lankan Tamil and even to an extent to the far-flung Tamil diaspora.

So far, structural sociolinguistic continuity with the classical and medieval past is very striking—and much the same can be said for the more general cultural arena, despite the dramatic transformations I have briefly discussed. Major themes and concepts that came up in the chapters of this book are still very much alive, and still evolving, in today's Tamil culture, often unconsciously so and thus deserving of even more respect. To name a few: recall the deep foundation of the person, the unitary, resilient *uyir,* or life breath, along with its inherent form of intuitive awareness, *uṇarvu;* the rule-bound, proliferating domains of in-ness, *akam,* and their complex links to objectified outness, *puṟam,* and the living subject at home in a real, that is, really imagined, world; the mantic nature of Tamil speech and the pragmatics of syllable magic and true utterance, *vāymŏḻi,* as autonomous forces released into this world; the always central role of grammar, broadly conceived, in both regulating speech—including figurative usage, a primary feature of all speech forms—and in generating the conditions of exceeding or subverting normative rules; the powers of graphic recording of poetic speech, especially by engraving it with bodily gestures on open space; the tensile and dynamic complementarities of right and left in the Tamil social and political body; the properties of musical utterance, including grammaticalized auralization and the shamanic internalization that can make a goddess come alive; the multifaceted divinity of the Tamil language itself, especially when juxtaposed with those strands of the classical tradition that insist on the entirely human origins of Tamil grammar.[102] Even in this partial list we can see the decisive cultural and conceptual significance of grammar, the *ālapanam* of this long essay.

We began with a few sentences by the great master of modern Tamil prose, Na. Muthuswamy. I want to conclude, first, with one more Muthuswamy sentence that shows more clearly than any analytic paraphrase the vastly expanded expressive potential available in good, lyrical, contemporary Tamil. It's a long sentence, this time from a play, "England," thus imprinted with strong traces of the spoken language. I give the Tamil first for those who can read it and hear its music. The translation is the work of S. Ramakrishnan and myself. The context is a depiction of a village with its Dalit neighborhood or *ceri* and a pond, once cool and clean, that has slowly been stopped up by deposits of refuse. Someone clearly has to collect this refuse and dump it in the pond:

> *[uṉ ceriyiṉ naṭukkuṭṭaiyai tūrttu viṭṭārkaḷ.] nava-nākarikat tĕrukkaḷil cekaritta kuppaiyap purātaṉa vaṇṭikaḷil uyir uraintu uṭal pāṭam pĕṟṟu ĕntiramāy iyaṅkum paḻaiya niṉaiviṉ paṭivukaḷai acaipoṭum iṟanta kālam pārtta aṟait tūkka viḻi māṭukaḷ pūṭṭiya vaṇṭikaḷil uruṇṭu uruṇṭu accum uḷḷāḻiyum teyntu taḷarntu cāyntu āṭum cakkaraṅkaḷ pūṭṭiya vaṇṭikaḷil vaittu vaittut teynta nukattaṭi māṭṭiṉ kaḻuttil ammik kuḻaviyāy aṟaittu māṭṭu kaḻuttuk kāyttut tŏṅkiya varum māṭukaḷ pūṭṭiya vaṇṭikaḷil paḻakkam āki niṉaiv'aṟṟu ŏru kaiyil talaikkayiṟum maṟṟ'ŏru kai viralil pallil taṭavik kŏḷḷa cĕṉṟa yukattil vaḻitta vĕṇ cuṇṇāmpum kuntiya ŏru kālum tŏṅki āṭum ŏru kālumāka nilaittu talai-muṟaikaḷ māṟi vara oṭṭi varum ŏruvaṉ cerik kuṭṭaiyait tūrttu viṭṭāṉ.*
>
> [They stopped up the pond at the center of your *cheri.*] Some cartman, with his life frozen and body embalmed, ruminating on deposits of old memories, bulls with half-asleep eyes harnessed to his cart that had seen better days, its axle and hub worn out, its wheels wobbly, its worn-out yoke rubbing against the bulls' necks like a grinding stone and the flesh on their necks calloused and hanging low, the cartman without any memories, one hand holding the reins and a finger of the other hand covered with lime from the previous century to rub on his gums, has stopped up the pond with refuse collected from new-fangled streets as he sits, one leg dangling and the other bent, driving the bulls as he has been doing for generations.

Even in translation, you can see the lush lexis, the complexity of thought, image, and syntax, the gently hyperglossic and hypotactic style worthy of Proust or, even better, of Ativīrarāma Pāṇṭiyaṉ's *Naiṭatam* (probably the highest compliment I can pay this sentence). In fact, to tell the truth, not even the *Naiṭatam* achieved this level of flexible lyrical precision, a trait proper to Tamil modernism, along with the equally modern, self-conscious marshaling of a remembered past haunting the present and the very syllables that bring us into that present. The frozen *uyir* and embalmed body are also very much to the point I want to make.

Finally, here is a contemporary Tamil poem by Manushya Puthiran in which the old *akam* grammar of in-ness in relation to a projected, imagined, and therefore objective out-ness has miraculously surfaced. This poem is recognizably, though perhaps a little ironically, linked to Tamil poems from the oldest stratum we have. As in any great classical literature in modern guise, it is those same nonexplicit links that impart a unique depth to the experience of reading the words—in this case, words that could almost have been spoken or sung by a lovesick Sangam-period heroine to her companion, or to herself, as a somewhat desolate present-future rejoins its own past:

Lost Love *(iḻanta kātal)*

A tree from my garden
tired of standing
came to me for comfort,
ascending the steps gently.

Since I knew
that trees could not walk
I thought it was a strange dream
and tarried long
before welcoming it.
Feeling slighted,
filled with the sorrow of rejection
to the tips of its thousand leaves
and roots,
there goes my garden tree
descending the steps.[103]

# Notes

Classical texts are cited in standard modern editions that include, in most cases, the medieval commentaries mentioned in the notes.

## 1. BEGINNINGS

*Ālāpana:* Opening improvisation.

1. Cuntaramūrtti *Tevāram* 36.3.
2. See Shulman 1987.
3. *Tiruviḷaiyāṭaṟ-purāṇam* 54 (see "The Grammarian's Blessing and Curse" in this chapter); *Tirukkuṟṟālat-talapurāṇam* 2.3; *Kanta-purāṇam* 2.23–28; Zvelebil 1992: 241.
4. *Puṟappŏruḷ vĕṇpā mālai,* preamble.
5. Wentworth 2011b.
6. *Pāṇṭikkovai* 219 in *Iṟaiyaṉār akappŏruḷ:* the heroine has a "nature gentle as the Tamil land" *(tamiḻ nāṭ' aṉṉa mĕlliyalāy).*
7. *nīrmai* can also mean "goodness," "nature," or "essence."
8. Zvelebil 1992: ix–xvii.
9. *Kādambarī* of Bāṇa (seventh century): 194.
10. *Daśa-kumāra-carita* 11.
11. *Kādambarī* of Bāṇa: 224; *Harṣa-carita* of Bāṇa: 76.
12. The discovery of an Indo-European family was famously announced by William Jones in Calcutta in 1786, although Muslim scholars such as Siraj al-Din 'Ali Khan Arzu in early eighteenth-century north India were aware, at least, that Persian and Sanskrit were genealogically related.
13. Trautmann 2006. To this fine study we can now add the pioneering work by Kovintarajan (2016) on early colonial predecessors to Ellis in the scientific study of Tamil.
14. See Chapter 5, "Maṇi-pravāḷam, Rubies and Coral."
15. *Līlā-tilakam* 5 at v. 5.
16. See Govindakutty Menon 1972. In addition to the features noted by Govindakutty Menon, Venugopala Panicker has pointed to Mal. *l* substituting for Skt. *t*: *ulsavam* for *utsavam*, for example. Tamil *uṟcavam* must preserve the original *l* (before *sandhi*). Thus "Malayalam phonetic evaluation of Sanskrit is older than the Tamil evaluation" (personal communication).
17. Caminat'aiyar 1968.

18. Such as the common uses of nonfinite verbal forms. Some types of Sanskrit nominal compounds are typically left-branching; historically, these compounds tended to become ever longer and to constitute the kind of clause structure typical of Dravidian.
19. Muthuswamy 2009: 156, translated by S. Ramakrishnan and myself.
20. See lengthy discussion by Rajam (1992b): 855–85.
21. Burrow and Emeneau 1961: 599.
22. Ibid. 600.
23. Meenakshisundaram 1965: 31.
24. Rajam 1985.
25. *Tŏl. Cŏl.* 401–2.
26. Muthuswamy 2009: 289. Translation by S. Ramakrishnan and D. Shulman, in press.
27. Monier-Williams 2001.
28. Muthuswamy 2009: 282.
29. Ibid.: 78.
30. See Chapter 7, "Dravidian Dreams."
31. We know from the ancient *Tŏlkāppiyam* grammar that this was the situation already long ago.
32. See Mitchell 2009 for detailed discussion of the linguistic history of twentieth-century Telugu; see Chapter 7, "Tillāṉā."
33. Lubotsky 2001; Witzel 1999; see also Kuiper 1948.
34. Witzel 1999: 19.
35. Southworth 1979.
36. Mayrhofer 1986–2001.
37. See *Puṟanāṉūṟu* 235. Mayrhofer assumes an indigenous source, perhaps from something like Tamil *nāṟṟam*+*kāy*, "aromatic fruit." Think of Spanish *naranja*.
38. Emeneau 1967: 159, discussed in Southworth 1979.
39. Southworth 1979: 297.
40. Ibid.
41. See Shulman 2014a.
42. McAlpin 1974 and 1975.
43. Zvelebil 1985.
44. Allchin 1982; but see Witzel 1999.
45. On the megaliths, see Sudyka 2011.
46. As Hart (1975) argued long ago.
47. Lienhard 1986.
48. See Neeman 2002.
49. Witzel 1999: 30.

50. Rabin 1971.
51. Parpola 1994; Knorozov, Albedil, and Volchok 1981; Mahadevan 2011.
52. See Rajan and Yatheeskumar 2013. I thank Sascha Ebeling for bringing this important essay to my attention and Gideon Shelach, Kesavan Veluthat, and Richard Salomon for helpful discussion of the carbon datings.
53. Salomon 1998: 34–36; see Mahadevan 2014.
54. *Tirukkuṟaḷ* 1.1. See also Chapter 6, "Tantric Tamil."
55. Girnar Rock Edict II.
56. Tieken 2008: 591; K. G. Krishnan 1970–1971.
57. See Nagaswamy 1995: 85–90, and Nagaswamy "Kollip-purai," n.d.; Gros 1983; Mahadevan 2014.
58. See Champakalakshmi 1996; Subrahmanian 1966.
59. Megasthenes' report survived as cited by the second-century A.D. author Arrian in *Indica;* see Nilakanta Sastri 1966: 27.
60. Recent debate on the date of the *Periplus* has now settled on the first century A.D. as the most likely.
61. See Begley 1983; Nagaswamy 1995: 77–78.
62. Gros 1968: 17, as translated by M. P. Boseman in Gros 2009: 75.
63. See, e.g., *Tŏlkāppiyam, Pŏruḷatikāram* (*Tŏl. Pŏruḷ.*) 649, commentary by Perāciriyar.
64. *Brihaddevatā* 5: 149–53.
65. Ibid.: 153.
66. See also *Rāmāyaṇa* 3.12 on Rāma's visit to Agastya's ashram.
67. *Raghu-vaṃśa* 6.61. Tamil inscriptions of the Chola period refer to the Pandya king as Agastya's pupil *(śishya)*: see survey by Zvelebil 1992: 244ff. (with some inaccuracies).
68. *Raghu-vaṃśa* 13.36, with Mallinātha's commentary; see Hiltebeitel 1977.
69. *Maṇimekalai, patikam* 9–12.
70. See material cited by Chevillard 2009: 260–61; also the enigmatic and elliptical reference in *Cilappatikāram* 15.14.
71. I put aside for the moment the laconic reference to the "first book(s)," *muntu nūl,* in the preface to the *Tŏlkāppiyam* (ascribed to Paṉampāraṉār).
72. See the recent comprehensive study by Wilden (2014).
73. Note, however, that some scholars doubt that the commentary on the first *sūtra* of *IA* actually belongs with the rest of this work; it may well have been added somewhat later.
74. For the mythic geography, see Aṭiyārkkunallār's commentary on *Cilappatikāram* 8.1–2; Nacciṉārkk'iṉiyar on the preface to *Tŏl.;* Perāciriyar on *Tŏl. Poruḷ. Mar.* 94; Shulman 1980: 55–75.

75. Takahashi (2015) convincingly identifies the *kūttu, vari, ciṟṟicai,* and *pericai* of the *IA* commentary with the *Malaipaṭukaṭām, Pŏrunar-āṟṟuppaṭai, Ciṟu-pāṇ-āṟṟuppaṭai* and *Pĕrumpāṇ-āṟṟuppaṭai,* respectively, all from the Ten Songs.
76. Possibly adumbrated in the Nakkīraṉār list. See also Perāciriyar on *Tŏl. Pŏruḷ. Cĕy.* 149.
77. For the first categorical distinction between the anthologies, *tŏkai,* and the long songs, *pāṭṭu,* see Perāciriyar on *Tŏl. Pŏruḷ. Mar.* 94; Mayilainātar on *Naṉṉūl* 387, offering the number eight for the anthologies *(ĕṇ pĕrut tŏkai)* and ten for the songs; cf. Zvelebil 1973b: 25.
78. See Zvelebil 1973b: 48–49.
79. *mahābhāratan tamiḻ paṭuttum madhurāpuriccaṅkam vaittum:* line 103 of the Tamil portion. See Chapter 2, "Pandyas, Pallavas, and the Carriers of Tamil Knowledge."
80. See Marr 1985: 12–13; Cox 2002; Freeman 2013: 306. Marr notes that the commentator on the Tamil version of Daṇḍin, the *Taṇṭiyalaṅkāram* (v. 5), lists four of the Sangam anthologies as examples of *tŏkai=saṅghāta.*
81. *Ādiparvan* 1.23; translated by Narayana Rao and Shulman (2002: 60).
82. Note that the Telugu tradition also at times offers Agastya a similar role: see, among other sources, *Pāṇḍuraṅga-māhātmyamu* of Tĕnāli Rāma-krishṇa, Canto 1. And see Wilden 2014 for a detailed discussion of the Agastya origin story in Tamil.
83. There is a sequel to this story involving a certain Ataṅkoṭṭācāṉ, who is mentioned by name in the preamble to the *Tŏlkāppiyam* as a teacher whose doubts were resolved by Tŏlkāppiyaṉār. The latter wished to have his grammar approved by a jury of experts, including Ataṅkoṭṭācaṉ; but Agastya had forbidden this teacher from even hearing the book *(nūl)* recited out loud. Despite the threat of Agastya's curse, Ataṅkoṭṭācaṉ did listen to the public recitation but raised doubts about the correctness of the grammatical rules it contained. The author of the preamble proudly tells us that Tŏlkāppiyaṉār successfully overcame these objections. See Chevillard 2009: 263.
84. See Iḷampūraṇār on *Tŏl. Cŏl.* 274.
85. *IA* 1: 7.
86. On these materials, see the fine studies by Aravamuthan (1931 and 1932); also see Zvelebil 1973a; Filliozat 1960: i–xi; Fisher 2013: 220–22, 231. Parañcoti was a student of the great sixteenth-century poet Nirampavaḻakiya Tecikar. Fisher sees the *Hālâsya-māhātmya* and Parañcoti's *Tiruviḷaiyāṭaṟ-purāṇam* as "twin texts" composed roughly at the same time, the *Hālâsya* being, in her view, "most likely re-Sanskritized directly from Parañcoti's

fabulously successful TVP" (2013: 231). I remain convinced on the basis of a close reading of both works that the *Hālâsya* is the older source. See also Wilden 2014: 268: "It [the *Tiruviḷaiyāṭal*] is clearly a re-creation in Tamil of the *Hālāsya Māhātmya,* taking over all of the latter's innovations and making a few of his own."

87. *See Tŏl., Ĕḻuttu* 8 and 46. In the *Pāṇinīya-śikṣā,* vowels, *svara,* are characterized as *prāṇa,* "life-breath." But Parañcoti is much closer to the linguistic metaphysics of the Kashmiri Tantra, where vowels, as *bīja,* "seeds," actually give birth to the consonants. See Padoux 1990: 230–31.
88. Perhaps, following the modern commentator Na. Mu. Venkatacami Nattar, the fifteen Sanskrit vowels and diphthongs and the thirty-three plosives, nasals, sibilants, semivowels, and the voiced *h.* There are, however, other ways to count; *Hālâsya-māhātmya (HM)* 57.12–18 identifies Śiva not with *a* but with *h.*
89. See Shulman 2007. On Tamil "proto Śrī-vidyā esotericism" and the *Tirumantiram,* see also Fisher 2013: 229.
90. *Kāḷahasti-māhātmyamu* of Dhūrjaṭi, 3.131.
91. *HM* 57.60ff. See also a seventeenth-century version of the story: *Śivalīlârṇava* of Nīlakaṇṭha Dīkshitar 20.24.
92. *Tiruviḷaiyāṭaṟ-purāṇam* 51.30–35.
93. First in the narrative presented in Pĕrumpaṟṟappuliyūr Nampi's *Tiruviḷaiyāṭaṟ-purāṇam* and then in the Sanskrit *Hālâsya;* I have followed the latter here. For details see Wilden 2014: 256–68.
94. My thanks to Velcheru Narayana Rao for discussion of this point.
95. *HM* 57.78–118.
96. See discussion in Shulman 2001: 120–27.
97. *Hālâsya-māhātmya (HM)* 60; *Tiruviḷaiyāṭaṟ-purāṇam* 54.
98. *Tiruvilaiyāṭaṟ-purāṇam* 54.11–12. In *HM,* Agastya says to the god: "When I go south to the Malaya Mountain, the Tamil-speaking people *(drāmiḍā janāḥ)* there will be eager to know Tamil words. Please teach me at once the Tamil *sūtras* so that I can teach them, and also for my own understanding."
99. *Tŏlkāppiyac cūttira virutti* 1.
100. *Vīracoḻiyam, pāyiram* 2.
101. Aṭiyārkkunallār on *Cilappatikāram* 3.12; Nacciṉārkk'iṉiyar on *Maturaikkāñci* 40–42.
102. As Chevillard (2009: 263) says, "It is all very well to attribute a grammatical work to a supernatural character like Agastya, as long as he is not asked to really compose a text."
103. See Zvelebil 1973c: 146–47 and 1992: 243, with reference to Aṭiyārkkunallār on *Cilappatikāram* 11.91; Mu. Irakav'aiyankar 1938: 306–9.

104. Chevillard 2009; Davis 2000; see also Clare 2011: 23–24.
105. See Maloney 1970.

## 2. FIRST BUDDING: TAMIL FROM THE INSIDE

*Pallavi:* Refrain.

1. *Tŏl. Pŏruḷ. Akattiṇai* 11. See "Tamil Landscapes" in this chapter at n. 11.
2. *varaivu nīṭṭittavaḻit talaimakaḷ taṉatu āṟṟāmai toṉṉat toḻikkuk kūṟiyatu.*
3. Eva Wilden's disciplined philological work on the corpus is an exception to the norm of near-total dependence on the colophons.
4. For *uḷḷuṟaiy uvamam,* see *Tŏl. Pŏruḷ. Akattiṇai* 48–50, with the medieval commentators; this form of implicit simile is clearly distinguished by the poetic grammar from other *(eṉai),* explicit, "ordinary" forms (*uvamam* < Skt. *upamā*).
5. I have discussed this problem at length in Shulman 2002a.
6. *Kuṟuntŏkai* 38, commentary (p. 98).
7. See Wilden 2006: 323–24.
8. Ramanujan 1985: 15.
9. For a trenchant example, chosen at random, see *Tirumayilait tirip'antāti* of Irāmaiyyar, verse 7 (an unusually eloquent eighteenth-century work).
10. Pandian 2009: 214 and 2010: 67–68, 74.
11. See *Iṟaiyaṉār akappŏruḷ,* p. 18, citing *Tŏl. Pŏr.* 2.
12. See the charts in Ramanujan 1985: 252 and Zvelebil 1973c: 100.
13. See Rajam 2008, which extends the semantic range of *kaikkiḷai* in important ways.
14. Ramanujan 1970: 106.
15. *IA,* p. 18.
16. For the perhaps unconscious persistence of *akam* scenarios, structured by classic *tiṇai* conventions, in modern Tamil prose, see, for example, chapter 1 of Sundara Ramaswamy's *Tamarind History* (2013).
17. *Tŏl. Pŏruḷ. Puṟattiṇai* 75; *Madras Tamil Lexicon.*
18. *Tŏl. Pŏruḷ. Puṟ.* 77. Again, see Rajam 2008.
19. For one striking example—the poet Māṅkuṭi Marutaṉ, named in *Puṟan.* 72—see discussion in "Clusters of Time" in this chapter. For a list of heroes' names, see *Puṟan.* 158.
20. *Puṟappŏruḷ vĕṇpā mālai* 4.6.
21. Thus the old commentary on *Puṟanāṉūṟu* 350 cited by U. Ve. Caminat'aiyar, and similarly by Auvai. Cu. Turaicamippillai 419. Translators such as Hart and Thangappa provide variations on this optimistic exhortation.
22. Hart and Heifetz 1999: 179.
23. E.g., *Puṟan.* 295.

24. The poem is also discussed in an interesting way by the medieval commentator Iḷampūraṇar (on *Tŏl. Pŏruḷ. Kaḷavu* 11), who remains close to the colophon.
25. As Ramanujan (1985: 262–66) clearly noted.
26. See Chapter 1, "The Grammarian's Blessing and Curse."
27. =Murugan, son of Śiva.
28. *IA* commentary, pp. 6–8.
29. See Zvelebil's discussion (1973a).
30. On this, see Wilden 2002: 17; Gros 1983; 2009: 39.
31. See Nagaswamy, n.d.
32. *ampalam*—more probably, "shrines."
33. Buck and Paramasivam 1997: 247.
34. Ibid.: 248.
35. Better: "Descending from high golden peaks and ridges. . . ."
36. *IA,* section 2, commentary, translated by Buck and Paramasivam (1997: 31–32).
37. Following the lists given by the medieval commentators Perāciriyar and Mayilainātar; see Chapter 1. On *Pattuppāṭṭu* as part of the Sangam corpus, see remarks by Marr (1985: 8).
38. On the internal stratigraphy of the *Tŏlkāppiyam,* see Takahashi 1989: 17–34; Wilden 2006: 133–37.
39. As must also have been the case with the *patikams* of *Patiṟṟuppattu:* see Marr 1971.
40. *Puṟan.* 255, translated by Hart (1979: 195).
41. For example, in the summaries of the acting manuals, *Āṭṭa-prakāram,* which are still handed out at Kūṭiyāṭṭam performances in Kerala to explain what will happen on stage in a given night's performance.
42. *Taṉippāṭaṟ ṟiraṭṭu* 437–39. On the dating of Opp'ilāmaṇippulavar, see Zvelebil 1995: 501–2 (there are two poets of this name); for the literary career of these verses, see *Puṟattiraṭṭu* 1179; *Tamil-nāvalar-caritai,* verses 15–17; and helpful remarks in Wilden 2014: 285–88.
43. Tieken 2001: 119.
44. Ibid.: 116.
45. Takahashi 1989: 42–50.
46. Hardy 1979 and 2016.
47. See the classic study by Paris (1912).
48. See discussion in Shulman 1990: xxxv–xxxix.
49. Nallantuvaṉār's supposed composition of the *nĕytal* section in *Kalittŏkai* is mentioned in a stray *vĕṇpā* verse, probably very late; for the text of the verse, see the introduction to this section in the 1938 SISSWPS edition.

50. Critical work on the *Kalittŏkai* text and surrounding materials, including these attributions, is still lacking.
51. E.g., *Akanāṉūṟu*. 43; *Naṟṟiṇai* 88. See detailed discussion by Gros (1968).
52. Ibid.: xix–xx; also Gros 2009: 78.
53. Marr (1985:138–43) argues that Marutaṉ Iḷanākaṉ could be the son of Māṅkuṭi Marutaṉ, mentioned *by name* in *Puṟan*. 73. If that is the case, then *Puṟan*. 73—and perhaps many other poems linked to Marutaṉ Iḷanākaṉ, including a major chunk of *Kalittŏkai*—would have to be added to the emerging cluster.
54. Wilden 2006: 158–59.
55. Wilden 2002: 21; Takahashi 1989: 51–60.
56. Gros 1968.
57. Tieken 2008: 597.
58. Nagaswamy 1991: 70–81.
59. Tieken has ingeniously argued that the archaic morphemes in Sangam texts reflect not chronological priority but a formalized and somewhat artificial literary language (or languages), as we find in the various Prakrits. But here the Prakrit model breaks down. Literary Tamil (as opposed to spoken Tamil) does not lend itself to genre-specific dialects spread over a wide cultural and social continuum, any more than old Telugu and old Kannada do. Seen in relation to the Tamil works of the seventh and eighth centuries onward, the language of the Sangam corpus looks clearly older; developments in Malayalam, assuming it did indeed break off from Tamil before the middle of the first millennium A.D., support this view.
60. See Chapter 1, "On Beginnings."
61. Nagaswamy 1995: 9–11.
62. Ibid., and 16–18. In private conversation, Dr. Nagaswamy suggested that the Chera images were fashioned after the images of the emperor Tiberius. It is likely that Roman craftsmen, present in south India over generations, cast many of the Karur coins.
63. *Puṟan*. 78, translated by Hart (1979: 156).
64. Neṭuñcĕḻiyaṉ was a big name, no doubt remembered for generations, so, in theory, one could posit a Homeric scenario—a much later poet revisiting this king and his exploits. But a great many of the *puṟam* poems deal with minor, highly local heroes unconnected to the main royal lineages. It is much more difficult to imagine a poet reviving, or inventing, their *gestes* centuries after they lived.
65. As Cox (2002) has said, Tieken's wide-angle reading of the *Paripāṭal* and *Kalittŏkai* collections deserves to be studied seriously in any future work on these texts. On the consolidation of the Greek literary canon by the

great Alexandrian scholars of Hellenistic time, see Finkelberg 2012 and Nünlist 2012; here is a parallel of some relevance to the Tamil case.

66. Champakalakshmi 1996.
67. Sivathamby 1998.
68. Shulman 1992a.
69. See Narayana Rao 1986.
70. Francis 2013b.
71. *Pĕrumpāṇāṟṟuppaṭai* 454; see also line 37, on the legendary Pallava king Tiraiyaṉ.
72. Nilakanta Sastri 1966: 146–72.
73. *Maturaikkāñci* 217–19 in *Pattuppāṭṭu.*
74. For an insightful study of the Velvikuti grant, see Gillet 2014.
75. Krishna Sastri 1923–24: 291–309.
76. Gillet 2014.
77. Ibid.; Veluthat 2010: 19–60.
78. *South Indian Inscriptions* 1929: 441ff.
79. It may not be wholly accidental that this period roughly coincides with the efflorescence of Sanskrit *kāvya* at the Gupta court.
80. As Takahashi (1989: 60) also suggests.
81. Hart 1975: 154–55.
82. See Smith 1991.
83. For recent work on the status and meaning of Homeric formulae, see Finkelberg 2000. See also Kailasapathy 1968.
84. It is again George Hart who originally stressed this point: 1975: 147–52.
85. See, for example, *Puṟan.* 202, discussed in Shulman 1992b: 93–94.
86. See Shulman 2014a and the summary at the end of Chapter 6 in this volume.
87. Takahashi 2010: 5.
88. Ibid.: 5–6.
89. Personal communication, August 2010.
90. The commentary also reads the two dance modes mentioned in the text itself *(iruvakai kūttiṉ ilakkaṇam)* as referring to classical *(mārga)* and local *(deśi)*; and see Aṭiyārkkunallār's comments on this passage in *Cilappatikāram* of Iḷaṅkovaṭikaḷ. On performance of ancient Tamil poetry more generally, see Dubianski 2000: 44–52; Gros 1968: xv–xvi.
91. On *abhinaya* here, see the commentary just cited.
92. See Chapter 3, "Inscribing (1)."
93. Although there are some couplets that appear to have a 3+4 pattern, as was noted already by Beschi, who translated the *Tirukkuṟaḷ* into Latin in the eighteenth century. See Rajam 1992a.
94. *Tirukkuṟaḷ* 24.5; Sundaram 1992: 42.

95. See Cutler 1992.
96. On the erotic section of this work, see Gros 1992.
97. For a summary see Zvelebil 1973c: 169–71; Glazov 1967: 113–76.
98. Often printed with the text itself in modern editions; studied by Gros (1992) and Blackburn (2000).
99. Ibid.
100. See the detailed critical discussion by Gros (1992).
101. See Zvelebil 1973c: 167–69.
102. There is an alternative reading—*ta<u>n</u>* for *ni<u>n</u>* at the end of the first line—which turns the statement into the third person: "Tell me if he is *not* going . . ." (Sundaram 1992: 138). I much prefer the direct second-person formulation of this thought which, like probably all readers of this note, I've heard myself in several variants.
103. A fine essay by M. G. S. Narayanan (1972: 17–22) argues on the basis of inscriptional and archaeological evidence from central Kerala that the *Cilappatikāram* could not predate the eighth century. The evidence, however, is not decisive, and a somewhat earlier date remains possible.
104. The translation is by R. Parthasarathy (1993:81). We are fortunate in having Parthasarathy's very fine translation of this work.
105. Marr (1971) has shown that there is a strong link between the *Vañcikkāṇṭam* and the *patikams* to the *Pati<u>rr</u>uppattu;* this connection does not, however, speak to the question of the coherence of the *Tale* with all its three sections.
106. On *Tĕyyam,* see Freeman 1991.
107. See Shulman 1980.
108. Studied by Obeyesekere (1984).
109. On this question, see Ziffren 1984.
110. Parthasarathy 1993: 168.
111. Though this epithet also serves to qualify royal personages and prestigious sages as well.
112. *Cilappatikāram* 30.160—however, this reading is not secure; in place of *kāyavāku* we also find *kāval(venta<u>n</u>).*
113. Zvelebil 1973c: 176. See also discussion by Tieken (2003 and 2008).
114. See Monius 2001:13–115; Richman 1988; Shulman 2001: 213–51.
115. Parthasarathy 1993: 277.
116. Pollock 2006.
117. Francis 2013b: 398.
118. Ibid.: 396.

## 3. SECOND BUDDING: THE MUSICAL SELF

*Anupallavi:* Secondary refrain.

1. These terms are close to, though not isomorphic with, Sanskrit *prāṇa.*
2. As Friedhelm Hardy (1983) showed. See the beautiful translation of the *Tiruviruttam* and the detailed essay by Venkatesan (2014b).
3. *Madras Tamil Lexicon.*
4. Venkatesan 2014b: 27.
5. See ibid.: 142–56, for the interpretative modes in which the Śrīvaishṇava commentators gloss such poetic instants.
6. The commentators read the relevant phrase differently, referring *matana(m),* "desire," to the god, who is the father of the Love God: see Venkatesan's translation, 2014b: 28.
7. See Handelman and Shulman 1998.
8. Vishṇu.
9. See Venkatesan 2014b: 134–35.
10. See discussion of Kamban's Tamil *Rāmāyaṇa* by Ramanujan (2004).
11. See Chapter 1, "The Grammarian's Blessing and Curse"; *Tirukkuṟaḷ* of Tiruvaḷḷuvar 1.1.
12. See Ceṉāvaraiyar on *Tŏl. Cŏl.* 13; discussion by Chevillard 2008a: 444–45.
13. See Kamban's *Irāmâvatāram* 3.8.51 *(cetaṉai maṉṉ uyir).* In *Vīracoḻiyam* 5.1, *uyir* is the carrier of meaning, *pŏruḷ,* while the body is the site of words, *urai* (in the context of literary figuration).
14. Thus the Mantakappattu inscription: see Francis 2013b: 272 and sources cited there.
15. Dirks 1976.
16. See Dhavamony 1971: 101–2.
17. *Bhāgavata-purāṇa* 11.5.39–41. Cf. *Padma-purāṇa, Uttara.* 189.51: *Bhakti* tells us she arose *(utpannā)* in the Tamil country *(drāviḍe)* and, interestingly, grew up *(vṛddhiṃ gatā)* in Karnataka.
18. On Dehalīśa, see Hardy: 1979 and 2016. See *Divya-sūri-carita* 2.19.
19. Nīlakaṇṭha-Śiva swallowed the black Hālāhala poison that emerged during the churning of the Ocean of Milk and held it in his throat.
20. Venkatesan 2016.
21. *Nācciyār Tirumŏḻi* 13.8, translated by Archana Venkatesan (2016).
22. *Tiruvācakam, tiruccatakam* 22.
23. See Yocum 1982; Harris 2008; and "Inscribing (2)" in this chapter.
24. Among other things, these "heretics" are accused of not knowing good Tamil: see Harris 2008: 132.

25. See Shulman 2001: 120–27; Chapter 5, "Tamil as Goddess"; and Chapter 6, "Tantric Tamil."
26. Kāḻi is Cirkali, in the eastern Kaveri delta.
27. Tiruñāṉacampantar *Tevāram* 2.93.11.
28. See Ramanujan 1970.
29. See Chapter 4, "The Inner Borders." Umāpati Civâcāriyar (early fourteenth century) claims in his *Tiruttŏṇṭarpurāṇa varalāṟu* 20–21 (prefaced to *Pĕriya Purāṇam*) that Cekkiḻār composed his *Pĕriya Purāṇam* in order to displace the "false" Jain *Cintāmaṇi*.
30. See Srinivasan 2014.
31. Meenakshisundaram 1966; Filliozat 1972: vii. And see Chapter 4, "Horizons."
32. See Hardy 1979: 36.
33. See Chapter 5.
34. *Līlā-tilakam, śilpa* 1, commentary. See Chapter 5, "Maṇi-pravāḷam, Rubies and Coral."
35. Halbertal 1997: 29. See citation and illuminating discussion of these markers of canonicity by Finkelberg (2012).
36. See Leonhardt 2013: 124–31.
37. Interestingly, the *Tiruviruttam,* with its complex *akam* poetics, is equated by the early tradition with the Rig Veda: *Divya-sūri-carita* 4.73.
38. See Chapter 5, "Maṇi-pravāḷam, Rubies and Coral," on *Līlā-tilakam:* Telugu and Kannada are excluded from the Draviḍa group because they are too remote from the language of the "Tamil Veda" (commentary on *śilpa* 1).
39. Riddle: *cĕttatiṉ vayiṟṟil ciṟiyatu piṟantāl/ĕttait tiṉṟu ĕṅke kiṭakkum//* Answer: *attait tiṉṟu aṅke kiṭakkum//.*
40. *Divya-sūri-carita* 4.68: *vedârtha-garbhā vihitā bhāṣâbhūd drāmiḍī stutiḥ.*
41. Younger 1982; Cutler 1987: 44–45; Venkatesan 2013. A tradition noted by the *Koyil ŏḻuku* temple record ascribes the foundation of the *Adhyayanotsava* to the poet Tirumaṅkaiyāḻvār. See Younger 1982.
42. *Koyil ŏḻuku,* cited in Younger 1982; Venkatesan 2014a.
43. See Chapter 1, "What Is Tamil?"
44. Venkatesan 2014a.
45. *Divya-sūri-carita* 16.22.
46. Hardy 1979: 42.
47. E.g., Tiruvaimozhi (5–5) by Sri Srirama Bharati—STD Pathasala.
48. Since the *Tiruppāvai* of Āṇṭāḷ is also enacted by the Araiyar at Srivilliputtur.
49. What follows is based primarily on Venkatesan 2005, 2013, and 2014a; see also Colas 2002.

50. The performed text is thus, at particular points, close to the "received" text—that is, the known and recited selection of beloved verses—as opposed to the "recorded" (linear, consecutive, complete) text, as defined by Velcheru Narayana Rao (1978).
51. See Narayana Rao 1978.
52. Venkatesan 2013: 15 (my emphasis).
53. My thanks to Don Handelman for discussion of this point.
54. Venkatesan 2005: 24.
55. See Chapter 5, "Maṇi-pravāḷam, Rubies and Coral."
56. See Chapter 2, "Pandyas, Pallavas, and the Carriers of Tamil Knowledge."
57. My thanks again to Archana Venkatesan for discussing this point.
58. See Cutler 1987.
59. Venkatesan 2013.
60. See Shulman 1990 for translation of these decades.
61. If we want to historicize this account, we will probably identify this king with Rājarāja I (985–ca. 1016).
62. *Tirumuṟaikaṇṭa purāṇam* of Umāpati civâcāriyar, often appended to editions of Cekkiḻār's *Pĕriya Purāṇam.*
63. See discussion in Cutler 1987: 49–50.
64. See the fine survey by Venkatacami (1959).
65. See Venkatesan 2013.
66. De Bary 1958: 70.
67. *Pĕriya Purāṇam* 28.2709–55. The episode is noteworthy also because Cekkiḻār, the author of the hagiographical account just cited, offers a long poetic exegesis of the *Tiruppācuram* in the course of telling his story (2720–43). Moreover, both the text of the *Tiruppācuram* itself (v. 11) and that of a decade supposedly composed immediately after it on the lord of Tiruveṭakam (3.32.11), where Campantar's palm leaf was fished out of the river by the Pandya queen, seem to refer to the story—specifically to the leaf floating upstream—and thus perhaps fit the textual model discussed in Chapter 2, "What to Do with the Colophons," with reference to the Sangam colophons.
68. See Chapter 2, "Toward an Integrated Cultural World."
69. *Vinota-raca-mañcari* 165–67.
70. *Cīvaka-cintāmaṇi* 1879. On this text, see Chapter 4, "The Inner Borders." For another palm-leaf message sent by a heartbroken lover, see *Cilappatikāram* 13.77–93.
71. Ibid. 668–70.
72. Ibid. 683.
73. See *Aitareya Āraṇyaka* 5.3.3.

74. Chapter 2, "Back to Stolen Love."
75. Today this spot in the Cidambaram temple is known as the *pancākkarappaṭi*, the step of the five-syllable mantra *namaḥ śivāya*.
76. *Tiruvātavūr-aṭikaḷ purāṇam* 7.511–15, 517–39.
77. More or less the same process continued to be enacted right through the mid-nineteenth century and is attested in historical sources about the major poet Tiricirapuram Minatcicuntaram Pillai (see Chapter 7, "Recovery and the Gap"). A "real" poet composes silently in his mind and then dictates the work to an amanuensis.
78. *Paṭṭiṉatt'aṭikaḷ tiruppāṭaṟ ṟiraṭṭu* 1–22; *Tiruviṭaimarutūr tirukkoyil tiruttala-varalāṟu* 41–43; Zvelebil 1973b: 92.
79. *Āmukta-mālyada* of Krishṇa-deva-rāya 2.75–78.
80. A particularly charming case, well worth an essay in its own right, is the story of the late-seventeenth-century *Kuḻaikkātar pā-mālai* of Nārāyaṇa Dīkshitar, once a very popular text; see the introduction to the edition; see also Caminat'aiyar 1968: 130–38.
81. Francis 2013b. See also Chapter 2, "Pandyas, Pallavas, and the Carriers of Tamil Knowledge."
82. The poet-king Mahendravarman I is said to have spent part of his youth at the Vishṇukundin court.
83. See Rabe 2001: 145–42.
84. See further in Chapters 5 and 6.
85. See Ollett 2015 and discussion in Chapter 4, "The Inner Borders."
86. See Chapter 5. The commentators do note that north Indian shrines did not have the privilege of being celebrated by the Āḻvārs. Aḻakiyamaṇavāḷappĕrumāḷ Nāyaṉār says that "northern Venkaṭam" (Tirupati, today just over the Andhra border), because of its northern situation, is inhabited by people who cannot understand the Veda without *itihāsa-purāṇa* commentary, whereas every speaker of Tamil can easily understand the poems of Tiruppāṇāḻvār. Venkatachari 1978: 29.
87. See discussion in ibid.: 28–29.
88. The authorship of the second of these works is still in dispute.
89. Rabe 2001; see also the balanced evaluation by Bronner (2010: 92–99).
90. *Avanti-sundarī-kathā* 13–15; see Rabe 2001: 46–47; Tieken 2013.
91. See Minakshi [1938] 1977: 224–32.
92. Stein 1980: 68–69.
93. Minakshi [1938] 1977: 233–36.
94. Stein 1980: 70–71.
95. Ibid.: 71.
96. Francis 2013b: 382–84; Minakshi 1941.

97. Beautifully analyzed by Francis 2013b: 386–90 and Francis 2016.
98. *Nantikkalampakam* v. 7 (3 in other numberings of the verses).
99. Francis 2013b: 389.
100. The fourth stanza of the *Uttiyoga paruvam* refers to the royal victor at Tĕḷḷāṟu, a battle regularly mentioned in the inscriptions of Nandin III; but see Francis 2013b: 387–90.
101. Also striking is the powerful portrait of Narasiṃhavarman I on the Dharmarāja Ratha. See Lockwood 1993.
102. See Kaimal 1988 for the definitive study of early portraiture.
103. Nagaswamy, n.d., no. 30; see Chapter 2, "Back to Stolen Love."
104. *Tiruvāymŏḻi* 1.5.11.
105. *pāl ey tamiḻar icaikārar pattar.*
106. See the detailed discussion by Venkatachari 1978: 89–90.
107. Marr 1972; Premalatha 1986.

## 4. THE IMPERIAL MOMENT, TRUTH, AND SOUND

*Caraṇam* 1: First verse.

1. For an overview, see Karashima and Subbarayalu 2009; also Balambal 1998: 120, 206. On the thirteenth-century Burma inscription, see Salomon 1998: 155.
2. Spencer 1983: 101–37.
3. See Lo Hsiang-Lin 1966; Wolters 1974.
4. There were subsequent Chola missions to China in 1020 and 1033—indications that southern China had become a known entity in Chola-period cultural-political maps of the sea routes to the east.
5. See Subbarayalu 2002; Balambal 1998: 125.
6. Lee 2009 and 2012 (chapter 5).
7. Wolters 1970; Spencer 1983: 147.
8. Text and translation in Kulke, Kesavapany, and Sakhuja 2009: 272–73; see discussion in Seshadri 2009 and Balambal 1998: 121–22.
9. Balambal 1998: 123; Seshadri 2009.
10. Kulke 2009; and see the brilliant essay by V. Narayanan (2013).
11. A cache of outstanding, locally stylized bronzes was uncovered in one of these shrines; they can be seen today in the Colombo Museum. Several other Chola temples were built at various sites on the island during the period of Chola incursions.
12. See Spencer 1983: 46–65.
13. See Heitzman 1987 and 1997; Karashima 1984; also Hall 1981.
14. As Talbot (2001) has shown for the Kakatiyas.
15. See Heitzman 1987.

16. Ibid.
17. *Travancore Archaeological Series (TAS)* 3, no. 34: 87–158.
18. See Chapter 2, "Pandyas, Pallavas, and the Carriers of Tamil Knowledge."
19. For an illuminating study of this work, see Cox, in press.
20. On *ulā* see the comprehensive study by Wentworth (2011a); also Ali 2004.
21. On *Tŏl. Pŏruḷ. Puṟ.* 82; Wentworth 2011a: 153–54; on the *pāṭṭ'iyal,* see "The New Cultural Ecology" in this chapter.
22. There are occasional exceptions to this generalization: see Shulman 1985: 312–24.
23. In the *Irācarācacoḻaṉ ulā,* Rājarāja II (ca. 1146–1173) is also identified with Lord Vishṇu: see Wentworth 2011a: 200. Kulottuṅga II (1133–1150) receives lavish praise in his *ulā* for having renovated the Cidambaram shrine.
24. *Irācarācacoḻaṉ ulā* 46.
25. See Ali 2004.
26. The *periḷampĕṇ.*
27. *Vikkiramacoḻaṉ ulā* 311–17, 21–26, in Wentworth 2011a: 213–14.
28. Wentworth 2011a: 213.
29. *Vikkiramacoḻaṉ ulā* 14 in *Mūvar ulā* of Ŏṭṭakkūttar; see *Kaliṅkattupparaṇi* 195; *Kulottuṅkacoḻaṉ ulā* 20 in *Mūvar ulā* of Ŏṭṭakkūttar. The memory of this mythic king survives into early modern times: see *Maturai cŏkkanātar tamiḻ viṭu tūtu* 79. Pŏykai was, it is said, the court-poet of a Cera king conquered in battle by Koccĕṅkaṭcoḻaṉ; by composing this work, the poet succeeded in having his patron released from his chains. See also commentary on *Vīracoḻiyam* 178.
30. With thanks to Whitney Cox for this suggestion.
31. The Tamil has a pun: flowers, *malar,* and the name of the poet's village, Malari. The verse is quoted as an illustration of the figure of "difference / excelling," *veṟṟumaiccamam. Taṇṭiyalaṅkāram* 112. See also Wentworth 2011a:144–45.
32. *Vinota-raca-mañcari* 147–48; and see Chapter 5, "Classicism."
33. *Vinota-raca-mañcari* 220–41.
34. Rajamani and Shulman 2011; *Tiyākarājaccarukkam* and *Tiruviḻāccarukkam* in *Tiruvārūrppurāṇam* of Campantamuṉivar.
35. Kulke 1970: 155–213. On Kulottuṅga, see now Cox (in press).
36. In later times, this quintessential form of political pragmatics—the hierarchical ranking of the devotees, with the king at the apex—is called "honor," *mariyātai.* See Kulke 1993: 51–81, on Orissan kingship.
37. Spencer 1969.

38. Heitzman 1997: 121–42. Heitzman, like all modern historians of Chola-period Tamil Nadu, relies heavily on the pioneering work of Y. Subbarayalu (1973) on the political geography of the Kaveri delta.
39. See *South Indian Inscriptions (SII)* 1913: 2.3.66.
40. See Sriraman 2011.
41. Chola paintings that antedate the Tanjavur masterpieces, possibly from the early tenth century, were discovered in 2014 at the temple of Tiruvorriyur, in the northern part of the city of Chennai.
42. *Takka-yākap-paraṇi* 246.
43. See, for example, Nilakanta Sastri 1975.
44. See Spencer 1983.
45. And probably in modern south Indian politics as well: see Shulman 1985.
46. Francis 2013a and 2013b; also Francis 2016.
47. See the careful summary and analysis by Orr (2009); also see Subbarayalu (2009).
48. See Veluppillai 1971.
49. Venkayya, Introduction to *SII* 2, Part I (1913): 15–16.
50. On later Tamil prose, see Chapter 6, "Prose, History, Realism."
51. See Narayana Rao, Shulman, and Subrahmanyam 1992.
52. See "Display" in this chapter.
53. See note 41 above.
54. In *Tŏl. Pŏruḷ. Cĕy.* 75, *vāymŏḻi* is listed as a genre.
55. Referring to Rāma.
56. *Irāmâvatāram* of Kamban 2.334–38. Verse 338 reads in Tamil:

    *mŏym māṇ viṉai ver aṟa vĕṉṟ' uyarvāṉ mŏḻiyā muṉṉam*
    *vimmāv aḻuvāḷ aracaṉ mĕyyiṟ ṟirivāṉ ĕṉṉiṉ*
    *immāv ulakatt' uyiroṭ' iṉi vāḻv' ukaveṉ ĕṉ cŏl*
    *pŏym māṇāmaṟk' iṉṟe pŏṉṟāt' ŏḻiyeṉ ĕṉṟāḷ*

57. In this sense, the south Indian notion of true speech differs from the Mīmāṃsā view of statements as self-authorizing and thus true unless disproved.
58. *Irāmâvatāram* 2.347–50.
59. See Chapter 2, "Pandyas, Pallavas, and the Carriers of Tamil Knowledge." On Tamil notions of truth and falsehood, see the fine essay by Ra. Irakav'aiyankar (1987: 76–84).
60. *cĕllun cŏl vallāṉ*.
61. *tĕṉ cŏl*=Tamil.
62. *Irāmâvatāram* 2.431–33.

63. *kŏllāta viratattār taṅ kaṭavuḷar kūṭṭam ŏttār.* The story appears in *Vinota-raca-mañcari* 147–220; see also Shulman 2001: 113–20.
64. On metrics, a Jain speciality, see discussion in "The New Cultural Ecology" in this chapter; in lexicography, we have Maṇṭalapuruṭar's *Cūṭāmaṇi,* from post-Chola times; in grammar, the important and idiosyncratic *Nemināthum.* For the *Vĕṇpā pāṭṭ'iyal,* see "The New Cultural Ecology."
65. That the Jains continued to value this work can be seen in the extant sixteenth-century commentary by a Jain scholar, Camaṇa Tivākara Vāmaṉa Muṉivar.
66. The name presumably means "Lively."
67. On Chola urbanization, see Hall 1980; Champakalakshmi 1996.
68. On *kathā,* see Narayana Rao 1978 and 1986; van Buitenen 1959: 1–9.
69. See verse 3143 with Nacciṉārkk'iṉiyar's commentary and the note by the editor, U. Ve. Caminat'aiyar.
70. Following Naccinārkk'iṉiyar here.
71. Recall that Kāntaruvatattai and her parents are Vidyādharas, inhabiting a world of continual delight and, in particular, plenty of fine music.
72. See Chapter 7, "Recovery and the Gap."
73. A Jain work of unknown date. See Mu. Irakav'aiyankar [1938] 1984: 446–50.
74. See Caminat'aiyar's introduction to his edition of *Cīvaka-cintāmaṇi* (1969): 16–19.
75. Monius 2001: 120; Zvelebil 1995: 587, citing various other possible datings.
76. Monius 2001: 118. Thus, for example, the definition of words as case-inflected and the typology of compounds follows Pāṇiniyan categories; rules of phonetic classification and combination are similarly adapted to the Sanskrit model.
77. *Vīracoḻiyam* 141, 198.
78. Monius 2001: 119; see Monius 2000 for a penetrating discussion of the relations between the Sanskrit and Tamil texts.
79. *Vīracoḻiyam* 180; see Chapter 5, "Maṇi-pravāḷam, Rubies and Coral."
80. See Chapter 1, "Agastya and the Origin of Tamil Speech."
81. Ollett 2015.
82. Ibid., chapter 4.
83. Chevillard 2008a: 17.
84. See discussion in Wilden 2009.
85. See Chapter 3, "Inscribing (1)."
86. Tubb 1998: 54; see also Clare 2011: 30.
87. *Āndhra Mahābhāratamu* of Nannayya 1.1.23; see also Chapter 1, "Agastya and the Origin of Tamil Speech."

88. Somanātha's *Vrishâdhipa śatakamu* in praise of the Śaiva Kannada poet Basavanna, ostensibly in Telugu, includes verses in all the languages just mentioned.
89. Pollock 2006.
90. Ibid.: 383–86.
91. Monius 2001: 133.
92. Ibid.: 136. See also the summary to Chapter 2 in this volume.
93. See Clare 2011: 34.
94. See ibid.: 29–30.
95. See Chapter 2, "In-ness."
96. See Narayana Rao and Shulman 1998.
97. Clare 2011: 52–53.
98. On *svabhāvokti* in the Sanskrit tradition, see Raghavan 1973: 102–30; and see Shulman 2011 on this figure in relation to *bhāvika,* the "imaginative" figure, in Sanskrit and Tamil. A systematic treatment of Chola-period poetics, including the new uses of figuration and suggestion, is being prepared by Jennifer Clare, Anne Monius, Jean-Luc Chevillard, and myself in the context of a far-reaching comparative study of Daṇḍin's poetics led by Yigal Bronner.
99. Clare 2011: 59–83.
100. See Shulman 2007 for examples.
101. See Shulman 2010; also Chapter 1, "The Grammarian's Blessing and Curse."
102. See detailed discussion by Clare (2011: 72–80).
103. *Paṉṉiru pāṭṭ'iyal* 19.
104. Ibid. 22.
105. See Niklas's introduction to *Yāpp'arunkala-kārikai* of Amitacākarar (1993: vii).
106. Monius 2001: 135. All such epithets could be analyzed as exocentric compounds (*bahu-vrīhi, aṉmŏḻittŏkai*).
107. *Vīracoḻiyam* 7.7.

## 5. REPUBLIC OF SYLLABLES

*Caraṇam* 2: Second verse.

1. *Vinota-raca-mañcari* 300.
2. For the text of the poem and commentary, see *Taṉippāṭaṟ ṟiraṭṭu* 19.
3. Bronner 2010.
4. On *bhāvanā,* see Shulman 2012.
5. *Taṉippāṭaṟ ṟiraṭṭu* 24.
6. Pagis 1986 and 1996: 100–102.
7. See Salomon 1996.

8. For the expanded story, see *Vinota-raca-mañcari* 293–325.
9. See Chapter 4, "Horizons."
10. See Ludden 1985: 50–52.
11. See Narayana Rao, Shulman, and Subrahmanyam 1992.
12. See Karashima 1984: 16–17; Ludden 1985: 49–50.
13. See Pollock 2006: 186. Note that hyperglossia as an analytical concept corresponds nicely to a Sanskrit term from *Nāṭya-śāstra: ati-bhāshā,* the language spoken by gods.
14. As in the comparable Kannada case: see Pollock 2006: 432; see also "Classicism: Perāciriyar and the New Poetics" in this chapter.
15. *Tiruvāṉaikkā ulā* 213.
16. Clare 2011: 12–31.
17. *Tŏl. Pŏruḷ. Mar.* 94.
18. Commentary on *Tŏl. Pŏruḷ. Mar.* 90.
19. Ibid., translated by Clare 2011: 18; see also Perāciriyar on *Tŏl. Pŏruḷ. Mar.* 105.
20. Comment on *Tŏl.Pŏruḷ. Cĕy.* 80, end.
21. Ibid.
22. Clare 2011: 28: "Whether in the field of metrics, literary genres or the reinterpretation of Caṅkam conventions, the Virutti commentary represents the heteroglossia which threatens the cohesiveness of the Tamil tradition." See also Chapter 4, "The New Cultural Ecology."
23. *Mahābhāshya* of Patañjali 3.173–74; see Cardona 1988: 639–43.
24. *Tŏl. Pŏruḷ. Mar.* 92. *Uyarntor* is taken from the definition of *vaḻakku* by *Tŏlkāppiyam* in this *sūtra.*
25. Clare 2011: 21.
26. *Tŏl. Pŏruḷ. Mar.* 93.
27. See Chapter 3, "Breath and Life" and "Inscribing (2)."
28. See the pointed remarks by Wilden (2014: 221–22 and 236).
29. My thanks to Archana Venakatesan for this reference.
30. Wilden 2014: 241.
31. For an impressive example, see Vergiani 2013.
32. Chevillard 2008a: 17; see Chapter 4, "The Inner Borders."
33. Vergiani 2013: 191.
34. Ibid.
35. See Chapter 3, "North and South."
36. See Monius 2000.
37. See Chapter 6, "The Tenkasi Breakthrough."
38. On *vĕṇpā* see Chapter 2, "Toward an Integrated Cultural World," and Rajam 1992a. On Pukaḻenti's *Naḷavĕṇpā,* see Shulman 2011a.

39. *Naiṣadhīya-carita* 3.10.
40. See Shulman 2007.
41. Technically, an *utprekṣā/taṟkuṟipp'eṟṟavaṇi,* "flight of fancy," transferring features from one existential domain to another.
42. *Vinota-raca-mañcari* 1876: 265–66.
43. Ibid.: 266–68. See further comment in Shulman 2011a.
44. See Chapter 6 summary.
45. *Bhagavad-viṣayam* 9:63 (on 9.2.8): Pĕriyavāccāṉ Piḷḷai; see also the *Īṭu,* and discussion by Venkatachari 1978: 43–44.
46. See Narayana Rao and Shulman 1998: 45.
47. My thanks to Whitney Cox for supplying me with scanned texts of these passages on short notice.
48. *Tamiḻ-nāvalar-caritai* 10–11.
49. The language of this *sūtra* is very close to *Tirukkuṟaḷ* 6.8.
50. See Chapter 1, "The Grammarian's Blessing and Curse," and Chapter 2, "Back to Stolen Love."
51. More modern versions say that the potter claimed that only Sanskrit syllables could kill someone or bring that person back to life.
52. See a laconic reading of the verses in question in Mutaliyar and Mutaliyar 1981: 916–17.
53. *Kāppu* 14 in the edition of Kopalakirusnamācāriyar; see Raman 2007: 7, 182.
54. Jagadeesan 1977: 194–206.
55. See Hardy 2016: 305–20.
56. Ibid.: 317.
57. Srinivas 1952.
58. On the inadequacy of the terms "Sanskritization" and "hybridization," see Ollett 2015: 59–66.
59. *Vīracoḻiyam* 180, 283. See discussion by Monius (2001:119); also see Venkatachari 1978: 4.
60. Raman 2007: 63; Monius 2001: 211.
61. Venkatachari 1978 and Nanacuntaram 1989.
62. Venkatachari 1978: 168.
63. With reference to Sangam literature, this criterion is ambiguous: see Gros 1968: 17 and Gros 1983; also Chapter 1, "On Beginnings."
64. Shulman 1996; Narayana Rao and Shulman 2012.
65. See McCann 2015.
66. See Raman 2007: 64–68; Venkatachari 1978: 159.
67. Raman 2007: 64, citing Jagadeesan 1989.
68. Discussed by Venkatachari (1978: 158–59).

69. Tamil alveolar *ṟ* is transcribed by the Telugu *śakaṭa-repha*, which, like its Tamil equivalent, is keyed to a sound that ceased to be phonemic.
70. On the date, see Freeman 1998: 42; Gopala Pillai 1985. I am a little skeptical about the commonly accepted dating to the fourteenth century; much about the *LT* suggests the cultural milieu of the late fifteenth or early sixteenth century.
71. See Chapter 1, "What Is Tamil?"
72. The *Tŏlkāppiyam* was composed, at least in part, in Kerala; we can easily list many major Tamil works from this region.
73. On the emergence of a self-conscious Malayalam identity, see the dissertation by Ellen Alexis Ambrosone at the University of Chicago (2016).
74. On this term, see Chapter 1, "What Is Tamil?" See also *LT*, commentary on *śilpa* 1.1 (p. 112).
75. See Freeman's excellent essays: 1998 and 2013.
76. Lucidly discussed by Freeman in ibid.
77. *LT*, commentary on the first *śilpa* (1.1, p. 111).
78. *LT* 2.7, exemplary verse 25.
79. Ibid., verses 28 and 26, respectively. Verse 29, replete with such forms, in the Sanskrit perfect, is discussed by Freeman (2013: 213).
80. See, e.g., the unpublished *Āṭṭa-prakāram* to *Subhadrā-dhanañjayam* Act 1.
81. See examples and discussion in Freeman 2013: 214.
82. *LT* 1.1, 112–13. My thanks to Sivan Goren for discussing this passage, and to Venugopala Panikkar.
83. This point is elaborated by Freeman (1998).
84. See Ollett 2015.
85. See the formulation of the argument by Freeman (2013: 210).
86. *LT* 116: *na bhāṣāyāṃ bhāṣântarā samāviśati vyavasthā-vilaya-prasaṅgāt.*
87. See Freeman 2013.
88. Freeman 1998: 59.
89. *LT* 116.
90. Freeman 2013: 209.
91. There is good reason to think that the *LT* was composed in Travancore, although the surviving manuscripts all come from farther north.
92. See Chapter 4, "The New Cultural Ecology."
93. Leonhardt 2013: 122–63; see also Pollock 2006: 443–49.
94. This surmise was put forward by Venugopala Panicker (oral communication).
95. My thanks to my student Maayan Nidbach for having spotted a copy of this rare work buried in the midst of hundreds of other works in a bookshop in Palakkadu.

96. *Naiṭatam* of Ativīrarāma Pāṇṭiyaṉ, *cuyamvarappaṭalam* 7.
97. See Chapter 6, "Tantric Tamil"; and compare Chapter 1, "The Grammarian's Blessing and Curse."
98. See Chapter 3, "Inscribing (2)."
99. Richman 1997.
100. Richman 1997: 9–14.
101. See Handelman 2014.
102. On the child poet Tiruñāṉacampantar's contest with his Jain opponents, during which a Tamil poem *(patikam)* he had inscribed on a palm leaf floated upstream in the Vaikai river, see Chapter 3, "Inscribing (2)."
103. In the Madurai temple.
104. Sarasvatī, goddess of poetry and music, and Lakshmī or Śrī.
105. See Chapter 3, "Inscribing (2)."
106. The poem addresses a bee:

> You who spend your life in flight,
> seeking a hidden sweetness:
> don't tell me what I want to hear,
> tell me what you really see.
> I love a woman, love everything
> about her—the way she walks,
> just like a peacock; her teeth,
> her long dark hair, more fragrant,
> I think, than any flower—but only you can say.

For the story that provides a context to this poem, see Shulman 2001: 121.

107. See Chapter 2, "In-ness."
108. See Egnore 1978.
109. I thank Charles Hallisey for insightful comments on this verse.
110. See *Maturaiccŏkkanātar ulā* of Purāṇa Tirumalainātar, verses 5, 7, 36. Verse 36 tells us that the god is accompanied in his procession by the *Tiruvācakam*, the *Tiruvicaippā*, the sweet songs of Sangam Tamil, and verses from the *Tirumantiram* of Tirumūlar. Note the continuing, necessary presence in this early-sixteenth-century work of the Sangam corpus alongside canonical devotional works and the esoteric masterpiece of Tirumūlar.

## 6. A TAMIL MODERNITY

*Caraṇam* 3: Third verse.

1. See Narayana Rao 2007: 159–67. On multiple modernities, see the programmatic essay by S. N. Eisenstadt (2000).

2. See *Pāṇḍya-kulodaya* of Maṇḍala-kavi; Orr 2014.
3. Orr 2014 and 2015; Seastrand 2013; cf. Sethuraman 1994.
4. See Chapter 5, "Tamil as Goddess."
5. See Shulman 2012: 155–204.
6. See Mu. Irakav'aiyankar 1907–1908; the text was published in installments in *Cĕntamiḻ* over the years 1923–1925. My thanks to Ofer Peres for bringing to light this remarkable work.
7. Shulman 2012.
8. Thus, says the modern commentator, blue sapphire for the woman's eyes, pearls for her teeth, coral for her lips, and so on.
9. *Naiṭatam* of Ativīrarāma Pāṇṭiyaṉ, *Aṉṉattaittūtu viṭṭa paṭalam* 111.
10. See discussion in Shulman 2012: 181–82, with reference to the *Naiṭatam*.
11. Borges 1962: 45–55.
12. See Chapter 5, "Classicism."
13. *Naiṭatam, Iḷaveṉiṟ paṭalam* 10.
14. See Malayil, in press; Shulman 2016.
15. See Raj 2010.
16. See *Vacu-carittiram* of Tŏṇṭaimāṉtuṟai Ampalatt'āṭum Ayyaṉ, introduction by the editor, T. Chandrasekharan.
17. See Chapter 7, "New Ambrosia in Old Vessels."
18. See Chevillard 2008b.
19. See Chapter 4, "Temples and Tamil Prose."
20. See Chapter 2, "Back to Stolen Love."
21. See Zvelebil 1973c: 271; Venkatacami 1962: 122–32, and sources cited there.
22. See Rajamani and Shulman 2011, with notes on the semicolloquial style of these captions.
23. Zvelebil 1973c: 264–76.
24. Ebeling 2010: 196.
25. Narayana Rao, Shulman, and Subrahmanyam 2001: 93–139.
26. See Chapter 7, "Tillāṉā"; Narayana Rao 2004; Ebeling 2010: 158–64.
27. See *Koyil-ŏḻuku*, introductions by Parthasarathy (1954) and Hari Rao (1961); see also Jagadeesan 1977: 29–30; Spencer 1978. My thanks to Vasudha Narayanan for making the Tamil text and secondary literature available to me.
28. Narayana Rao, Shulman, and Subrahmanyam 2001: 243–48; and see Motzkin 1992 on eighteenth-century French historiography.
29. See Ebeling 2010: 197.
30. See Zvelebil 1973c: 273–75; on Ananda Ranga Pillai, see Shulman 2004.
31. Tieken 2015.

32. Shulman 2012.
33. My thanks to Margalit Finkelberg for articulating this idea.
34. See, e.g., Narayana Rao, Shulman, and Subrahmanyan 2001: 292–303, on the *Cĕytakāti-nŏṇṭi-nāṭakam* featuring the famous Muslim merchant Cītakkāti (late-seventeenth- and early-eighteenth centuries), discussed later in this section.
35. See, e.g., the ongoing studies by Bronner (e.g., 2015) on the intellectual milieu of Appaya Dikshitar (sixteenth century).
36. *Cīkāḷatti -purāṇam* of Karuṇaippirakāca cuvāmikaḷ, Civappirakāca cuvāmikaḷ, and Velaiya cuvāmikaḷ, verse 1.14, which is attributed to Karuṇaippirakācar. See also the next verse on the Sangam poets and the Sangam "plank" and the chapter on Nakkīrar, discussed in Wilden 2014: 271–74.
37. See Chapter 2, "Back to Stolen Love."
38. See *Madras Tamil Lexicon,* also *uṟaḻcci,* "rivalry, competition"; *uṟaḻvu,* "enmity, resemblance, likeness."
39. On *ślesha,* see the definitive study by Bronner (2010).
40. See Ebeling 2010: 141–42.
41. See editor's introduction to *Camuttira-vilācam* of Kaṭikaimuttuppulavar, p. 8.
42. On *maṭakku,* see the insightful remarks by Bate (2009: 130–32).
43. See Dubianski 2005, and "Tantric Tamil" in this chapter.
44. See later in this section, on the Jaffna poet Ciṉṉattampi.
45. On Cītakkāti, see Narayana Rao, Shulman, and Subrahmanyam 1992: 264–303.
46. See Shulman 1984:174–75 and sources cited there.
47. See V. Narayanan 2003; Tschacher 2001; Bayly 1989; Schomberg 2003; Shulman 1984 and 2002b.
48. Tschacher 2001.
49. Ricci 2011: 13–20.
50. Shulman 2002b: 87.
51. Ibid.; Tschacher 2009; McGilvray 1998 and 2004.
52. Ibid.
53. Home to the pilgrimage site of the Sufi saint Shahul Hamid or Mīrān Sāhib, known in Tamil as Nākūr Āṇṭavar, claimed as a descendent of 'Abd al-Qādir al-Gīlāni, the founder of the Qādiri Sufi order; a purāṇic biography of the latter exists in poetic Tamil as the *Kutpu nāyakam* or *Mukiyittīṉ purāṇam* of Cĕyku Aptul kātir Nayiṉār Lĕppai. Shahul Hamid is connected to the Tanjavur Nāyaka king Acyutappa Nāyaka (1529–1542),

who is said to have been cured by the saint of an illness caused by black magic (a pigeon pierced by mantric needles; the saint found the pigeon in the palace and removed the needles).

54. See Kokan 1974.
55. Narayana Rao, Shulman, and Subrahmanyam 1992: 274–92.
56. Kalvaḷai is known now as Sandilipay, associated with tragic events during the Sri Lankan civil war.
57. See Dharmadasa 1976 and the more careful study by Seneviratne (1976).
58. See Wilden 2014: 351; Sumathi Ramaswamy 1998.
59. Sumathi Ramaswamy 1998.
60. Ibid.: 75.
61. For a full analysis of the *TVT* and the Tamil messenger poems generally, see Shulman, in press.
62. For an introduction to the linguistic metaphysics of the northern Śaiva schools—including the Śrīvidyā, which took root in the far south—see Padoux 1990, and the magisterial study by Sanderson (2009).
63. See Sanderson 2002 for this school and its historical relations to Kubjikā and the Western Tradition.
64. See, e.g., Rajamani and Shulman 2011; on Cidambaram, see Cox 2006.
65. As Fisher (2013) has shown in a pathbreaking study.
66. See Wilke 2012; on Bhāsakarāya, an outstanding, complex, and multifaceted figure among the Kaveri Kaula theoreticians, see Brooks 1990. There is evidence, still awaiting detailed study, that several Andhra lines of transmission extended deep into the Tamil area during this period.
67. For "nondualist Śaiva Siddhânta" in the seventeenth century, in particular in the work of Nīlakaṇṭha Dīkshitar, see Fisher 2013: 75–76.
68. Ibid.: 85–101.
69. On Tantric grammar, see Shulman 2007.
70. See Chevillard 2014; Clare 2011: 115–32.
71. For examples, see Shulman 2007.
72. *Ānanta-laharī* 5.
73. Interestingly, this work was one of the very first to make the transition into the emergent print culture of the mid-nineteenth century; it was published by Arumuka Navalar in 1849.
74. See Kuppuswami 1991: v.
75. See Lakshmīdhara on this verse in *Saundarya-laharī;* more generally on theories of authorship, see the Ḍiṇḍima commentary, introductory verses 3 and 4. The commentators offer several competing stories about the identity of the "Tamil boy."
76. Kuppuswami 1991: vi.

77. *Ānanta-laharī* and *Sauntarya-laharī* of Vīrai Kavirāja Paṇṭitar, *pāyiram* 3–4.
78. The fifteenth-century devotional poet Aruṇakirinātar says disparagingly of himself that he is an unlettered fool who cannot write on palm leaf *(eṭ' ĕḻutā muḻu eḻai): Tiruppukaḻ* of Aruṇakirinātar, *Tiruccĕntūr* 17.
79. E.g., the Telugu *Bhīmeśvara-purāṇamu* of Śrīnātha 1.12.
80. *Pāṇḍuraṅga-māhātmya* of Tĕnāli Rāmakrishṇa, 3.24.
81. Manickam Naicker [1917] 1985.
82. *Āṉanta-laharī* 31–32.
83. See Shulman 2007: 338.
84. Soneji has shown the pivotal impact of the Maratha *bhajan* on the evolution of modern Carnatic music. On Maratha-period Tanjavur, see the ongoing studies by Peterson (1999, 2011, 2015).
85. See discussion in Narayana Rao, Shulman, and Subrahmanyam 1992: 202–16. This text provides fascinating documentation for Kaveri delta spoken Tamil of this period.
86. See Peterson 2011; Soneji 2012a.
87. Peterson 2011: 312.
88. Soneji 2012b: 48; see also Soneji 2012a: 142–43.
89. On *kuṟavañci*, see Muilwijk 1996; Peterson 1998.
90. Soneji 2012b: 62–66; Narayana Rao, Ramanujan, and Shulman 1994.
91. Subbarāma Dīkshitulu 1904: 1:27.
92. Shulman 2014a.
93. For example, in King Tulaja's *Saṅgīta-sārâmṛta;* see Krishnan 2008.
94. Fisher 2013: 244.
95. Ibid.: 245–46.
96. Ibid.: 183.

## 7. BEYOND THE MERELY MODERN

*Rāgamālikā:* Garland of rāga modes.

1. Clare 2011: 134, 136.
2. For nineteenth-century Tamil, see Ebeling 2010 and Venkatacami 1962. For the linguistic metaphysics of the nationalists, see Sumathi Ramaswamy 1997; Irschick 1969 and 1986; and Barnett 1976. For the tale of recovery, Rajesh 2014 and Venkatachalapathy 2006: 89–113. On the intellectual and sociopolitical ferment of nineteenth- and twentieth-century Tamil Nadu, see Blackburn 2003; also Washbrook 1989; Baker 1975; and Trautmann 2006.
3. Blackburn 2003.
4. See Malten 1997. Traditional Tamil lexicons were arranged primarily as lists of synonyms, as in Sanskrit lexicography.

5. Blackburn 2003: 61.
6. See Ebeling 2010.
7. Ibid.: 159.
8. Ibid.: 162.
9. Ibid.: 33–102.
10. Caminat'aiyar [1938] 1986.
11. On the projected childhood of the goddess at Jambukesvaram near Srirangam, on the island in the Kaveri at Tirucchirapalli.
12. *Akilāṇṭa nāyaki piḷḷaittamiḻ* 1, in Caminat'aiyar [1938] 1986: 1:48.
13. Ebeling 2010: 157.
14. See the arrogant and obtuse statements collected by Ebeling (2010: 16–19).
15. See Blackburn 2003: 180 and the careful distinctions he introduces there.
16. Narayana Rao, in press.
17. A particularly salient and tragic example is that of the Telugu *Vasucaritramu,* one of the high points of the classical literature; as late as a century ago, there were scholars who still knew the *rāgas* in which each verse of this text was meant to be sung, but that knowledge—crucial for understanding the work—has been irrevocably lost. On the received and recorded texts, see Chapter 3, "Inscribing (1)."
18. See Chapter 3, "Inscribing (1)."
19. See Chapter 5, "Who Knows Tamil?"
20. See Narayana Rao and Shulman 1998: 190–96.
21. We know of nineteenth-century poets of this type who prefixed *aṭṭâvadhāṉi* or *catâvadhāṉi* to their names, e.g., Aṭṭâvatāṉam Caravaṇap Pĕrumāḷ Kavirāyar at the Ramnad court. A substantial list of names is given by Venkatacami (1962: 66–68), along with a live description of *avadhānam* performance from a *Viṟali viṭu tūtu* text; here the improvising poet is playing both dice and chess as he makes the rounds of the *pricchakas.* This stratum of modern Tamil literary production remains to be studied.
22. Ebeling 2010: 205–45. *Kamalambal* has been translated into English by Blackburn (1998).
23. Ebeling 2010: 198. I would subject the term "sanskritization" to the kind of constraints mentioned earlier, especially in Chapter 5, "Maṇi-pravāḷam, Rubies and Coral."
24. See Ebeling 2010: 210; Tschacher 2001: 49. On the "City of Brass," see Hamori 1974.
25. I want at least to mention another pioneering modernist work from ca. 1899, Villiyappa Piḷḷai's *Pañcalakshaṇat tirumuka-vilācam,* "A Letter about Famine, in Good Grammar and Meter, by God," published by oral

recitation at the Sivagangai zamindari court near Ramnad. The title plays on *pañcam,* "famine," and Skt. *pañca,* "five," in this case the five standard topics *(lakshaṇa)* of Tamil grammar and, perhaps, the five most prevalent Tamil meters or metrical "families." This poem of bitter realistic parody shows a hypermodern consciousness at work in a relatively remote corner of the Tamil country. The intellectual trajectory of modern Tamil cannot be understood without reference to this great text.

26. The title is amenable to another interpretation, if we take *uṉmaṇi* not as an irregular or mistaken Tamilization of Skt. *unmanas* / *unmanī* (as in the state of awareness linked to the god Tyāgarāja at Tiruvarur) but as the very rare *uṉmaṇi,* "a gem lying on the surface" (seemingly attested only in the medieval lexicons). The heroine would thus be the "apparent gem of the mind."
27. See Narayana Rao 2007.
28. See Venkatacami 1962: 218.
29. He calls it a *rūpaka-mālâlaṅkāram,* a "sequential metaphoric superimposition" (Tamil introduction, p. 21), and says that the text requires an imaginative reading along these lines *(immuṟaiye pāvittu uytt'uṇarntu kŏḷḷa veṇṭiyatu).*
30. This work is discussed at length in Shulman 2012: 232–65.
31. See also Sumathi Ramaswamy 1997: 17–18; Wentworth 2011b. The first verse of the invocation became the official "prayer song" of the Tamil Nadu government in 1970. On *Maṉoṉmaṇīyam* see also Bate 2009: 39–59.
32. The commentator interestingly says that people still use Sanskrit, the language of the gods *(teva-pāshai),* because the vernaculars in all countries eventually cease to be used. The line I have just paraphrased is somewhat ambiguous, amenable to an opposite reading.
33. See also Chapter 5, "Tamil as Goddess," at n. 106.
34. See Chapter 3, "Inscribing (2)."
35. That is, the normative *Laws of Manu.*
36. Final lines of the *pāyiram* preface. This section is the equivalent of the conventional apology, *avaiyaṭakkam,* offered by the author to "real" scholars and poets.
37. Caminat'aiyar 1982: 530–32. English readers can find a translation of this famous passage in Zvelebil 1992: 190–92; also Venkatachalapathy 2006: 91–92.
38. Caminat'aiyar 1982: 555–56; see Wilden 2014: 355–56.
39. Wilden 2014.
40. See Wilden 2014: 32–33; also Rajesh 2014: 100–49.
41. Caminat'aiyar 1982: 570–76.

42. Cited by Zvelebil (1992: 177).
43. Venkatachalapathy 2006: 101.
44. E.g., Caminat'aiyar 1982.
45. Wilden 2014: 316.
46. *Ilakkaṇak-kŏttu* 1.7, commentary. See the judicious discussion by Wilden (2014: 348–51).
47. Zvelebil 1992: 35. Cf. Venkatachalapathy 2006: 109.
48. Ibid.
49. See Chapter 3, "North and South."
50. *Māraṉ-alaṅkaram* and *Māraṉ-akappŏruḷ;* see the edition of the latter by Gopal Iyer.
51. See Ebeling 2010: 54–55.
52. See Wilden 2014: 32, 358, 380–81.
53. One originally oral version of it, in Sanskrit, turns up in the so-called Tukkā poems in the Andhra tradition, possibly from the mid-seventeenth century; see Shulman 2008. On Sanskrit translations of this poem in the *Hālâsya-māhātmya* and the *Śiva-līlârṇava* of Nilakaṇṭha Dīkshitar, see Wilden 2014: 265 and Fisher 2013.
54. These materials have now been lucidly and comprehensively discussed by Wilden (2014).
55. See Clare 2011: 115–32, on the integrative *Ilakkaṇa viḷakkam;* also Wilden 2014: 345.
56. Wilden 2014: 30; see also 357.
57. Rajesh 2014: 22.
58. Venkatachalapathy 2006: 103.
59. See Chapter 5, "Classicism," at n. 29. See also Wentworth 2011b; Pollock 2006: 508–10.
60. Venkatachalapathy 2006: 103–9.
61. See Irschick 1969: 282–83.
62. See Chapter 1, "What Is Tamil?"
63. Irschick 1969: 284.
64. Ponemballem Pillai 1909.
65. The figures are given in Irschick 1969: 12–19.
66. Stein 1980: 69, 71; see also Chapter 3, "North and South."
67. Irschick 1969: 289.
68. Kanakasabhai Pillai [1904] 1956.
69. See Sumathi Ramaswamy 1997: 25–28; Zvelebil 1992: 258.
70. See the detailed discussion in Sumathi Ramaswamy 1997: 24–34.
71. See Raman 2009.
72. Ibid.: 144–54; Nambi Arooran 1980; see also Annamalai 2011: 13–34.

73. Irschick 1969: 22, 47–50.
74. Ibid.: 186–88, 339.
75. Venkatachalapathy 2006: 115.
76. Cited by Sumathi Ramaswamy (1997:125), from a text in the Dravidianist journal *Kuṭi aracu*, 1939.
77. Sumathi Ramaswamy 1997: 235.
78. Well described by Venkatachalapathy (2006: 114–42).
79. Bate 2009: 4.
80. See Chapter 5, "Maṇi-pravāḷam, Rubies and Coral." For Dravidian as only Tamil, see Sumathi Ramaswamy 1997: 63.
81. See Zvelebil 1973b; Buck 1976.
82. Weiss 2009.
83. See Blackburn 2003: 161–62.
84. See Arunachalam 1989; Weidman 2006: 166–91.
85. Venkatachalapathy 2006: 106. On Ramalinga, see also Weiss 2015.
86. Venkatachalapathy 2006: 104–05; Zvelebil 1992: 101.
87. Fisher 2013: 209, 212.
88. Blackburn 2003: 161–65.
89. Gover 1871: 14.
90. Quoted in Irschick 1969: 281.
91. Ibid.
92. See Ebeling 2009.
93. See Narayana Rao and Sreenivas 2014.
94. For a remarkable portrait of the resilience of Tamil Brahmins over recent decades, see Fuller and Narasimhan 2014.
95. Annamalai 2011: 75; see also Bate 2009: 9–17 on Tamil diglossia in general.
96. See Mitchell 2009.
97. Bate 2009: 27–67.
98. Ibid.: 65.
99. Ibid.
100. For an interesting speculative prediction of a different sort, see Annamalai 2011: 54–55. Annamalai notes here that "in many cases, frequency of use of CT [colloquial Tamil] forms in LT [literary Tamil] is increasing at the morphophonemic, morphological and syntactical levels." It remains uncertain how to interpret this undoubtedly correct observation.
101. Annamalai 2011: 92–109.
102. For the latter, see Chevillard 2008a: 10.
103. Kanaganayakakam 2013: 110–11. Compare *Kuṟuntŏkai* 30. Manushya Puthiran is the pen name of S. Abdul Hameed, born in Thuravankuricci in 1967.

# References

## LIST OF ABBREVIATIONS

| | |
|---|---|
| *EI* | *Epigraphia Indica* |
| *HM* | *Hālâsya-māhātmya* |
| *IA* | *Iṟaiyaṉār akappŏruḷ, Grammar of Stolen Love* |
| *LT* | *Līlā-tilakam* |
| *Puṟan.* | *Puṟanāṉūṟu* |
| *SII* | *South Indian Inscriptions* |
| SISSWPS | South Indian Saiva Siddhanta Works Publishing Society |
| *Tŏl.* | *Tŏlkāppiyam, Ĕḻutt'atikāram* |
| *Tŏl. Cŏl.* | *Tŏlkāppiyam, Cŏllatikāram* |
| *Tŏl. Pŏruḷ.* | *Tŏlkāppiyam, Pŏruḷatikāram* |
| *Tŏl. Pŏruḷ., Ak.* | *Tŏlkāppiyam Pŏruḷatikāram, Akattiṇai* |
| *Tŏl. Pŏruḷ. Cĕy.* | *Tŏlkāppiyam Pŏruḷatikāram Cĕyyuḷiyal* |
| *Tŏl. Pŏruḷ. Mar.* | *Tŏlkāppiyam Pŏruḷatikāram Marap'iyal* |
| *Tŏl. Pŏruḷ. Puṟ.* | *Tŏlkāppiyam Pŏruḷatikāram Puṟattiṇai* |
| *TVT* | *Maturai cŏkkanātar tamiḻ viṭu tūtu* |
| UVCN | U. Ve. Caminat'aiyar Nul Nilaiyam |

## PRIMARY SOURCES


*Aiṅkuṟunūṟu.* Edited by Po. Ve. Comacuntaranar. Madras: SISSWPS, 1972.

*Aitareya Āraṇyaka.* Edited by Arthur Berriedale Keith. Oxford, U.K.: Clarendon Press, 1909.

*Akanāṉūṟu.* Edited by Na. Mu. Venkattacami Nattar, Ka. Kaviyaracu Venkattacalam Pillai. Madras: SISSWPS, 1943–1944.

*Āmukta-mālyada* of Krishṇa-deva-rāya. Edited by Vedamu Venkataraya Sastri. Madras: Vedam Venkataraya Sastri and Brothers, 1964.

*Āṉanta-laharī* and *Sauntarya-laharī* of Vīrai Kavirāja Paṇṭitar. In A. Ve. Ra. Kirusnacami Rettiyar, ed., *Sauntarya-laharī (yantiram, pirayokam nuṭpaṅkaḷuṭaṉ),* 30–45. Tirucci: Tiruvatippatippakam, 1977.

*Āndhra Mahābhāratamu* of Nannayya. Hyderabad: Telugu University, n.d.

*Avanti-sundarī-kathā* of Daṇḍin. Trivandrum: University of Travancore, Trivandrum Sanskrit Series, 1954.

*Bhagavad-viṣayam.* Edited by Ce. Kirushnamacariyar. Tiruvallikeni: Sriranganacciyar Press, 1929; reprinted 1999.

*Bhāgavata-purāṇa*. Gorakpur: Gita Press, Samvat 2022.

*Bhīmeśvara-purāṇamu* of Śrīnātha. Guntur: Phalaksha Pracurana, 1997.

*Brihaddevatā* of Śaunaka. Edited by A. A. Macdonell. Cambridge, Mass.: Harvard University Press, 1904.

*Camuttira-vilācam* of Kaṭikaimuttuppulavar. With a commentary by Cĕ. Rĕ. Iramacamippillai. Madras: SISSWPS, 1956.

*Cīkāḷatti-purāṇam* of Karuṇaippirakāca cuvāmikaḷ, Civappirakāca cuvāmikaḷ, and Velaiya cuvāmikaḷ. Madras: Memorial Press, 1948.

*Cilappatikāram* of Iḷaṅkovaṭikaḷ. Tiruvanmiyur: U. Ve. Caminat'aiyar Library, 1978.

———. Translated by R. Parthasarathy as *The Tale of an Anklet*. New York: Columbia University Press, 1993.

*Cīṟāppurāṇam* of Umaṟuppulavar. Utayamarttantapuram: Naccikulattar, 1974.

*Cīvaka-cintāmaṇi* of Tiruttakkatevar. Edited by U. Ve. Caminat'aiyar. 7th edition. Madras: Kabeer Printing Works, 1969.

———. Translated by James D. Ryan as *Cīvakacintāmaṇi: The Hero Cīvakaṉ, the Gem that Fulfills All Wishes*. Fremont, Calif.: Jain Publishing Company, 2005.

*Civarāttiri purāṇam* of Varatarāca kavirāyar. Yalppanam: Srikanta Press, 1970.

*Daśa-kumāra-carita* of Daṇḍin. Edited by M. R. Kale. Delhi: Motilal Banarsidass, 1966.

*Divya-sūri-carita* of Garuḍa-vāhana. Edited by T. A. Sampath Kumaracharya and K. K. A. Venkatachari. Bombay: Anathacharya Research Institute, 1978.

*Hālâsya-māhātmya*. Madras: Sastra-sanjivini Press, 1911.

*Harṣa-carita* of Bāṇa. Edited by P. V. Kane. Delhi: Motilal Banarsidass, 1918/1986.

*Ilakkaṇak-kŏttu* of Cuvāminàta Tecikar. Chennai: Vittiyanupalana Press, 1925.

*Iṟaiyaṉār akappŏruḷ*. Madras: SISSWPS, 1976.

———. Translated by David C. Buck and K. Paramasivam as *The Study of Stolen Love*. Atlanta: Scholars Press, 1997.

*Irāmâvatāram* of Kamban. 8 vols. Tiruvanmiyur: UVCN, 1946–1963.

*Kādambarī* of Bāṇa. Edited by P. Peterson. Bombay: Government Central Book Depot, 1899–1900.

———. Edited by Kashinath Pandurang Parab and revised by Wasudeva Laxmana Shastri Pansikar. Delhi: Nag Publications, 1985.

*Kāḷahasti-māhātmyamu* of Dhūrjaṭi. Madras: Vavilla Ramasvami Sastrulu and Sons, 1966.

*Kaliṅkattupparaṇi* of Cayaṅkŏṇṭār. Madras: Tamsan Kampeni, 1898.

*Kalittŏkai*. Madras: SISSWPS, 1938.

*Kalvaḷaiyantâti* of Yāḻppāṇam Nallūr Ciṉṉattampip pulavar. Madras: SISSWPS, 1964.

*Kanta-purāṇam* of Kacciyappa Civâcāriyar. Tiruppanantal: Srikacimatam, 1952–1953.

*Kāvyâdarśa* of Daṇḍin. Edited with Telugu commentary by Pullela Sriramachandradu. Hyderabad: Andhra Pradesh Sahitya Akademi, 1981.

*Koyil-ŏḻuku*. Madras: Ananta Press, 1909.

———. Translated and summarized by V. N. Hari Rao. Madras: Rochouse and Sons, 1961.

———. Translated by T. S. Parthasarathy as *The Koyil Olugu (History of the Srirangam Temple)*. Tirupati: Tirumala-Tirupati Devasthanams, 1954.

*Kuḻaikkātar pā-mālai* of Nārāyaṇa Dīkshitar. Tirunelveli: Cirri Accakattar, ca. 1975.

*Kuṟuntŏkai*. Edited by U. Ve. Caminat'aiyar. Madras: Kapir Press, 1947.

*Līlā-tilakam*. Edited by Ilankulam Kunjan Pillai. Kottayam: National Book Stall, 2011.

*Mahābhāshya* of Patañjali. Varanasi: Chaukhamba, 1984.

*Maṇimekalai* of Cīttalaiccāttaṉār. Edited by Po. Ve. Comacuntaranar. Madras: SISSWPS, 1971.

*Maṉoṉmaṇīyam* of Cuntaram Piḷḷai. Coimbatore: Merkkuri Puttaka Company, 1968.

*Manu-caritramu* of Pĕddana. Madras: R. Venkateswar, 1919.

*Māraṉakappŏruḷ* and *Tiruppatikkovai* of Tirukkurukaip Pĕrumāḷ Kavirāyar. *A Treatise on Tamil Poetics illustrated with a narrative poem*. Edited by T. V. Gopal Iyer. Pondichéry: Institut Français de Pondichéry and École Française d'Extrême-Orient, 2005.

*Maturaiccŏkkanātar ulā* of Purāṇat Tirumalainātar. Chennai: Kecari accukkutam, 1931.

*Maturai cokkanātar tamiḻ viṭu tūtu*. With notes by U. Ve. Caminat'aiyar. Besant Nagar: U. Ve. Caminat'aiyar Library, 2004.

*Maturai mīṉâṭciyammai Piḷḷaittamiḻ* of Kumarakuruparar cuvāmikaḷ. Edited by Pu. Ci. Punnaivananata Mutaliyar. Tirunelveli: SISSWPS, 1965.

*Mūvar ulā* of Ŏṭṭakkūttar. Tirunelveli: SISSWPS, 1967.

*Naiṣadhīya-carita* of Śrīharṣa. With commentary by Nārāyaṇa. Delhi: Meharchand Lacchmandas Publications, 1986.

*Naiṭatam* of Ativīrarāma Pāṇṭiyaṉ. Madras: n.p., ca. 1907.

*Nālāyira-tivya-prabandham*. Chennai: Alvar Ayvu maiyam, 1993.

*Naṉṉūl* of Pavaṇanti. Edited by Arumuka Navalar. Tanjavur: Tanjavur University, 1984.

*Nantikkalampakam*. Edited by Pu. Ci. Punnaivanata Mutaliyar. Tirunelveli: SISSWPS, 1961.

*Naṟṟiṇai*. Edited by A. Narayanacami Aiyar. Tirunelveli: SISSWPS, 1954.

———. Critical Edition and Annotated Translation plus Glossary, edited by E. Wilden. Chennai: École Française d'Extrême-Orient / Tamilman patippakam, 2008.

*Nāṭya-śāstra*. Edited by Manomohan Ghosh. Calcutta: Manisha Granthalaya, 1967.

*Neminātham* of Kuṇavīrapaṇṭitar. Edited and translated by M. Elayaperumal. Trivandrum: Kerala University, 1984.

*Padma-purāṇa*. Benares: Anandasrama, India, 1894.

*Pāṇḍuraṅga-māhātmya* of Tĕnāli Rāmakrishṇa. With commentary by Bulusu Venkataramanayya. Madras: Ramaswami Sastruly and Sons, 1968.

*Pāṇḍya-kulodaya* of Maṇḍala-kavi. Hoshiarpur: Vishveshvaranand Visha Bandhu Institute of Sanskrit and Indological Studies, Panjab University, 1981.

*Paṉṉiru pāṭṭ'iyal*. Tirunelveli: SISSWPS, 1963.

*Paripāṭal*. Tiruvanmiyur: U. Ve. Caminat'aiyar Library, 1980.

———. Edited and translated by F. Gros as *Le Paripāṭal*. Pondichéry: Institut Français d'Indologie, 1968.

*Patiṟṟuppattu*. Edited by Auvai. Cu. Turaicamippillai. Tirunelveli: SISSWPS, 1973.

*Paṭṭiṉatt'aṭikaḷ tiruppāṭaṟ ṟiraṭṭu*. Chennai: B. Irattina Nayakar Sons, 1968.

*Pattuppāṭṭu*. Tirunelveli: SISSWPS, 1976.

*Pĕriya Purāṇam*. See *Tiruttŏṇṭar purāṇam* of Cekkiḻār.

*Puṟanāṉūṟu*. Edited by U. Ve. Caminat'aiyar. Tiruvanmiyur: U. Ve. Caminat'aiyar Library, 1971.

———. Edited with commentary by Auvai. Cu. Turaicamippillai. Tirunelveli: SISSWPS, 1973.

———. Translated by George L. Hart and Hank Heifetz as *The Four Hundred Songs of War and Wisdom*. New York: Columbia University Press, 1999.

*Puṟappŏruḷ vĕṇpā mālai*. Edited by Po. Ce. Comacuntaranar. Madras: SISSWPS, 1955.

*Puṟattiraṭṭu*. Tirunelveli: SISSWPS, 1972.

*Purūrava-caritai* of Ayyam Pĕrumāḷ Civanta Kavirācar. *Cĕntamiḻ* 20, nos. 3–9, 12; 21, nos. 10–11; 22, nos. 10–12; 23–27, nos. 9–11 (c. 1923–1925).

*Raghu-vaṃśa* of Kālidāsa. Delhi: Motilal Banarsidass, 1982.

*Rāmāyaṇa* of Vālmīki. Edited by K. Chinnaswami Sastrigal and V. H. Subrahmanya Sastri. Madras: Ramaratnam, 1958.

*Saundarya-laharī*. Edited with many commentaries by A. Kuppuswami. Delhi: Nag Publishers, 1991.
*Śiva-līlârṇava* of Nīlakaṇṭha Dīkshitar. Srirangam: Srivanivilasa Press, 1911.
*Takka-yākap-paraṇi* of Ŏṭṭakkūttar. Tiruvanmiyur: UVCN, 1960.
*Tamiḻ-nāvalar-caritai*. Edited by Auvai Cu. Turaicamippillai. Madras: SISSWPC, 1972.
*Taṉippāṭaṟ ṟiraṭṭu*. M. Viraver Pillai. Madras: P. Na. Citampara Mutaliyar Brothers, n.d.
*Taṇṭiyalaṅkāram*. Edited by Ko. Iramalinkattampiran. Madras: SISSWPC, 1997.
*Tevāram*. 7 vols. Tarumapuram: Tarumapura Atinam, 1953–1964.
*Tirukkuṟaḷ* of Tiruvaḷḷuvar. New Delhi: Asian Educational Services, 1989.
———. Translated by P. S. Sundaram as *The Kural*. New Delhi: Penguin Books, 1992.
———. Translated and annotated by F. Gros as *Tiruvaḷḷuvar: Le Livre de l'amour*. Paris: Gallimard, 1992.
*Tirukkuṟṟālat-talapurāṇam* of Tirikūṭarācappan. Edited by Mu. Ra. Arunacalakkavirayar. Madurai, India. 1910.
*Tirumayilait tirip'antāti* of Irāmaiyyar. Edited by U. Ve. Caminat'aiyar. Tiruvanmiyur: U. Ve. Caminat'aiyar Library, 1997.
*Tiruppāvai* of Āṇṭāḷ. Edited and translated by Jean Filliozat as *Un Texte tamoul de dévotion vishnouite*. Pondichéry: Institut Français d'Indologie, 1972.
*Tiruppukaḻ* of Aruṇakirinātar. Chennai: Vanati patippakam, 1977.
*Tiruttŏṇṭar purāṇam* of Cekkiḻār. Edited with commentary by Ci. Ke. Cuppiramaniya Mutaliyar. Koyamputtur: Kovaittamiḻccaṅkam, 1975.
*Tiruvācakam* of Māṇikkavācakar. Tirunelveli: SISSWPS, 1976.
*Tiruvāṉaikkā ulā* of Kāḷamekappulavar. Edited by Mu. Arunacalam. Cokkanatapuram: Cĕntamiḻk kaḷakam, 1944.
*Tiruvārūrppurāṇam* of Campantamuṉivar. Edited by Cu. Cuvaminata Tecikar. Madras: Comacuntara Mutaliyar, 1894.
*Tiruvātavūr-aṭikaḷ purāṇam* of Kaṭavuḷ māmuṉivar. Edited by Pu. Ci. Punnaivanata Mutaliyar. Tirunelveli: SISSWPS, 1967.
*Tiruvāymŏḻi* of Nammāḻvār. See *Nālāyira-tivya-prabandham*.
*Tiruviḷaiyāṭaṟpurāṇam* of Parañcoti muṉivar. Madras: Vittiyanupalana Press, 1907.
*Tiruviruttam* of Nammāḻvar. Madras: Visishtadvaita Pracharini Sabha, 1967.
———. *See* Venkatesan, Archana, trans. 2014b.
*Tiruviṭaimarutūr tirukkoyil tiruttala-varalāṟu*. Tiruvavatuturai: Tiruvavatuturai atinam, 2013.

*Tŏlkāppiyac cūttira virutti* of Civañāṉa Muṉivar. Chennai: Vittiyanupalana Accakam, 1956.

*Tŏlkāppiyam, Cŏllatikāram.* With Ceṉāvaraiyam. Annamalainagar: Annamalai University, 1981.

*Tŏlkāppiyam, Ĕḻutt'atikāram.* Tirunelveli: SISSWPS, 1923.

*Tŏlkāppiyam, Pŏruḷatikāram.* With commentary by Perāciriyar. Edited by Ku. Cuntaramurtti. Annamalainagar: Annamalai University, 2012.

———. With commentary of Iḷampūraṇar. Tirunelveli: SISSWPS, 1961.

*Vacu-carittiram* of Tŏṇṭaimāṉturai Ampalatt'āṭum Ayyaṉ. Edited by T. Chandrasekharan. Madras: Madras Government Oriental Manuscripts Series 17, 1952.

*Vinota-raca-mañcari* of Aṭṭâvatāṉam of Vīracāmi Cĕṭṭiyar. Madras: Vidya Ratnakaram Press, 1888.

*Vīracoḻiyam* of Puttamittiraṉ. Edited by K. R. Kovintaraja Mutaliyar. Madras: SISSWPS, 1970.

*Virāṭa-parva-maṇi-pravāḷa-mañjarī* of Viśvanātha Suri. Edited by K. Ramachandrasarma. Madras: Adyar Library and Research Center, 1985.

*Yāpp'aruṅkalam [paḻaiya virutti uraiyuṭaṉ]* of Amitacākarar. Edited by I. Ilankumara. Tirunelveli: SISSWPS, 1973.

*Yāpp'aruṅkala-kārikai* of Amitacākarar. With commentary of Kuṇacākarar. Tiruvanmiyur: U. Ve. Caminat'aiyar Library, 1968.

———. Translated by Ulrike Niklas as *The Verses on the Precious Jewel Prosody composed by Amitacākarar with the commentary by Kuṇacākarar.* Pondichéry: Institut Français de Pondichéry, 1993.

## SECONDARY SOURCES

Ali, Daud. 2004. *Courtly Culture and Political Life in Early Medieval India.* New York: Cambridge University Press.

Allchin, Bridget. 1982. *The Rise of Civilization in India and Pakistan.* New York: Cambridge University Press.

Ambrosone, Ellen Alexis. 2016. "Making Modern Malayalam: Literary and Educational Practices in Nineteenth-Century Kerala." Ph.D. dissertation, University of Chicago.

Annamalai, E. 2011. *Social Dimensions of Modern Tamil.* Chennai: Cre-A.

Aravamuthan, T. G. 1931. "The Maturai Chronicles and the Tamil Academies." *Journal of Oriental Research, Madras* 5: 108–24, 196–214.

———. 1932. "The Maturai Chronicles and the Tamil Academies." *Journal of Oriental Research, Madras* 6: 89–105, 274–94, 322–40.

Arunachalam, M. 1989. *Musical Tradition of Tamilnadu.* Madras: International Society for the Investigation of Ancient Civilizations.

Baker, Christopher J. 1975. "Temples and Political Development." In C. J. Baker and D. A. Washbrook, eds., *South India: Political Institutions and Political Change, 1880–1940*, 6–97. Delhi: Macmillan.

Balambal, V. 1998. *Studies in Chola History*. Delhi: Kalinga Publications.

Barnett, Marguerite. 1976. *The Politics of Cultural Nationalism in South India*. Princeton, N.J.: Princeton University Press.

Baskaran, Theodore. 2011. "Royal Touch." *Frontline* 28: 19 (September 10–23).

Bate, Bernard. 2009. *Tamil Oratory and the Dravidian Aesthetic [Democratic Practice in South India]*. New York: Columbia University Press.

Bayly, Susan. 1989. *Saints, Goddesses and Kings: Muslims and Christians in South Indian Society, 1700–1900*. Cambridge, U.K.: Cambridge University Press.

Begley, Vimala. 1983. "Arikamedu Reconsidered." *American Journal of Archaeology* 87: 461–81.

Blackburn, Stuart. 2000. "Corruption and Redemption: The Legend of Vaḷḷuvar and Tamil Literary History." *Modern Asian Studies* 34 (2000): 449–82.

———. 2003. *Print, Folklore, and Nationalism in Colonial South India*. Delhi: Permanent Black.

———, trans. 1998. *The Fatal Rumour: A Nineteenth-Century Novel*, by B. R. Rajam Aiyar. Delhi: Oxford University Press.

Borges, Jorge Luis. 1962. *Ficciones*. New York: Grove Press.

Bronner, Yigal. 2010. *Extreme Poetry: The South Asian Movement of Simultaneous Narration*. New York: Columbia University Press.

———. 2015. "South Meets North: Banaras from the Perspective of Appayya Dīkṣita." *South Asian History and Culture* 6.1 (2015): 10–31.

Bronner, Yigal, and David Shulman, eds. Forthcoming. *Mapping the World through Courier Poetry*.

Brooks, Douglas Renfrew. 1990. *The Secret of the Three Cities: An Introduction to Hindu Śākta Tantrism*. Chicago and London: University of Chicago Press.

Buck, David C. 1976. *Dance, Snake! Dance. The Song of Pampatti-cittar*. Calcutta: Writers Workshop.

Buck, David C., and K. Paramasivam, trans. 1997. *Iṟaiyaṉār akappŏruḷ*. Translated as *The Study of Stolen Love*. Atlanta: Scholars Press.

Burrow, T., and M. B. Emeneau. 1961. *Dravidian Etymological Dictionary*. Oxford, U.K.: Clarendon Press.

Caminat'aiyar, U. Ve. [1938] 1986. *Śrī Mīṉâṭcicuntaram avarkaḷiṉ carittiram*. Tanjavur: Tamil University.

———. 1968. *Putiyatum paḻaiyatum*. Madras: Kabeer Printing Works.

———. 1982. *Ĕṉ carittiram*. Tiruvanmiyur: U. Ve. Caminat'aiyar Library.

Cardona, George. 1988. *Pāṇini: His Work and Its Traditions.* Delhi: Motilal Banarsidass.

Champakalakshmi, R. 1996. *Trade, Ideology and Urbanization: South India 300 B.C. to A.D. 1300.* Delhi: Oxford University Press.

Chevillard, Jean-Luc. 1996. *Le commentaire de Cēṉāvaraiyar sur le Collatikāram du Tolkāppiyam.* Pondichéry: Institut Français de Pondichéry and École Française d'Extrême-Orient.

———. 2008a. *Companion Volume to the Cēṉāvaraiyam on Tamil Morphology and Syntax. Le commentaire de Cĕṉāvaraiyar sur le Collatikāram du Tolkāppiyam.* Vol. 2. Pondichéry: Institut Français de Pondichéry and École Française d'Extrême-Orient.

———. 2008b. "The Concept of *ticai-c-col* in Tamil Grammatical Literature and the Regional Diversity of Classical Tamil Literature." In M. Kannan, ed. *Streams of Language: Dialects in Tamil*, 21–50. Pondichéry: Institut Français de Pondichéry.

———. 2009. "The Pantheon of Tamil Grammarians: A Short History of the Myth of Agastya's Twelve Disciples." In *Écrire et Transmettre en Inde Classique,* ed. Colas Gérard and Gerschheimer Gerdi. Paris: École française d'Extrême-Orient.

———. 2014. "Snapshots of the Tamil Scholarly Tradition." In S. Archaimbault, J-M. Fournier, and V. Raby, eds., *Penser l'histoire des saviors linguistiques. Homage à Sylvani Auroux*, 255–71. Lyon: ÉNS Editions.

Clare, Jennifer Steele. 2011. "Canons, Conventions and Creativity: Defining Literary Tradition in Premodern Tamil South India." Ph.D. dissertation, University of California, Berkeley.

Colas, Gerard. 2002. "Variations sur la pâmoison dévote: A propos d'un poème de Vēdāntadeśika et du theatre des araiyar." In V. Bouillier and G. Tarabout, *Images du corps dans le monde hindou*, 275–324. Paris: CNRS.

Cox, Whitney. 2002. Review of *Kāvya in South India* by Herman Tieken. *Journal of the Royal Asiatic Society* 12, no. 3: 407–10.

———. 2006. "Making a *tantra* in Medieval South India: The *Mahārthamañjarī* and the Textual Culture of Co̱la Cidambaram." Ph.D. dissertation, University of Chicago.

———. In press. *Politics, Kingship, and Poetry in Medieval South India: Moonset on Sunrise Mountain.* Cambridge, U.K.: Cambridge University Press.

Cutler, Norman. 1987. *Songs of Experience: The Poetics of Tamil Devotion.* Bloomington: Indiana University Press.

———. 1992. "Interpreting Tirukkuṟaḷ: The Role of Commentary in the Creation of a Text." *Journal of the American Oriental Society* 112, no. 4: 549–56.

Davis, William. 2000. "Agastya: The Southern Sage from the North." Ph.D. dissertation, University of Chicago.

de Bary, Wm. Theodore, ed. 1958. *Sources of Indian Tradition.* Vol. 1. New York: Columbia University Press.

Dessigane, R., P. Z. Pattabiramin, and J. Filliozat. 1960. *La légende des jeux de Çiva à Maturai.* Pondichérry: Institut Français d'Indologie.

Dharmadasa, K. N. O. 1976. "The Sinhala-Buddhist Identity and the Nayakkar Dynasty in the Politics of the Kandyan Kingdom, 1739–1815." *Ceylon Journal of Historical and Social Studies,* n.s. 6, no. 1: 1–23.

Dhavamony, Mariasusai. 1971. *Love of God according to Śaiva Siddhānta.* Oxford, U.K.: Clarendon Press.

Dirks, Nicholas. 1976. "Political Authority and Structural Change in Early South Indian History." *Indian Economic and Social History Review* 13: 125–57.

Dubianski, Alexander M. 2000. *Ritual and Mythological Sources of the Early Tamil Poetry.* Groningen, The Netherlands: Egbert Forsten.

———. 2005. "Messenger-Poems in Tamil Poetry." In Lidia Sudykal, ed., *Love and Nature in Kāvya Literature,* 259–74. Cracow Indological Studies 7. Krakow: Jagiellonian University, Institute of Oriental Philology.

Ebeling, Sascha. 2009. "The College of Fort St. George and the Transformation of Tamil Philology during the Nineteenth Century." In Thomas R. Trautmann, ed., *The Madras School of Orientalism: Producing Knowledge in Colonial South India,* 233–60. Delhi: Oxford University Press.

———. 2010. *Colonizing the Realm of Words: The Transformation of Tamil Literature in Nineteenth-Century South India.* Albany: SUNY Press.

Egnore, Margaret. 1978. "The Sacred Spell and Other Conceptions of Life in Tamil Culture." Ph.D. dissertation, University of Chicago.

Eisenstadt, S. N. 2000. "Multiple Modernities." *Daedalus* 129 (Winter): 1–29.

Emeneau, M. B. 1967. *Collected Papers (On Dravidian Linguistics, Ethnology and Folktales).* Annamalainagar, India: Annamalai University.

Filliozat, J. 1960. "Introduction." In R. Dessigane, P. Z. Pattabiramin, and J. Filliozat, *La légende des jeux de Çiva à Maturai.* Pondichéry: Institut Français d'Indologie.

———. 1972. See *Tiruppāvai.*

Finkelberg, Margalit. 2000. "The *Cypria,* the *Iliad,* and the Problem of Multiformity in Oral and Written Tradition." *Classical Philology* 95: 1–11.

———. 2012. "Canonising and Decanonising Homer: Reception of the Homeric Poems in Antiquity and Modernity." In Maren Niehoff, ed., *Homer and the Bible in the Eyes of Ancient Interpreters,* 15–28. Leiden, The Netherlands: Brill.

Fisher, Elaine. 2013. "A New Public Theology: Sanskrit and Society in Seventeenth Century South India." Ph.D. dissertation, Columbia University.

Francis, Emmanuel. 2013a. *Le discours royal dans l'Inde du Sud ancienne. Inscriptions et monuments pallava (IVème– IXème siècles).* Louvaine-La-Neuve: Université catholique de Louvain.

———. 2013b. "Praising the King in Tamil during the Pallava Period." In Whitney Cox and Vincenzo Vergiani, eds., *Bilingual Discourse and Cross-Cultural Fertilisation: Sanskrit and Tamil in Medieval India*, 359–409. Pondichéry: Institut Français de Pondichéry.

———. 2016. "Forerunners of the Cōḻa *Meykkīrtis*." In K. M. Bhadri and S. Swaminathan, eds., *K. V. Ramesh Felicitation Volume.* Mysore: K. V. Ramesh Felicitation Committee.

Freeman, John Richardson. 1991. "Purity and Violence: Sacred Power in the *Teyyam* Worship of Malabar." Ph.D. dissertation, University of Pennsylvania.

———. 1998. "Rubies and Coral: The Lapidary Crafting of Language in Kerala." *Journal of Asian Studies* 57: 38–65.

———. 2013. "Caught in Translation: Ideologies of Literary Language in the *Līlātilakam*." In Whitney Cox and Vincenzo Vergiani, eds., *Bilingual Discourse and Cross-cultural Fertilisation: Sanskrit and Tamil in Medieval India*, 199–240. Pondichéry: Institut Français de Pondichéry and École Française d'Extrême-Orient.

Fuller, Chris, and Haripriya Narasimhan. 2014. *Tamil Brahmans: The Making of a Middle-Class Caste.* Chicago: University of Chicago Press.

Gillet, Valérie. 2014. "The Dark Period: Myth or Reality?" *Indian Economic and Social History Review.*

Glazov, J. J. 1967. *Introduction to the Historical Grammar of the Tamil Language.* Moscow: Nauka Publishing.

Gopala Pillai, A. R. 1985. *Linguistic Interpretation of Līlātilakam.* Trivandrum, India: Dravidian Linguistics Association.

Gover, Charles E. 1871. *The Folk-songs of Southern India.* Madras: Higginbotham.

Govindakutty Menon, Achutan. 1972. "From Proto-Tamil-Malayalam to West Coast Dialects," *Indo-Iranian Journal* 14: 52–60.

Gros, François. 1968. *Le Paripāṭal. Introduction, Traduction et Notes.* Pondichéry: Institut Français d'Indologie.

———. 1983. "La littérature du Sangam et son public." *Purusartha* 7: 77–107.

———, trans. 1992. *Tirukkuṟaḷ* of Tiruvaḷḷuvar. Translated and annotated as *Tiruvaḷḷuvar: Le Livre de l'amour.* Paris: Gallimard.

———. 2009. *Deep Rivers: Selected Writings on Tamil Literature.* Translated by M. P. Boseman. Edited by M. Kannan and Jennifer Clare. Pondichéry:

Institut Français de Pondichéry and Department of South and Southeast Asian Studies, University of California.

Halbertal, Moshe. 1997. *People of the Book: Canon, Meaning, and Authority.* Cambridge, Mass.: Harvard University Press.

Hall, Kenneth. 1980. *Trade and Statecraft in the Age of the Chōlas.* New Delhi: Abhinav Publications.

———. 1981. "Peasant State and Society in Chola Times: A View from the Tiruvidaimarudur Urban Complex." *Indian Economic and Social History Review* 18 (July): 393–410.

Hamori, Andras. 1974. *On the Art of Medieval Arabic Literature.* Princeton, N.J.: Princeton University Press.

Handelman, Don. 2014. *One God, Two Goddesses, Three Studies of South Indian Cosmology.* Leiden, The Netherlands: Brill.

Handelman, Don, and David Shulman. 1998. *God Inside Out: Śiva's Game of Dice.* New York: Oxford University Press.

Hardgrave, Robert. 1965. *The Dravidian Movement.* Bombay: Popular Prakasan.

Hardy, Friedhelm. 1979. "The Tamil Veda of a Śūdra Saint. The Śrīvaiṣṇava Interpretation of Nammāḻvār." In Gopal Krishna, ed., *Contributions to South Asian Studies* 1: 29–87.

———. 1983. *Viraha-bhakti.* Delhi: Oxford University Press.

———. 2016. *Collected Essays: Studies in South Indian Śrīvaisṇavism.* Edited by Aruna Hardy and D. Shulman. Delhi: Motilal Banarsidass.

Harris, Anthony Gardner. 2008. "Obtaining Grace: Locating the Origins of a Tamil Śaiva Precept." Ph.D. dissertation, University of Texas.

Hart, George. 1975. *The Poems of Ancient Tamil: Their Milieu and Their Sanskrit Counterparts.* Berkeley: University of California Press.

———. 1979. *Poets of the Tamil Anthologies.* Princeton, N.J.: Princeton University Press.

Hart, George, and Hank Heifetz, trans. 1999. *Puṟanāṉūṟu.* Translated as *The Four Hundred Songs of War and Wisdom.* New York: Columbia University Press, 1999.

Heitzman, James. 1987. "State Formation in South India, 850–1280." *Indian Economic and Social History Review* 24: 35–61.

———. 1997. *Gifts of Power. Lordship in an Early Indian State.* Delhi: Oxford University Press.

Hiltebeitel, Alf. 1977. "Nahuṣa in the Skies: A Human King of Heaven." *History of Religions* 16: 59–60.

Irakav'aiyankar, Mu. 1907–1908. "Nūl-ārāycci: Purūravā-caritai." *Cĕntamiḻ.*

———. [1938] 1984. *Ārāyccit tŏkuti.* Tancavur, India: Tamil University.

Irakav'aiyankar, Ra. 1904. "Editor's Note." *Cĕntamiḻ*, Vol. 3, 43.

———. ca. 1987. *Ārāyccik kaṭṭuraikaḷ*. Chennai: New Era Publications.

Irschick, Eugene F. 1969. *Politics and Social Conflict in South India: The Non-Brahman Movement and Tamil Separatism, 1916–1929*. Berkeley: University of California Press.

———. 1986. *Tamil Revivalism in the 1930s*. Madras: Cre-A.

———. 1994. *Dialogue and History: Constructing South India, 1795–1895*. Berkeley: University of California Press.

Jagadeesan, N. 1977. *History of Sri Vaishnavism in the Tamil Country (Post-Ramanuja)*. Madurai, India: Koodal Publishers.

———. 1989. "Sri Vaishṇava Written and Spoken Tamil." In *Collected Papers on Tamil Vaishṇavism*, 64–76. Madurai: New Rathna Press.

Kailasapathy, K. 1968. *Tamil Heroic Poetry*. Oxford, U.K.: Clarendon Press.

Kaimal, Padma. 1988. "Stone Portrait Sculpture at Pallava and Early Cola Temples: Kings, Patrons and Individual Identity." Ph.D. dissertation, University of California, Berkeley.

Kanaganayakam, Chelva. 2013. *In Our Translated World: Contemporary Global Tamil Poetry*. Toronto: TSAR Publications.

Kanakasabhai Pillai, V. [1904] 1956. *The Tamils 1800 Years Ago*. Tirunelveli: SISSWPS.

Karashima, Noboru. 1984. *South Indian History and Society: South Indian Inscriptions 850–1800*. Delhi: Oxford University Press, 1984.

Karashima, Noboru, and Y. Subbarayalu. 2009. "Ancient and Medieval Tamil and Sanskrit Inscriptions Relating to Southeast Asia and China." In H. Kulke, K. Kesavapany, and Vijay Sakhuja, eds., *Nagapattinam to Suvarnadwipa: Reflections on the Chola Naval Expeditions to Southeast Asia*, 271–91. Singapore: Institute of Southeast Asian Studies.

Knorozov, Y. V., M. F. Albedil, and B. Y. Volchok. 1981. *Proto-India: 1979. Report on the Investigation of the Proto-Indian Texts*. Moscow: Nauka Publishing House.

Kokan, Muhammad Yousuf. 1974. *Arabic and Persian in Carnatic, 1710–1960*. Madras: Ameera.

Kovintarajan, N. 2016. *Atikāramum tamiḻp pulamaiyum. Tamiḻiliruntu mutal āṅkila mŏḻipĕyarppukaḷ*. Chennai: Cre-A.

Krishna Sastri, H. [1923–1924] 1983. "Velvikudi Grant of Nedunjadaiyan: The Third Year of Reign." *Epigraphia Indica* 17: 291–309.

Krishnan, Hari. 2008. "Inscribing Practice: Reconfigurations and Textualizations of Devadasi Repertoire in Nineteenth and Early Twentieth Century South India." In Indira Viswanathan Peterson and Davesh Soneji, eds.,

*Performing Pasts: Reinventing the Arts in Modern South India*, 71–89. New Delhi: Oxford University Press.

Krishnan, K. G. 1970–1971. "Cēra Kings of the Pukalūr Inscriptions." *Journal of Ancient Indian History* 4: 137–43.

Kuiper, F. B. J. 1948. *Proto-Munda Words in Sanskrit.* Amsterdam: Verhandlingenden Koninklijke Nederlandse Akademie von Wetenschappen 51/3.

Kulke, Hermann. 1970. *Cidambara-māhātmya.* Wiesbaden, Germany: Harrassowitz.

———. 1993. *Kings and Cults: State Formation and Legitimation in India and Southeast Asia.* Delhi: Manohar.

———. 2009. "The Naval Expeditions of the Cholas in the Context of Asian History," In Hermann Kulke, K. Kesavapany, and Vijay Sakhuja, eds., *Nagapattinam to Suvarnadwipa: Reflections on the Chola Naval Expeditions to Southeast Asia*, 1–19. Singapore: Institute of Southeast Asian Studies.

Kulke, Hermann, K. Kesavapany, and Vijay Sakhuja, eds. 2009. *Nagapattinam to Suvarnadwipa: Reflections on the Chola Naval Expeditions to Southeast Asia.* Singapore: Institute of Southeast Asian Studies.

Kuppuswami, A. 1991. See *Saundarya-laharī.*

Lee, Risha. 2009. "Rethinking Community: The Indic Carvings of Quanzhou." In Hermann Kulke, K. Kesavapany, and Vijay Sakhuja, eds., *Nagapattinam to Suvarnadwipa: Reflections on the Chola Naval Expeditions to Southeast Asia* 240–70. Singapore: Institute of Southeast Asian Studies.

———. 2012. "Tamil Merchant Temples in India and China." Ph.D. dissertation, Columbia University.

Leonhardt, Jürgen. 2013. *Latin: Story of a World Language.* Cambridge, Mass.: Harvard University Press.

Lienhard, S. 1986. "Sanskrit *kapi* and *kareṇu*." In W. Morgenroth, ed., *Proceedings of the Fourth World Sanskrit Conference of the International Association of Sanskrit Studies. Weimar 1979*, 348–52. Schriften zur Geschichte und Kultur des Alten Orients 18. Berlin: Akademie Verlag.

Lo Hsiang-Lin. 1966. "On the Voyage of Soli Samudra, Chola's Envoy to China in A.D. 1015." *Proceedings of the First International Conference Seminar on Tamil,* Kuala Lumpur. International Association of Tamil Research.

Lockwood, Michael. 1993. *Māmallapuram: A Guide to the Monuments.* Madras: Tambaram Research Associates.

Lubotsky, Alexander. 2001. "The Indo-Iranian Substratum. Early Contacts between Uralic and Indo-European: Linguistic and ArchaeologicalConsiderations."

In C. Carpelan, A. Parpola, and P. Koskikallio, eds., *Mémoires de la Société Finno-ougrienne*, 301–17. Helsinki. Available at https://openaccess.leidenuniv.nl/handle/1887/2691.

Ludden, David. 1985. *Peasant History in South India*. Princeton, N.J.: Princeton University Press.

*Madras Tamil Lexicon*. 1924–1936. Madras: University of Madras.

Mahadevan, Iravatham. 1971. "Tamil-Brahmin Inscriptions of the Sangam Age." In R. E. Asher, ed., *Proceedings of the Second International Conference Seminar of Tamil Studies, Madras, India, January 1968*, 1, 73–106. Madras: International Association of Tamil Research.

———. 2011. "The Indus Fish Swam in the Great Bath: A New Solution to an Old Riddle." *Bulletin of the Indus Research Centre*, Roja Muthiah Research Library 2: 1–70.

———. 2014. *Early Tamil Epigraphy: Tamil-Brahmi Inscriptions*. Revised and enlarged 2nd ed. Vol. 1. Chennai: Central Institute of Classical Tamil.

Malayil, Abhilash. In press. "Recipes of Fire: Firework Varieties in Veṭikkampavidhi, an Early Malayalam Text on Early-Modern Pyrotechny." *Indian Journal of History of Science*.

Maloney, Clarence. 1970. "The Beginnings of Civilization in South India." *Journal of Asian Studies* 29: 603–16.

Malten, Thomas. 1997. "Antam de Proença's Tamil-Portuguese Dictionary, Printed in India in 1679." In Helmut Feldmann and Charles J. Borges, eds., *Goa and Portugal: Cultural Links*, 271–29. New Delhi: Concept Publishing Company.

Manickam Naicker, P. V. [1917] 1985. *The Tamil Alphabet and Its Mystic Aspect*. New Delhi: Asian Educational Services.

Marr, John Ralston. 1971. "The Lost Decades of Patiṟṟuppattu." In R. E. Asher, *Proceedings of the Second International Conference Seminar of Tamil Studies, Madras, India, January 1968*, 1, 19–24. Madras: International Association of Tamil Research.

———. 1972. "The Kuṭumiyāmalai Music Inscription." *Bulletin of the School of Oriental and African Studies* 35: 615–20.

———. 1985. *The Eight Anthologies: A Study in Early Tamil Literature*. Tiruvanmiyur: Institute of Asian Studies.

Mayrhofer, Manfred. 1986–2001. *Etymologisches Wörterbuch des Altindoarischen*. Heidelberg: C. Winter.

McAlpin, David W. 1974. "Towards Proto-Elamo-Dravidian." *Language* 50: 89–101.

———. 1975. "Elamite and Dravidian: Further Evidence of Relationship." *Current Anthropology* 16: 105–15.

McCann, Erin. 2015. "Ācāryābhimānam: Agency, Ontology, and Salvation in Piḷḷai Lokācārya's Śrīvacanabhūṣaṇam." Ph.D. dissertation, McGill University.

McGilvray, Dennis B. 1998. "Arabs, Moors and Muslims: Sri Lankan Muslim Ethnicity in Regional Perspective." *Contributions to Indian Sociology* (n.s.) 32: 433–83.

———. 2004. "Jailani: A Sufi Shrine in Sri Lanka." In Imtiaz Ahmad and Helmut Reifeld, eds., *Lived Islam in South Asia: Adaptation, Accommodation and Conflict*, 273–89. Delhi: Social Science Press.

Meenakshisundaram, T. P. 1965. *A History of Tamil Language*. Poona: Deccan College.

———. 1966. "*Tiruppavai, Tiruvempavai* in South-East Asia." *Proceedings of the First International Conference-Seminar of Tamil Studies*, Kuala Lumpur. International Association of Tamil Studies.

Minakshi, C. [1938] 1977. *Administration and Social Life under the Pallavas*. Madras: University of Madras.

———. 1941. *The Historical Sculptures of the Vaikuṇṭhaperumāḷ Temple, Kāñcī. Memoirs of the Archaeological Survey of India*, no. 63. Delhi: Archaeological Survey of India.

Mitchell, Lisa. 2009. *Language, Emotion, and Politics in South India: The Making of a Mother Tongue*. Bloomington: Indiana University Press.

Monier-Williams, M. 2001. *English Sanskrit Dictionary*. New Delhi: Asian Educational Services.

Monius, Anne E. 2000. "The Many Lives of Daṇḍin: The *Kāvyādarśa* in Sanskrit and Tamil." *International Journal of Hindu Studies* 4, no. 2: 195–223.

———. 2001. *Imagining a Place for Buddhism: Literary Culture and Religious Community in Tamil-Speaking South India*. New York: Oxford University Press.

———. 2011. "U. Ve. Cāminātaiyar and the Construction of Tamil Literary 'Tradition'." *Journal of Indian Philosophy* 39: 589–97.

Motzkin, G. 1992. *Time and Transcendence: Secular History, the Catholic Reaction, and the Rediscovery of the Future*. Dordrecht: Springer Verlag.

Muilwijk, M. 1996. *The Divine Kuṟa Tribe: Kuṟavañci and other Prabandhams*. Groningen, The Netherlands: Egbert Forsten.

Mutaliyar, A. Cinkaravelu, and A. Civappirakaca Mutaliyar. 1981. *Apitāṉa cintāmani*. New Delhi: Asian Educational Services.

Muthukumar, Vangal N. 2011. "Poetics of Place in Early Tamil Literature." Ph.D. dissertation, University of California, Berkeley.

Muthuswamy, Na. 2009. *Meṟkattik kŏmpu māṭukaḷ*. Chennai: Cre-A.

Nagaswamy, R. 1991. "Alagankulam: An Indo-Roman Trading Port." In C. Margabandhu et al., eds., *Indian Archaeological Heritage: Sri K. V. Soundara Rajan Festschrift*, 247–54. Delhi: Agam Kala Prakashan.

———. 1995. *Roman Karur.* Madras: Brahad Prakashan.

———. n.d. "Kollip-purai: An Inscribed Tamil Coin." http://tamilartsacademy.com/articles/article48.xml.

———. "Arikesari and Pandikkovai." http://tamilartsacademy.com/articles/article48.xml.

———. "A New Pandya Record and the Dates of Nayanmars and Alvars." http://tamilartsacademy.com/articles/article48.xml.

Nambi Arooran, K. 1980. *Tamil Renaissance and Dravidian Nationalism, 1905–1944.* Madurai, India: Koodal.

Nanacuntaram, Te. 1989. *Vaiṣṇava urai-vaḷam.* Madras: Tayammai Patippakam.

Narayana Rao, Velcheru. 1978. *Tĕlugulo kavitā viplavāla svarūpam.* Vijayawada: Visalandhra.

———. 1986. "Epics and Ideologies: Six Telugu Folk Epics." In Stuart H. Blackburn and A. K. Ramanujan, eds., *Another Harmony: New Essays on the Folklore of India*, 131–64. Berkeley: University of California Press.

———. 2004. "Print and Prose: Pundits, Karanams, and the East India Company in the Making of Modern Telugu." In Stuart Blackburn and Vasudha Dalmia, eds., *India's Literary History: Essays on the Nineteenth Century*, 146–66. Delhi: Permanent Black.

———. 2007. *Girls for Sale: Kanyāśulkam, a Play from Colonial India.* Bloomington: Indiana University Press.

———. In press. "Print and Silence."

Narayana Rao, Velcheru, and David Shulman. 1998. *A Poem at the Right Moment: Remembered Verses from Premodern South India.* Berkeley: University of California Press.

Narayana Rao, Velcheru, with David Shulman. 2002. *Classical Telugu Poetry: An Anthology.* Berkeley: University of California Press.

———. 2012. *Śrīnātha: The Poet who Made Gods and Kings.* New York: Oxford University Press.

Narayana Rao, Velcheru, with Paruchuri Sreenivas. 2014. "Manaku tĕliyani Brown Dora: Charles Philip Brown." *Eemata* (May).

Narayana Rao, Velcheru, with A. K. Ramanujan and David Shulman. 1994. *When God Is a Customer: Telugu Courtesan Songs by Kshetrayya and Others.* Berkeley: University of California Press.

Narayana Rao, Velcheru, with David Shulman and Sanjay Subrahmanyam. 1992. *Symbols of Substance: Court and State in Nāyaka Period Tamil Nadu.* Delhi: Oxford University Press.

——. 2001. *Textures of Time: Writing History in South India, 1600–1800.* Delhi: Permanent Black.

Narayanan, M. G. S. 1972. *Cultural Symbiosis in Kerala.* Trivandrum, India: Kerala Historical Society.

Narayanan, Vasudha. 2003. "Religious Vocabulary and Regional Identity: A Study of the Tamil *Cīṟāppurāṇam* ('Life of the Prophet')." In Richard M. Eaton, ed., *India's Islamic Traditions, 711–1750*, 393–410. Delhi: Oxford University Press.

——. 2013. "Who Is the Strong-Armed Monkey Who Churns the Ocean of Milk?" *Udaya: Journal of Khmer Studies* 11: 3–28.

Neeman, Nadav. 2002. *Ha-avar ha-mechonen et ha-hoveh: itzuvah shel ha-historiografia ha-mikrait be-sof yemai ha-bayit ha-rishon uleahar ha-hurban.* Jerusalem: Yeriot.

Niehof, Maren R. 2012. *Homer and the Bible in the Eyes of Ancient Interpreters.* Leiden, The Netherlands: Brill.

Niklas, Ulrike. 1987. *Einfuhrung in das Muttoḷḷāyiram.* Inaugural-Dissertation, Universität Köln.

——. 1993. See *Yāpp'aruṅkala-kārikai.*

Nilakanta Sastri, K. A. 1966. *A History of South India.* Oxford, U.K., and Delhi: Oxford University Press.

——. 1975. *The Cōḷas.* Madras: University of Madras.

Nünlist, René. 2012. "*Topos didaskalikos* and *anaphora*—Two Interrelated Principles in Aristarchus' Commentaries." In Maren Niehoff, ed., *Homer and the Bible in the Eyes of Ancient Interpreters*, 113–26. Leiden, The Netherlands: Brill.

Obeyesekere, Gananatha. 1984. *The Cult of the Goddess Pattini.* Chicago: University of Chicago Press.

Ollett, Andrew. 2015. "Language of the Snakes: Prakrit, Sanskrit, and the Language Order of Premodern India." Ph.D. dissertation, Columbia University.

Orr, Leslie. 2009. "Tamil and Sanskrit in the Epigraphical Context." In M. Kannan and Jennifer Clare, eds., *Passages: Relations between Tamil and Sanskrit*, 96–114. Pondichéry: Institut Français de Pondichéry and Tamil Chair, Department of South and Southeast Asian Studies, University of California.

——. 2014 (in press). "Mythologizing, Archaizing, and Localizing: Royal Glory and the Tenkasi Pandyas." Lecture, Paris.

——. 2015. "Making Place in a Small Space: The Sacred Worlds of the Tenkasi Pandyas." Lecture, Association of Asian Studies, Chicago.

Padoux, André. 1990. *Vāc: The Concept of the Word in Selected Hindu Tantras.* Albany: SUNY Press.

Pagis, Dan. 1986. *Al sod hatum [A Secret Sealed: The History of the Hebrew Riddle in Italy and Holland]*. Jerusalem: Magnes Press.

———. 1996. "Toward a Theory of the Literary Riddle." In Galit Hasan-Rokem and David Shulman, eds., *Untying the Knot: On Riddles and Other Enigmatic Modes*. New York: Oxford University Press: 81–108.

Pandian, Anand. 2009. *Crooked Stalks: Cultivating Virtue in South India*. Durham, N.C., and London: Duke University Press.

———. 2010. "Interior Horizons: An Ethical Space for Selfhood in South India." *Journal of the Royal Anthropological Institute* 16: 64–83.

Paris, Gaston. 1912. *Mélanges de littérature française du moyen âge*. Paris: H. Champion.

Parpola, Asko. 1994. *Deciphering the Indus Script*. Cambridge, U.K.: Cambridge University Press.

Parthasarathy, R., trans. 1993. *Cilappatikāram* of Iḷaṅkovaṭikaḷ. Translated as *The Tale of an Anklet*. New York: Columbia University Press, 1993.

Peterson, Indira Viswanathan. 1998. "The Evolution of the Kuṟavañci Dance-Drama in Tamil Nadu: Negotiating the 'Folk' and the 'Classical' in the Bharata Nāṭyam Canon." *South Asia Research* 18: 39–72.

———. 1999. "The Cabinet of King Serfoji of Tanjore." *Journal of the History of Collections* 11: 71–93.

———. 2011. "Multilingual Dramas at the Thanjavur Maratha Court and Literary Cultures in Early Modern South India." *Medieval History Journal* 14: 285–321.

———. 2015. "The Sequence of King Śarabhendra's Sacred Places: Pilgrimage and Kingship in a Marathi Text from Nineteenth-century Thanjavur." In Anna Aurelia Esposito, Heike Oberlin, Karin Juliana Steiner, and B. A. Viveka Rai, eds., *In ihrer rechten Hand hielt sie ein silbernes Messer mit Glöckchen . . . Setubandinīvandanakaumudī*, 275–81. Festscrift Heidrun Brückner. Wiesbaden, Germany: Harrassowitz.

Piatigorsky, A. 1962. *Materiali po istorii indiskoi filosofi*. Moscow: Izdatelstvo vostochnoi literatury.

Pollock, Sheldon. 2006. *The Language of the Gods in the World of Men: Sanskrit, Culture, and Power in Pre-Modern India*. Berkeley: University of California Press.

Ponemballem Pillai, T. 1909. "The Morality of the Ramayana," *Malabar Quarterly Review* 8 (June): 83.

Premalatha, Venkataraman. 1986. *Kudumiyanmalai Inscription on Music*. Madurai, India: Published by the author.

Rabe, Michael D. 2001. *The Great Penance at Māmallapuram*. Chennai: Institute of Asian Studies.

Rabin, Chaim. 1971. "Loanword Evidence in Biblical Hebrew for Trade between Tamil Nad and Palestine in the First Millennium B.C." In R. E. Asher, ed., *Proceedings of the Second International Conference Seminar of Tamil Studies, Madras, India, January 1968*, 1, 432–40. Madras: International Association of Tamil Research.

Raghavan, V. 1973. *Studies on Some Concepts of the Alaṃkāra Śāstra*. Madras: Adyar Library and Research Center.

Raj, Kapil. 2010. *Relocating Modern Science: Circulation and the Construction of Knowledge in South Asia and Europe, 1650–1900*. London: Palgrave Macmillan.

Rajam, V. S. 1985. "The Duration of an Action—Real or Aspectual? The Evolution of the Present Tense in Tamil." *Journal of the American Oriental Society* 105: 277–91.

———. 1992a. "The Evolution of *veṇpa:* as an Independent Entity." *PILC Journal of Dravidic Studies* 2, no. 2: 163–84.

———. 1992b. *A Reference Grammar of Classical Tamil Poetry*. Philadelphia: American Philosophical Society.

———. 2008. "Revisiting *kaikkiḷai* and *peruntiṇai* in Light of *Kuṟuntokai, Puṟanāṉūṟu*, and the *Tolkāppiyam*." Unpublished ms.

Rajam Aiyar, B. R. 1994. *Āpattukk'iṭamāṉa apavātam allatu kamalâmpāḷ carittiram*. Chennai: New Century Book House.

———. 1998. *The Fatal Rumour: A Nineteenth-Century Indian Novel*. Translated by Stuart Blackburn. Delhi: Oxford University Press.

Rajamani, V. K., and D. Shulman. 2011. The *Mucukunda Murals in the Tyāgarājasvāmi Temple, Tiruvārūr*. Chennai: Prakriti Foundation.

Rajan, K., and V. P. Yatheeskumar. 2013. "New Evidences on Scientific Date for Brahmi Script as Revealed from Porunthal and Kodumanal Excavations." *Pragdhara* 21–22: 279–95.

Rajesh, V. 2014. *Manuscripts, Memory and History: Classical Tamil Literature in Colonial India*. Delhi: Foundation Books.

Raman, Srilata. 2007. *Self-Surrender (Prapatti) to God in Śrīvaiṣṇavism: Tamil Cats and Sanskrit Monkeys*. London: Routledge.

———. 2009. "Who Are the Velalas? Twentieth-Century Construction and Contestations of Tamil Identity in Maraimalai Adigal (1876–1950)." In Kelly Pemberton and Michael Nijhawan, eds., *Shared Idioms, Sacred Symbols, and the Articulation of Identities in South Asia*, 78–95. New York: Routledge.

Ramanujan, A. K. 1970. *The Interior Landscape*. London: Peter Owen.

———. 1973. *Speaking of Śiva*. Harmondsworth: Penguin Books.

———. 1985. *Poems of Love and War: From the Eight Anthologies and the Ten Long Poems of Classical Tamil.* New York: Columbia University Press.
———. 2004. "Three Hundred *Rāmāyaṇas:* Five Examples and Three Thoughts on Translation." In Vinay Dharwardker, ed., *The Collected Essays of A. K. Ramanujan,* 131–60. Delhi: Oxford University Press.
Ramaswamy, Sumathi. 1997. *Passions of the Tongue: Language Devotion in Tamil India, 1891–1970.* Berkeley: University of California Press.
———. 1998. "Language of the People in the World of Gods: Ideologies of Tamil before the Nation." *Journal of Asian Studies* 57: 66–92.
———. 2004. *The Lost Land of Lemuria: Fabulous Geographies, Catastrophic Histories.* Berkeley: University of California Press.
Ramaswamy, Sundara. 1966. *Ŏru puḷiya marattiṉ katai.* Chennai: Tamilp puttakalayam.
———. 2013. *Tamarind History.* Translated by Blake Wentworth. Gurgaon: Penguin Books India.
Ricci, Ronit. 2011. *Islam Translated: Literature, Conversion, and the Arabic Cosmopolis of South and Southeast Asia.* Chicago: University of Chicago Press.
Richman, Paula. 1988. *Women, Branch Stories, and Religious Rhetoric in a Tamil Buddhist Text.* Syracuse, N.Y.: Syracuse University.
———. 1997. *Extraordinary Child: Poems from a South Indian Devotional Genre.* Honolulu: University of Hawai'i Press.
Salomon, Richard. 1996. "When Is a Riddle Not a Riddle? Some Comments on Riddling and Related Poetic Devices in Classical Sanskrit." In Galit Hasan-Rokem and David Shulman, eds., *Untying the Knot: On Riddles and Other Enigmatic Modes,* 168–78. New York: Oxford University Press.
———. 1998. *Indian Epigraphy: A Guide to the Study of Inscriptions in Sanskrit, Prakrit, and the Other Indo-Aryan Languages.* New York: Oxford University Press.
Sanderson, Alexis. 2002. "Remarks on the Text of the Kubjikāmatatantra." *Indo-Iranian Journal* 45: 1–24.
———. 2009. "The Śaiva Age—The Rise and Dominance of Śaivism during the Early Medieval Period." In Shingo Einoo, ed., *Genesis and Development of Tantrism,* 41–349. Tokyo: University of Tokyo, Institute of Oriental Culture.
Schomburg, Susan Elizabeth. 2003. "'Reviving Religion': The Qādirī Sufi Order, Popular Devotion to Sufi Saint Muḥyīuddīn 'Abdul Qādir al-Gīlāni, and Processes of 'Islamization' in Tamil Nadu and Sri Lanka." Ph.D. dissertation, Harvard University.
Seastrand, Anna. 2013. "Praise, Politics and Language: South Indian Murals, 1500–1800." Ph.D. dissertation, Columbia University.

Seneviratne, H. L. 1976. "The Alien King: Nayakkars on the Throne of Kandy." *Ceylon Journal of Historical and Social Studies*, n.s. 6, no.1: 55–61.

Seshadri, Gokul. 2009. "New Perspectives on Nagapattinam, the Medieval Port City in the Context of Political, Religious, and Commercial Exchanges between South India, Southeast Asia, and China." In H. Kulke, K. Kesavapany, and Vijay Sakhuja, eds., *Nagapattinam to Suvarnadwipa: Reflections on the Chola Naval Expeditions to Southeast Asia*, 102–34. Singapore: Institute of Southeast Asian Studies.

Sethuraman, N. 1994. "The Later Pandyas (1371–1750)." *Journal of the Epigraphic Society of India* 20: 96–116.

Shulman, David. 1980. *Tamil Temple Myths: Sacrifice and Divine Marriage in the South Indian Śaiva Tradition*. Princeton, N.J.: Princeton University Press.

———. 1984. "Muslim Popular Literature in Tamil." In Yohanan Friedmann, ed., *Islam in Asia*, Vol. 1, 174–207. Jerusalem: Magnes Press.

———1985. *The King and the Clown in South Indian Myth and Poetry*. Princeton, N.J.: Princeton University Press.

———. 1987. "The Scent of Memory in Hindu South India." *Res: Anthropology and Aesthetics* 13: 123–33.

———. 1990. *Songs of the Harsh Devotee: The Tevāram of Cuntaramūrttināyaṉār*. Philadelphia: Department of South Asia Regional Studies, University of Pennsylvania.

———1992a. "Die Dynamik der Sektenbildung im mittelalterlichen Südindien." In S. N. Eisenstadt, ed., *Kulturen der Achsenzeit II*, 102–28. Frankfurt: Suhrkamp.

———1992b. "Poets and Patrons in Tamil Literature and Literary Legend." In Barbara Stoler Miller, ed., *The Powers of Art: Patronage in Indian Culture*, 89–119. Delhi: Oxford University Press.

———1996. "Playing at Sanskrit: Notes on the Linguistic Textures of Śrīnātha." In Friedrich Wilhelm, ed., *Festschrift Dieter Schlingloff*, 239–56. Reinbek, Germany: Verlag für Orientalistische Fachpublikationen.

———. 2001. *The Wisdom of Poets*. Delhi: Oxford University Press.

———. 2002a. "Suga be-suga 'asuya be-sifrut hatamilit ha-atika," In N. Wasserman, ed., *Hutim Nitvim*, 111–24. Jerusalem: Magnes Press.

———. 2002b. "Tamil Praises of the Prophet: Kācimpulavar's *Tiruppukaḻ*." *Jerusalem Studies in Arabic and Islam* 27: 86–108.

———. 2004. "Cowherd or King? The Sanskrit Biography of Ananda Ranga Pillai." In David Arnold and Stuart Blackburn, eds., *Telling Lives in India: Biography, Autobiography, and Life History*, 175–202. Delhi: Permanent Black.

———. 2005. "The Buzz of God and the Click of Delight." In Angela Hobart and Bruce Kapferer, eds., *Aesthetics in Performance: Formations of Symbolic Construction and Experience*, 43–63. New York: Berghahn Books.

———. 2007. "How to Bring a Goddess into Being through Visible Sound." In Sergio La Porta and David Shulman, eds., *The Poetics of Grammar and the Metaphysics of Sound and Sign*, 305–42. Leiden, The Netherlands: Brill.

———. 2008. "Tukkā and Krishṇarāya: Notes on Kings and Bees." In D. Shulman and Shalva Weill, eds., *Karmic Passages: Israeli Scholarship on India*, 11–34. Delhi: Oxford University Press.

———. 2010. "Notes on Camatkāra." In D. Shulman, ed., *Language, Ritual and Poetics in Ancient India and Iran: Studies in Honor of Shaul Migron*, 249–76. Jerusalem: Israel Academy of Sciences and Humanities.

———. 2011a. "Nala Unhinged: Pukaḻentippulavar's *Naḷavĕṇpā*." In Susan S. Wadley, ed., *Damayanti and Nala: The Many Lives of a Story*, 283–315. New Delhi: Chronicle Books.

———. 2011b. "Notes on *Bhāvikālaṅkāra*." In Peter Schalk and Ruth Van Nahl, eds., *The Tamils from the Past to the Present. Celebratory Volume in Honour of Professor Alvapillai Veluppillai at the Occasion of His 75th Birthday*. Uppsala, Sweden: Uppsala University, and Colombo, Sri Lanka: Kumaran Book House.

———. 2012. *More Than Real. A History of the Imagination in South India*. Cambridge, Mass.: Harvard University Press.

———. 2014a. "Muttusvāmi Dīkṣitar and the Invention of Modern Carnatic Music: The Abhayâmba Vibhakti-kṛtis." Gonda lecture, Royal Netherlands Academy of Arts and Sciences.

———. 2014b. "Śākalya Malla's Telangana Rāmāyaṇa: The Udāra Rāghava." In Yigal Bronner, David Shulman, and Gary Tubb, eds., *Innovations and Turning Points: Toward a History of Kāvya Literature*, 613–47. Delhi: Oxford University Press.

———. 2016. "Empirical Observation and Embodied Nature in Sixteenth-Century South India." In Wendy Doniger, Peter Galison, and Susan Neiman, eds., *What Reason Promises: Essays on Reason, Nature, and History*, 142–54. Berlin: de Gruyter.

———. In press. "Tamil Messenger Poems." In Y. Bronner and D. Shulman, eds., *Mapping the World through Courier Poetry*.

Sivaramamurti, C. 1964. *Royal Conquests and Cultural Migrations in South India and the Deccan*. Calcutta: Indian Museum.

Sivathamby, K. S. 1998. *Studies in Ancient Tamil Society: Economy, Society and State Formation*. Madras: New Century Book House.

Smith, John D. 1991. *The Epic of Pābūjī: A Study, Transcription, and Translation.* Cambridge, U.K.: Cambridge University Press.

Soneji, Davesh. 2012a. "The Śaṅkara Pallaki Seva Prabandhamu: An Essay." In *Pallaki Seva Prabandhamu: An Opera by Sahaji Maharaja*, 137–49. Chennai: C. P. Ramaswami Aiyar Foundation.

———. 2012b. *Unfinished Gestures: Devadāsīs, Memory, and Modernity in South India.* Chicago: University of Chicago Press.

*South Indian Inscriptions.* 1913 and 1929, Vols. 2 and 3. Madras: Government Press. Madras: Government Press.

Southworth, Franklin C. 1979. "Lexical Evidence for Early Contacts between Indo-Aryan and Dravidian." In Madhava M. Deshpande and Peter Edwin Hook, eds., *Aryan and Non-Aryan in India.* Michigan Papers on South and Southeast Asia no. 14; Ann Arbor: University of Michigan Center for South and Southeast Asian Studies.

Spencer, George W. 1969. "Religious Networks and Royal Influence in Eleventh-Century South India." *Journal of Economic and Social History* 12: 42–56.

———. 1978. "Crisis of Authority in a Hindu Temple under the Impact of Islam." In Bardwell L. Smith, ed., *Religion and the Legitimation of Power in South Asia*, 14–27. Leiden, The Netherlands: Brill.

———. 1983. *The Politics of Expansion: The Chola Conquest of Sri Lanka and Sri Vijaya.* Madras: New Era Publications.

Srinivas, M. N. [1952] 2003. *Religion and Society among the Coorgs of South India.* New York: Oxford University Press.

Srinivasan, M. P. 2014. *Periyalwar.* Delhi: Sahitya Akademi.

Sriraman, P. S. 2011. *Chola Murals: Documentation and Study of the Chola Murals of Brihadisvara temple, Thanjavur.* Delhi: Archaeological Survey of India.

Stein, Burton. 1980. *Peasant State and Society in Medieval South India.* Delhi: Oxford University Press.

Subbarāma Dīkshitulu. 1904. *Saṅgīta-sampradāya-pradarśini.* Ettayapuram, India: Vidyavilasini Press.

Subbarayalu, Y. 1973. *The Political Geography of the Chola Country.* Madras: State Department of Archaeology.

———. 2002. "The Tamil Merchant-Guild Inscription at Barus: A Rediscovery." In N. Karashima, ed., *Ancient and Medieval Commercial Activities in the Indian Ocean.* Tokyo: Taisho University, 19–26.

———. 2009. "Sanskrit in Tamil Inscriptions." In M. Kannan and Jennifer Clare, eds., *Passages: Relations between Tamil and Sanskrit*, 115–24. Pondichéry: Institut Français de Pondichéry and Tamil Chair, Department of South and Southeast Asian Studies, University of California.

Subrahmanian, N. 1966. *Śaṅgam Polity: The Administration and Social Life of the Śaṅgam Tamils.* London: Asia Publishing House.

Sudyka, Joanna. 2011. "The 'Megalithic' Iron Age Culture in South India—Some General Remarks." *Analecta Archaeologica Ressoviensia* 5: 359–401.

Sundaram, P. S., trans. 1992. *Tirukkuṟaḷ* of Tiruvaḷḷuvar. Translated as *The Kural.* New Delhi: Penguin Books, 1992.

Takahashi, Takanobu. 1989. "Poetry and Poetics: Literary Conventions of Tamil Love Poetry." Ph.D. dissertation, University of Utrecht.

———. 2010. "The Origin of the Colophons to Tamil Love Poems." Unpublished ms.

———. 2015. "A New Interpretation of the 'Sangam Legend.'" *Journal of Indian and Buddhist Studies* 63: 80–88.

Talbot, Cynthia. 2001. *Precolonial India in Practice: Society, Region, and Identity in Medieval Andhra.* New York: Oxford University Press.

Thangappa, M. L. 2010. *Love Stands Alone: Selections from Tamil Sangam Poetry.* Edited and introduced by A. R. Venkatachalapathy. New Delhi: Penguin / Viking.

Tieken, Herman. 2001. *Kāvya in South India.* Groningen, The Netherlands: Egbert Forsten.

———. 2003. "Old Tamil Caṅkam Literature and the So-Called Caṅkam Period." *Indian Economic and Social History Review* 40: 247–78.

———. 2008. "A Propos Three Recent Publications on the Question of the Dating of Old Tamil Caṅkam Poetry." *Asiatische Studien / Études Asiatiques* 62: 575–605.

———. 2013. "Daṇḍin, the *Daśakumāracarita*, and the *Avantīsundarīkathā*." *Bulletin d'Etudes Indiennes:* 231–52.

———. 2015. *Between Colombo and the Cape: Letters in Tamil, Dutch and Sinhala, Sent to Nicolaas Ondaatje from Ceylon, Exile at the Cape of Good Hope (1728–1737).* New Delhi: Manohar.

———. n.d. "The Origin of the Colophons to Tamil Love Poems." Unpublished ms.

Trautmann, Thomas. 2006. *Languages and Nations: The Dravidian Proof in Colonial Madras.* Berkeley: University of California Press.

Tschacher, Torsten. 2001. *Islam in Tamilnadu: Varia.* Halle, Germany: Südasienwissenschaftliche Arbeitsblätter 2.

———. 2009. "Circulating Islam: Convergence and Divergence in the Islamic Traditions of Ma'bar and Nusantara." In R. Michael Feener and Terenjit Sevea, eds., *Islamic Connections: Muslim Societies in South and Southeast Asia,* 48–67. Singapore: Institute of Southeast Asian Studies.

Tubb, Gary. 1998. "Hemacandra and Sanskrit Poetics." In John Cort, ed., *Open Boundaries: Jain Communities and Culture in Indian History,* 53–66. Albany: SUNY Press.

Van Buitenen, J. A. B. 1959. *Tales of Ancient India*. Chicago: University of Chicago Press.

Vedanayakam Pillai, S. 1994. *Piratāpa Mutaliyār Carittiram*. Chennai: New Century Book House.

Veluppillai, A. 1971. "*Viracoozhiyam* as a Grammar for Inscriptional Tamil." In R. E. Asher, ed., *Proceedings of the Second International Conference Seminar of Tamil Studies, January 1968*, 1, 345–48. Madras: International Association of Tamil Research.

Veluthat, Kesavan. 2010. *The Early Medieval in South India*. Delhi: Oxford University Press.

Venkatacami, Mayilai Cini. 1959. *Maṟainta poṉa tamiḻ nūlkaḷ*. Chennai: Cantinulakam.

———. 1962. *Pattŏṉpatām nūṟṟ'āṇṭil tamiḻ ilakkiyam*. Chennai: Cantinulakam.

Venkatachalapathy, A. R. 2006. *In Those Days There Was No Coffee: Writings in Cultural History*. New Delhi: Yoda Press.

Venkatachari, K. K. A. 1978. *The Maṇipravāala Literature of the Srīvaiṣṇava Ācāryas, 12th to 15th century A.D.* Bombay: Ananthacharya Research Institute.

Venkatesan, Archana. 2005. "Divining the Future of a Goddess: The *Araiyar Cēvai* as Commentary at the Śrīvilliputtūr Āṇṭāḷ Temple." *Nidān: The International Journal of Hinduism* 17: 19–51.

———. 2013. "The Service of Kings: Dance, Music, and Recitation at a South Indian Temple." Lecture, McGill University.

———. 2014a. "A Tale of Two Cēvais: Araiyar Cēvai and Kaittala Cēvai at the Āṇṭāḷ Temple in Srivilliputtur." *Journal of Vaishnava Studies* 22 (Spring): 125–46.

———, trans. 2014b. *Nammāḻvār. A Hundred Measures of Time. Tiruviruttam*. Gurgaon: Penguin Books India.

———. 2016. *The Secret Garland: Andal's Tiruppāvai and Nācciyār Tirumoḻi*. Noida: HarperCollins Publishers India.

Venkayya, V. 1913. *Introduction to South Indian Inscriptions*. Vol. 2. Madras: Government Press.

Vergiani, Vincenzo. 2013. "The Adoption of Bhartṛhari's Classification of the Grammatical Object in Cēṉāvaraiyar's Commentary on the *Tolkāppiyam*." In Whitney Cox and Vincenzo Vergiani, eds., *Bilingual Discourse and Cross-Cultural Fertilisation: Sanskrit and Tamil in Medieval India*, 161–98. Pondichéry: Institut Français de Pondichéry and École Française d'Extrême-Orient.

Washbrook, David. 1989. "Caste, Class and Dominance in Modern Tamil Nadu: Non-Brahmanism, Dravidianism and Tamil Nationalism." In F. Francel and M. S. A. Rao, eds., *Dominance and State Power in Modern India*. New Delhi: Oxford University Press.

Weidman, Amanda J. 2006. *Singing the Classical, Voicing the Modern: The Post-colonial Politics of Music in South India*. Durham, N.C., and London: Duke University Press.

Weiss, Rick. 2009. *Recipes for Immortality: Healing, Religion, and Community in South India*. New York: Oxford University Press.

———. 2015. "Print, Religion, and Canon in Colonial India: The Publication of Ramalinga Adigal's *Tiruvaruṭpā*." *Modern Asian Studies* 49: 650–77.

Wentworth, Blake. 2011a. "Yearning for a Dreamed Real: The Procession of the Lord in the Tamil *Ulās*." Ph.D. dissertation, University of Chicago.

———. 2011b. "Insiders, Outsiders, and the Tamil Tongue." In Y. Bronner, Whitney Cox, and Lawrence McCrea, eds., *South Asian Texts in History: Critical Engagements with Sheldon Pollock*, 153–76. Ann Arbor, Mich.: Association of Asian Studies.

Wilden, Eva. 2002. "Towards an Internal Chronology of Old Tamil Caṅkam Literature or How to Trace the Laws of a Poetic Universe." *Wiener Zeitschrift für die Kunde Südasiens* 46: 105–33.

———. 2006. *Literary Techniques in Old Tamil Caṅkam Poetry. The Kuṟuntokai*. Wiesbaden, Germany: Harrassowitz.

———. 2009. "Canonisation of Classical Tamil Texts in the Mirror of the Poetological Commentaries." In E. Wilden, ed., *Between Preservation and Recreation: Tamil Traditions of Commentary*, 145–67. Pondichéry: Institut Français de Pondichéry and École Française d'Extrême-Orient.

———. 2014. *Manuscript, Script, and Memory: Relics of the Caṅkam in Tamilnadu*. Berlin: de Gruyter.

Wilke, Annette. 2012. "Negotiating Tantra and Veda in the Paraśurāma-Kalpa Tradition." In F. Neubert and U. Hüsken, eds., *Negotiating Rites*. New York: Oxford University Press.

Witzel, Michael. 1999. "Early Sources for South Asian Substrate Languages." *Mother Tongue* (October): 1–75.

Wolters, O. W. 1970. *The Fall of Śrīvijaya in Malay History*. Ithaca, N.Y.: Cornell University Press.

———. 1974. "North-western Cambodia in the Seventh Century," *Bulletin of the School of Oriental and African Studies* 37: 355–84.

Yocum, Glenn E. 1982. *Hymns to the Dancing Siva*. Columbia, Mo.: South Asia Books.

Younger, Paul. 1982. "Singing the Tamil Hymnbook in the Tradition of Rāmānuja: The Adhyayanōtsava Festival in Śrīraṅkam." *History of Religions* 21: 272–93.

Ziffren, Abby. 1984. "Human Effort and Destiny: A Study of Beliefs among the Tamil People of South India." Ph.D. dissertation, University of Wisconsin.

Zvelebil, Kamil. 1973a. "The Earliest Account of the Tamil Academies." *Indo-Iranian Journal* 15: 109–35.

———. 1973b. *The Poets of the Powers*. London: Rider.

———. 1973c. *The Smile of Murugan*. Leiden, The Netherlands: Brill.

———. 1974. *Tamil Literature*. Vol. 10.1 of *A History of Indian Literature*. Edited by J. Gonda. Wiesbaden, Germany: Harrassowitz.

———. 1985. Review of *Proto-Elamo-Dravidian* by David McAlpin. *Journal of the American Oriental Society* 105: 364–72.

———. 1992. *Companion Studies to the History of Tamil Literature*. Leiden, The Netherlands: Brill.

———. 1995. *Lexicon of Tamil Literature*. Leiden, The Netherlands: Brill.

# Credits

## CHAPTER 2

*Kuruntŏkai* 60, from *Poems of Love and War: From the Eight Anthologies and the Ten Long Poems of Classical Tamil,* selected and translated by A. K. Ramanujan (New York: Columbia University Press, 1985). Copyright © 1985 by Columbia University Press. Reprinted with permission of the publisher.

*Puṟanāṉūṟu* 310, from *The Four Hundred Songs of War and Wisdom: An Anthology of Poems from Classical Tamil, The Puṟanāṉūṟu,* translated and edited by George L. Hart and Hank Heifetz (New York: Columbia University Press, 1999). Copyright © 1999 by Columbia University Press. Reprinted with permission of the publisher.

Extract from *The Study of Stolen Love,* by David Buck and K. Paramasivam (Oxford: Oxford University Press, 1997). Reprinted by permission of Oxford University Press.

*Puṟanānūṟu* 78 and 255, from *Poets of the Tamil Anthologies: Ancient Poems of Love and War* by George L. Hart III (Princeton: Princeton University Press, 1979). Copyright © 1979 by Princeton University Press. Reprinted with permission of the publisher.

Epilogue verse by Iḷaṅkō Aṭikaḷ. From *The Tale of an Anklet: An Epic of South India, The Cilappatikāram of Iḷaṅkō Aṭikaḷ,* translated by R. Parthasarathy (New York: Columbia University Press, 1993). Copyright © 1993 by Columbia University Press. Reprinted with permission of the publisher.

## CHAPTER 3

Two poems from *Nācciyār Tirumŏḻi*, from *The Secret Garland: Andal's Tiruppāvai and Nācciyār Tirumoḻi,* translated with an introduction and commentary by Archana Venkatesan (Noida: HarperCollins Publishers India, 2016). Copyright © Archana Venkatesan. Reprinted with permission of the publisher.

## CHAPTER 4

Translation of part of the *periḷampĕṉ* section of the *Vikramacoḻaṉ ulā* by Ŏṭṭakkūttar, from Blake Tucker Wentworth, "Yearning for a Dreamed Real: The Procession of the Lord in the Tamil Ulās," PhD dissertation, University of Chicago Divinity School, December 2011. Copyright © 2011 by Blake Tucker Wentworth. Reproduced courtesy of the author.

## CHAPTER 5

"Five, four, three," from *A Poem at the Right Moment: Remembered Verses from Premodern South India,* collected and translated by Velcheru Narayana Rao and David Shulman (Berkeley: University of California Press, 1998). Copyright © 1998 by the Regents of the University of California.

## CHAPTER 7

Lost Love (*iḻanta kātal*) by Manushya Puthiran (S. Abdul Hameed). From *In Our Translated World: Contemporary Global Tamil Poetry,* edited by Chelva Kanaganayakam (Toronto: TSAR Publications and the Tamil Literary Garden, 2013). Reproduced courtesy of Manushya Puthiran.

# Index


Abhinavagupta, 221, 276
*abhinaya* (gestures language), 91, 126, 127, 129, 131, 137
academies, ancient, 26, 27, 28, 29. *See also* mutt *(maṭha)* academies
*Ācārya-hridayam* (Aḻakiya Maṇavāḷap Pĕrumāḷ Nāyaṉār), 220–221
*Adhyayanotsava* (Festival of Recitation), 126, 127, 132, 336n41
Agastya, 25–26; and Ataṅkoṭṭācāṉ, 328n83; cultural role of, 40–41, 328n82; and esoteric practices, 40; and fissure in transmission, 30–31, 40; as foundational grammarian, 4, 25, 26, 27–28, 38, 39, 42, 329n102; learning of Tamil by, 38–39, 329n98; and Pandya king, 327n67; and Perāciriyar, 205
agglutination, 7
Aiyaṉāritaṉār, 50, 188–189
*akam* (in-ness), 45; characters in poems about, 91, 178; continued use of, 330n16; language-oriented aspect of, 172; Nāṟkavirāca Nampi on, 207; performance of, 91; *Tiruviruttam* poems as, 108; and *uyir* (breath of life), 131–132. See also *puṟam* (out-ness) poems
*akam* (in-ness) and *puṟam* (out-ness): in Chola period, 188; and colophons, 68; continued relevance of, 306, 321; interweavings between, 45, 47–48, 49, 59–60; in poem by Manushya Puthiran, 323; in *ulā* genre, 158. *See also* landscapes *(tiṇai)*
*Akanāṉūru*, 28, 63, 77–78, 78–79
*Akattiyam* (Agastya), 25, 27–28, 38. *See also* Agastya
*Akilāṇṭa Nāyaki Piḷḷaittamiḻ* (Minatcicuntaram Pillai), 288–289, 352n11
Aḻakiya Maṇavāḷap Pĕrumāḷ Nāyaṉār, 220–221, 222, 338n86
Āḻvārs (Vaishṇava poets), 113, 115–116, 127, 207–208, 216, 338n86. *See also* Vaishṇava canon
Amitacākarar, 182, 187, 192, 304
*Āmukta-mālyada* (Krishṇa-deva-rāya), 317
Ananda Ranga Pillai, 257–258
Andhra poetry, 190, 292
*aṅkatam* genre, 219
Annadurai, C. N., 310, 319
Annamalai, E., 318, 355n100
Āṇṭāḷ, 113, 118–119, 121. See also *Tiruppāvai*
*antâti* genre, 268
antinomianism, 121, 273, 312
Appar, 113, 121, 175
Appa Rao, Gurujada, 293
Arabic, 261, 266, 319
*araiyar cevai* performance, 128–129, 130–131
Arikamedu, 24
Arikesari Parâṅkuśa Māravarmaṉ, 63, 79, 147
*Aruḷiccĕyalrahasyam* (Aḻakiya Maṇavāḷap Pĕrumāḷ Nāyaṉār), 222
Arumuka Navalar, 301–302, 314, 350n73
Aruṇâcalakkavirāyar, 279
Aruṇakirinātar, 266, 351n78
Arwi script, 266
Aryan philosophy/civilization, 307
aspect, 11–12
Ataṅkoṭṭācaṉ, 328n83
Athenaeus, 293